# Music Copyright Law

David J. Moser and Cheryl L. Slay

**Course Technology PTR**
*A part of Cengage Learning*

COURSE TECHNOLOGY
CENGAGE Learning·

Australia • Brazil • Japan • Korea • Mexico • Singapore • Spain • United Kingdom • United States

# COURSE TECHNOLOGY
## CENGAGE Learning

**Music Copyright Law**
**David J. Moser**
**Cheryl L. Slay**

Publisher and General Manager, Course Technology PTR: Stacy L. Hiquet

Associate Director of Marketing: Sarah Panella

Manager of Editorial Services: Heather Talbot

Marketing Manager: Mark Hughes

Project Editor: Cathleen D. Small

Copy Editor: Sandy Doell

Technical Reviewer: Tara Aaron

Interior Layout Tech: MPS Limited, a Macmillan Company

Cover Designer: Luke Fletcher

Indexer: Sharon Shock

Proofreader: Gene Redding

Library of Congress Control Number: 2011936036

ISBN-13: 978-1-4354-5972-4

ISBN-10: 1-4354-5972-5

**Course Technology, a part of Cengage Learning**

20 Channel Center Street

Boston, MA 02210

USA

Cengage Learning is a leading provider of customized learning solutions with office locations around the globe, including Singapore, the United Kingdom, Australia, Mexico, Brazil, and Japan. Locate your local office at: **international.cengage.com/region**

Cengage Learning products are represented in Canada by Nelson Education, Ltd.

For your lifelong learning solutions, visit **courseptr.com**

Visit our corporate website at **cengage.com**

Printed in the United States of America
2 3 4 5 6 7 17 16 15 14

# Foreword

As an entertainment attorney, recognition and conversation about the impact of copyrights and copyright law is a daily occurrence. Whether reviewing, negotiating, or drafting an agreement on behalf of an artist/writer/creator or a record company/publisher/owner, I will always take an extra moment to think about the application of copyright law, while randomly recalling lessons learned in any other music business class or contracts course in law school. In representing many different types of clients, from notable artists to first-time professional songwriters, from record distributors to digital service providers, and from catalog builders to artist estates, my counsel will always include a conversation about both the aesthetic and the market value of music—which are defined, affected, or controlled by copyright law.

From the separate bundles of rights embodied in one song to the new media and methods of distributing and exploiting that song, copyright is a current and healthy topic of debate. We are witnesses to a defining moment of evolution in the music industry (or maybe a revolution). The former business-run industry is now a consumer-driven industry being chased by business and Congress. Time has proven that creativity and innovation cannot be curbed because of holes in or lack of copyright law; but rather, creativity is necessary to better define copyright law. I sometimes say that you need to know the rules before you can break them, and a fundamental understanding of copyright basics is essential for anyone who is considering constructing new-model systems and practices and competing in the next music industry.

I live in a world of legal theory but need to constantly apply this theory in practice. *Music Copyright Law* is a substantial outline on music copyright. David Moser and Cheryl Slay do a great job complementing their discourse on history and current issues with diverse theories and practical, real-world examples to help explain (and challenge) these rules and principles in a very contemporary manner.

Kent Marcus, Esq.

*(Kent represents many clients in the entertainment industry, including the group Kings of Leon.)*

# Acknowledgments

The authors would like to thank all of the people who have assisted in the creation of this book and provided feedback about it. Although the list is too long to include (and we would be afraid to leave someone out), many individuals including attorneys, music industry professionals, professors, and students have reviewed chapters and offered suggestions.

# About the Authors

**David J. Moser** is an attorney and a professor specializing in copyright law, entertainment law, and business law. He has been a professor at the Mike Curb College of Entertainment and Music Business at Belmont University, Middle Tennessee State University, and Xiamen University of Technology in China. As an attorney, Moser has more than 15 years of experience in intellectual property and entertainment law. He also teaches an online copyright course at UCLA Extension and is a recipient of a Fulbright Scholar Award to conduct research on intellectual property piracy in the Philippines.

**Cheryl L. Slay** is an entertainment and intellectual property (IP) attorney and assistant professor of music business at Belmont University. In 2000, Slay launched an entertainment and IP law firm with a particular focus on developing creative business and legal solutions for arts and entertainment professionals. She has more than 12 years of experience in representing independent and emerging filmmakers, novelists, record companies, musicians, technology companies, visual artists, and other arts, technology, and business professionals. Combining her arts focus with 17 years of experience in managing and advising public sector programs on matters ranging from consumer protection to administrative law, Slay developed a progressive practice to provide clients with cutting-edge counsel on changes in the entertainment industry and trends in IP law and policy. A frequent presenter, writer, and researcher, Ms. Slay speaks extensively on arts and IP matters, including in television appearances and as a presenter for numerous organizations, universities, and conferences. She has authored numerous publications on matters ranging from strategies for success in the music business to trademark issues in reality television. She holds a Juris Doctor degree from the University of Maryland School of Law, a Master of Public Administration from Atlanta University, and a Bachelor of Arts from the University of Michigan. She completed the Harvard Law School Program of Continuing Education for Lawyers in International and Comparative Intellectual Property in 2004. In 2005, she was selected as a Maryland Bar Foundation Fellow. She has served on the board of directors for Maryland Volunteer Lawyers for the Arts and is an alumnus of the 2010 class of Leadership Music. Ms. Slay is also a vocalist with more than 25 years of performance experience. Additional information is available at www.slaylaw.com.

# Contents

# Chapter 3
# What Can Be Protected by Copyright?    **25**

# Chapter 4
# Ownership of Copyright    **47**

# Chapter 9
# Copyright Formalities                                                    153

# Chapter 10
# Infringement of Copyright                                               179

# Chapter 11
# Defenses to Infringement

**203**

# Chapter 12
# Remedies for Copyright Infringement

**221**

# Chapter 13
# International Copyright Protection

**235**

## Chapter 14
## Copyright and Digital Technology                                      249

## Chapter 15
## The Online Music War                                                 271

# Introduction

We have entered what may be one of the greatest periods of growth in creative expression. This growth is primarily the result of advances in technology that have made it easier and much less costly to produce and distribute creative works on a worldwide basis. Civilization experienced an explosion in creativity in the eighteenth century after the invention of the printing press and the development of a print publishing industry. The end of the twentieth century may have begun a similar explosion in creativity as well as a means of distributing the products of that creativity using digital technology and the Internet.

Technological change, however, brings challenges as well as opportunities. New technologies have made it much easier to copy and distribute creative works. These new technologies have also made it much easier to infringe upon the rights of the creators and owners of creative works. Part of Internet culture revolves around the notion that everything available over the Internet should be free. Many people still mistakenly believe that they can copy and exchange music and other creative works freely over the Internet, even though numerous lawsuits involving Internet infringements have held otherwise.

Copyright law has always involved a tension between two important competing interests. On one hand, creative works should be readily accessible to the public so that society can benefit from them. On the other hand, authors and publishers who invest their time and money in the creation and marketing of these works should be compensated for their efforts. The United States was founded upon the principles of liberty and justice. The principle of liberty suggests that people should have free access to creative works. Justice, however, sometimes imposes limitations on liberty. The principle of justice suggests that even though society benefits from having access to creative works, it is not fair that some members of society can appropriate other member's creations without permission or payment. Copyright law attempts to strike a balance between the competing principles of liberty and justice by providing authors with a right to be compensated in order to encourage them to create new works that will be made available to the public.

Whether or not we realize it, copyright law affects us all during virtually every day of our lives. For instance, consider whether a day goes by in your life in which you do not turn on the radio or television; listen to a CD or an MP3; read a book, newspaper, or magazine; watch a movie; run software on your computer; or surf the web. If you do any of these things, you have had access to copyrighted materials. While we tend to take the availability of all of these materials for granted, many of them would not exist or be as readily available if creators and publishers did not have legal protection that allows them to profit from their efforts.

While copyright law and the ownership of intellectual property may be a confusing concept to many people, it is the lifeblood of many industries, a crucial part of the American economy and a necessity to authors and producers of creative works. Many of the businesses that comprise the entertainment industry—book publishing, motion pictures, computer software, and music—are based on the ownership and use of copyrighted works.

While music existed long before copyright and would continue to exist without copyright, there would not likely be any music industry without copyright. This is due to the fact that the main assets of the music industry (songs and sound recordings) are forms of property that are protected by copyright. Without copyright, songwriters and music publishers could not own and derive income from songs; artists and record companies could not own and derive income from sound recordings. However, many participants in the music industry (from songwriters to record company executives) fail to understand and appreciate the importance that copyright law has on their careers and their livelihoods. There are many common inaccurate beliefs about some of the basic principles of copyright law. For example, the belief that copyright allows people to control ideas is a mistaken one. As discussed in Chapter 1, copyright only protects certain ways that ideas are expressed rather than the ideas themselves. Although some aspects of copyright law are technical in nature and very complicated, certain basic principles should be understood by everyone who works in the music industry.

The idea for the original edition of this book (then entitled *Music Copyright for the New Millennium*) originated when David Moser started teaching copyright law classes to college students in a music business program. The class had been using a law school casebook (a collection of court decisions) as a text. Although that may work well for teaching law school copyright classes using the Socratic method (teaching primarily by asking questions rather than providing answers), it doesn't necessarily work as well for undergraduate music business students, especially because relatively few of the cases dealt with music. Previous editions of this book have been adopted as a text for courses in copyright law and music business at higher educational institutions, such as Belmont University, Fordham University Law School, Loyola University (New Orleans), New York University, Northeastern University, University of California (Santa Barbara), University of Memphis, University of North Alabama, and the University of Southern California (Los Angeles).

The goal of this book is therefore to provide an overall understanding of copyright law as it applies specifically to music and the music industry. Some of the main issues that this book covers are:

- What is copyright and why is it important?
- How did copyright law originate and how has it evolved?
- What types of creations are protected by copyright and what is not protected by copyright?
- What provisions of copyright law are especially relevant to music?

- What is copyright infringement?

- How do you know who owns the rights to a copyrighted work and how can you get permission to use it?

- How has copyright law responded to advances in technology?

- What are the main challenges to copyright posed by digital technology and the Internet?

In writing this book, the authors have attempted to arrange the material in a logical fashion and to explain provisions of the law as simply as possible. Unfortunately, however, some provisions of copyright law are technical and complex. We have also incorporated many examples and practical tips to illustrate how specific provisions of the law are applied. We hope that the result is an informative and useful reference.

A few basic things to keep in mind when reading the material presented are: (1) all references to "the Copyright Act" refer to the United States Copyright Act of 1976 as amended unless otherwise specified; (2) the Copyright Act is part of the United States Code, which is a collection of federal statutes; (3) the Copyright Act comprises Chapter 17 of the United States Code; (4) the Copyright Act is organized by chapters and sections within those chapters (for example, the first section of the Copyright Act, Section 101, contains several pages of defined terms; the legal citation to this section is 17 U.S.C. § 101); (5) the symbol "§" means "section" and refers to specific section numbers of the Copyright Act; and (6) the full text of the Copyright Act is available from the Copyright Office website at http://www.copyright.gov/title17/.

## Note on This Edition

This title is in essence a new edition of a previous book, entitled *Moser on Music Copyright*, which was in turn a revision of a book entitled *Music Copyright for the New Millennium*. The current edition contains revised and updated information current as of mid-2011. Since the publication of the first edition in 2002, many significant copyright cases have been decided, many of which deal with online music and are covered in Chapter 15. Over the past 10 years, the application of copyright law has been evolving at a more rapid pace than ever before as new technologies and new businesses built based upon those technologies continue to arise and evolve. While we have tried to keep as up to date as possible, the reality is that even shortly after this book is published, there will be new developments in existing controversies and challenges that lead to new controversies. At the least, we hope that this book will give readers a sufficient background in the basic principles and provisions of copyright law so that they will be able to understand important issues that do arise.

## Disclaimer

It is hoped that the information provided in this book will be helpful to readers. Every effort has been made to make this book as complete and accurate as possible. To the authors' best knowledge, the information presented was accurate at the time of its writing. However, legislative changes to the law and court decisions interpreting and applying the law are made on a continuing basis. Consequently, it is impossible to guarantee absolute up-to-date accuracy. Accordingly, readers should not rely on this book as their sole source of legal information or as a substitute for qualified legal counsel. This book is sold with the understanding that the publisher and authors are not rendering specific legal advice and the publisher and authors shall not be liable or responsible to any person or entity with respect to any loss or damage caused or alleged to be caused, directly or indirectly, by the information contained in this book.

## Quotes about *Music Copyright for the New Millennium*

"A vital resource for anyone contemplating or pursuing a career in this exciting and ever-changing industry." Mike Curb, president, Curb Records

"Whether you've been in the music business for 2 weeks or 25 years, *Music Copyright for the New Millennium* is a must read." John Burns, former executive vice-president, Giant Records

"Straightforward and easy to comprehend." Kent Dunlap, principal legal advisor for the General Counsel, U.S. Copyright Office

"Of note is Moser's use of case study material to illustrate points. He has done a fine job of making the arcane matter of copyright law understandable for the legal layperson." Robert Garfrerick, Entertainment Industry Center, University of North Alabama

"This work will help fill the void for a textbook in music copyright law classes for undergraduate and graduate music industry programs as well as law schools. In addition, practicing entertainment attorneys and music industry executives will find this a valuable resource." Dr. Richard Barnet, professor of recording industry, Middle Tennessee State University

"In recent years the U.S. Copyright laws have been criticized for becoming as difficult to understand as the tax code. David Moser presents these complex rules in a straightforward practical delivery." Richard D. Rose, former vice president, Legal Affairs & Business Development, Copyright.net

"Students will appreciate a straightforward approach that doesn't assume a law student's sensitivities." Professor Edward Samuels, New York Law School

"From the Statute of Anne in the early eighteenth century to recent lawsuits against MP3-swapping services, this is the most comprehensive guide to music copyright ever created." Music Books Plus

"An up-to-date and vastly informative handbook on current music copyright law, with needed attention paid to issues germane to the age of MP3, Napster, and the Internet. The text is rife with excellent examples concerning copyright infringement, authorship/ownership, registration, fair use, piracy, performance rights, etc." Martin Brady, *Nashville Scene*

# 1 What Is Copyright?

*[handwritten: Clear understanding of copyright:*
*• what it is*
*• type of copyright]*

*"Music is such a tremendou[s] [handwritten: Positive] PLANS ....ment supervision.... I also advocate*
*much more rigid laws so thi[s] many who enjoy glory plus financial*
*gain's abundance, even in the ...... ...es or sweeping the streets. Lack of*
*proper protection causes this."[1]*

—Jelly Roll Morton (ragtime jazz pianist of the early twentieth century)

The quotation above by Jelly Roll Morton is from 1938. If Morton knew how much easier it is today to copy and use music without the author or copyright owner's permission over the Internet and with digital technology, he would probably be rolling over in his grave. This quotation is a good starting point for this book because it indicates that music and other forms of artistic works need some form of government supervision (i.e., laws) in order to provide authors and companies that invest in the creation, distribution, and marketing of artistic creations with protection for the works they create and make available, which ultimately benefits society at large. That, in essence, is what copyright seeks to accomplish.

## I. Copyright: A Type of Property

Copyright is a form of property ownership for certain types of artistic and creative works. Copyright can be defined as a way that the law gives creators and owners of creative works the right to control and profit from the use of their creations. The law provides this means of control by giving copyright owners certain exclusive rights over the use of their works. These exclusive rights are discussed in more detail in later chapters, but include the rights to reproduce, distribute, adapt (or creative derivative works), publicly perform, and publicly display a copyrighted work. Copyright law protects many types of original creative expression. Some, but by no means all, of the types of works that can be protected by copyright are songs, sound recordings, movies, television shows, plays, dance routines, books, poems, photographs, paintings, sculpture, computer programs, and websites.

In general, there are two broad categories of property: real property and personal property. Real property protects land or things that are built on land, such as houses and buildings. Personal property basically protects everything that can be owned other than real property. A car, for instance, would be personal property. One subcategory of personal property is intellectual property, which protects certain products of the mind and affords ownership rights to things that

1

have no physical existence. The main categories of intellectual property are copyrights, patents, and trademarks.

The concept of copyright is difficult for many people to understand, in part because it protects intangible rather than tangible property. Tangible or physical property is easier to visualize and understand because it can be possessed. People generally do not find it hard to understand that things such as houses, cars, food, and compact discs are property. These types of property can be seen, touched, and sometimes tasted, smelled, or heard.

Intellectual property, on the other hand, cannot be possessed by anyone, although this does not mean that it cannot be owned. You cannot, for example, possess a song although you can certainly own one. You cannot see, touch, taste, or smell a song. In fact, you cannot even hear a song, although you can hear a particular performance of a song. In other words, the thing to which the property right applies (the song) is not subject to direct perception by the senses and cannot be possessed in itself. It's a bit easier to understand if you realize that property refers not to the actual possession of a thing, but to the right to use it and control its use. A copyright owner's right to prevent the unauthorized use of a work is therefore somewhat analogous to a homeowner's right to prevent trespassing on his or her property.

The idea behind the law of copyright is that products created by a person's mind (such as songs, books, and films) are just as much the creator's property as products created by a person's hands. Unfortunately, it is difficult to draw clear boundaries around intellectual property. Over 150 years ago, in a case involving an infringing biography that contained letters written by George Washington, the United States Supreme Court recognized this difficulty, stating that:

> Copyrights approach, nearer than any other class of cases belonging to forensic discussions, to what may be called the metaphysics of the law, where the distinctions are, or at the least may be, very subtle and refined, and sometimes almost evanescent.

Many people find it difficult to regard mental creations, such as those protected by copyright, as a form of property. This may be because the rights granted by copyright law conflict with many expectations people have with respect to their rights to use tangible property. Most people believe that when they purchase something, they have the right to do anything they want with it. However, if that property is a compact disc that contains copyrighted works, the owner of the compact disc cannot do whatever she wants with that piece of property (at least not legally). For example, the owner of the compact disc cannot legally make copies of the compact disc except for the owner's personal use. Although the majority of people would probably agree that it is wrong (not to mention illegal) to go to a store and shoplift a compact disc, a much smaller percentage of people are likely to consider it wrong to make a copy of a compact disc they own and give it to someone else. The harm to the record store due to the stolen compact disc is much more apparent than the harm to the copyright owners of the intangible works infringed upon by the copying of the compact disc.

To make things more confusing, although copyright law protects intangible property, copyrighted works are embodied or contained in physical objects, which can be possessed. For example, a song can be embodied in a recording (whether on tape, compact disc, MP3 or other type of digital file, or other recording medium) or in written notation on paper or stored on a computer (such as sheet music). So, although you cannot actually possess a copyrighted work, you can possess physical objects in which the copyrighted work is embodied. However, it is important to understand that possession of a physical object embodying a copyrighted work does not equate to ownership of the copyrighted work. If you buy a compact disc from a record store, you are the owner of that compact disc. Acquiring ownership of that compact disc, however, does not give you any ownership rights to the copyrighted works embodied on that disc (i.e., songs and recordings). Similarly, if you purchase a recording of a song by download from an online music store such as iTunes, you do not own the song or the recording of the song. Instead, you merely have the right to use the downloaded recording according to the license from the online music store (which reflects rights granted to the store by copyright owners). Copyrighted works are separate pieces of property from any tangible property—a compact disc, a DVD, a computer file, or any other physical object—that they may be embodied in.

One major disadvantage of intangible property (such as copyright) as opposed to tangible property is that it can be easily infringed upon. If you own a car, and someone takes it without your permission, that person has stolen your property. Similarly, if someone uses your copyrighted work without your permission and without any legal defense, that person has infringed upon your copyright. If someone steals your car, it probably won't take you long to figure out that it has been stolen. However, when someone infringes upon your copyright, you may not be aware that the infringement has taken place because a copyright is not a physical object. If someone wants to steal your car, he has to take possession of it. However, if someone wants to infringe on the copyright to your song, he can do so without taking possession of any physical object and quite possibly without your awareness of the infringement. Further, someone can infringe upon the copyright to your song from thousands of miles away. Finally, if that wasn't bad enough, a copyright can be infringed upon by more than one person at the same time.

Initially, copyright involved only the right to copy literary works and applied only to printed material. Over the past several centuries, copyright law has evolved and now gives authors of all kinds of creative works certain exclusive rights to their works. These rights include the right to reproduce, adapt, distribute, publicly perform, and publicly display the copyrighted work. By granting these rights exclusively to copyright owners, copyright law also prevents others from using copyrighted works without the copyright owner's permission. It is the exercise of these exclusive rights that allows copyright owners the possibility of making money from the use of their works. Permission to use a work is usually granted by a license, which is an agreement (or contract) stating how the work may be used and what compensation the copyright owner will be paid for allowing the use. There are different kinds of licenses for different types of uses, and the compensation paid to a copyright owner under a license is usually in the form of royalties (i.e., a percentage of the price paid for the use).

## II. Why Do We Need Copyright?

For society to function smoothly, it is necessary to have rules governing who owns and who can exert control over intangible as well as tangible creations. Copyright law provides such a set of rules to govern the ownership and control of certain intangible creative works.

Before discussing the development of copyright, it is important to understand why copyright law exists in the first place. The issue of whether copyright should be recognized in creative works challenges fundamental assumptions about why society has created property rights. Historically, most property rights arose from the act of possession. However, intellectual property is unlike physical property because, once it is made available to the public, it is not subject to exclusive possession. The Supreme Court has stated that:

> The general rule of law is, that the noblest of human productions—knowledge, truths ascertained, conceptions, and ideas—become, after voluntary communication to others, free as the air to common use.[2]

There are several potential justifications for copyright. One involves considerations of privacy. An author may not want a work he or she has created to be made available to the public. Copyright gives the author the right to decide whether or not to make works available. Another justification involves the belief that an author who creates an artistic work should be able to control how that work is used. Finally, there are strong economic justifications for copyright. It can cost a lot of money to produce and market artistic works. For instance, the average recording released by a major record company involves an investment of at least several hundred thousand dollars, while a major motion picture typically involves an investment of over $50 million. Although recording costs have decreased with the advent of new technologies, the recording process still represents a substantial economic and artistic investment. Consequently, authors and copyright owners rely on the hope that potential revenues from their copyrighted works will repay their investment and allow them to make a profit.

---

**Example 1.1**

A songwriter transfers her copyright ownership in a son [*IMPortance of copyright*] in
return for an advance and potential royalties based on ( er
then attempts to exploit the song by licensing its use ne
(e.g., recordings, movie and television soundtracks, comm nd
the publisher's actions are based, at least partly, on econo up
their investment and make a profit.

*Positive* PLANS

---

Although most people agree that authors should be compensated for their work, it is also important to realize that copyright protection comes at a price. If copyright gives control to one person (the author or owner), it takes away some degree of freedom to use the work from others (the public). This does not mean that the public will be totally denied access to copyrighted works. Rather, it means that the public will sometimes be forced to pay for this access. The right to prevent the use of a copyrighted work also implies the power to allow the use of that work for a price. Most physical property, once used, is gone forever. However, because use of copyrighted works generally involves copies of the work rather than the original work, the price paid is usually a relatively small amount per copy or use.

Additionally, copyright is not an unlimited right and is subject to many limitations. The fair use defense, for example, allows people to use copyrighted works without permission and without paying for their use in certain circumstances, thereby preventing copyright from acting as a deterrent to free speech. The Supreme Court has stated that:

> It should not be forgotten that the Framers intended copyright itself to be the engine of free expression and only if that engine is adequately fueled will public access to literary, musical and artistic creations be ensured.[3]

Since the beginnings of copyright, a fundamental, philosophical debate has taken place involving whether copyright should be expanded to encompass new technologies so that authors and publishers can obtain the benefits of their works' value in the marketplace. Alternatively, should copyright be limited in order to ensure that the public has free or at least inexpensive access to new works and new uses? This debate revolves around the issue of whether copyright should be viewed as an author's right (primarily benefiting authors) or a user's right (primarily benefiting consumers).

## A. The Author's Right Philosophy

Under the author's right (or natural right) philosophy, an author is believed to be morally entitled to control and exploit the products of the author's intellect. This includes the right to be credited as the author and the right to prevent the work from being changed substantially. The author's right philosophy extends copyright protection automatically, as a matter of principle, to every new form of artistic work. It is based on the idea that an author should be allowed to obtain the reward for his contribution to society and to protect the integrity of his creation as an extension of his personality. One of the earliest and most well-known advocates of the author's right philosophy was the English philosopher, John Locke. Locke believed that because authors own their bodies, they also own the labor of their bodies and the fruits of their labor. According to Locke, property [...] d, but man acquired ownership of things by exerting labor a [...] ng useful.[4] Under the author's right philosophy, a songwriter [...] the right to control the song's use and to be compensated fo [...] be compensated for selling the crops he produces. Additional [...] ociety and may continue to do so in the future, the author s[...] sated to the full extent of the song's success. While a piece o [...] is eaten, a song can be enjoyed by many people indefinitely. T [...] owed, at least to some extent, by many European countries, [...] ight statutes as author's rights (also known as *moral rights*) la... ......... .. copyright laws (e.g., *droit d'auteur* in France, *Urheberrecht* in Germany, and *diritto d'autore* in Italy). In endorsing this concept of author's rights, an English court in 1769 stated that:

> It is just, that an author should reap the pecuniary profits of his own ingenuity and labor. It is just, that another should not use his name, without his consent. It is fit, that he should judge when to publish, or whether he even will publish. It is fit he should not only choose the time, but the manner of publication; how many; what volume; what print. It is fit, he should choose to whose care he will trust the accuracy and correctness of the impression; in whose honesty he will confide; not to foist in additions; with other reasoning of the same effect.[5]

## B. The Utilitarian Philosophy

The primary purpose of copyright law under the utilitarian (which might also be referred to as a "user's right" or "rights balancing") philosophy is to encourage the widest possible production and availability of artistic works. Copyright law is designed to achieve this objective by granting to authors property rights that provide them with financial incentives to produce and distribute creative works. The utilitarian philosophy assumes that authors (as well as publishers who finance the creation, distribution, and marketing of artistic works) will only invest sufficient resources in creating and publishing new works if they will have ownership rights that will enable them to control and profit from their works' distribution to the public. However, copyright law also recognizes that all creative efforts necessarily build on the creative efforts that precede them, and if copyright law is to promote the availability of information, it must allow subsequent creators to draw on copyrighted works for their inspiration and education.

The free market economic system disfavors monopolies unless there is a compelling justification for them. Although copyright is a limited form of monopoly, its justification is that it is necessary to ensure that creators have sufficient incentives to create. This results in a major difference between property rights in physical property and intellectual property. While the owner of physical property has absolute ownership rights to that property, intellectual property rights are not absolute. Copyright is a limited monopoly granted for a specified period of time. This limited copyright duration gives the copyright owner a chance to benefit financially from its property in order to recoup its investment and earn profits, thereby encouraging the creation and dissemination of new works of authorship. Because copyright ownership is limited in duration, all copyrighted works will eventually fall into the public domain, where they will be free for all to use. Copyright is also limited in other ways: Its scope is limited to original works of authorship, it protects only expression rather than ideas, and certain uses of copyrighted works are permitted without the copyright owner's consent.

Copyright law attempts to strike a balance between the incentives that authors and publishers need to produce original works and the freedom that creators need to draw on earlier copyrighted works. As stated by the Supreme Court:

> The limited scope of the copyright holder's statutory monopoly, like the limited copyright duration required by the Constitution, reflects a balance of competing claims upon the public interest: Creative work is to be encouraged and rewarded, but private motivation must ultimately serve the cause of promoting broad public availability of literature, music and other arts.[6]

Under the utilitarian philosophy, the costs and benefits of extending copyright to a new type of work or a new type of use must be balanced against each other. A plausible argument can be made that copyright protection does not significantly affect the extent to which authors will create new works. It is certainly likely that many authors would still create works even knowing that they could not own them or profit from them. However, it is also conceivable that other authors would not or would create fewer works if they had no financial incentive.

**Example 1.2**

> Although writing this book has been somewhat a labor of love, and the authors do not expect to earn a fortune from it, it probably would not have been written if there were no possibility of receiving some compensation. The authors have spent a great deal of time creating this book and, like most authors, hope that people will find their creation useful enough that they are willing to pay for it.

A criticism that has been aimed at copyright law is that since it is often large companies rather than authors who end up owning copyrighted works, copyright law does not really provide much incentive for authors to create. However, it is the author's decision to transfer ownership of a copyrighted work. In many situations, the only way the work will be made available to the general public is through a publisher's financing, marketing, and distribution. Even when an author transfers ownership to a publisher, the author will normally still receive royalties based on the publisher's distribution of the work, so financial incentives still exist. Further, it certainly seems fair that publishers are compensated for taking the financial risk necessary to make works available to the public. Copyright is a necessary incentive for distributors of creative works such as publishers as well as authors. Without the possibility of financial gain, publishers would certainly not be willing to invest the often substantial sums of money required to produce, market, and distribute creative works. Without that investment by publishers, far fewer works would be likely to reach the public, even assuming that authors were still willing to create them.

Copyright law involves striking a balance between providing sufficient incentives to authors to create works while also assuring that the public can have access to those works. The goal is to assure the greatest possible production and availability of creative works. Eventually, all works will enter the public domain, where they will be free to all people to use.

American copyright law is based on the utilitarian philosophy. In fact, Congress has specifically rejected the author's right philosophy as it recorded in the House Report on the 1909 Copyright Act:

> *The enactment of copyright legislation by Congress under the terms of the Constitution is not based upon any natural right that the author has in his writings... but upon the ground that the welfare of the public will be served and progress of science and useful arts will be promoted by securing to authors for limited periods the exclusive rights to their writings.*

## C. Other Philosophies

The United States' economy, as well as the economies of most Western nations, is based on the free market system and the belief that profits are the just reward for labor expended in creative endeavors. However, other countries are based on different economic foundations and have different viewpoints on the concept of authorship. Many nations' economies are related to the philosophies and religions of Confucianism, Buddhism, and Islam, which are more communally oriented. According to these countries' economic systems, profits should be shared within society. Under the authorship philosophies of some Asian countries, creative works have historically been viewed not as private property belonging to their authors, but as goods for everybody to share freely. In these countries, cultural esteem rather than financial gain was the main incentive for creativity, although this has changed somewhat in more recent history due largely to increasingly capitalistic business practices, rapid economic growth, and the corresponding potential for greater financial gain in countries such as Japan, South Korea, and China.

In feudal China, Confucian literary and artistic culture was based upon interaction with the past and discouraged bold innovation. Much of this background survived in the People's Republic of China, which has been hostile to the concept of private ownership rights in intellectual property. However, China has been forced, due in large part to foreign economic pressure, to adopt a copyright system highly similar to those of most Western nations. The forced nature of copyright is a probable reason for the enforcement problems that have been prevalent in China as well as other countries.

In many cultures, copying of copyrighted works is tolerated to a much greater extent than in the United States. In Islamic countries, where piracy is rampant, the rationale is that copying of original material should not be prevented because the most widespread dissemination of knowledge benefits the public good. Similarly, in countries such as China, South Korea, and Singapore, imitation and reproduction of ideas, art, and scholarship are considered a token of honor and respect.

## D. Economic Rights Philosophy

American copyright law, although historically based upon the user's right philosophy, may be more accurately described as an economic rights (or trade-based) philosophy. The United States is the world's largest producer and exporter of intellectual property. The main copyright industries (i.e., newspapers, books, music, motion pictures, software, radio, and television) account for about 6.44 percent of the annual gross domestic product ($889 billion) in the United States and employ about 4 percent (5.35 million) of the United States' workforce.[7] Copyrights bring more revenue into the United States than many other major industries, including aircraft, automobiles, and agriculture.

As copyrighted works have become a larger part of international trade, they have also become one of the few positive components in the otherwise unfavorable United States trade balance (i.e., the United States imports more of just about everything than it exports). One major exception is copyrighted works, where the United States has a surplus trade balance with every country in the world. Although foreigners are not buying huge quantities of American physical products such as cars, stereos, or computers, foreign sales of American intellectual property products such as music, movies, television programs, and computer programs are substantial. Consequently, the United States has taken a much more active role in expanding copyright's reach and enforcing copyright on an international basis, often without much consideration of either author's or user's rights. For example, the United States extended the duration of copyright by 20 years in 1998. It seems unlikely that this additional 20 years of copyright protection will make authors more likely to create artistic works. In reality, the two primary motivating factors for the 20-year extension were: (1) to preserve many valuable copyrights—including the copyrights to the Disney character

Mickey Mouse and songs written by George Gershwin—that were about to expire; and (2) to bring the term of American copyright protection in line with many European countries.

Although these reasons may be economically important for some copyrighted works, they have little to do with encouraging authors to create new works. There was no evidence presented to suggest that authors would be less likely to create new works without the additional 20 years of protection. The passage of the term extension amendment was due primarily to lobbying efforts of copyright owners of very valuable copyrighted works such as Disney and the Gershwin estate, with only token consideration given to providing incentives to authors or public access. This goes against the ideological basis for copyright, but it reflects the reality of our political and economic systems.

## III. Other Types of Intellectual Property Protection

Many people confuse copyright with other types of intellectual property. Each category of intellectual property law is aimed at a particular type of creation or information, but there is often a degree of overlap between these categories. For example, some patentable materials may be protected by trade secret law before a patent is granted, and although song titles are not protected under copyright law, they may be protected as trademarks under limited circumstances.

### A. Patents

Patent law provides protection for certain inventions, discoveries, and product designs. Patent protection is obtained by filing an application with the United States Patent & Trademark Office (PTO). Obtaining a patent is a time-consuming and often expensive process. The PTO examines the application to make sure that it complies with legal requirements and reviews prior patents and literature to determine whether the invention or design is eligible for patent protection. It is much more difficult to get a patent issued than it is to obtain an IP right, because patent protection requires that the invention be novel and nonobvious, while a copyright merely has to be original and fixed in tangible form. Patents, although providing the greatest degree of protection of any type of intellectual property, have a relatively short duration of 20 years.

### B. Trademarks

A trademark is any word, name, symbol, or device or any combination thereof used to identify products or services and to distinguish them from those manufactured or sold by others.[8] Trademark law can be used to protect names, designs, logos, slogans, symbols, colors, packaging, containers, and any other marks used by businesses to identify the source of their goods and services.

In the United States, trademark rights are acquired through use of a mark in commerce. In other words, the first person to use a mark will have rights in the mark, at least in the geographic area where the mark is used. Trademark rights last indefinitely, as long as the mark is being used to identify a product or service.

A trademark owner has the exclusive right to use its mark to identify its product or service. This allows a trademark owner to prevent others from using the same or a confusingly similar mark to identify the same or similar products or services. Although trademarks benefit their owners, they are primarily intended to benefit the public by preventing consumers from being misled or confused as to the source of goods and services.

Although not required, trademarks can be registered with the federal government as well as state governments. A federal trademark registration is obtained from the United States Patent & Trademark Office. State registrations are generally obtained from the secretary of state's office. Federally registered trademarks must bear a notice using the symbol ® (which denotes a federally "registered" mark) in order to obtain certain benefits provided by registration. The symbol ™ may be used for unregistered marks or marks covered by state registration.

### C. Trade Secrets

A trade secret is any business information that is kept secret and gives a business a competitive advantage. Trade secrets may include designs, devices, processes, databases, computer programs, formulas, recipes, customer lists, and business plans. Some materials subject to protection as trade secrets, such as computer programs, may also be protected by copyright and patent law. There is no registration process for trade secrets. Instead, trade secret protection lasts as long as the information is kept secret.

## IV. Copyright's Importance to the Economy and the Music Industry

The United States economy has evolved from the industrial age to the post-industrial information age. In the industrial age, economic power was measured by the number of physical products a nation produced. In the information age, intellectual property is more important than any physical commodities. This is illustrated by the fact that the wealthiest individual in the world at the beginning of the twenty-first century was Bill Gates, who made his fortune from the intellectual property contained in Microsoft's computer software.

The importance of intellectual pro... rent with the prevalence of digital technology and the Internet... tury, intellectual property's importance is sure to increase. Pro... power, and in the twenty-first century, intellectual property... will be a crucial source of economic power and prosperity.

*Revenue Streams*

Copyright is vital to the existence ... dustry is based upon ownership of certain creative works, p... *Positive* PLANS ... use the rights provided by copyright law exist to protect crea... of authorship, it is important to understand what these rights are, how they are exercised, and how they are enforced. This understanding will enable you to comprehend what ownership rights different parties in the music industry routinely have in different types of works. It will also enable you to know when certain rights are being violated and prevent you from violating other people's rights.

One of the criticisms leveled against copyright in recent years is that huge entertainment corporations use it to exercise control over content. Although it is certainly true that companies such as the major record company conglomerates own vast numbers of valuable copyrights, it is very inaccurate to imply that only these major companies benefit from copyright law. In reality, many people have jobs and make a living due to copyright law. Artists from Aerosmith (whose recordings are owned by Sony through their record label, Columbia Records) to Ani DiFranco (who owns and releases her recordings independently) are dependent on copyright law. In addition to famous musicians, there are also many behind-the-scenes individuals whose livelihoods are dependent on copyright law, such as songwriters, record producers, recording engineers, entertainment attorneys, etc.

Despite its critics, copyright law is here to stay. It is by no means a perfect system, but it has proved to be a fairly successful one. Its success is based on the fact that copyright law does provide incentives for authors to create new works that are generally made available to the public. Although the public often has to pay a price for access to these works, this price results in compensation to authors (and companies that finance authors' creations) that allows them to keep creating. Although copyright will remain with us, it is also certain to change. As discussed in the next chapter, copyright's history reflects a continuous evolution based on technological advances. The challenge for copyright law is to accommodate technological advances while still guaranteeing that creators and producers have the right to control and profit from the use of their creations.

## Endnotes

1. "I Created Jazz in 1902, Not W.C.". Handy, *Down Beat*, Aug.–Sept. 1938, reprinted in *Down Beat*, July 1994, at 10.
2. *International News Service v. Associated Press*, 248 U.S. 215, 250 (1918).
3. *Harper & Row v. Nation Enterprises*, 471 U.S. 539 (1985).
4. J. Locke, *Treatise of Government*, Chapter 5 (1690).
5. *Millar v. Taylor*, (1769) 98 ER 201 at 252.
6. *Twentieth Century Music Corp. v. Aiken*, 422 U.S. 151, 156 (1975).
7. "Copyright Industries in the U.S. Economy: The 2003–2007 Report," prepared for IIPA by Economists, Inc., June 2009, available at http://www.iipa.com.
8. 15 U.S.C. § 1127 (2010).

# 2 The History of Copyright

*"The progress of copyright law does not take place by revolutions, but by successive stages. It resembles the growth of a city in which, as time goes on, some parts are torn down and others are devoted to new uses, while the plan remains the same and the great historic structures are preserved."[1]*

—Richard C. DeWolf

Although the main intention of this book is to discuss copyright law's current and future applications, before examining copyright law in the twenty-first century, it is first necessary to examine the evolution of copyright to the present. Many of the issues currently being raised about copyright law's application in the era of digital technology have been raised in the past in other contexts.

Copyright has existed in the United States since the nation's birth and in England since the beginning of the eighteenth century. Although copyright as a form of ownership did not exist prior to that, the economic origins of copyright go back even further and can be traced back to ancient Greece, where singers were paid for their performances of music. Copyright has evolved over the past three centuries primarily because new technologies have resulted in new forms of creative expression, new media in which creative works are used, and new businesses that are in some way dependent on the use of copyrighted works. Consequently, to deal with these developments, copyright law has involved the gradual expansion of the types of works protected by copyright as well as the rights encompassed by copyright. As advances in technology have expanded the range of economically valuable uses of copyrighted works, the types of works protected and the scope of exclusive rights in these works have also been expanded in order to enable creators and copyright owners to realize the benefits of their works in these new mediums of expression.

## I. The World before Copyright

Prior to the eighteenth century, most creators were regarded as craftsmen who worked toward the creation of a product. At the beginning of the first millennium, a book trade in the Roman Empire developed. However, book manufacturing at this time consisted of slaves transcribing written works onto papyrus sheets that were then assembled into scrolls, which was a cumbersome process. More commonly, creative works were communicated orally. In the Greek states in the middle of the first millennium, authors read their works and musicians performed their works at public gatherings. Because there was no law protecting creative works of art, Greek states such as Athens

13

relied on government sponsorship of the arts rather than any form of private ownership and commercialization of artistic creations. However, even in these ancient, pre-copyright times, there was some idea that an author should have the right to control the use of his creations.

**Example 2.1**

In the middle of the first millennium, the monk Columba transcribed the abbot Finnian's manuscript of the Psalms. In a precursor of many copyright disputes to come, Finnian objected to the unauthorized transcription, and Celtic King Diarmait reportedly resolved the dispute by stating "to every cow her calf, to every book its copy." Although copyright law did not yet exist, this was an early recognition of the idea that creative works might be treated as some form of property.

Copyright's origins were in part a delayed response to important technological advances. In 1436, Johannes Gutenberg invented the printing press. This innovation in technology made it possible to make cheaper multiple copies of written works. One result of the invention of the printing press was that many more literary works were made available to the public than ever before. Another result was that the issue of who would be entitled to own and profit from the production and distribution of these works arose. The Internet may be the twenty-first century's equivalent of the printing press because it has allowed many works to be made easily and cheaply available while also spawning controversy over who (if anyone) should have the right to control and profit from the digital distribution of copyrighted works.

**The Beginnings of Print**   Although Gutenberg is commonly credited as the inventor of the printing press in the fifteenth century, printing apparently originated in the eleventh century in China. However, for various cultural and economic reasons, a print publishing industry did not develop in China to anywhere near the extent that it did in Europe after Gutenberg's printing press. Consequently, the concept of copyright was relatively unknown and of little importance in China until the nineteenth century.

During the seventeenth century, authors rarely owned or controlled the works they created. A book trade developed with printers purchasing the right to print copies from authors and then owning the books they published. As the book trade grew, printers and distributors formed guilds to avoid competition. At the same time, governments engaged in censorship to avoid religious and political dissent. To do so, many European nations instituted monopolies for favored publishers who, in return for agreeing not to publish any heretical or objectionable works, were able to prevent other publishers from competing with them.

**Example 2.2**

Musicians were generally even worse off than their literary counterparts, mostly working in the streets or as servants. Classical composers such as Haydn and Mozart spent most of their lives working under the sponsorship of a monarch and received little financial compensation for their creations.

# II. Copyright's English Origins

As a result of the competition among book publishers after the introduction of the printing press in England, the English Crown became concerned about the possibility of books being published that advocated religious heresy and political dissent. In 1534, to prevent such dissent, the Crown passed a law known as the Licensing Act, which required that anyone who wanted to publish written works must first obtain a license. The Licensing Act led to a publishing monopoly by a group of English printers and booksellers known as the Stationers' Company.

In 1557, a revised version of the Licensing Act was passed that required all books to be registered with the Stationers' Company, which recorded who owned the "copy-right" (i.e., the right to print copies of the work). The Licensing Act effectively gave the Stationers' Company a monopoly on printing. The Stationers' Company also had the authority to search out, seize, and destroy any offending works, thereby operating as a mechanism of government control of printed works. This precursor to copyright was therefore a means of censorship rather than a means of protection for authors.

In 1694, the Licensing Act expired, and the Stationers' Company started having competition from new printers, many of whom published cheaper versions of books previously published by the Stationers. The Stationers' Company lobbied in Parliament for legislative protection to maintain its monopoly. However, it made the fatal mistake of attempting to persuade Parliament that a law was needed not solely to allow them to profit from publishing, but also to provide authors with incentives to create new works. Their lobbying efforts eventually resulted in the world's first copyright statute. This was not the result that the Stationers had hoped for because rather than re-creating the monopoly the Stationers had previously enjoyed, it gave ownership rights to authors.

## A. The Statute of Anne

By the early eighteenth century, the mercantilist regimes that had dominated the previous century had given way to a less regulatory form of government. In this more relaxed regulatory environment, individuals became increasingly free to think, work, and create without intervention. This environment led to the birth of copyright laws that recognized the importance of authorship. The notion that creators of artistic works should be accorded ownership of the works they produced began to emerge. The idea that authorship justified ownership was based on the degree of originality involved in the creation of most artistic works.

In 1710, the English Parliament passed the Statute of Anne, which was formally titled "An Act for the Encouragement of Learning, by vesting the Copies of Printed Books in the Authors or Purchasers of such Copies, during the Times therein mentioned." The Statute of Anne stated its purpose as follows:

> *Whereas printers, booksellers, and other persons have of late frequently taken the liberty of printing, reprinting and publishing... books and other writings, without the consent of the authors or proprietors of such books and writings, to their very great detriment, and too often to the ruin of them and their families: for preventing therefor such practices for the future and for the encouragement of learned men to*

*compose and write useful books; may it please your Majesty, that it may be enacted… that the author of any book or books… and his assignee or assigns, shall have the sole liberty of printing and reprinting such books for the term of fourteen years, to commence from the day of the first publishing the same, and no longer.*

Although the Statute of Anne confirmed the Stationers' rights in their existing books for a period of 21 years, it granted protection in new works to their authors. An author could obtain copyright protection by registering his work on the Stationers' register. Commonly, due to the high cost involved in printing and distributing books, authors sold their works to one of the Stationers for a lump sum payment. The Stationer then registered the work in its own name with no further compensation paid to the author.

The Statute of Anne provided that authors received a 14-year term of copyright protection, with an additional 14-year term if the author was still alive. The reason for dividing the term of protection into two periods was that even if an author transferred his copyright to a publisher, the copyright returned to the author at the end of the initial 14-year period. In order to receive protection, the copyright owner had to register the title of the book with the Stationers' Company before publication. Infringement occurred when someone other than the author or owner printed a book without the author's permission. Once the copyright expired, anyone was free to copy the work and distribute copies.

Copyright under the Statute of Anne was much more limited than modern copyright and applied solely to the printing and selling of books. Copyright therefore covered the right to make copies by printing and to prevent others from making copies without permission. The Statute of Anne did not confer any protection on musical works. It was not until 1842 that the Victoria Statutes recognized the copyrightability of music in England,[2] although an earlier court case brought by the son of Johann Sebastian Bach had decided that the Statute of Anne was applicable to music.[3]

# III. Copyright in the United States

In the early history of the United States, many areas of law including copyright were largely based on British law. Prior to the founding of the United States, most of the American colonies enacted copyright laws modeled on British law. Even after establishing its political independence from England, the new nation's leaders continued to rely heavily on British law as the basis for much of the American legal system. It should therefore not be surprising that the United States' first copyright law was very similar to England's Statute of Anne.

## A. The Colonial States

The development of copyright law in the United States was very similar to the evolution of copyright law in England. Several authors campaigned for copyright protection in the colonial states, including Noah Webster—author of the *Grammatical Institute of the English Language*, which sold over 70 million copies—and Thomas Paine (author, inventor, and one of the Founding Fathers of the United States). The first state copyright statute was passed in 1783 by Connecticut; by 1786, 12 of the 13 colonial states had passed copyright statutes.[4]

The fact that 12 of the 13 colonial states each had its own copyright laws created problems with consistency and enforcement from one state to the next. Consequently, by the time of the Constitutional Convention, it had become apparent that a uniform, national copyright law was needed.

### B. The Constitutional Copyright Clause

On March 10, 1783, the Continental Congress established a committee to "consider the most proper means of cherishing genius and useful arts through the United States by securing to the authors or publishers of new books their property in such works." The representatives at the Constitutional Convention drafted a clause giving the federal government the authority to pass laws dealing with copyright, which passed unanimously. Article I, section 8, clause 8 of the Constitution, commonly known as the Copyright and Patent clause, states that Congress will have the power:

> To promote the progress of Science and the Useful Arts, by securing for limited times to Authors and Inventors the exclusive right to their writings and discoveries.

The constitutional clause's language, "to promote the progress of Science and the Useful Arts," established that the primary purpose of copyright law in the United States is to promote the creation and dissemination of creative works to the public. Copyright law in the United States is therefore supposed to ultimately benefit the public. Rewarding authors for their creations is only a secondary purpose. The rationale for rewarding authors is based on the idea that the best way to encourage people to create works of authorship is to provide financial incentives to do so. If no such financial incentives existed, people would be less likely to create new works. Over the years, courts have expressed this belief repeatedly. For instance, the Supreme Court has stated that:

> [T]he encouragement of individual effort by personal gain is the best way to advance public welfare through the talents of authors.[5]

### C. The Copyright Act of 1790

In 1790, Congress exercised its right under the copyright clause of the Constitution and passed the first American copyright statute, which was largely based on England's Statute of Anne and signed into law by President George Washington. Copyright protection under the 1790 Act was limited to books, maps, and charts. The 1790 Act provided for an initial term of copyright protection consisting of 14 years and a renewal term of 14 years, thus allowing for a maximum of 28 years of protection.

### D. The Copyright Act of 1831

In 1831, the first general revision of the United States Copyright Act took place. The Copyright Act of 1831 changed the initial term of copyright protection to 28 years in order to give American copyright owners the same period of protection that many foreign authors enjoyed at that time. The 1831 Act also allowed the renewal right to pass to the author's widow or children if the author was not alive at the end of the initial term. The 1831 Act also included musical compositions as a class of copyrightable subject matter, although a public performance right was not included until 1897.

## E. The Copyright Act of 1909

In 1905, President Theodore Roosevelt called for a complete revision of the Copyright Act in order to bring it in line with technological advances that had taken place. One of the main changes made by the 1909 Act was that, instead of individually specifying the types of works that can be subject to copyright, it simply stated that copyright protection is applicable to "all the writings of an author."[6] The term "writings" was interpreted by the Supreme Court to include works that are based upon the creative powers of the mind and are the fruits of intellectual labor. This broad meaning of the term, therefore, included most types of artistic works.

Under the 1909 Act, the renewal period of copyright protection was extended to 28 years, increasing the maximum period of copyright protection to 56 years (i.e., a 28-year initial period plus a 28-year renewal period). The 1909 Act protected only published works, leaving unpublished works protected by common-law copyright (copyright protection recognized by court decisions rather than a statute).

One major shortcoming of the 1909 Act was that it failed to bring American copyright law in line with the terms required to join the main international copyright treaty (the Berne Convention) due to its insistence on formalities and a shorter term of protection. Unlike the United States, most foreign countries did not condition copyright protection upon any formalities such as registration and notice. However, the United States felt strongly that these requirements were important, and the 1909 Act, like the copyright statutes before it, conditioned copyright protection upon these formalities.

A new and very important provision for copyright owners of musical works was incorporated into the 1909 Act. This provision created a compulsory (i.e., mandatory) mechanical license to reproduce and distribute sound recordings of musical compositions. It provided for a two-cent royalty to be paid to the copyright owner of a song for each record distributed containing that song, provided that the copyright owner had previously authorized the first recording and distribution of the song. In the early 1900s, the main formats in which recordings were reproduced were piano rolls, discs, and cylinder recordings, all of which were made mechanically. However, the mechanical license is now applicable to all types of reproduction (other than audio-visual reproduction) regardless of the format that the recording takes. Consequently, the license required to record a copyrighted song, regardless of the type of recording (e.g., mechanical, analog, digital, etc.), is called a mechanical license (see Chapter 5, "The Reproduction Right," regarding the current compulsory mechanical license provisions).

Sound recordings were not protected under the 1909 Copyright Act, but an amendment was passed giving a limited degree of copyright protection to sound recordings for the first time in the United States, as of February 15, 1972. This amendment prohibits the actual copying of a sound recording but does not prohibit independently recording an imitation of a sound recording. It also did not include a right of public performance for sound recordings.

Although the 1909 Act has been replaced by the 1976 Act, it continues to be applicable in some respects for works created before January 1, 1978—the date the 1976 Copyright Act became effective—subject to certain amendments that have since been passed.

### F. The Copyright Act of 1976

In 1955, Congress authorized a copyright revision project that—after 21 years of lobbying, studies, and hearings—resulted in the passage of a new and substantially revised copyright statute. The 1976 Copyright Act is a much more detailed statute than previous copyright statutes. In many of its provisions, rather than specifying general rules, the 1976 Act takes a more regulatory approach, much of which resulted from extensive lobbying by special interest groups. The following are some of the more important changes made by the 1976 Copyright Act, all of which are discussed in greater detail in subsequent chapters:

**Protection:** Copyright begins automatically when a copyrightable work is fixed in a tangible form without any registration requirement (see Chapter 3, "What Can Be Protected by Copyright").

**Preemption:** Section 301 of the 1976 Act states that because copyright applies to any works fixed in tangible form, there would no longer be any common law copyright for unpublished works. Any copyrightable work created on or after January 1, 1978, whether published or unpublished, is protected by the 1976 Copyright Act.

**Subject Matter:** Any original works of authorship can be protected by copyright. The 1976 Act specifies broad illustrative categories of the types of works that are copyrightable, including musical works and sound recordings (see Chapter 3).

**Ownership:** The 1976 Act made copyright divisible, meaning that a copyright owner can transfer less than its full ownership interest to others. Copyrights can therefore be split into many shares and in many different ways (see Chapter 4, "Ownership of Copyright").

**Duration:** The 1976 Act changed the basic term of copyright protection to a period based on the life of the author plus 50 years, which has since been increased to the life of the author plus 70 years (see Chapter 8, "Duration of Copyright").

**Termination Right:** The 1976 Act conferred an important new right on authors, allowing them to terminate transfers of copyright ownership and regain full ownership of their works (see Chapter 4).

**Formalities:** Copyright notice continued to be required for published works. Registration and recordation of copyright transfers remained conditions to bringing suit for infringement, although these formalities were later made optional (see Chapter 9, "Copyright Formalities").

**Fair Use:** The 1976 Act made the fair use doctrine, which had developed in the courts, a part of the copyright statute. Fair use is the broadest exception to the copyright owner's exclusive rights, giving others the right to use copyrighted works without permission in certain circumstances and for certain purposes (see Chapter 11, "Defenses to Infringement").

**Compulsory Licenses:** The 1976 Act carried forward the 1909 Act's compulsory mechanical license, but provided for increases in mechanical royalty rates (see Chapter 5). It also added several other compulsory licenses that allow the use of copyrighted works upon compliance with certain procedures and payment of specified fees (cable television compulsory license, jukebox compulsory license, and public broadcasting compulsory license)

Even though the 1976 Copyright Act was designed to be a flexible statute that could be applied to new types of works and new uses of copyrighted works, it has been amended over 30 times since its passage. The copyright timeline at the end of this chapter lists some of the more important of these amendments.

# IV. International Developments

During the nineteenth century, the United States generally refused to extend any copyright protection to foreign works, and many American book publishers freely pirated English books. Similarly, the French book publishing industry was subject to rampant piracy in Belgium until the French government threatened trade reprisals. Eventually, France and Belgium entered into a treaty providing for copyright protection of each other's works. Other treaties between countries followed among various European nations, resulting in a network of laws providing for copyright protection among nations.

As the international market for copyrighted works increased, the system of bilateral treaties among individual countries made less sense. Instead, many countries started to realize that some type of uniform body of law binding as many countries as possible was needed. After years of negotiation, a small group of countries formed the Berne Convention in 1886. Under the Berne Convention, each member country agreed to give foreign works the same degree of protection as its law provided for domestic works. Over the next century, more countries gradually joined the Berne Convention. The United States, however, resisted joining the Berne Convention until 1989.

Over the latter half of the twentieth century, the importance of copyright has increased dramatically on an international basis. Virtually every country in the world recognizes some form of copyright law. Although copyright law varies from country to country, international treaties such as the Berne Convention guarantee at least certain minimum levels of copyright protection.

# V. Summary

In the sixteenth and seventeenth centuries, governments attempted to combat piracy and exercise censorship by enacting legislation that limited the variety of works that reached the public. In the early eighteenth century, copyright laws began to develop that gave ownership rights to authors. Commonly, authors sold their rights to publishers who manufactured, distributed, and marketed their works. From the mid-nineteenth century to the present, copyright has been adapted and expanded to accommodate many advances in technology.

In the nineteenth century, new industries arose based on producing and distributing copyrighted works. Many of these industries (e.g., film, television, and music) are highly cost intensive, competitive, and global in nature. Consequently, copyright has become increasingly important as a means of protecting the investment made by companies from piracy by others who wish to appropriate that investment without paying for it. In recent years, due to the ability to distribute copyrighted works worldwide, the importance of copyright has been increasingly recognized on an international scale.

## Table 2.1  Copyright Timeline

| | |
|---|---|
| 1436 | Johannes Gutenberg invented the printing press, making the mass production ... works possible. |
| 1534 | The English Crown passed the Licensing Act, which required that anyone who wanted to publish written works must first obtain a license. The Licensing Act led to a publishing monopoly by the Stationers' Company. |
| 1557 | A new version of the Licensing Act was passed. It required that all books had to be licensed by registering them with the Stationers' Company, which recorded who owned the "copy-right" (i.e., the right to print copies of the work). |
| 1694 | The Licensing Act expired, and the Stationers' Company started having competition from new printers who published their own cheaper versions of books published by the Stationers. |
| 1710 | The English Parliament passed the Statute of Anne, the world's first copyright law. |
| 1783 | Connecticut passed the first copyright statute of the colonial United States. |
| 1787 | James Madison submitted to the framers of the Constitution a provision "to secure to literary authors their copyrights for a limited time." |
| 1790 | Congress passed the first United States Copyright Act, which protected books, charts, and maps. The first copyrighted work registered in the United States was *The Philadelphia Spelling Book* by John Barry. |
| 1831 | The first general revision of the Copyright Act was made. Music was added to the types of works protected by copyright. The first term of copyright was extended to 28 years with a renewal term of 14 years. |
| 1841 | The case of *Folsom v. Marsh* introduced the concept of fair use into copyright law. Fair use makes it possible to use copyrighted works without the copyright owner's permission in certain limited circumstances. For a more detailed explanation of fair use, see Chapter 11. |
| 1851 | The first performing rights organization, *Societe des Auteurs, Compositeurs et Editeurs de Musique* (SACEM), was formed in France. |
| 1856 | Dramatic works were added to the types of works protected by copyright. |
| 1865 | Photographs were added to the types of works protected by copyright. |
| 1877 | Thomas Edison invented the phonograph. |
| 1886 | The Berne Convention became the first international copyright treaty. The United States did not join until 1989. |
| 1891 | The first U.S. copyright law authorizing the establishment of copyright relations with foreign countries was passed. |
| 1897 | The public performance right was made applicable to musical works. The Copyright Office was established as a department of the Library of Congress. |
| 1909 | The Copyright Act of 1909 was passed. |
| 1912 | Motion pictures, previously registered as photographs, were added to the types of works protected by copyright. |

*(Continues)*

**Table 2.1** Copyright Timeline (*Continued*)

| | |
|---|---|
| 1914 | The American Society of Composers, Authors and Publishers (ASCAP), the first performing rights society in the United States, was formed. |
| 1940 | Broadcast Music Incorporated (BMI), a performing rights organization, was formed to compete with ASCAP. |
| 1955 | The Universal Copyright Convention became effective in the United States. |
| 1970 | The World Intellectual Property Organization (WIPO) was established to protect creators and owners of intellectual property on an international basis. |
| 1972 | An amendment to the 1909 Copyright Act, which provided limited copyright protection to sound recordings fixed and published on or after February 15, 1972, became effective. |
| 1974 | The United States became a member of the Convention for the Protection of Producers of Phonograms Against Unauthorized Duplication of Their Phonograms. |
| 1976 | The fourth general revision of the United States Copyright Act was signed into law by President Ford. |
| 1978 | The 1976 Copyright Act became effective. |
| 1982 | § 506(a) of the Copyright Act was amended to provide that persons who infringe copyright willfully and for purposes of commercial advantage or private financial gain shall be subject to criminal copyright infringement. |
| 1984 | The Record Rental Amendment became effective. This amendment granted the copyright owner of a sound recording the right to authorize or prohibit the rental, lease, or lending of phonorecords for direct or indirect commercial purposes. |
| 1984 | The Supreme Court ruled, in *Sony v. Universal Studios*, that the videotaping of television shows using videocassette recorders in order to watch the shows at more convenient times is fair use. This decision, which has become the mantra of file sharing companies sued for copyright infringement, ensures that new forms of technology that can be used to infringe copyrights cannot be banned as long as they also have substantial non-infringing uses. |
| 1989 | The United States became a member of the Berne Convention (effective March 1, 1989). The Berne Convention Implementation Act made several changes to U.S. copyright law. Most importantly, copyright notice was made optional rather than mandatory. |
| 1992 | Renewal registration was made optional. Works copyrighted between January 1, 1964, and December 31, 1977, were automatically renewed even if renewal registration was not made. |
| 1992 | The Audio Home Recording Act was passed. This Act required serial copy management systems in digital audio recorders, imposed royalties on the sale of digital audio recording devices and media, and exempted individuals from liability for copyright infringement for private, non-commercial copying (i.e., home taping). |
| 1994 | The Uruguay Round Agreements Act restored copyright to certain foreign works that were in the public domain in the United States and created legal measures to prohibit the unauthorized fixation and trafficking in sound recordings of live musical performances and music videos. |
| 1995 | The Performance Right in Sound Recordings Act was passed. It provided for a limited performance right in sound recordings, which applies to digital audio transmissions of recordings. |

1997    The No Electronic Theft Act amended criminal copyright infringement provisions to permit the government to prosecute not only those who sell copies of copyrighted works without permission but also individuals who merely give away copies. This reversed the decision of *United States v. La Macchia*, in which a bulletin board system operator was found not liable for unlicensed distribution by providing free pirated copies of copyrighted software.

1998    The Sonny Bono Copyright Term Extension Act was passed, increasing the term of copyright protection in the United States to the life of the author plus 70 years.

1998    The Fairness in Music Licensing Act was passed. This law broadened the exemption to the public performance right in music for certain restaurants and other retail establishments, depending on the size of the establishment and the number and size of speakers.

1998    Congress passed the Digital Millennium Copyright Act (DMCA), which implemented two international treaties designed to provide greater protection for copyrighted works in the digital environment (see Chapter 14, "Copyright and Digital Technology").

1999    Congress passed the Digital Theft Deterrence and Copyright Damages Improvement Act of 1999, which increased the minimum statutory damages amounts under § 504(c) of the Copyright Act.

1999    Congress passed an amendment to the Copyright Act, which added sound recordings to the classes of works that are eligible to be treated as specially ordered or commissioned works made for hire under § 101(2). This amendment provoked much criticism and was repealed the following year.

2000    In the first major lawsuit against a file sharing company, a U.S. district court ruled that the Napster file sharing company was likely liable for infringements committed by users of its file sharing software. The decision was upheld on appeal, and Napster shortly thereafter went bankrupt.

2002    In *Eldred v. Ashcroft*, the U.S. Supreme Court upheld the Sonny Bono Copyright Term Extension Act enacted in 1998. The Act had been challenged by a group of publishers of public domain materials who claimed that the Act violated the Constitution, which says that copyrights can only be for "limited times." The Supreme Court held that the Constitution specifically gives Congress the right to determine how long copyrights should last and, because the amended copyright term was for a limited (although a long) time, the Act did not violate the Constitution.

2003    In *MGM Studios, Inc. v. Grokster, Ltd.*, a federal district court ruled that file sharing companies Grokster and Streamcast were not liable for copyright infringements committed by users of their file sharing software because file sharing software can be used for legal as well as illegal purposes and because the court believed the file sharing companies were unable to prevent infringements from occurring. In 2004, this decision was upheld by a federal appeals court (but overruled in 2005 by the Supreme Court).

2005    The U.S. Supreme Court reversed the decisions of the district and appeals courts in *MGM Studios, Inc. v. Grokster, Ltd.*, holding that file sharing companies may be held liable for copyright infringement if they actively encourage or induce infringement by users of their file sharing software.

2005    Congress enacted the Family Entertainment and Copyright Act, which does the following things: (1) makes it a criminal offense to use video cameras or other recording devices to record movies in movie theaters; (2) makes it a criminal offense to make copyrighted works that have not yet been released available on the Internet; (3) authorizes the

*(Continues)*

**Table 2.1**  Copyright Timeline (*Continued*)

|  | Register of Copyrights to issue regulations for preregistration of certain types of works prone to infringement before publication; and (4) creates an exemption from copyright infringement for editing objectionable content (e.g., profanity, nudity, violence) from legally acquired copies of copyrighted movies for private home viewing. |
|---|---|
| 2008 | Congress enacted the Prioritizing Resources and Organization for Intellectual Property Act, which added several provisions to the Copyright Act, including increasing civil and criminal penalties for copyright infringement; providing for increased funding for the investigation and prosecution of intellectual property crimes; and establishing a new federal government office called the Office of the United States Intellectual Property Enforcement Representative, which is responsible for coordinating plans to fight piracy of intellectual property by federal government departments. |

# Endnotes

1.  *An Outline of Copyright Law,* viii (1925).
2.  1842, 5 & 6 Vict., ch. 45, § 2.
3.  *Bach v. Longman*, 98 Eng. Rep. 1274 (K.B. 1777).
4.  Delaware was the only state that had not passed a copyright statute.
5.  *Mazer v. Stein*, 347 U.S. 201 (1954).
6.  17 U.S.C. § 4 (superseded 1976).

# 3 What Can Be Protected by Copyright?

*"In truth, in literature, in science and in art, there are, and can be, few, if any, things, which, in an abstract sense, are strictly new and original throughout. Every book in literature, science and art, borrows, and must necessarily borrow, and use much which was well known and used before."*

*–Emerson v. Davies, 8 F. Cas. 615, 619 (C.C.D. Mass. 1845)*

Many different types of creations are capable of being protected by copyright. This is partly due to the fact that when Congress passed the 1976 Copyright Act, it chose to adopt a very broad definition of authorship, recognizing that authors are constantly developing new ways to express themselves. Generally, all forms of literary, musical, visual, and other artistic works can be protected by copyright if they fit the requirements specified by the Copyright Act. Copyrightable works include, among other things, books, magazines, newspapers, scripts, speeches, personal and business correspondence (including e-mail), computer programs, product packaging, musical compositions (with or without lyrics), sound recordings, motion pictures, videos, photographs, paintings, drawings, and sculpture.

It is important to understand that copyright protection is not based on any aesthetic consideration of the value of a work. Subjective judgments as to whether a work is good or bad are irrelevant as far as copyright protection is concerned. In a famous Supreme Court opinion from 1903, Justice Holmes stated that:

> It would be a dangerous undertaking for persons trained only to the law to constitute themselves final judges of the worth of pictorial illustrations outside of the narrowest and most obvious limits.[1]

Holmes was in effect saying that judges are not necessarily the best qualified people to make judgments about the artistic value of creative works and that, aside from determining whether the Copyright Act's requirements for copyrightable subject matter are met, courts should not have to evaluate the artistic merit of works.

## I. Requirements for Copyright

There are three basic requirements for a work to be capable of copyright protection: originality, expression, and fixation. Section 102(a) of the Copyright Act specifies that copyright protection is available to:

*original works of authorship fixed in any **tangible** medium of **expression**, now or later developed, from which they can be perceived, reproduced, or otherwise communicated, either directly or with the aid of a machine or device.*

## A. Originality

The first requirement that a work must satisfy in order for it to be copyrightable is that it must be original. Although this requirement may seem straightforward, the originality requirement is a common source of confusion. As the quote beginning this chapter illustrates, very little is totally original because virtually all creativity draws on already existing elements. Music composers select and arrange musical notes and rhythms that have existed for centuries, and literary authors use words already in existence rather than creating their own.

How original does a work have to be in order to be entitled to copyright protection? The term "original" was purposely left undefined by the Copyright Act because Congress intended to let courts establish standards of originality and to allow the categories of copyrightable works to expand in response to technological advances. The first Copyright Act in the United States protected only books, charts, and maps, but Congress has added other types of works over the years by passing amendments bringing works such as photographs, musical compositions, sound recordings, and computer programs within the scope of copyright. Rather than attempt to specify an all-encompassing list of works protected by copyright, the 1976 Copyright Act provides copyright protection to all "original works of authorship," regardless of the type of work or form of authorship.

At its simplest, originality means that a work has been independently created by its author rather than copied from another work. Originality does not require any measure of novelty,[2] ingenuity, or aesthetic merit. According to one court:

*Originality is…distinguished from novelty; there must be independent creation, but it need not be invention in the sense of striking uniqueness, ingeniousness, or novelty… Originality means that the work owes its creation to the author and this in turn means that the work must not consist of actual copying.[3]*

In *Sheldon v. Metro-Goldwyn Pictures Corp.*, Judge Learned Hand, who decided many important copyright cases, described the originality requirement, stating that:

*…if by some magic a man who had never known it were to compose anew Keats's "Ode on a Grecian Urn," he would be an "author," and, if he copyrighted it, others might not copy the poem, though they might of course copy Keats's.[4]*

Substituting a song for Keats's "Ode," if two different songwriters each composed exactly identical songs without copying from the other, each would own the copyright in his song. Although this situation would involve a very unlikely coincidence, it illustrates that originality is based upon independent creation.

In addition to independent creation, originality also requires a minimal amount of creativity. The reason for this requirement is that some works, although independently created, are too trivial or insignificant to justify copyright protection. The Supreme Court has held that, in addition to being independently created, a work must also possess "at least some minimal degree of creativity," although "the requisite level of creativity is extremely low" and "even a slight amount will suffice."[5] The Court went on to state that "the vast majority of works make the grade quite easily, as they possess some creative spark."

Although some degree of creativity is required, creativity is a subjective concept, and courts have struggled with defining and measuring creativity. One thing that courts have agreed on is that the amount of creativity required is minimal. Courts have variously expressed the creativity requirement as requiring more than "merely trivial" variation,[6] a "modicum of creativity,"[7] a "touch of fresh authorship,"[8] and a "distinguishable variation."[9] Because the primary purpose of copyright is to encourage the production of the widest possible variety of literary and artistic expression, the low originality requirement helps to achieve that purpose by allowing protection for works that differ only minimally from earlier works.

The degree of originality required will vary somewhat for different types of works. Originality is easily found in highly artistic works such as literary works of fiction and musical works. In contrast, originality will be examined more closely in factual works (such as telephone directories) and functional works (such as accounting forms) because there is a limited amount of variation possible.

---

**Example 3.1**

---

In *ZZ Top v. Chrysler Corp.*,[10] ZZ Top sued Chrysler over its use of the distinctive guitar riff from their song "La Grange" in a press conference to debut the Plymouth Prowler. Chrysler argued that the riff was substantially similar to riffs in earlier songs, including "Boogie Chillen" by John Lee Hooker and "Spirit in the Sky" by Norman Greenbaum. However, the court found the ZZ Top riff to be sufficiently original to be protected by copyright despite these similarities.

---

## B. Expression

All songs are made up of notes, chords, and rhythms that exist apart from that work and that have been used in many other songs before. All books are written with words and ideas that exist apart from and predate the book. This leads us to the second requirement for copyrightable subject matter, which is that a work must contain some original expression of the author rather than mere ideas, even if the ideas are totally original. This requirement is expressed in Section 102(b) of the Copyright Act:

> *In no case does copyright protection for an original work of authorship extend to any idea, procedure, process, system, method of operation, concept, principle, or discovery, regardless of the form in which it is described, explained, illustrated, or embodied in such work.*

The distinction between ideas and the expression of ideas is crucial to understanding copyright law. One of the most common criticisms of copyright is based on the misconception that copyright law allows people to own and monopolize the use of ideas. In actuality, ideas can never be protected by copyright, although an author's original way of expressing ideas may be protected. If an author expresses an idea in an original manner and fixes that expression in tangible form, the author's expression will be protected by copyright law. However, the author's copyright will not prevent another person from using the same idea to create another original work because ideas are free for everyone to use. The expression requirement, although closely related, is not the same as the originality requirement because some ideas will be original. However, even if an author comes up with an original idea, the idea will still not be entitled to copyright protection, although the author's particular expression of that idea may be copyrightable.

The reason that copyright protection is limited to expression rather than ideas is completely consistent with the primary purpose behind copyright protection. In order to encourage the production of the greatest possible number of artistic works, ideas must be free for use by all authors because they are the building blocks of creative expression.

---

**Example 3.2**

Suppose I have the idea to write a song about love. Although I'm fairly sure that a few songwriters have already written songs about this topic, let's assume for argument's sake that I'm the first person to have this idea. It would be contrary to the rationale behind copyright law for me to have exclusive use of the idea of a song about love because I would have a monopoly on love songs and could prevent everyone else from writing love songs (or at least become very rich licensing my idea to others). The idea of writing a song about love is certainly a very general idea because there are obviously many different types of possible love songs, and to allow any individual to monopolize that idea would hinder the creation of artistic works. Consequently, all songwriters are free to write love songs as long as their particular expression of the idea is original.

---

Distinguishing ideas from their expression is not always easy, but it is a distinction that must be made in order to know which elements of a work are unprotected and which elements are protected. In literary works, such uncopyrightable elements would include the work's plot, stock characters, and settings. As far as visual works of art are concerned, colors and shapes would certainly be considered uncopyrightable building blocks. For musical works, uncopyrightable elements will generally include a song's theme, individual words, individual notes, short musical phrases, rhythm, and harmony.

## C. Fixation

The third requirement for a work to be copyrightable is that the work must be fixed in tangible form. Section 102(a) of the Copyright Act, in addition to requiring originality, states that copyrightable works must be

*…fixed in any tangible medium of expression, now known or later developed, from which they can be perceived, reproduced, or otherwise communicated, either directly or with the aid of a machine or device.*

According to Section 101's definition of fixation:

*…a work is fixed in a tangible medium of expression when its embodiment in a copy or phonorecord, by or under the authority of the copyright owner, is sufficiently permanent or stable to permit it to be perceived, reproduced, or otherwise communicated for a period of more than transitory duration.*

At first, it might seem odd that, although copyright protects intangible property, copyright protection is only available to works that are fixed in tangible form. Although a song is intangible, it must be produced in some kind of tangible form such as a recording or sheet music before it is capable of being protected by copyright. However, the reasoning for this requirement is simple practicality. If an intangible work was not made available in some tangible form, it could be very difficult to prove its existence.

The Copyright Act specifies two types of material objects that copyrighted works can be fixed in: copies and phonorecords. Both copies and phonorecords are physical objects from which a work can be perceived, reproduced, or otherwise communicated. Section 101 of the Copyright Act defines "phonorecords" as:

> ...material objects in which sounds, other than those accompanying a motion picture or other audiovisual work, are fixed by any method now known or later developed, and from which the sounds can be perceived, reproduced, or otherwise communicated, either directly or with the aid of a machine or device.

Phonorecords therefore include cassette tapes, compact discs, digital audio tapes, MP3 files, and other media capable of capturing and storing sound. A sound recording is fixed by definition because the recording process results in some type of phonorecord. Phonorecords are distinguished from copies. Section 101 of the Copyright Act defines "copies" as:

> ...material objects other than phonorecords, in which a work is fixed by any method now known or later developed, and from which the work can be perceived, reproduced, or otherwise communicated, either directly or with the aid of a machine or device.

This definition of copies in the Copyright Act does not imply only duplicates of works. Rather, copies encompass any material objects other than phonorecords. A musical work could be fixed in several different types of copies such as a lead sheet, written lyric, musical score, etc. Similarly, literary works could be embodied in copies or phonorecords such as books, periodicals, microfilm, tape recordings, etc.

The language of Section 102(a) states that fixation can be in a medium "now known or later developed." This is intended to include fixation in media brought about by technological advances. All that is required to satisfy the fixation requirement is that a work be embodied in some tangible medium. It does not matter what the form, manner, or method of fixation may be—words, numbers, notes, sounds, pictures, or any other graphic or symbolic indicia—as long as it is embodied in a physical object.

### Example 3.3

In 1908, the Supreme Court decided a case brought by the composer of "Little Cotton Dolly" and "Kentucky Babe."[11] The composer alleged that his songs had been infringed by a company that transcribed them onto perforated piano rolls used in player pianos, which were very popular at the time. Piano rolls operated by allowing air to rush through perforations in the rolls, placing pressure on the individual piano keys that in turn played the song. The Copyright Act in effect at that time provided protection for musical works. The composer argued that copyright law protected all means of expression that could permit the song to be played and heard. The Supreme Court, however, took a narrow view and held that piano rolls were not copies because the musical compositions could not be visually perceived by looking at the rolls. Piano rolls could not be read and understood by most people and were part of a machine, rather than copies such as sheet music, which was protected by copyright law. This decision was harshly criticized and overruled a year later by the 1909 Copyright Act, which included piano rolls and phonograph records as tangible objects that could contain copyrightable works. The 1909 Copyright Act, however, made both piano rolls and recordings subject to a compulsory license to address the concern that granting copyright protection to recorded music might result in a monopoly to one large, dominant player-piano manufacturer of the time.

## II. Categories of Copyrightable Works

In addition to specifying the general requirements for copyrightable subject matter, Section 102(a) of the Copyright Act specifies eight specific categories of copyrightable works to illustrate the types of works that may be copyrightable. These categories are

Literary works

Musical works

Dramatic works

Pantomimes and choreographic works

Pictorial, graphic, and sculptural works

Motion pictures and other audiovisual works

Sound recordings

Architectural works

Some of these categories are not defined by the Copyright Act because Congress believed that they have commonly understood meanings. Moreover, it is possible, in some circumstances, for a work to fit more than one of these categories. For example, a sound recording could be part of a motion picture. The overlap may affect the particular rights in a work because Section 106 specifies different rights for different categories of works, and Sections 108 through 120 specify limitations on some rights to certain categories of works.

It is also important to keep in mind that the eight categories specified are not necessarily the only categories of copyrightable works. It is conceivable that some new type of work could be created that does not fit within any of the eight categories. The fact that the Copyright Act lists only eight categories does not imply that there cannot be additional categories. This is supported by Section 102(a), which states that protected works of authorship "include" the eight listed categories. In Section 101, the term "including" is defined as "illustrative and not limitative." Other sections of the Copyright Act protect different, less traditional kinds of works, such as boat hulls, but a different set of rights is granted to these kinds of work.

The next sections will examine the eight different categories of copyrightable works in Section 102(a), first examining the two categories of most importance to the music industry, musical works and sound recordings, then briefly the other categories of copyrightable works.

### A. Musical Works

Section 102(a)(2) of the Copyright Act specifies that "musical works, including any accompanying words," are subject matter suitable for protection. Generally, a musical work consists of a combination of melody, harmony, and rhythm, regardless of the material object in which it is embodied. In order to be protected by copyright, musical compositions must be original, contain expression, and be fixed in tangible form.

The term "musical works" includes songs consisting of music and lyrics as well as solely instrumental compositions. In the case of a musical composition that includes both music and lyrics, copyright will protect the combination of music and lyrics, the music alone, and the lyrics alone. In one case, a court described this relationship between music and lyrics as follows:

*The popularity of a song turns upon both the words and the music; the share of each in its success cannot be appraised; they interpenetrate each other as much as the notes of the melody, or separate words of the "lyric."[12]*

Accordingly, if a person copies only the music or only the lyrics from a composition, he will be liable for infringement of the work to the same extent as if he had copied both the music and the lyrics.(1)

### (1) The Originality and Expression Requirements for Musical Works
Musical compositions are generally comprised of several elements, which can include lyrics, melody, harmony, and rhythm. Not every composition will contain all of these elements, and the amount of originality and expression present in any of these elements will vary from one composition to the next.

### (a) Lyrics
Some musical compositions contain lyrics as well as music. If words are written independently of music without any intention at the time of creation that they will be combined with music, the work will be considered to be a literary work. However, if created to be combined with music, the words will be part of a musical work.

Lyrics may be copyrightable if they contain original expression. Just as the expression requirement means that individual words or notes are not copyrightable, it also prevents people from claiming copyright ownership in short and simple phrases. For instance, in *O'Brien v. Chappel & Co.*, it was held that a phrase from the song "I've Grown Accustomed to Your Face" in the musical *My Fair Lady* was not an infringement. The phrase consisted of the lyrics "I've grown accustomed to the tune you whistle night and noon," while the plaintiff's song contained the following lyrics:

*I've grown accustomed to the tune you whistle night and noon. Sharing my dreams with a star, asking the moon if it's soon when you'll be mine, night and noon.*

Although the plaintiff may have created a catchy lyrical phrase, the court refused to recognize any ownership rights in that phrase, stating that:

*The plaintiff apparently thinks that he can get sole rights to the use of the phrase 'night and noon' no matter in what context the phrase is used. Such a common phrase in and of itself is not susceptible of copyright nor of appropriation by any individual. It is well established that copyright or literary rights do not extend to words or phrases isolated from their context, nor do they extend to abstract ideas or situations.*

In another case, *Acuff-Rose Music, Inc. v. Jostens, Inc.*,[13] music publisher Acuff-Rose alleged that Jostens infringed upon its copyrighted song "You've Got to Stand for Something," which was written and recorded by country artist Aaron Tippin. The song is based on the theme of a father giving advice to his son to stand up for his principles. Jostens, a company that sells school rings, had developed an advertising campaign based on the slogan "If You Don't Stand for Something, You'll Fall for Anything." Even though the court believed that Jostens had copied its slogan from the song, it held that Jostens was not guilty of infringement because the lyrics involved lacked the requisite originality. The court noted that:

> *While especially creative phrases may be protected, there is nothing unique[14] about the use of standing/ falling imagery to convey the importance of living a principled life.*

It is possible that a musical composition containing music and lyrics that would not be sufficiently original or expressive to be copyrightable by themselves could be copyrightable as a whole. In such a situation, a person who copied just the music or just the lyrics would not be liable for infringement of the work because he would only have copied elements not subject to protection. It is also possible that a musical composition that contains music and lyrics may not be copyrightable at all due to lack of originality or expression.

### (b) Melody

Melody has been defined as "a pleasing succession or arrangement of sounds" or "a rhythmically organized sequence of single tones so related to one another as to make up a particular phrase or idea."[15] At its simplest form, melody consists of the musical notes, the duration of these notes, and the order or arrangement of notes. For most musical compositions, melody is the most recognizable element. Although a melody must be original in order to be copyrightable, the components of melodic composition are very limited. First, melody is limited by the number of notes in the musical scale, which, as far as popular music is concerned, is 12. Second, even though the 12 notes can be arranged in many different ways, the options are further limited by certain musical conventions. In contrast, there are many more than 12 words commonly used in the creation of literary works. Consequently, it is generally a bit easier to find the requisite originality in literary works than in musical works.

Additionally, the distinction between ideas and expression is also important in the context of melody. Short musical phrases may be held to be ideas rather than expression and therefore not copyrightable in and of themselves.

---

**Example 3.4**

---

In *Smith v. George E. Muehlebach Brewing Co.*, a jingle for a beer company that consisted of the phrase "Tic Toc, Tic Toc, Time for Muehlebach," scored to the notes "C" and "G" in the musical key of "C" to mimic the sound of a clock ticking, was held not to be copyrightable.[16] According to the court, if all a composer does is "add a mechanical application of sound to a word that is itself not copyrightable, and adds the same to a descriptive phrase (Time for Muehlebach) already dedicated to the public domain, without the use of even the most simple harmonious chords, he has no musical composition subject to copyright."

---

Unfortunately, copyright law does not provide any strict rule to determine how long or creative a melody must be in order to be copyrightable. A common misconception among musicians, sometimes referred to as "the six-bar rule," is that any melody that lasts for less than six bars is not copyrightable. This misconception apparently developed in response to one particular court decision, *Marks v. Leo Feist, Inc.*[17] Marks was the copyright owner of a song entitled "Wedding Dance Waltz" and alleged that a song owned by Feist called "Swanee River Moon" infringed its copyright. The court held that there was no infringement even though "Swanee River Moon" contained six bars of music that were very similar to "Wedding Dance Waltz." The court stated that:

> *Musical signs available for combinations are about 13 in number. They are tones produced by striking in succession the white and black keys as they are found on the keyboard of the piano. It is called the chromatic scale. In a popular song, the composer must write a composition arranging combinations of these tones limited by the range of the ordinary voice and by the skill of the ordinary player. To be successful, it must be a combination of tones that can be played as well as sung by almost anyone. Necessarily, within these limits, there will be found some similarity of tone succession. To constitute an infringement of the appellant's composition, it would be necessary to find a substantial copying of a substantial and material part of it. The exclusive right granted to the appellant by his copyright to print, reprint, publish, copy, and vend does not exclude the appellee from the use of 6 similar bars, when used in a composition of 450 bars."*

The holding in *Marks*, however, was limited to the particular factual situation and was not intended to set a limit as to how many bars of music are necessary to be copyrightable. In fact, other courts have held that as few as two to four bars of music may be protected by copyright.[18]

### (c) Harmony

Harmony can be defined as "the structure, progression, and relation of chords."[19] The chord progression that makes up a harmony is, by definition, structured based on the melody. Because harmony is generally dictated by melody, harmony on its own will rarely be sufficiently original to be copyrightable. However, in a case involving an ownership dispute over a derivative version of the jazz classic "Satin Doll," the court refused to say that harmony can never be copyrightable.[20] While recognizing that a melody usually implies a limited range of chords to accompany it, the court also believed that a composer may exercise creativity in selecting chords and that the choice of chords indicates the mood, feel, and sound of the composition. Consequently, the court ruled that harmony may be capable of copyright protection in certain circumstances, although it will not be in most circumstances. Although harmony by itself will rarely be copyrightable, it can certainly contribute to the copyrightability of a musical composition as a whole.

### (d) Rhythm

Another basic element of musical composition is rhythm, which is "a regular pattern formed by a series of notes of differing duration and stress."[21] Simply put, rhythm is the beat that a musical composition follows. The vast majority of popular musical compositions have a steady, unvarying rhythm. Consequently, rhythm alone will rarely be sufficiently original to merit copyright protection. One court has stated that:

> *Rhythm is simply the tempo in which the composition is written. It is the background for the melody. There is only a limited amount of tempos; these appear to have been long since exhausted; originality of rhythm is a rarity, if not an impossibility.*[22]

Although this court's view is perhaps a bit too limited, it is true, at least with respect to popular music, that rhythm alone will rarely be copyrightable. However, there are instances in which courts have found the potential for copyrightability in rhythmic components of songs. This is notable in light of a progression toward the composition of music "beats" and beats sampling. In *Vargas v. Pfizer*,[23] the composer of "Bust Dat Groove Without Ride" brought suit against Pfizer, Inc. and other defendants alleging that Pfizer had used musical themes from the composition and sound recording of the same title in its national advertising campaign for Celebrex. The defendants maintained that the work was not copyrightable, asserting that it was "a basic percussion pattern that has existed in other musical works and instructional text books for decades." Alternatively, the plaintiff contended that "the high hat and snare drum elements of the composition are original because of Vargas' creative choice in selecting and combining them." The court, citing the modest originality requirements established under *Feist Publications, Inc. v. Rural Telephone Service Co.*, discussed later in this chapter, found that a jury could find originality despite similarity between the plaintiff's composition and others so long as it was independently created. The copyrightability of individual beats and beat tracks has become extremely important to the hip-hop and rap industries—selling beats is an important source of income for many producers.

### (2) The Fixation Requirement for Musical Works

Under the 1909 Copyright Act, musical compositions had to be reduced to readable form in order to be protected. In a case decided in 1908, the Supreme Court held that a perforated musical roll used in a player piano was not a "copy" of a musical composition and therefore could not infringe the right to make copies of the copyrighted composition because it was not "a written or printed record in intelligible notation."[24] However, under the 1976 Copyright Act, a musical composition may be fixed in either copies or phonorecords. Consequently, musical compositions can be fixed in the form of written musical notation or recorded on tape, disk, or other media. According to the Copyright Office:

> A musical composition would be copyrightable if it is written or recorded in words or any kind of visible notation, in Braille, on a phonograph disk, on a film sound track, on magnetic tape, or on punch cards.[25]

In fact, the majority of musical compositions registered with the Copyright Office are fixed in some type of recording rather than written musical notation.

### B. Sound Recordings

It is very important to understand the distinction between musical works and sound recordings. Section 102(a)(7) of the Copyright Act includes sound recordings as one of the categories of copyrightable subject matter. Sound recordings are defined as:

> Works that result from the fixation of a series of musical, spoken or other sounds, but not including the sounds accompanying a motion picture or other audiovisual work, regardless of the nature of the material objects, such as disks, tapes, or other phonorecords, in which they are embodied.[26]

Sound recordings are separate and distinct from the underlying musical, literary, or dramatic works whose performance may be contained on the recording. For example, a recording of a song constitutes a sound recording, separately copyrightable from the song recorded. If the song is protected by copyright, the recording artist or record company must obtain a license from the copyright owner of the song to reproduce the song in phonorecords. If such a license is not obtained, the artist and record company will be liable for infringement of the song. Further, without such a license, the sound recording produced will not be protected by copyright because a sound recording is a derivative work and, under Section 103(a), protection for a derivative work utilizing "preexisting material in which copyright subsists does not extend to any part of the work in which such material has been used unlawfully."

The distinction between the copyright in sound recordings and the copyright in musical compositions is often difficult to comprehend because both the sound recording and the musical composition are fixed in the same physical object, a phonorecord. The copyright in the sound recording covers the rendition or performance of the musical composition rather than the composition itself. The copyright in the musical composition covers the sequence of musical notes and phrases, lyrics, and rhythm. The copyright in a sound recording covers the particular combination of sounds recorded and is expressed in the physical medium in which the recording is embodied (such as a compact disc, cassette, or computer file).

Sound recordings are not limited to recordings of musical compositions. A sound recording can consist of synthesized sounds, mechanical sounds, or sounds that occur in nature (e.g., wind blowing, ocean sounds, etc.).

---

**Example 3.5**

*Songs of the Humpback Whale* is a recording of whales singing. Even though the performers were not human, this sound recording is just as copyrightable as a sound recording of Mozart symphonies or Madonna pop songs. Apparently, humpback whales are prolific songwriters; they supposedly compose new songs each year. Although their music takes a little time to get used to, some of them are probably better singers than some humans.

---

Sound recordings have not always been protected by copyright and still enjoy less protection than other types of works. Congress first granted copyright protection to sound recordings by passing an amendment to the 1909 Copyright Act that gave copyright protection to recordings fixed, published, and copyrighted on and after February 15, 1972.[27] The 1976 Copyright Act incorporated this amendment into Section 301(c).

Sound recordings fixed before February 15, 1972, although not protected under federal copyright law, may be protected under state statutory and common law.[28] In *Goldstein v. California*, the Supreme Court held that state laws prohibiting the copying of sound recordings fixed before February 15, 1972, were valid and enforceable.[29] However, because common law copyright generally lasts indefinitely, the 1976 Copyright Act imposed a time limitation on the duration of common law copyright for sound recordings fixed before February 15, 1972. Section 301(c) of the 1976 Act states that:

*With respect to sound recordings fixed before February 15, 1972, any rights or remedies under the common law or statutes of any State shall not be annulled or limited by this title until February 15, 2067...*

*and the preemptive provisions of subsection (a) shall apply to any such rights and remedies pertaining to any cause of action arising from undertakings commenced on and after February 15, 2067.*

Consequently, all sound recordings made prior to February 15, 1972, that are protected by common law copyright will enter the public domain on February 15, 2067, or before that if the law of the relevant state does not protect those recordings for that long. This expiration date ensures that all such recordings will be protected for at least 95 years (1972 to 2067).

Like all other types of copyrightable works, sound recordings must contain originality and expression. Congress has stated that copyrightable elements of sound recordings may include the contributions:

*...of the performers whose performance is captured and on the part of the record producer responsible for setting up the recording session, capturing and electronically processing the sounds, and compiling and editing them to make the final sound recording."[30]*

Copyrightable elements of authorship in a sound recording can include the way the musical composition is sung by a vocalist, played by musicians, arranged by a musical director or producer, mixed by a recording engineer, and so on. However, it is possible that only some of these individuals will contribute authorship. For instance, the record producer's contribution may be so minimal that the performance is the only copyrightable element in the work. In other situations, the record producer's contribution may be the only copyrightable contribution to a sound recording such as recordings of naturally occurring sounds (e.g., a thunderstorm, birdcalls, etc.). Because sound recordings often involve authorship by multiple individuals, determining who the authors and owners of the copyright in a sound recording are can be difficult. When sound recordings are made under a record contract between a recording artist and a record company, this difficulty is typically resolved through a contractual provision in which the various creators (artist, musicians and vocalists, producers, etc.) transfer any ownership interest they may have to the record company (see Chapter 4, "Ownership of Copyright," for a more in-depth discussion of copyright ownership of sound recordings).

In the context of sound recordings as well as all other copyrightable works, there must at least be some minimal degree of originality contributed–for example, by selecting the particular sounds to be recorded, selecting the specific point in time to record those sounds, and selecting the distance and angle between the microphone and the performers–in order for a contributor to have a copyright interest in the recording.

An important limitation on the copyrightability of sound recordings under Section 114(b) of the Copyright Act is that the reproduction right in sound recordings is limited to works "that directly or indirectly recapture the actual sounds fixed in the recording." In other words, the copyright in a sound recording only protects against actual copying of the recorded sounds and not against imitation of those sounds.

### Example 3.6

If we (the authors of this book) hired musicians to record a cover version of the song "Baby," imitating the musical performance of Justin Bieber, our recording, even if it sounded virtually identical to young Mr. Bieber's version (which is admittedly not likely), would not be an infringement of the Bieber sound recording (owned by Island Records). We would need a license to record the copyrighted song (which could be obtained under the Section 115 compulsory mechanical license provision of the 1976

Copyright Act), but if we were to create our own recording rather than taking the sounds from the Bieber recording, we would not have violated Island's copyright in the sound recording. However, if we sold phonorecords of our recording, we might be sued by Bieber for violating his publicity rights if we imitated his voice. It is important to realize that copyright does not operate in a vacuum, and even though we would not have violated copyright law, we probably would have violated other related laws.

## C. Literary Works

Literary works are defined as "works, other than audiovisual works, expressed in words, numbers, or other verbal or numerical symbols or indicia, regardless of the nature of the material objects, such as books, periodicals, manuscripts, phonorecords, film, tapes, disks, or cards, in which they are embodied."[31] This category includes novels, magazine articles, poems, catalogs, directories, instructional works, compilations of data, computer databases, computer programs, etc. For example, computer software programs–like the Word program used to write this book–are classified as literary works because they are expressed in computer languages that use letters, words, and numbers.

Generally, copyright protection in a literary work is based upon the arrangement of words that an author uses to express ideas. No individual words or ideas are copyrightable in and of themselves. Accordingly, copyright does not protect a literary work's theme, general plot, factual information, or other common elements and ideas. Although copyright protection in literary works is based on the arrangement of words used by the author, this does not mean that a literary work can be infringed upon only by exact copying of the work. Even if a person paraphrases the work, he will still be liable for infringement if the paraphrase is based upon the work's expression rather than just its underlying ideas.

### Example 3.7

The book you are reading is a "copy" of a copyrighted literary work. Although you own the particular copy you are reading (assuming you acquired it lawfully), Course Technology PTR (with which we have a contract to publish this book) is the only party that has the right to manufacture and sell the book. If you were to photocopy this book and give the photocopy to a friend, you would have committed copyright infringement. Although the publisher owns the copyright in this book, that does not prevent anyone else from writing his own book about copyright, because the idea of writing a book about copyright is not copyrightable. Copyright does, however, make it illegal for someone to copy the copyrightable expression from this book without permission.

## D. Dramatic Works

Section 102(a)(3) specifies that "dramatic works, including any accompanying music," may be copyrightable works. Although the Copyright Act does not define the term, dramatic works tell a story through action, dialog, and narration. A dramatic work may also include music, such as the musical play *West Side Story*.

There is often a degree of overlap between a dramatic work and other types of works. First, because dramatic works are generally expressed using words, they may also qualify as literary works. Dramatic works may also be expressed by the use of actions and may therefore also qualify as pantomimes or choreographic works. If a dramatic work is fixed in an audiovisual medium such as film or videotape, it may also qualify as a motion picture. Finally, because the Copyright Act states that dramatic works may include "any accompanying music," parts of dramatic works may also qualify as musical works.

### E. Pantomines and Choreographic Works

Pantomimes and choreographic works are generally expressed by movement (such as dance) or physical attitudes and are usually fixed on videotape or film. However, a dance routine could also be fixed in a written description. Pantomimes comprise a drama presented by gestures and action without words. Choreographic works consist of recorded or notated movements of a dancer. Although choreographic works can include dance routines, dance steps and simple dance routines are not copyrightable due to lack of sufficient originality or expression.

### F. Pictorial, Graphic, and Sculptural Works

Pictorial, graphic, and sculptural works are defined as "two-dimensional and three-dimensional works of fine, graphic, and applied art, photographs, prints and art reproductions, maps, globes, charts, diagrams, models, and technical drawings, including architectural plans."[32] A simple photograph, for instance, will generally qualify as a pictorial work because, as one court observed, "no photograph, however simple, can be unaffected by the personal influence of the author."[33] However, individual elements of a pictorial, graphic, or sculptural work such as color, perspective, and shapes will be considered ideas rather than expression and will not be protected by copyright unless combined and arranged in a way that constitutes expression.

Visually depicted characters, such as cartoon characters, may be copyrightable as pictorial, graphic, or sculptural works.[34] Several cases have involved the Superman character and have held that although the character itself is copyrightable, this does not prevent others from creating characters possessing similar attributes such as miraculous strength, flight, X-ray vision, and imperviousness to bullets.[35]

### G. Motion Pictures and Other Audiovisual Works

Section 102(a)(6) includes motion pictures and other audiovisual works as copyrightable works. Audiovisual works are "works that consist of a series of related images which are intrinsically intended to be shown by the use of machines or devices such as projectors, viewers, or electronic equipment, together with accompanying sounds, if any, regardless of the nature of the material objects, such as films or tapes, in which the works are embodied."[36] Motion pictures are "audiovisual works consisting of a series of related images which, when shown in succession, impart an impression of motion, together with accompanying sounds, if any."[37]

Audiovisual works may include other types of copyrightable works. For instance, a musical composition contained in an audiovisual work is considered part of the audiovisual work rather than a musical work.[38] Consequently, a song included in an audiovisual work such as a movie or music video will not be subject to the compulsory license provisions of Section 115 if it has only been embodied in a copy rather than a phonorecord as required under Section 115(a)(1).

Another important distinction involves motion picture soundtracks. Within the music industry, the term "soundtrack" is often used to refer to the songs played during the film, which are often made available for sale separately as a "soundtrack album." However, a motion picture soundtrack actually consists of all sounds that are part of the film: dialogue, sound effects, and musical sounds as well. The definition of a sound recording under Section 101 excludes "the sounds accompanying a motion picture or other audiovisual work." However, the recorded sounds contained in the soundtrack to a motion picture are copyrightable as part of the motion picture. Due to the limited rights afforded to sound recordings, a recording that is part of a motion picture soundtrack will have greater rights than a sound recording. Specifically, the sounds contained in a soundtrack will be subject to the full performance right and the right against imitation as well as against dubbing.

## III. Compilations

Section 103 of the Copyright Act provides that compilations may be copyrightable. Within the music industry the term "compilation" is generally used to refer to an album or collection of music. However, the Copyright Act provides a different definition that is not limited to music or musical works. Compilations are special types of works that overlap the categories of copyrightable works specified in Section 102(a). Consequently, they may be literary, musical, dramatic, or other types of works. Section 101 defines a compilation as:

> *A work formed by the collection and assembling of preexisting materials or of data that are selected, coordinated, or arranged in such a way that the resulting work as a whole constitutes an original work of authorship.*

Like all copyrightable works, compilations are subject to the requirements of originality, expression, and fixation. They differ from other types of works due to the fact that they are based upon preexisting material. Consequently, the requisite originality and expression must be found in the selection and arrangement of the preexisting materials.

There are two important rules concerning compilations. First, under Section 103(b), the copyright in a compilation

> *…extends only to the material contributed by the author of such work, as distinguished from the preexisting material employed in the work, and does not imply any exclusive right in the preexisting material. The copyright in such work is independent of, and does not affect or enlarge the scope, duration, ownership, or subsistence of, any copyright protection in the preexisting material.*

Second, under Section 103(a), "protection for a work employing preexisting material in which copyright subsists does not extend to any part of the work in which such material has been used unlawfully."

The copyright in a compilation results from the selection, coordination, and arrangement of the preexisting materials in such a way that the resulting work constitutes an original work of authorship. The term "selection" refers to the choice of material, regardless of whether it is taken from one source or from multiple sources. The terms "arrangement" and "coordination" refer to the ordering or grouping of material, which must be more than mere mechanical grouping of data, such as alphabetical or chronological listings of data. The copyright in a compilation protects the author's original expression in the arrangement of the compilation itself and not any of the ideas or materials compiled.

Although a compilation may consist of individually copyrighted works (such as a compilation of songs), a compilation may also consist of preexisting material that is not protected by copyright. A famous Supreme Court case dealing with compilations involved a dispute over telephone directories. In *Feist Publications, Inc. v. Rural Telephone Service Co.*, Rural published white and yellow page telephone directories for its service area. Feist published an area-wide telephone directory that covered 11 different telephone service areas, including Rural's. Feist requested a license from Rural to copy its white page listings, which was refused. Feist, however, went ahead and copied Rural's listings. Feist's directory differed from Rural's, but 1,309 of Feist's 46,878 listings were identical to Rural's, including four fictitious listings included by Rural to detect copiers.

Both the district and appellate courts found in favor of Rural because it was clear that Feist had copied Rural's listings. The Supreme Court, however, reversed this decision, holding that although Feist copied Rural's listings, those listings were not copyrightable. The reasoning for its decision was based on the rule that facts such as names and telephone numbers are not original and therefore not copyrightable.

According to the Court, facts themselves can never be copyrightable, although compilations of facts may be. The originality requirement is the key to the different treatment between facts and factual compilations. The distinction is between creation and discovery; facts are discovered, while compilations of facts are created. If the creation of a compilation possesses the requisite originality, the compilation will be copyrightable. Originality in a compilation is found in the materials selected by the author and the way in which those materials are arranged. However, in *Feist*, the selection or arrangement was not original because it consisted of the residences in Rural's telephone service area arranged in alphabetical order. The Court stated that "there is nothing remotely creative about arranging names alphabetically in a white pages directory."

The Court also rejected what had become known as the sweat of the brow theory for copyright protection that some lower courts had recognized. The Court's ruling means that regardless of the time and effort spent in researching and accumulating information for a compilation, the research and accumulation will not qualify the results for copyright protection. A compilation will only be copyrightable if it contains originality of expression.

---

**Example 3.8**

In *Consolidated Music Publishers, Inc. v. Ashley Publications, Inc.*,[39] the plaintiff sued to prevent the defendant from manufacturing and distributing a compilation of sheet music entitled *World's Favorite Classic to Contemporary Piano Music*, which the plaintiff alleged was an infringement of its compilation entitled *Easy Classics to Moderns*. Both compilations consisted entirely of public domain musical compositions. The plaintiff's compilation was originally published in 1956 and contained 142 compositions.

The defendant's compilation was published in 1961 and contained 83 compositions, 29 of which were contained in the plaintiff's compilation. Additionally, the defendant's compilation contained editorial material allegedly copied from the plaintiff's, and there were several errors common to both works. The court found that the plaintiff's compilation exhibited originality in the fingering, dynamic marks, tempo indications, slurs, and phrasing, as well as the selection and arrangement of the compositions. The court consequently held that the defendant was guilty of infringement because it utilized the same titles arbitrarily chosen by the plaintiff for several compositions, duplicated a selection already in its book under a different title, misspelled an author's name in the same manner as the plaintiff, and repeated another notational error made by the plaintiff. It is important to note that the court's ruling does not mean that no one else can create a compilation using the same compositions. However, it does mean that one cannot merely copy parts of the plaintiff's compilation that exhibit originality and are therefore copyrightable.

**Elements of a Copyrightable Compilation**

The following elements are required in order to have a copyrightable compilation:

1. Collection and assembly of pre-existing material, facts, or data.

2. Selection, coordination, and arrangement of those materials.

3. Creation, through the selection, coordination, and arrangement, of an original work of authorship.

## A. Collective Works

A collective work is a type of compilation and is defined as "a work, such as a periodical issue, anthology, or encyclopedia, in which a number of contributions, constituting separate and independent works in themselves, are assembled into a collective whole." In other words, a collective work is a compilation of copyrighted works. As with other types of compilations, originality in a collective work will usually be found in the author's selection and arrangement of the works included. If the method of arrangement is very simple or is dictated by function (such as alphabetical arrangements and chronological order), the collection may not be copyrightable due to its lack of originality.

**Example 3.9**

A songbook containing a group of previously existing copyrighted songs such as the top 10 songs of 1999 would be a collective work. In order to compile such a work, the author of the collective work must have print licenses from the copyright owners of each of the songs in the songbook. If, however, the songbook contained 10 public domain songs such as the top 10 songs of 1899, no licenses would be required. Whether the songbook contained copyrighted or public domain songs, the copyright in the resulting compilation would only cover the author's particular selection and arrangement of songs (assuming such selection and arrangement is original and not merely a copy of the Billboard Top 10, for example) and would not give the author any rights in the individual songs. Similarly, a record album consisting of 10 individual copyrighted master recordings is a collective work, although such works are commonly called compilation albums in the music industry if the recordings were previously released on other albums.

**Example 3.10**

In *Caffey v. Cook*, the court found that where the producer of a live music show selected and ordered 32 songs from a universe of possible musical compositions based on the producer's sense of musicality, the audience's familiarity with the songs, the physical demands of performance, the suggestions of the defendants based on their own repertoire, and creation of text of dialogue in combination with a compilation of song lyrics, the combination qualified for copyright protection as an original compilation—specifically, a collective work–incorporating the selection and ordering of preexisting musical compositions.[40]

**Example 3.11**

Compilations of musical compositions selected and arranged by the disc jockey Khia Edgerton (known as "K-Swift") were held to be copyrightable in *Edgerton v. UPI Holdings, Inc.*[41] The defendants challenged Edgerton's copyright ownership of CDs comprised of songs she had selected and arranged since the collection of songs was not composed by Edgerton. The court acknowledged her skill in the selection of music and found that her selections and arrangements contained the minimum degree of creativity required under *Feist*.

# IV. What Is Not Protected by Copyright?

The Constitutional Patent and Copyright clause established broad parameters for Congress in terms of limiting the types of works that merit copyright protection. Therefore, in addition to limiting the duration of copyright for creative works, copyright law limits the types of works that merit copyright protection.

## A. The Public Domain

Creative works that are not protected by copyright are considered to be in the public domain. A work that is in the public domain is not owned by anyone. Therefore any member of the public is free to use the work without having to obtain permission and without having to make any payment for the use. Because virtually all authorship borrows to some extent from prior works of authorship, the public domain encourages the creation of new works through the use of old works. As stated by one legal scholar:

> *Transformation is the essence of the authorship process. An author transforms her memories, experiences, inspirations, and influences into a new work. That work inevitably echoes expressive elements of prior works.*[42]

There are several ways by which a work can enter the public domain. First, when the copyright to a work expires, the work enters the public domain. Additionally, some works published before 1964 for which the copyright was not renewed are in the public domain. Some works for which the author did not take the proper steps to secure copyright, such as works published before March 1, 1989, without copyright notice, may also be in the public domain. Finally, a work may enter the public domain due to the copyright owner's abandonment of the work.

## B. Ideas versus Expression

Section 102(b) of the Copyright Act provides that ideas, procedures, processes, systems, methods of operation, concepts, principles, and discoveries are not copyrightable and are therefore part of the public domain. The notion that ideas cannot be copyrighted is fundamental to copyright law because to allow authors to monopolize ideas would inhibit authorship rather than encourage it. Instead, copyright protection is limited to an author's particular expression of ideas. Although anyone is free to use an author's ideas, the public is not free to copy the author's expression of an idea. Legal disputes usually arise over where to draw the line between a work's expression and its underlying ideas.

## C. Facts

Copyright law does not protect facts of any kind. The reason is similar to the distinction between ideas and expression. Like ideas, if the first author to write about a specific fact could gain a monopoly over that fact, the creation of other works of authorship using the same fact would be severely restricted. A further reason for not allowing facts to be copyrightable is that facts, although they may be discovered by an author, are not created by an author.

## D. Names, Titles, Slogans, and Short Phrases

Although there can be creativity and originality in names, titles, slogans, and short phrases, these materials are not subject to copyright protection.[43] This is because names and titles usually consist of short phrases that are either unoriginal or constitute ideas rather than expression.

---

**Example 3.12**

There are at least 129 songs entitled "Love Is a Wonderful Thing" registered with the Copyright Office (two of which were the subject of a lawsuit by the Isley Brothers against Michael Bolton, discussed in Chapter 10, "Infringement of Copyright"). Although all of these songs are protected by copyright, none of the copyright owners of these songs has any copyright ownership in the title itself.

---

Although names, titles, and slogans are not protected by copyright, they may receive protection under trademark law. These types of protection are essentially based on use of the name, title, or slogan (legally known as the "mark") in commerce and prevent uses that are likely to cause confusion among consumers as to the source of goods or services.

---

**Example 3.13**

Short phrases and slogans such as "just do it" as used by Nike are not protected by copyright. Similarly, the use of the often-used blues lyric phrase "got my mojo working" was held not to be copyrightable,[44] as was the phrase "that which does not kill us makes us stronger" when used in the hook of a song.[45] However, slogans can be protected by trademark law if they become closely associated with a product or service. Nike has trademark rights in the slogan "just do it" because it has spent millions of dollars advertising its products using that slogan and consequently developing a close association among consumers between the slogan and Nike products.

---

## E. Unfixed Works

Because fixation in tangible form is one of the requirements for copyright protection, any work that is not fixed in tangible form will not be protected by copyright. Although most musical works are fixed in tangible form as part of the creation process, there are some musical works that are created without fixation. For example, works that are improvised during a performance are not ordinarily fixed in tangible form unless the performance is recorded. An improvised work is, by definition, actually created spontaneously during a performance. Improvisation therefore combines the activities of authorship and performance that, for most musical works, are done separately. Improvisation is one of the defining compositional elements of jazz, and there are consequently many improvised musical compositions by jazz artists that are not protected by copyright.[46]

Although improvisation and other unfixed works are not protected under copyright law, they can be protected under other legal doctrines. For instance, some states protect works that are not fixed in tangible form. States are prevented from passing laws affecting the rights protected by federal copyright law under the doctrine of preemption, because unfixed works are not protected by copyright; however, preemption is not applicable. California, however, is the only state that has enacted a statute providing protection for improvised works. This statute states that "the author of any original work of authorship that is not fixed in any tangible medium of expression shall receive exclusive ownership in the representation or expression thereof."[47]

One way for improvisational authors to protect themselves is to record their performances, thereby fixing an improvisational performance in tangible form as it occurs. This gives the performer a copyright in the underlying musical composition as well as the sound recording of the performance.

Another source of protection for unfixed works is found in Section 1101 of the United States Code (commonly referred to as the anti-bootlegging statute).[48] This provision prohibits the unauthorized fixation of "sounds or sounds and images of a live musical performance" and was intended to provide protection to performers rather than authors by prohibiting the bootlegging of live performances. Although it does not give a performer of an improvisational work a copyright in the improvised musical composition, it does have the practical effect of preventing bootleggers from making recordings, which also indirectly protects against unauthorized reproduction of the underlying musical composition.

## F. Works of the United States Government

Under Section 105 of the Copyright Act, copyright protection is not available to works created by the United States government. A work of the United States government is defined as a work prepared by an officer or employee of the United States government as part of that person's official duties. This means that government works such as federal judicial opinions and legislative enactments are part of the public domain and can be used freely by all. Additionally, all publications of the Copyright Office, the Trademark Office, and the IRS are in the public domain.

It is important to note that Section 105 applies only to the federal government and does not prevent states from claiming copyright ownership of works created by state employees. Further,

Section 105 does not prevent the United States government from owning copyrights that are transferred to it rather than created by the federal government.

## Endnotes

1. *Bleistein v. Donaldson Lithographing Co.*, 188 U.S. 239 (1903).
2. Although novelty is not required, its existence can be used to help prove that a work is original.
3. *Batlin & Son, Inc. v. Snyder,* 536 F.2d 486, 490 (2d Cir. 1976).
4. 81 F.2d 49, 54 (2d Cir.).
5. *Feist Publications, Inc. v. Rural Telephone Service Co.*, 499 U.S. at 345.
6. *Alfred Bell & Co., Ltd. v. Catalda Fine Arts, Inc.*, 191 F.2d 99, 103 (2d Cir. 1951).
7. *Universal Athletic Sales Co. v. Salkeld*, 511 F.2d 904, 908 (3d Cir. 1975).
8. *Kuddle Toy, Inc. v. Pussycat-Toy Co.*, 183 U.S.P.Q. 642, 663 (E.D.N.Y. 1974).
9. *L. Batlin & Sons, Inc. v. Snyder*, 536 F.2d 486, 490 (2d Cir. 1976).
10. 54 F. Supp. 2d 983.
11. *White-Smith Music Publishing Co. v. Apollo Co.*, 209 U.S. 1 (1908).
12. *Edward B. Marks Music Corp. v. Jerry Vogel Music Co.*, 140 F.2d 266 at 267 (2d Cir. 1944).
13. 45 U.S.P.Q. 2d (BNA) 1452 (1997).
14. Although the court's reasoning is correct, its use of the word "unique" is unfortunate because copyright only requires originality rather than uniqueness.
15. *The American Heritage Dictionary of the English Language*, Third Edition, Houghton Mifflin Company (1992).
16. *Smith v. George E. Muehlebach Brewing Co.*, 140 F. Supp. 729 (W.D. Mo. 1956).
17. 290 F. 959, 960 (2d Cir. 1923) ("The exclusive right granted to the appellant by his copyright to print, reprint, publish, copy and vend does not exclude the appellee from the use of 6 similar bars, when used in a composition of 450 bars.").
18. *Boosey v. Empire Music Co.*, 224 F. 646, 647 (S.D.N.Y. 1915).
19. *The American Heritage Dictionary of the English Language*, Third Edition, Houghton Mifflin Company (1992).
20. *Tempo Music, Inc. v. Famous Music Corporation v. Gregory A. Morris*, 838 F. Supp. 162 (1993).
21. *The American Heritage Dictionary of the English Language*, Third Edition, Houghton Mifflin Company (1992).
22. *Northern Music Corp. v. King Record Distrib. Co.*, 105 F. Supp. 393, 400 (S.D.N.Y. 1952).
23. 418 F. Supp.2d 369 (S.D. NY 2005). Affirmed on appeal. 352 Fed.Appx. 458 C.A.2 (N.Y.), 2009.
24. *White-Smith Music Publishing Co. v. Apollo Co.*, 209 U.S. 1, 17 (1908).
25. See Register's Supplementary Report, 4.
26. 17 U.S.C. § 101.

27. Pub. L. No. 92–140, 85 Stat. 391 (1971), as amended, Pub. L. No. 93–573, 88 Stat. 1873 (1974).

28. For example, California enacted a statute protecting sound recordings created prior to February 15, 1972. Cal. Civ. Code § 980.

29. 412 U.S. 546, 178 (1973).

30. The House Report on the 1976 Act at 56.

31. 17 U.S.C. § 101.

32. 17 U.S.C. § 101.

33. *Jeweler's Circular Publishing Co. v. Keystone Publishing Co.*, 274 F. 932, 934 (S.D.N.Y. 1921).

34. See, e.g., *Walt Disney Prods. v. Air Pirates*, 581 F.2d 751, 756, 199 U.S.P.Q. 769 (9th Cir. 1978); *Detective Comics, Inc. v. Bruns Publications, Inc.*, 111 F.2d 432, 433–434 (2d Cir. 1940).

35. See, e.g., *Warner Bros., Inc. v. American Broadcasting Cos.*, 720 F.2d 231, 243 (2d Cir. 1983); *Detective Comics, Inc. v. Bruns Publications, Inc.*, 111 F.2d 432, 433 (2d Cir. 1940); *DC Comics, Inc. v. Unlimited Monkey Business, Inc.*, 598 F. Supp. 110, 118–119 (N.D. Ga. 1984).

36. 17 U.S.C. § 101.

37. 17 U.S.C. § 101.

38. *WGN Continental Broadcasting Co. v. United Video, Inc.*, 693 F.2d 622, 627 (7th Cir. 1982).

39. 197 F. Supp. 17 (1961).

40. 409 F. Supp. 2d 484 (S.D.N.Y. 2006). Copyright protection for the collective work was granted by the court notwithstanding plaintiffs' failure to obtain prior authorization for the inclusion of those compositions in the show, since there was no evidence that the compositions were used without payment of applicable royalties.

41. *Edgerton v. UPI Holdings, Inc.* 2010 WL 2651304 (D.Md. 2010)

42. Litman, The Public Domain, 39 Emory Law Journal 965 (1990).

43. 37 C.F.R. §202.1(a) (1993).

44. *Stratchborneo v. Arc Music Corp.*, 357 F. Supp. 1393 (S.D.N.Y. 1973).

45. *Peters v. West*, 2011 WL 831137 (N.D.Ill. 2011)).

46. See H.R. Rep. No. 94-1476, at 52 ("an improvisation ... would not be eligible for Federal statutory protection under Section 102").

47. Cal. Civ. Code 980(a)(1).

48. The constitutionality of the civil anti-bootlegging provision of 17 U.S.C. § 1101(a)(3) was challenged but upheld in *KISS Catalog, Ltd., et al. v. Passport International Productions Inc., et al.*, 405 F. Supp. 2d 1169 (C.D.Cal., 2005). A separate anti-bootlegging provision that imposes criminal penalties for violation, 18 U.S.C. § 2319A, has also been challenged on constitutional grounds and upheld in *United States v. Martignon*, 492 F.3d. 140 (2d Circuit 2007). However § 2319A was upheld by distinguishing it from § 1101(a)(3), therefore some copyright scholars believe § 1101(a)(3) may be vulnerable to future constitutional challenges.

# 4 Ownership of Copyright

*"The songs I create mean many things to me. Foremost among them is my goal, and I think the goal of every artist, to connect with and communicate my thoughts, emotions, and beliefs to my audience... But, my songs also are my livelihood. If I can't earn a living from them, I'll have to do something else... I love what I do. But this is a tough business. And to illustrate that, I would ask each of you on this distinguished committee to think about this question: Have you ever seen in the classified section of any newspaper an ad which reads: 'Songwriter wanted. Good salary. Paid vacation. Health benefits and many other perks.' I'm sure you haven't. Most songwriters are lonely entrepreneurs trying again and again for that hit which will help them take care of their families and keep them writing in the hopes of another hit down the road, so that songwriting can be a career, not a part-time unpaid struggle. However, success would be meaningless without strong copyright laws... For it is only through the protection of the copyright law... that our right to earn a living from our creative work is assured."[1]*

*—Lyle Lovett, testifying before the House Subcommittee on Courts, the Internet and Intellectual Property, May 17, 2001*

Owning a copyright is, in many ways, like owning other types of property, although there are some important differences. Like other types of property, a copyright can be owned by one or more people and can be transferred from one owner to another. Just as a car owner can sell her car, a copyright owner can sell her copyright. A major difference is that when an author sells a copyrighted work (commonly known as a transfer or assignment of copyright), the author usually retains a contractual right to receive income from uses of the work. In many situations, in order to earn income from their copyrighted works, authors must transfer their copyrights to publishers so that the publisher can commercially exploit the work. Primarily due to the fact that copyright is intangible property, there are some strict rules for transferring copyrights that must be followed.

It is crucial to understand the difference between ownership of copyright as opposed to ownership of physical objects that copyrighted works may be embodied in. Section 202 of the Copyright Act provides that:

> *Transfer of ownership of any material object, including the copy or phonorecord in which the work is first fixed, does not of itself convey any rights in the copyrighted work embodied in the object.*

For example, the transfer of ownership of a compact disc would not constitute a transfer of copyright ownership. The purchaser of the compact disc owns the physical object embodying the copyrighted works contained on the compact disc, but does not acquire any ownership rights in the copyrighted works (songs and sound recordings) contained on the disc. Similarly, the purchaser of a song download from iTunes or other website from which one can legally acquire music owns (or, depending on the terms of the website's agreement with the purchaser, has a license to use) the digital file containing the copyrighted music, but does not acquire any ownership rights in the copyrighted works contained in the file.

# I. Initial Ownership

Copyright ownership arises from and begins upon creation of a work. Many people confuse copyright ownership with copyright registration and assume that you have to apply for or register a work in order for it to be copyrighted. In fact, a work is automatically protected by copyright from the moment it is created, as long as it satisfies the requirements for copyrightable subject matter discussed in the previous chapter. Although registration of a work does provide important benefits to the copyright owner, copyright ownership is not conditioned upon registration (see Chapter 9, "Copyright Formalities," for information on copyright registration).

Section 201(a) of the Copyright Act provides that the author of a work is the initial owner of the copyright. Although in most situations it is obvious who the author of a work is, there are some situations where this may not be clear, such as when there is more than one author and when one person creates a work on behalf of another. In general, the author of a work is the person who creates the work or translates an idea into fixed, tangible expression. The Supreme Court has stated that the term "author" should be interpreted in a broad sense and defined the term author as "he to whom anything owes its origin."[2]

---

**Example 4.1**

Suppose rap artist Jay XYZ writes a song entitled "Copyright State of Mind." As the author, Jay XYZ would be the copyright owner of the song (assuming that the song is an original expression and fixed in tangible form).

---

The owner of a copyrighted work may exercise any of the rights provided by copyright law or may authorize others to exercise any of those rights. The owner may also transfer copyright ownership to others.

---

**Example 4.2**

As the copyright owner of the song from the previous example, Jay XYZ could reproduce, adapt, distribute, and publicly perform his song, or he could allow others to do any of these things. If he wanted to, he could sell his song to a publisher, who would then become the owner of the song.

---

Obviously, knowing the identity of the author of a work is extremely important because all rights initially belong to the author. An author, however, does not necessarily have to perform all of the tasks involved in the creation of a work. For instance, copyright ownership in a sound recording may belong to the producer who directs and supervises the recording process, as well as to the performers themselves.

# II. Joint Ownership

It is not uncommon for more than one person to contribute to the creation of a work, and it is also quite common for more than one person or company to share ownership of copyrights. In fact, as far as published songs are concerned, it is rare for a single individual or entity to own the whole copyright to a song. One reason for this split ownership is that songwriters often collaborate in the creation of songs.

---

**Example 4.3**

---

If a song is written by a band consisting of five individuals with all five members contributing to its authorship, the copyright will be split among five co-authors. Ownership may be further divided due to transfers of ownership by the authors. If three of the band members have publishing contracts with three different music publishers, there could be as many as eight co-owners (i.e., the five band members and three publishing companies).

---

Even if a song is written by one author, copyright ownership may still be split among several parties. For instance, if a songwriter writes a song and pitches it to a record producer, the producer might insist on partial ownership in return for getting an artist to record it. Sometimes artists as well as some record companies will similarly insist on partial ownership of a song in return for recording it. The result is that a song written by one person may end up being owned by several different individuals and/or publishing companies.

Section 101 of the Copyright Act defines a joint work as a work prepared by two or more authors with the intention that their contributions be merged into inseparable or interdependent parts of a unitary whole. Under Section 201(a), the authors of a joint work are considered co-owners of the copyright in the work.

---

**Note:** The difference between inseparable and interdependent is that the contributions are inseparable when they have little or no independent meaning standing alone and interdependent when the parts have some significant meaning alone but achieve their primary significance because of their combined effect. For example, the music and lyrics of a song would be interdependent.

---

## A. Requirements for Joint Ownership

There are two requirements necessary for the creation of a joint work. First, two or more authors must contribute to the creation of the work. Second, each of the co-authors must make his contribution with the intention that the contributions be combined to form a single work.

### (1) Intent Requirement

In order for a work to qualify as a joint work, its authors must intend to combine their contributions into a unitary whole. The authors' intent to combine their contributions must exist at the time their contributions are created. When two or more co-authors work together at the same time and in the same place to create a work, it will be fairly obvious that they intend their contributions to be combined.

---

**Example 4.4**

Many music publishers in Nashville have "writer's rooms" where songwriters get together to collaborate on new songs. Songs created in this manner will almost always be joint works as long as each collaborator has made an independently copyrightable contribution. Similarly, when members of a band write songs together, the songs will usually be joint works.

---

It is not necessary, however, that authors work together at the same time and place or that they even know each other as long as each intends that his contribution will be combined with someone else's contribution to form a single work.

---

**Example 4.5**

In one case, a songwriter sold lyrics he had written to a music publisher, who then had another writer compose music for the lyrics. The court held that the resulting song was a joint work, stating that "It makes no difference whether the authors work in concert, or even whether they know each other; it is enough that they mean their contributions to be complementary in the sense that they are to be embodied in a single work to be performed as such."[3]

---

There are, however, situations in which separate works may be combined to form a single work and the resulting combination is not a joint work. For example, if one person writes a poem that she intends to be complete as is, and later, another person writes music to accompany the poem, the resulting song would not be a joint work because the intent to combine the poem with the music did not exist at the time the poem was composed. Instead, the song would be a derivative work based on the poem.

In order to determine whether authors possessed the intent to create a joint work, courts will generally look at several different factors. First, a court will examine the conduct of the contributors and any statements they may have made indicating their intent. Additionally, courts may consider the quality and quantity of the contribution. If the quality and quantity of a contribution are great, it is likely that a joint work was intended. Conversely, the fact that someone contributed a very small amount to a work might indicate that joint authorship was not intended. Finally, if the copyright to a work has been registered, courts will presume that the information identifying the authors in the registration application is accurate, and someone claiming to be an author who is not identified as such in the registration application will have the burden of proving that he is in fact a co-author.

### (2) Copyrightability of Individual Contributions
In addition to having the intent to create a joint work, each of the contributors must contribute some original expression that would be copyrightable on its own. This requirement results from

Section 101's definition of a joint work, which specifies that the work must be prepared by two or more "authors." In other words, each contributor must contribute copyrightable authorship in order to have a joint work.

---

**Example 4.6**

If a singer added a few words to the lyrics of a song written by someone else, the singer would not be a joint author because her contribution would not be copyrightable on its own. Similarly, if a singer has an idea for a song but, because she has no talent as a songwriter, tells someone else her idea and the other person writes the song, the singer would not be a joint author. The idea, no matter how important it is to the song, is not a copyrightable contribution.

---

Although uncopyrightable contributions will not qualify a contributor as an author, a contributor could still be a co-owner of the resulting work's copyright. For instance, if a singer has an idea for a song and wants someone else to write a song based on her idea, she could require the songwriter to sign a contract giving her partial copyright ownership in the song in return for disclosing the idea. In this situation, the singer would have acquired ownership from a transfer of ownership rather than from being an author. Sometimes, individuals who have not contributed authorship to a song will still be credited as authors. In some situations this results merely because the parties involved are not aware of the legal requirements for joint authorship. In other situations, the parties may agree to treat someone as a co-author even though they know that the person is not really an author, such as when a recording artist is credited as a co-author of a song when the artist merely makes minor, uncopyrightable lyric changes. The actual author of the song might be willing to credit a popular recording artist as a co-author, even though not legally accurate, in return for the artist's recording of the song, which may result in much greater exposure, popularity, and income than if the song were not recorded by a popular recording artist.

Although each co-author's contribution must be independently copyrightable, it is not necessary that each contribution be equal. In other words, it is possible for one author to contribute much less to the creation of a work than another but still be a co-author.

### B. Rights and Duties of Joint Owners

The Copyright Act provides some rules governing joint ownership of copyright. These rules can be thought of as default rules that apply unless co-owners make up their own rules. Co-owners are free to agree to any other ownership rules as long as they put their agreement in writing. However, if they do not agree otherwise in writing, the Copyright Act's rules apply.

#### (1) Equal, Undivided Ownership Interests

Section 201(a) provides that joint authors of a copyrighted work are co-owners of the copyright, and courts have interpreted this provision as providing for co-ownership in equal, undivided interests unless joint authors clearly indicate otherwise. This means that each co-author owns an equal share of the entire work. For instance, if two songwriters collaborate in the creation of a song, each will own 50 percent of the entire song. This is true regardless of the contributions made by the individual authors. Even if one author composes the music while the other writes the lyrics, both authors will own 50 percent of the entire song rather than one owning the music and the other owning the lyrics. The same rule holds true even if one songwriter contributes 90 percent of the song and the other contributes only 10 percent.

The joint work provisions operate under the assumption that co-authors usually contribute relatively equal portions and deserve an equal share of any profits derived from the work. There are two main reasons for this assumption. First, courts should not be put in the position of having to make subjective judgments about the relative value of co-authors' contributions. Second, in reality, co-authors rarely discuss how ownership should be shared prior to collaborating in the creation of a work. In many co-writing relationships between songwriters, it is assumed that each co-writer will own an equal share in the song. However, co-authors are perfectly free to alter this assumption of equality and agree upon any ownership split they choose as long as they put their agreement in writing.

---

**Example 4.7**

*Papa-June Music v. McLean*[4] involved an ownership dispute between co-authors of several songs. In 1989, Ramsey McLean sent some poems he had written to Harry Connick, Jr., who added music to them and recorded the resulting songs on an album. Connick and McLean entered into a co-publishing contract that provided that copyright ownership of the songs would be split 70 percent to Connick and 30 percent to McLean. Several years later, McLean sent Connick some new poems, which Connick added music to and recorded on another album. McLean then notified Connick that he wanted a 50/50 ownership split. Connick, however, thought the 70/30 split previously agreed to should apply. The court held that McLean was a joint owner of the copyrights for the songs, and because the parties did not have a written agreement specifying a different arrangement for these songs, McLean and Connick each owned 50 percent under Section 201(a) of the Copyright Act. This result illustrates the importance of having a written agreement if co-owners intend to share ownership in anything other than equal shares.

---

**Tips for Songwriters**   Many disputes arise over ownership of songs. In fact, this is one of the most common reasons for disputes between band members. The following are a few tips that can help avoid some of the more common disputes:

- Written collaboration agreements with co-writers can clarify how ownership and income will be shared and reduce the chance of misunderstandings.

- Do what the major record labels, famous recording artists, and Hollywood movie studios do: Do not accept or listen to any unsolicited material (demo recordings, etc. from people you do not know well or trust). By accepting unsolicited material, you make it easier for someone to prove access if they sue you for copyright infringement.

- Keep notes and/or recordings of writing sessions, especially with co-writers. Many professional writers keep journals in which they write down song ideas, lyrics, etc., and some use notebook computers or PDAs for the same purpose. Make sure you date your notes or recordings. If you are ever sued or have to sue someone else for infringement, these types of records can be important evidence.

## (2) Right to License

Because each joint owner of a copyrighted work owns an equal, undivided interest in the work, each joint owner has the right to use the work or to authorize others to use the work. This rule applies regardless of whether the author authorizing the use has the consent of the other authors. For instance, if three songwriters collaborate in the creation of a song, each would be free to record the song himself. Further, each of the songwriters would be free to issue a mechanical license authorizing someone else to record the song or use the song in a film or television commercial, even if one of the co-writers objects. The only exception is that a joint owner cannot grant an exclusive license because that would prevent co-owners from granting licenses. Practically, this rule can present licensing problems, but as with all of the joint ownership rules, co-owners are free to agree otherwise in writing. Even though one joint owner can grant non-exclusive licenses, many licensees will want to obtain a license from all joint owners. Contrary to American copyright law, many foreign countries require all joint owners to consent to the issuance of a license.

## (3) Duty to Account to Co-Owners

Although joint owners have the right to use and to authorize others to use the copyrighted work, they are required to account to their co-owners for their share of any profits derived from the use. Unless the co-owners have agreed otherwise in writing, each co-owner is entitled to an equal share of any income generated by a jointly owned work.

---

**Example 4.8**

A 1947 case, *Jerry Vogel Music Co. v. Miller Music, Inc.*[5] involved the song "I Love You California," which was composed by two authors, each of whom assigned his ownership interest to a different publisher. Universal Pictures asked Jerry Vogel Music Co. for a license quote for the use of the song in a movie, and Vogel quoted a fee of $1,000. Universal then obtained a license from Miller Music for $200. Vogel demanded half of the license fee, and after Miller refused, sued for an accounting. The court held that co-owners have a duty to account for profits from licensing to third parties. The court recognized that not having a duty to account to co-owners would lead to competition among co-owners for a low bid and encourage waste of copyrighted works. In other words, one co-owner cannot underbid another co-owner and keep the entire amount of income generated from the low bid.

---

## (4) Joint Authorship Problems

Problems frequently arise with respect to joint authorship of copyrighted works. Usually these problems are the result of authors who collaborate in the creation of a work but fail to discuss what their ownership interests will be. Disputes also tend to arise when songs are composed or worked on during recording sessions.

**Example 4.9**

In 1999, singer/songwriter Sarah McLachlan was sued in a Canadian court by Daryl Neudorf, who was hired by McLachlan's record company to work on the preproduction of her first album. Neudorf claimed that, during this working relationship, he co-wrote four songs with McLachlan that were included on her album. McLachlan contended that Neudorf only provided services as a musician and producer and that his contributions to the songs did not constitute authorship. The court found that although Neudorf did make contributions to the songs, his contributions to three of the songs were not sufficient to constitute original expression. However, even though the court believed that Neudorf had contributed original expression to the fourth song, it held the song was not a joint work because Neudorf failed to prove a mutual intent to co-author the song with McLachlan. The problem that arises from this decision is that, regardless of the extent of a musician or producer's songwriting contributions, a recording artist could potentially defeat the musician or producer's joint authorship claim by simply intending not to treat that person as a co-author. Instead, the artist could claim that any contributions the musician or producer may have made to songs were merely part of the services he was hired to perform.

The only practical solution is for the co-authors to have a written collaboration agreement for any co-written songs.

In recent years, the distinction between songwriters, musicians, and producers has become blurred. This is especially true in musical styles such as hip-hop, rap, and electronica that are largely dependent on beats and samples as opposed to more traditional melody- and lyric-based songs. In these types of music, the distinction between the creation of a song and the creation of a recording is often also blurred because songs often result as part of the recording process.

**Example 4.10**

In 1998, four individuals who worked on Lauryn Hill's album *The MisEducation of Lauryn Hill* sued Hill, claiming that they were co-authors of several songs on the album. Hill contended that she was the sole writer of the songs. Interestingly, the album's liner notes credit the individuals as performers, producers, or contributors of "additional music or lyrics," arguably indicating that they are co-authors. This lawsuit was reportedly settled, with the terms of the settlement confidential.

**Example 4.11**

In a 2004 case,[6] Demme Ulloa was a guest at a recording studio where popular rap recording artist Jay Z was working on recordings for his 2001 album *Blueprint*. While listening to an early demo recording of Jay Z's song "Izzo (H.O.V.A.)," Ulloa improvised and recorded a counter-melody (a secondary melody accompanying a primary melody), which was included on the recording eventually released by Jay Z and his record label, Universal Music Group. There was no agreement reached as to how Ulloa's contribution would be treated in connection with the Jay Z song, but Ulloa later claimed that she was a joint author of the song, which ultimately became a top 10 hit. Although the court believed that Ulloa may have made a copyrightable contribution to the song, it decided that Ulloa was not a joint author since there was no evidence that Jay Z intended to share authorship with her. The court stressed the importance of the joint authorship intent requirement, stating that "the parties must intend to share the rights of authorship rather than merely intend to enter into a relationship that results in the creation of a copyrightable work."

> However, the court left open the question of whether Ulloa's contribution could be considered a copyrightable derivative work, which may have been infringed by its inclusion in the Jay Z recording.

## C. Community Property

Nine states, including California, have community property laws specifying that property acquired while people are married belongs to both spouses equally. In such states, if a wife were to compose a musical composition, the copyright ownership in that composition would belong jointly to the husband and wife unless they agree otherwise. A California court has held that a copyright acquired by one spouse during marriage is community property. Property acquired before or after marriage is not considered community property.[7]

> **Note:** Other states that have community property laws include Arizona, Idaho, Louisiana, Nevada, New Mexico, Texas, Washington, and Wisconsin.

Under community property laws, either spouse would be entitled to sell a jointly owned copyright without the other's consent. Any income from such a sale would have to be shared jointly. However, a spouse cannot give away community property without the other spouse's consent. When one spouse dies, the other spouse would not necessarily inherit a copyright owned as community property because the deceased spouse may convey his or her share of the copyright by will to anyone. Upon divorce, the spouses are free to divide their jointly owned property in any way they choose. However, if they cannot agree, a court may end up splitting up the property. In such a situation, the judge could award a copyright entirely to one party and award the other cash or other property of equal value or could award each spouse half of the copyright.

> **Prenups and Copyrights**   An author or other copyright owner who is planning on getting married in a community property state and does not want to share ownership of copyrighted works can enter into a prenuptial agreement specifying that copyrights will be owned individually by the author. Even in non-community property states, it might be a good idea to enter into such an agreement to protect against a judge awarding a spouse ownership of property in a divorce settlement.

# III. Works Made for Hire

In some situations, the person who creates a work will not be considered the work's author and therefore not the initial copyright owner. Such situations can occur when a person creates a work on another's behalf. The work for hire doctrine is an exception to the general rule that copyright ownership vests initially in the work's creator. Instead, the person or party on whose behalf the work is created is considered to be the author and initial copyright owner. Section 201(b) of the Copyright Act provides that:

*In the case of a work made for hire, the employer or other person for whom the work was prepared is considered the author for purposes of this title and, unless the parties have expressly agreed otherwise in a written instrument signed by them, owns all of the rights comprised in the copyright.*

Under the work made for hire doctrine, an author does not have to be a human being. A corporation or other business entity can qualify as an author. The copyright owner of a work made for hire, whether an individual or a business, will have the same rights in the work that any author would have, with a few exceptions (such as the duration of copyright protection), and can exercise any of the exclusive rights or authorize others to do so. The actual creator of a work made for hire has no ownership rights in the work.

A work's classification as a work made for hire is important for several reasons. First, the initial ownership of a work made for hire belongs to the employer or commissioning party rather than the person who actually creates the work. Second, works made for hire have a different copyright term than other works (95 years from publication or 120 years from creation, whichever expires first). Third, there is no termination right applicable to works made for hire (see the "Termination of Transfers" section later in this chapter).

## A. Two Categories of Works Made for Hire

There are two situations in which a work made for hire can be created. The first involves works made by an employee as part of the employee's employment. The second involves certain types of works that are specially ordered or commissioned.

### (1) Works Prepared by Employees within the Scope of Employment

Under the work for hire definition of Section 101(1) of the Copyright Act, if an employee creates a copyrightable work as part of his or her job, the employer will own the copyright to the work. It is not necessary for the employer to tell employees that such works will be works made for hire, nor is it necessary to have a written contract stating so (although it may be advisable to do so).

### (a) Who Is an Employee?

In order to determine whether a work is made for hire, a determination must first be made as to whether the creator of the work is an employee rather than an independent contractor (a self-employed person who provides goods or services to another pursuant to a contractual agreement). Although the Copyright Act does not define the term "employee," the Supreme Court has held that a person is an employee if the party on whose behalf the work is performed has the right to control the manner and means by which the work is performed. This rule will be applicable regardless of how the parties classify their relationship. For instance, the fact that two parties have a written contract stating that a work created by one party is a work made for hire does not necessarily make it so. It also generally does not matter whether control is actually exercised by the employer, as long as it has the right to control.

In *Community for Creative Non-Violence v. Reid*,[8] the Supreme Court held that a sculptor who was hired to create a sculpture was an independent contractor rather than an employee. The Court considered a group of factors in reaching its conclusion to determine whether a person is an employee or an independent contractor. The following factors should be evaluated to determine whether the hiring party has the right to control the work of the hired party:

- The skill required to do the work
- The source of tools and materials used to create the work
- The location of the work performed
- The duration of the relationship between the parties
- Whether the hiring party has the right to assign additional projects to the hired party
- The extent of the hired party's discretion over when and how long to work
- The method of payment for the work
- Which party decides whether assistants will be used and which party pays them
- Whether the work is part of the regular business of the hiring party
- Whether the party creating the work is in business for itself
- Whether the hired party receives employee benefits from the hiring party
- The tax treatment of the hired party

In *Reid*, the Court evaluated these factors as follows: Reid was a sculptor, which is generally regarded as a skilled occupation; Reid supplied his own tools; Reid worked in his own studio; he was retained for less than two months; CCNV had no right to assign additional projects to Reid; Reid had control over when and how long he worked; CCNV paid Reid a $15,000 lump sum rather than a salary; Reid had authority to hire and pay assistants; creating sculptures was not part of CCNV's regular business; CCNV did not pay payroll or Social Security taxes; and CCNV did not provide any employee benefits to Reid.

Although none of the factors are individually determinative, three factors have generally weighed heavily in courts' evaluations. These are (1) whether the worker is paid a salary; (2) whether the hiring party provides employee benefits; and (3) whether the hiring party pays the worker's Social Security taxes. The reason for the importance of these factors is that it would be unfair for a company to be allowed to treat a worker as an independent contractor for tax purposes and as an employee for copyright ownership purposes. It is usually safe to assume that an employment relationship exists when an employee is paid a salary and provided with benefits and when the employer pays Social Security taxes for the employee.

---

**Tip:** Some states, such as California, require that employers who obtain copyright ownership from their employees as works made for hire must pay worker's compensation, unemployment insurance, and disability insurance.[9]

---

### (b) When Is a Work Prepared within the Scope of Employment?

After determining that an employment relationship exists, a determination must be made as to whether the work was created by the employee within the scope of employment. Generally, a work will be considered to be made within the scope of employment if (1) it is the type of work that the employee is paid to perform; (2) the work is performed substantially within work hours at the work place; and (3) the work is performed, at least in part, to benefit the employer.[10]

Any works created outside of the scope of an employment relationship will not be works made for hire unless the parties have a written agreement stating otherwise and the work fits within certain specified categories. An employer and employee are also free to agree that the employee will own the copyright in a work created within the scope of employment. To do so, there must be a written agreement transferring copyright ownership to the employee because the employer would still be considered to be the author of the work. In situations where it is uncertain whether an employment relationship exists, it is a good idea to have a written contract giving the hiring party ownership or the specific rights in the copyrighted work that are needed.

---

**Example 4.12**

Some music publishers, in contracts with songwriters, state that songs will be considered to be works made for hire. However, regardless of what a contract says, whether songs are works made for hire depends on whether the relationship between the publisher and songwriter is an employment or independent contractor relationship. If the songwriter is an employee, any songs written by the songwriter would be works made for hire, and the publisher would be considered the author. If the songwriter is an independent contractor, the songwriter would be considered the author, although the contract would provide that copyright ownership is transferred by the songwriter to the publisher. Either way, the publisher will own the copyrights to the songs; however, there are some important differences. For example, the duration of copyright protection will differ. Also, the author's termination right does not apply to works made for hire. In the vast majority of situations, songwriters will not be considered employees of publishers. Analyzing the *Reid* factors: Songwriting is generally regarded as a skilled occupation; songwriters generally work at times and places of their own choosing; songwriters are not usually paid a salary (although they may receive advances); publishers do not normally pay payroll or Social Security taxes; and publishers do not normally provide any employee benefits to songwriters.

---

### (2) Specially Ordered or Commissioned Works

If an employment relationship does not exist and one party hires another to create a copyrightable work, the work may still be a work made for hire if it is one of the types of specially ordered or commissioned works specified in Section 101(2). A specially ordered or commissioned work is created when the hiring party is the motivating factor in the creation of the work. In many circumstances, payment to the creator from the hiring party is considered to be the motivation for the creation of a work. Specially ordered or commissioned works can be works made for hire if the parties agree in writing and the work fits one of the following nine categories:

- A contribution to a collective work (e.g., an article in a magazine)
- A part of a motion picture or other audiovisual work (e.g., a screenplay)
- A translation
- A supplementary work—a work prepared for publication as a secondary part of a work by another author such as a foreword, pictorial illustration, musical arrangement, bibliography, appendix, etc.

- A compilation (e.g., individual sound recordings of songs created to be part of an album may be considered to be a compilation if the copyright owner of the songs only ever released them as an album)[11]
- An instructional text (e.g. a manual for stereo equipment)
- A test (e.g., ACT, LSAT)
- Answer material for a test
- An atlas

---

**Example 4.13**

A movie producer hires a composer to compose soundtrack music for a motion picture. In order for the music to be a work made for hire, the producer and composer must enter into a contract stating that the music is created as a work made for hire. Because the music is created to be a part of a motion picture—one of the nine specified categories—it would qualify as a work made for hire under Section 101(2).

---

In order for a work to be considered a work made for hire under Section 101(2), it must fit strictly within one of the nine specified categories. For example, one court held that advertising jingles did not fit the audiovisual works category because they did not have a visual component.[12] Instead, the jingles were sound recordings and therefore not works made for hire under Section 101(2).

If a work made for hire relationship does not exist, the party commissioning a work can have the creator transfer or assign the copyright to the commissioning party under a written contract. The only major disadvantage is that the creator will have the right to terminate the assignment in the future.

# IV. Transfer of Copyright Ownership

Like most types of property, copyright ownership can be transferred. As defined in Section 101 of the Copyright Act, a transfer of copyright includes:

> ... *an assignment, mortgage, exclusive license, or any other conveyance, alienation, or hypothecation of a copyright or of any of the exclusive rights comprised in a copyright, whether or not it is limited in time or place of effect, but not including a nonexclusive license.*

---

**Example 4.14**

Songwriters often transfer copyright ownership of songs they write to music publishers in return for the publisher's efforts at commercially exploiting the songs and the contractual right to receive royalties from any such exploitation. Similarly, musicians and producers often transfer copyright ownership of sound recordings they create to record companies.

---

The two most common types of transfers are assignments and exclusive licenses. An assignment occurs when a copyright owner transfers all or part of its ownership interest in a copyrighted work. An exclusive license occurs when a copyright owner transfers one or more of its exclusive rights but retains one or more rights as well. An exclusive licensee owns the rights transferred to it and, therefore, unless the license provides otherwise, has the right to sue infringers of its rights and to transfer its rights to others. Nonexclusive licenses, on the other hand, do not involve a transfer of ownership. Instead, a nonexclusive license gives someone the right to exercise one or more of the copyright owner's rights but does not restrict the copyright owner from letting others exercise the same right. Both exclusive and nonexclusive licenses may be limited in scope. For instance, a license can be limited in terms of duration, territory, or type of use.

Under the 1909 Copyright Act (which still applies to transfers made before January 1, 1978), copyright ownership was indivisible, meaning that a copyright owner's interest could not be divided. The 1976 Copyright Act changed this rule, making copyright ownership divisible. This means that a copyright can be divided without restriction. Consequently, a copyright owner can transfer its ownership interest in full or in part. Section 201(d)(1) provides that the author of a work may, as the initial owner of copyright, transfer his copyright by assigning all rights in the work, and his assignees and their assignees may similarly assign all rights in the work. Alternatively, under section 201(d)(2), the author and any assignees may transfer any one or more of the exclusive rights specified in Section 106. Finally, the author and any assignees may make transfers of subdivisions of the exclusive rights. It is also possible to transfer individual exclusive rights and to transfer different rights for different territories.

---

**Example 4.15**

Because copyright ownership is divisible, a songwriter can transfer partial ownership of songs to a publisher, retaining partial ownership (and a greater percentage of income earned). This type of arrangement between a songwriter and publisher is known as a co-publishing agreement and is quite common for commercially successful songwriters. Alternatively, a songwriter could grant copyright ownership to different publishers for different territories of the world (although this is not common).

---

### A. The Writing Requirement

The Copyright Act requires that transfers of copyright ownership must be made in writing. Section 204(a) provides that:

*A transfer of copyright ownership, other than by operation of law, is not valid unless an instrument of conveyance, or a note or memorandum of the transfer, is in writing and signed by the owner of the rights conveyed or such owner's duly authorized agent.*

Exclusive licenses, because they involve a transfer of ownership, must be made in writing except when made by operation of law. Nonexclusive licenses do not have to be made in writing, but it is best to do so anyway to specify the exact terms and rights involved.

The Copyright Act imposes the writing requirement to ensure that creators will not give away their copyright ownership inadvertently. It also forces someone who wants to use a copyrighted work to negotiate to determine precisely what rights are to be transferred and at what price.

### (1) What Kind of Writing Is Required?

Courts have tended to be very liberal in their interpretation of what form of writing is required to transfer copyright ownership. For example, courts have held that endorsed checks can fulfill the writing requirement. Obviously, it is better to use a clearly written document to avoid misunderstanding, but a complicated contract is not necessarily needed. Often, a simple letter or memo will be sufficient as long as the terms of the transfer are specified. At a minimum, any transfer document should be in writing, signed by the owner of the rights being transferred, specify the particular rights being transferred, specify who is acquiring the rights, and specify the duration of the transfer. Additionally, a license should always state whether it is exclusive or nonexclusive.

**Example 4.16**

In *Ballas v. Tedesco*,[13] a ballroom dancer (Ballas) wanted to record a compact disc (CD) containing music from the movie *Titanic* to be used at dance competitions. Ballas negotiated a deal through e-mail correspondence with a producer (Tedesco) to produce the CD. Ballas agreed to pay Tedesco $15,000 for making musical arrangements, producing, mixing, and mastering the CD. Ballas was to have the exclusive right to manufacture 5,000 copies of the CD for sale. Although they exchanged drafts of a proposed written agreement through e-mails, due to disagreements, the parties' relationship ceased and negotiations ended. Tedesco registered the copyright for the sound recordings embodied on the CD and began marketing it at dance competitions. Ballas sued claiming that Tedesco had breached the parties' contract. The court held that there was no written agreement evidencing any transfer of ownership to Ballas as required by Section 204(a) of the Copyright Act. The court disagreed with Ballas' contention that the exchange of e-mails satisfied the writing requirement because the e-mails were not signed by Tedesco. Tedesco was therefore the sole owner of the recordings.

**Tip:** It is a good idea to sign three copies of any transfer document: one for the transferor, one for the transferee, and one for recordation with the Copyright Office (see the following section, "Recording Copyright Transfers").

## B. Recording Copyright Transfers

Any document pertaining to a copyright may be recorded in the Copyright Office.[14] This includes transfers of ownership, exclusive or nonexclusive licenses, wills, contracts, etc. When a transfer is recorded, a copy is placed in the Copyright Office's files, which are indexed and available in the Copyright Office and online at the Copyright Office's website (www.copyright.gov) for public inspection. This is similar to the process for recording the deed to a house with a county recorder's office. The Copyright Office will also send a certificate of recordation to the recording party.

**Recordation versus Registration** Recordation, the process of recording transfers of copyright ownership, is not the same as copyright registration, which is the process for recording claims of copyright ownership (see Chapter 9 for a discussion of copyright registration). In a perfect world, the author of a work would register the copyright shortly after its creation, and any transfers of ownership would be recorded promptly after they occur. In the real world, which is far from perfect, many authors and copyright owners neglect to register their copyrights and record transfers of ownership. This often makes it difficult to determine who actually owns a copyrighted work.

Although recordation is not mandatory, there are several important benefits gained by recordation. Because copyright is intangible property that can be transferred without transferring possession of any physical object, it is easy for unscrupulous copyright owners to attempt to make multiple transfers of the same copyright interest. Recordation protects purchasers by establishing rules of priority between transferees when a copyright owner makes multiple transfers of the same interest. Most importantly, recordation gives constructive notice to the world of the facts specified in the recorded document. Constructive notice means that everyone is deemed to have knowledge of the transfer regardless of whether they actually have knowledge or not. The reasoning is that once a transfer is recorded, anyone can check the Copyright Office records to find out about it.

## (1) Priority Rules for Transfers

The Copyright Act provides the following rules regarding priority of copyright transfers:

- If there are conflicting transfers of copyright ownership of a registered work, the first transfer takes priority over any subsequent transfers if it is recorded first.

- If a subsequent transfer is recorded first, the first transfer will still take priority over the subsequent transfer if the first transfer is recorded within one month after it is made (or two months if the transfer was made outside of the United States).

- If the first transfer is not recorded or is recorded more than one month after it is made (or two months if outside of the United States), the transfer that is recorded first will take priority even if it is made subsequent to another transfer. There are two limitations to this rule. First, it is not applicable if the transfer was a gift or is inherited by will. Second, it is not applicable if the subsequent transferee had knowledge of the earlier transfer.

---

**Example 4.17**

Sammy Sleazeball writes a song, registers it with the Copyright Office, and then transfers it to Honest Abe's Music on March 1 in return for a $1,000 advance. A week later, after spending the $1,000, Sammy attempts to transfer the same song to Trustworthy Tunes for another advance.

(a) Who owns the copyright to the song if Honest Abe's records its transfer agreement on March 3? Honest Abe's, because the first transfer will always prevail if it is recorded first.

(b) Who owns the copyright to the song if Honest Abe's records its transfer agreement on March 31? Honest Abe's, because it has 30 days to record its transfer and still have priority over any subsequent transfers.

(c) Who owns the copyright to the song if Honest Abe's records its transfer agreement on April 31, but Trustworthy Tunes records its transfer agreement on April 30? Trustworthy, as long as it did not know of the previous transfer to Honest Abe. If, however, Trustworthy was not really trustworthy and knew of the previous transfer to Honest Abe's, Honest Abe's would own the copyright regardless of when it recorded its transfer.

---

**Tip:**  Before purchasing a copyrighted work, it is highly advisable to conduct a search of the Copyright Office records to make sure that the party you are buying the work from actually has the right to sell it to you. But remember that just because a transfer is not recorded in the Copyright Office, that does not mean that no prior transfers exist.

### (2) How to Record a Transfer

In order to record a transfer document, you should fill out a Document Cover Sheet form, which can be obtained from the Copyright Office. If the work has not previously been registered, a registration form should be filed as well. The Document Cover Sheet specifies basic information about the transfer document, such as the names of the parties (assignor and assignee), the titles of the works transferred, the number of copyrighted works included in the recorded document (used to determine the filing fee), and the date the document was signed or became effective. Additionally, it is important to include the address where the Copyright Office should send the certificate of recordation at the bottom of the page.

As of the date of this book's publication, the Copyright Office charges a fee of $105 for the first title and $30 for each group of up to 10 additional titles recorded. For example, if a document contains 2–11 titles, the fee will be $135. However, Copyright Office fees are subject to change, so it is advisable to check the Copyright Office website (www.copyright.gov) for current fees before submitting any documents. When you have filled out the Document Cover Sheet, send the original and one copy, along with the recordation fee and the document, to the Copyright Office at the address specified on the Document Cover Sheet. Within two to three months, you should receive a certificate of recordation along with the original transfer document. See Copyright Office Circular 12, available from the Copyright Office website (www.copyright.gov) for instructions on recording copyright transfer documents.

**Assignment of Copyright**  When a songwriter transfers ownership of a song to a music publisher, the parties will sign a contract. If the songs transferred were registered by the songwriter, the publisher could file a recordation using the contract as the transfer document. However, any document recorded will become a public record. Because publishing contracts typically contain many provisions in addition to the provisions transferring ownership, the parties will probably not want to make the whole contract available to the public. For instance, the parties may wish to keep royalty rates and advance amounts confidential. To do so, publishers commonly record an assignment of copyright form, which simply describes the transfer of ownership.

# V. Termination of Transfers

If you own any type of property, you are generally free to transfer ownership of that property to someone else. People commonly transfer property by selling it or giving it away. For example, you could sell a car or a house that you own. Once you transfer property to someone else, you no longer have any ownership rights to that property, so you wouldn't expect to be able to take back ownership of a car, house, or any other property transferred to someone else, especially if you have been paid to transfer the property. In this respect, copyrights are unique because the law provides authors of copyrighted works with a right to terminate certain transfers of copyright or, in other words, a right to take back ownership of property previously transferred. This may seem like a strange right, but it is based on the idea that copyrights are in some ways very different than other types of property.

## A. Rationale for the Termination Right

Although American copyright law has given authors the right to transfer copyright ownership, Congress has at the same time tried to protect authors from transfers that turn out to be bad deals for the author. Congress has attempted to provide this protection first with the renewal provisions of the 1909 Copyright Act and then with the termination provisions of the 1976 Copyright Act.

The renewal system under the 1909 Copyright Act was designed to allow authors and their heirs to regain ownership of copyrighted works that the author had previously transferred. Section 24 of the 1909 Act provided for an initial period of copyright protection lasting for 28 years from the date of the work's first publication. Section 24 also provided for a second 28-year period of protection for works that were renewed. The renewal right belonged to the author or to the author's heirs if the author died prior to the 28th year of the initial period. The rationale for having a renewal period was described by Congress as follows:

> It not infrequently happens that the author sells his copyright outright to a publisher for a comparatively small sum. If the work proves to be a great success and lives beyond the term of twenty-eight years, your committee felt that it should be the exclusive right of the author to take the renewal term.[15]

Unfortunately for authors, the renewal provision was largely unsuccessful in accomplishing its intended purpose. The 1909 Act did not address the question of whether an author could assign his rights to the renewal term. In *Fred Fisher Music Co. v. M. Witmark & Sons*,[16] the authors of the song "When Irish Eyes Are Smiling" assigned both the initial term and the renewal term to a music publisher. The Supreme Court ruled that the renewal term was assignable during the original copyright term, provided that the author survived beyond the end of the original term. In a subsequent case, *Miller Music Corp. v. Charles N. Daniels, Inc.*,[17] the Supreme Court held that when the author died before the 28th year of the initial term, the renewal right belonged to the author's heirs, regardless of any assignment to another party.

Many authors did not have the opportunity to take advantage of the renewal period because publishers routinely required authors and their likely heirs to assign their rights in the renewal term to the publisher. Consequently, if the author was alive at the time for renewal, the renewal right belonged to the publisher rather than the author.

The 1976 Copyright Act did away with the renewal system but added provisions designed to accomplish a similar result by giving authors the right to terminate transfers of copyright after a period of time. This is a highly unusual right and is unique to copyright law. For instance, when you sell any other kind of property, such as a car, you have no right to take back that property at some future point in time. According to Congress:

*A provision of this sort is needed because of the unequal bargaining position of authors, resulting in part from the impossibility of determining a work's value until it has been exploited.*

There are two different provisions in the 1976 Copyright Act dealing with termination.

Section 203 governs terminations of transfers made beginning in 1978, and Section 304 governs terminations of transfers made before 1978. Unlike the renewal right under the 1909 Copyright Act, the termination right cannot be waived by an author. In other words, even if a songwriter agrees in a contract with a publisher that he will not exercise his right to terminate, such a contractual agreement is not legally valid, and the author can still terminate the transfer. Works made for hire are not subject to termination because the rationale of protecting authors from unremunerative transfers does not really apply to employers.

The termination provisions are very detailed and complex, and it is important that they be fully complied with because the failure to do so can result in a loss of the termination right. In addition to the rules specified by Sections 203 and 304 of the Copyright Act, the Copyright Office is authorized to promulgate additional regulations, which are included in the U.S. Code of Federal Regulations, 37 C.F.R. § 201.10.

## B. Transfers Made Beginning January 1, 1978

The termination right under Section 203 applies to any "exclusive or nonexclusive grant of a transfer or license" of a copyright or any right under copyright that is made by the author on or after January 1, 1978. For purposes of the termination right, the most important date is not the date of a work's creation. Instead, the most important date is the date when a transfer of rights is made. For instance, if a song was composed in 1960 and transferred by its composer to a publisher in 1978, the transfer is subject to the Section 203 termination right. The fact that the song was created prior to 1978 does not matter as long as the transfer took place on or after January 1, 1978.

### (1) Who Can Terminate?

The termination right can be exercised by the author or the author's successors, as specified by Section 203, which provides a succession hierarchy that works basically as follows:

- If the author dies and is survived by a spouse but no children or grandchildren, the spouse gets the termination right.

- If the author dies and is survived by a spouse and children or grandchildren of a deceased child, the spouse gets half of the termination right, and the surviving children and grandchildren share the other half. Grandchildren get the share their deceased parent would have had.

- If the author dies and is survived by children and grandchildren of deceased children (but no spouse), the children and grandchildren get the termination right in equal shares.

- If the author dies leaving no surviving spouse, children, or grandchildren, the author's executor (as appointed by the author's will) gets the termination right.

A majority of the persons who hold the termination interest is required to exercise the termination right. If a work has more than one author, termination can be made by a majority of the authors or their successors.

---

**Example 4.18**

Peter, Paul, and Mary, joint authors of a song called "Blowing in the Wind," transfer the song to Dylan Music. If Peter dies, leaving a wife and two children, the termination can be made by either: (1) Paul and Mary; or (2) Paul or Mary and at least two of Peter's three successors.

---

### (2) When Can the Termination Right Be Exercised?

Termination can be made at any time during a five-year time period between 35 and 40 years after the date of transfer. However, if a transfer includes the right of publication (as most do), termination may be made during the five-year period beginning at the end of 35 years from publication or 40 years from the transfer date, whichever is earlier. Because most works are published shortly after they are transferred, 35 years from publication will usually be the beginning of the termination period rather than 40 years from the transfer date. The first terminations to be made under Section 203 will occur in 2013 (35 years after 1978).

---

**Example 4.19**

Tommy Tunesmith wrote a song and transferred the copyright to Deaf Mute Music in 1980. Tommy could terminate the transfer during the five-year period beginning in 2015 and ending in 2020.

---

### (3) What Must Be Done to Exercise the Termination Right?

In order to make a termination, the terminating party must give written notice, signed by the terminating party (or his or her agent) to the transferee. If the transferee has transferred the copyright to another party, the termination notice must be sent to that party if the terminating party knows of that party's identity. Before sending a termination notice, it is advisable to check the Copyright Office records as well as the records of the performing rights organizations (for songs) to verify who the current owner is. The notice must state the intended termination date and may be sent at any time between two and ten years before the termination date. A copy of the notice must also be filed with the Copyright Office.

**Example 4.20**

To exercise the termination right for the previous example in 2016, Tommy could send notice to Deaf Mute Music at any time from 2006 to 2014. If Tommy waited until 2015, the termination could not take place in 2016, although it could still take place during the remaining four years of the five-year termination period. If Deaf Mute Music had sold the copyright to Omniversal Music in 1990, the notice must be sent to Omniversal, although it couldn't hurt to send a copy to Deaf Mute as well if they are still in business.

### (4) What Happens after Termination?

Once a termination takes place, the copyright reverts to the author or the author's successors. If there is more than one author, even authors or successors who did not join in signing the termination notice will benefit from the termination and co-own the copyright.

An owner of a copyright acquired by termination has the same rights as any copyright owner, including the right to sell and license the work. However, these rights cannot be exercised prior to termination even if a termination notice has already been made. In other words, an author who sends a termination notice cannot assign his rights to a new transferee before the termination becomes effective. There is one exception to this rule: A new transfer may be made to the original transferee or the successor of the original transferee.

**Example 4.21**

Using the information from the previous example, if Tommy gives proper notice to terminate the transfer effective as of 2016, he cannot make a new transfer to anyone except Deaf Mute Music (or its transferee) before 2016. Beginning in 2016, Tommy can transfer or license the copyright to anyone.

### (5) Agreements to Transfer before Creation of a Work

In 2011, the U.S. Copyright Office attempted to address a potential problem involving notices of termination under Section 203 of the Copyright Act. The problem involves situations in which an author made a contractual agreement to transfer copyright in a work before 1978, but the work was created on or after January 1, 1978. This type of situation may be fairly common, such as when songwriters agree to transfer copyrights in songs to be created in the future under exclusive songwriting contracts with music publishers. For example, a songwriter might have entered into a contract in 1977 that provides that the songwriter will transfer copyrights to songs to be created over the next three years to a publisher. If the songwriter creates a song in 1978, what is the relevant date for recording a notice of termination with the Copyright Office? Since a transfer of copyright cannot be made before a work exists, the key date is 1978 in this example (even though the agreement to transfer was made in 1977). The Copyright Office amended its regulations to clarify that recordation of notices of termination must include the transfer date since that is the date on which termination rights are based. However, the Copyright Office also stated that it may be helpful (although not mandatory) to also include the date of creation, especially in situations involving works created on or after January 1, 1978, but subject to agreements to transfer made before 1978. The Copyright Office also indicated that it may issue additional regulations in the future to provide further clarification and alternatively recommended that Congress consider enacting legislation to resolve potential issues that may arise. For up-to-date information on termination regulations, see the Copyright Office website at www.copyright .gov/docs/termination/. Unless and until Congress or the Copyright Office more specifically addresses this issue, the best practice for recordation of termination notices under Section 203 seems to be to state the date of transfer and, if possible, also state the date of creation. It is also advisable to retain any documentation proving evidence of dates of creation as well as dates of transfer pertaining to copyrighted works to which the termination right may apply.

---

**Tip:** Publishers or other transferees who receive termination notices for valuable works may attempt to convince the author (or other terminating party) to re-transfer the copyright to them before the termination takes place. In order to do so, they will probably have to offer the author a better deal than the one under which they originally acquired the copyright (e.g., higher royalty rates, additional advances, co-publishing rights, etc.).

---

## C. Transfers Made before January 1, 1978

The termination provisions of Section 304 govern transfers made before 1978 and allow the author or the author's successors to recapture the 39-year extension of the renewal period provided by the 1976 Act and the Term Extension Act of 1998 (discussed in Chapter 8, "Duration of Copyright"). The provisions of Section 304 are very similar to those of Section 203, although there are a few important differences. One difference is that in addition to transfers made by authors, the termination right under Section 304 also applies to transfers made by the author's beneficiaries who are entitled to a renewal right under the 1909 Copyright Act (i.e., the author's spouse, children, executor, or next of kin). The five-year termination period begins 56 years after copyright is secured. If such a termination is made, the author or the author's beneficiaries would recapture copyright ownership for the last 39 years of the 95-year copyright term. Additionally, if an author fails to terminate during that period, he has a second chance during the five-year period beginning 75 years after the copyright was secured under the Term Extension Act of 1998. If a termination is made in this situation, the author or the author's beneficiaries would recapture copyright ownership for the last 19 years of the 95-year copyright term.

**Example 4.22**

Theresa Tunesmith writes a song and registers the copyright in 1940. If the copyright was transferred by Theresa before 1978, she could terminate the transfer during the five-year period from 1996 to 2000. If Theresa failed to exercise this termination right, she or her beneficiaries have a second chance to terminate from 2016 to 2020.

## D. The Derivative Works Exception

Even if a transfer is terminated, a derivative work made before termination can continue to be used by the transferee. This derivative works exception applies to transfers made before and after 1978 and states that:

*A derivative work prepared under authority of the grant before its termination may continue to be utilized under the terms of the grant after its termination, but this privilege does not extend to the preparation after the termination of other derivative works based upon the copyrighted work covered by the terminated grant.*[18]

---

### Example 4.23

A record company that received a license from a publisher to make sound recordings of a song is allowed to continue to sell sound recordings containing that song after the songwriter terminates its transfer to the publisher. Although the termination allows the author to recapture ownership of the song, the author cannot prevent the continued exploitation of derivative works (such as sound recordings) based on the song.

---

The rationale for the derivative works exception is that a substantial investment may be made in some derivative works, and it would be unfair to prevent someone who has made that investment from being able to continue using the derivative work. The exception only allows continued use of derivative works made before termination. It does not allow a transferee to make any derivative works after termination.

---

**Derivate Works Based on Works with Terminated Rights**   It is quite possible that transferees that receive termination notices will have derivative works created based on the work to which the termination applies. For instance, a music publisher might have a derivative musical composition made based on a musical composition to which its rights are to be terminated and then attempt to exploit the derivative composition as much as possible instead of the original composition. It does not appear that there is any way authors can prevent this practice (unless they have a contractual right of approval over derivative works), although they may be able to limit it by giving termination notices close to the latest possible date allowed (i.e., two years prior to termination).

---

# VI. Ownership of Sound Recordings

Determining who the authors of a sound recording are can often be a complicated matter. Anyone who has contributed original expression to the creation of a recording would legally be considered an author. Generally, the recording artist whose performance is recorded would be considered an author. In addition, the record producer (and in certain situations the recording engineer) who is responsible for setting up the recording sessions, capturing and electronically processing the sounds, and compiling and editing them to make the final recording may also be an author.[19] However, in some situations, the record producer's contribution may be so minimal that the recording artist's performance is the only copyrightable element in the work. In other situations, the record producer's contribution may be the only copyrightable contribution to a sound recording, such as recordings of naturally occurring sounds (e.g., a thunderstorm, bird-calls, etc.). Musicians hired by the featured recording artist, record company, or record producer may also contribute authorship in some circumstances.

Regardless of who the authors of a sound recording are, sound recordings made by artists under contract to record companies are virtually always owned by the record company, at least by assignment of copyright from the authors to the record company, and possibly as a work for hire.

Disputes can arise when an investor pays for recording studio time to enable an artist to make a recording. Often, the investor believes he or she owns the copyright in the recording produced simply because he or she paid for it. However, if the investor did not contribute any original material to the sound recording, he or she would not be legally entitled to claim authorship unless the recording was a work made for hire. Sometimes an investor will require the artist to sign a contract stating that the recordings produced will be works for hire. Regardless of what a contract says, such recordings may not qualify as works made for hire. Consequently, an investor might be better off having a contract under which the artist transfers ownership to the investor.

Most recording contracts provide that recordings made under the contract will be considered to be works made for hire. However, due to legal uncertainty as to whether sound recordings qualify as works made for hire, recording contracts also usually provide that if the recordings do not qualify as works made for hire, the artist transfers his copyright ownership to the record company.

In 1999, the Recording Industry Association of America (RIAA), a trade organization that represents record companies, got an amendment passed that added sound recordings as a category of works eligible for treatment as works made for hire under the specially ordered or commissioned works category of Section 101(2). Although the RIAA described the amendment as a technical clarification of existing law, it had potentially severe implications for recording artists and producers.

Under copyright law prior to the amendment, artists (and possibly producers and other contributors to the creation of sound recordings) who signed contracts with record companies beginning in 1978 would likely have the right to terminate the transfer of sound recording copyrights to record companies 35 years after the transfers were made. For valuable recordings, the artist would be in a much better bargaining position after termination than when the original transfer was made. The artist could sell or lease the sound recording back to the record company for a much greater share of the recording's revenue, sell or lease it to a different record company, or retain ownership and sell the recording to the public himself. However, the amendment, by allowing sound recordings to be treated as works made for hire, eliminated the possibility of termination by artists because the termination right is not available for works made for hire.

After the amendment's passage, several artists, entertainment attorneys, artists' managers, and journalists began to voice their objections to it. Some prominent recording artists such as Don Henley and Sheryl Crow also started to speak out about the amendment's impact on artists. Due to these efforts, Congress repealed the amendment retroactively, but rather than putting the law back exactly as it was, it added language to the definition of "work for hire" in Section 101 of the Copyright Act, which says that "neither the amendment... nor [its] deletion... shall be considered or otherwise given any legal significance." The definition goes on to say that works for hire should be analyzed as if the amendment "were never enacted...." This new language has apparently done nothing to reduce confusion regarding the status of sound recordings as works for hire, at least in part because it is still possible that sound recordings could be considered to be works made for hire under Section 101(2) under the categories of compilations and collective works, as courts have held that sound recordings, at least in the form of albums, are in fact compilations. Particularly because very valuable recording catalogs from artists such as Bruce Springsteen and Billy Joel are some of the first to be eligible for termination and to put the question to the test, litigation to resolve this issue is almost certain to commence in the near future.

---

**Sound Recordings**   In the authors' opinion, sound recordings frequently will not qualify as works made for hire because they are not usually created under an employment relationship and because, in many cases, they will potentially fit within only a few of the categories of specially ordered or commissioned works that can be works made for hire. However, transfers of copyright ownership of sound recordings may be subject to termination rights in some circumstances. Some artists are excited about this because they believe it will allow them to regain copyright ownership of valuable sound recordings. However, other individuals (producers, engineers, musicians, etc.) may have termination rights in addition to artists in some circumstances. This may result in situations where multiple parties attempt to terminate transfers of copyright ownership in a single sound recording. Problems arising from such situations will include determining which parties are actually authors and have termination rights, determining how many of these parties are necessary to effectuate termination (since a majority is legally required), and determining how a sound recording can be commercially exploited after termination when it is co-owned by multiple terminating parties.

---

# VII. Orphan Copyrights

For various reasons, it can sometimes be difficult or even impossible to determine whether a work is currently protected by copyright or, assuming a work is still protected, who the owner of the copyright is. For example, in some circumstances, a person might not know he or she is the owner of a copyright if ownership was acquired by an inheritance he is unaware of. In other situations, a company that owned a copyright may have gone out of business many years before, and it may not be possible to determine who copyright ownership was transferred to. Works for which the copyright owner cannot be located or contacted are referred to as "orphan works," and for the past several years there have been attempts to amend American copyright law to address the issue of orphan works.

Orphan works pose a problem for people who want to use these works but are unable to know whether they can be used freely or not. For instance, a filmmaker who wants to use music in a film but cannot identify the copyright owner would not be able to use the music without the risk of infringing the work's copyright. Additionally, libraries, educational institutions, and websites that want to digitize and make available old books, films, and recordings cannot always be sure they aren't infringing copyrights. Photographs are most often the subject of an orphan works problem, since they often have no copyright information attached to them. Since 2003, several attempts have been made by Congress to enact legislation dealing with orphan works, but none have been enacted as of this book's publication. While many people, including the authors, believe that allowing the use of orphan works is desirable, some organizations representing authors and publishers have opposed such proposals, especially early proposals that would have required copyright owners to file renewal registrations or lose their copyrights to the public domain. Some copyright owners also fear that orphan works legislation will be taken advantage of by people trying to avoid licensing and paying for the use of copyrighted works.

In 2006, the U.S. Copyright Office released a report on orphan works that recommended Congress amend the Copyright Act to allow people to use orphan works if they make a diligent search but are unable to identify the owner of a work.[20] If the copyright owner of a work later turned up, the user would have to pay a reasonable fee for continued use of the work but would not be subject to any other penalties for copyright infringement. The most recent attempt to enact orphan works legislation in 2008 included most of the recommendations of the Copyright Office report but, like previous attempts, was unsuccessful.[21]

Other countries (as well as the European Union, which issued a proposal recommending orphan works legislation in mid-2011)[22] have attempted to deal with the orphan works issue, but as of this book's publication, Canada is the only country to implement a law specifically dealing with orphan works.[23] The Canadian law provides that if a prospective user of an orphan work is not able to identify the copyright owner after making a reasonable effort to do so, the prospective user can apply to the Copyright Board of Canada for a license. If approved, the license allows use of the work as requested, but the user has to pay a fee determined by the Copyright Board that is held in escrow to be paid to the copyright owner if later identified.

# Endnotes

1. Testimony on the Internet Uses of Music Before the House Subcommittee on Courts, the Internet and Intellectual Property, May 17, 2001.
2. *Goldstein v. California*, 412 U.S. 546, 561 (1973) (quoting *Burrow-Giles Lithographic Co. v. Sarony*, 111 U.S. 53, 58 (1884)).
3. *Edward B. Marks Music Corp. v. Jerry Vogel Music Co.*, 140 F.2d 266, 267.
4. 921 F. Supp. 1154 (1996).
5. 73 F. Supp. 165, 168 (S.D.N.Y. 1947).
6. *Ulloa v. Universal*, 303 F. Supp. 2d 409 (S.D.N.Y. 2004).
7. *Marriage of Worth*, 195 Cal. App. 3d 768 (1987).
8. 490 U.S. 730, 753 (1989).
9. Cal. Lab. Code § 3252.5.
10. *Miller v. CP Chemicals, Inc.*, 808 F. Supp. 1238 (D.S.C. 1992) (quoting Restatement of Agency).
11. *Bryant v. Media Right Productions, Inc.*, 603 F.3d 135 (2d Cir. 2010).

12. *Lulirama Ltd. v. Axcess Broad. Servs., Inc.*, 128 F.3d 872 (5th Cir. 1997).

13. 41 F. Supp. 2D 531 (D.N.J. 1999).

14. 17 U.S.C. § 205.

15. H.R. REP. NO. 2222, 60th Cong., 2d Sess. 14 (1909).

16. 318 U.S. 643 (1943).

17. 362 U.S. 373 (1960).

18. 17 U.S.C. § 203(b)(1) and 304(c)(6)(A).

19. The House Report on the 1976 Act at 56.

20. See U.S. Copyright Office Report on Orphan Works, January 2006, available at http://www.copyright.gov/orphan/orphan-report-full.pdf.

21. Orphan Works Act of 2008, HR 5889, 110th Congress, available at http://www.thomas.gov/cgi-bin/query/z?c110:H.R.5889.

22. Proposal for a Directive of the European Parliament and of the Council on Certain Permitted Uses of Orphan Works, European Commission, May 24, 2011, available at http://ec.europa.eu/internal_market/copyright/docs/orphan-works/proposal_en.pdf.

23. Canadian Copyright Act (R.S.C., 1985, c.-C-42), section 77, available at http://laws.justice.gc.ca/eng/acts/C-42/.

# 5   The Reproduction Right

> *"We think of copyright as a bundle of rights—the reproduction right, the distribution right, and the performance right—and the reason for thinking that way is historical. In the beginning, when people copied manuscripts by hand, we had a 'copy' right, which gradually evolved over time to encompass newer technologies. The key idea behind all of these rights is giving copyright owners the ability to meaningfully exploit their works."*
>
> —Shira Perlmutter, former Associate Register for Policy and International Affairs, United States Copyright Office

The hallmark of copyright protection is the copyright owner's entitlement, subject to some important limitations, to exclusive use and control of her intellectual property. Accordingly, it is important to review and unde-rstand the scope of each of the exclusive rights encompassed in an owner's copyright.

## I. Introduction: Exclusive Rights

Section 106 of the Copyright Act provides for six exclusive rights that copyright owners may have, depending on the type of work involved. The exclusive rights have been referred to as a "bundle of rights" that may overlap, be subdivided, and be owned and enforced separately. These exclusive rights are the essence of copyright law because they allow the copyright owner to control the use of his work. The copyright owner can exercise any of the rights himself or authorize others to do so. Generally, no one other than the copyright owner can exercise any of the exclusive rights without obtaining the copyright owner's permission. If someone other than the copyright owner exercises one or more of the exclusive rights without the copyright owner's permission, that person has committed an infringement unless the use is permitted by any of the defenses to copyright infringement.

---

**Licenses for Different Uses of Music**   Permission to use a copyrighted work is normally granted by a license. A license is an agreement in which one party (the copyright owner or "licensor") gives another party (the "licensee") permission to do something (e.g., use a copyrighted work in a specified manner), usually for some type of compensation (i.e., a fee or royalty). There are different types of licenses for different uses of music, the most common of which are as follows:

- **Mechanical license:** Allows the licensee (record company or recording artist) to reproduce and distribute a copyrighted musical work in recordings such as compact discs and cassettes in return for a royalty (a percentage of the sale price) on recordings sold.

75

- **Performance license:** Allows the licensee (radio or television station, concert venue, business establishment, etc.) to publicly perform a copyrighted musical work in return for a royalty.

- **Synchronization license:** Allows the licensee (movie or television producer, etc.) to reproduce and distribute a copyrighted musical work in audiovisual recordings such as movies, television, and videocassettes in return for a flat fee and/or a royalty.

- **Print license:** Allows the licensee to reproduce and distribute a copyrighted musical work in printed form such as sheet music in return for a royalty.

- **Distribution license:** Allows the licensee to distribute a copyrighted musical work or sound recording in return for a distribution fee.

It is important to realize that the exclusive rights are not absolute and are subject to various exemptions, compulsory licenses, and defenses. In fact, while the exclusive rights are all specified in one section of the Copyright Act (i.e, Section 106), the limitations on the exclusive rights are specified in many sections (i.e., Section 107 through 120), some of which are quite lengthy and complicated.

# II. The Reproduction Right

Section 106(1) gives the copyright owner the exclusive right to reproduce, and to authorize others to reproduce, the copyrighted work. Reproduction involves producing a material object in which the copyrighted work is contained or embodied. The Copyright Act specifies two categories of material objects in which copyrighted works can be embodied: copies and phonorecords (discussed in Chapter 3, "What Can Be Protected by Copyright").

---

**Example 5.1**

Copyrighted works such as songs and sound recordings can be embodied on material objects such as recording tape, compact discs, and computer files, among other things. Although the copyrighted work cannot be directly perceived, reproduced, or communicated merely by possession of the object itself, it can be perceived, reproduced, and communicated with the aid of a machine or device such as a stereo system or computer.

---

## A. Reproduction of Musical Works

Licensing facilitates lawful reproduction of creative works. Mechanical and master use licensing are important vehicles for recording and distributing works in the music industry. It is important to distinguish reproduction of a musical composition from reproduction of a sound recording and to recognize issues involved in reproduction of sound recordings, such as sampling sound recording works.

### (1) The Compulsory Mechanical License

The most important limitation on the reproduction right for musical works is the compulsory mechanical license. A mechanical license gives the licensee (a record company or artist) permission to reproduce and distribute a copyrighted musical work in recordings. In most situations, licenses are negotiated, and if a copyright owner does not want to issue a license, it is free to decline to do so. However, the compulsory mechanical license provision of the Copyright Act says that under certain circumstances, a mechanical license can be obtained regardless of whether the copyright owner gives permission.

The compulsory license provision is contained in Section 115 of the 1976 Copyright Act and provides that once a musical composition has been distributed to the public in phonorecords in the United States with the copyright owner's permission, anyone may reproduce the composition. This means that the copyright owner has absolute control over the first recording of its song. However, once that first recording has been distributed, the copyright owner cannot prevent anyone else from recording his own version of the song. Distribution of phonorecords includes distribution of audio recordings of any type (cassette, compact disc, MP3 file, etc.) but does not include audiovisual works because audiovisual works are embodied in copies rather than phonorecords.

**Example 5.2**

A song contained in the soundtrack to a motion picture will not be subject to a compulsory license unless it is also contained on a phonorecord such as a soundtrack album that is distributed to the public.

The compulsory license applies only to non-dramatic musical works (i.e., musical compositions or songs). Accordingly, if you want to record a literary work or a dramatic musical work, the compulsory license is not available, and you must obtain the copyright owner's permission.

**Example 5.3**

Martin George, an aspiring producer, wants to record the Beatles' song "Yesterday." He can obtain a compulsory license because "Yesterday" is a non-dramatic musical composition that has been previously recorded and distributed. However, he cannot copy the Beatles' sound recording of "Yesterday" under the compulsory license. Instead, he would have to hire singers and musicians to record a new sound recording of the song. To use the Beatles' recording, he would have to obtain a license from the copyright owner of the sound recording (Capitol Records), which is referred to as a master-use license, as well as a mechanical license from the copyright owner of "Yesterday" (Sony/ATV).

## (a) Obtaining a Compulsory License

In order to obtain a compulsory license, you must comply with the provisions of Section 115 of the Copyright Act as well as the applicable regulations of the Copyright Office. The primary purpose for making your recording must be to distribute it to the public for private use. If you intend to make a recording of a song that will be sold on cassettes, compact discs, computer files, or some other audio-only recording format, that is exactly what the compulsory license is intended for. In contrast, if you intend to make a recording primarily to broadcast it or use it in connection with background music services such as Muzak, you cannot obtain a compulsory license. Instead, you would have to request a license directly from the copyright owner (which the copyright owner could refuse to grant).

You are allowed to make an arrangement of the copyrighted song to the extent necessary to conform the work to the style or manner of interpretation of your performance. This arrangement privilege is very limited and does not allow you to change the basic melody or fundamental character of the work. Minor changes to the work are permitted, such as recording the work in a different key than it was written in or changing pronouns from masculine to feminine or vice versa. If the changes are major, the result would be considered a derivative work, which cannot be made without the copyright owner's consent.

You must file a Notice of Intention to Obtain Compulsory License with the copyright owner. This notice must be made no later than 30 days after making your recording and before distributing it. If you fail to give this notice, you cannot get a compulsory license, and unless you have a negotiated license from the copyright owner, this subjects you to liability for infringement.

---

**Tip:**  If the copyright owner of a song you want to record is unknown and the Copyright Office records do not identify the owner, you can file the notice with the Copyright Office. If the copyright owner later registers its copyright, you only have to pay mechanical royalties for records sold after the registration was made.

---

You must pay the statutory mechanical royalty rate for each record made and distributed. This rate, which is set from time to time by the Copyright Royalty Board, applies to each song contained on a recording, so if your recording contains more than one song, you would pay a royalty for each song. At the time of this book's writing, the statutory royalty rate is 9.1 cents per song or 1.75 cents per minute, whichever is greater. In 1998, representatives from the music publishing and record industries negotiated a 10-year schedule for increases. A summary of the statutory mechanical royalty rate for physical phonorecords (as distinguished from digital phonorecords) is shown as Table 5.1. The Copyright Royalty Board, consisting of three Copyright Royalty Judges (CRJs), is an arm of the Library of Congress that sets the statutory rate in part by conducting public hearings to facilitate the rate setting process. The current rate was set to expire in 2009; therefore, hearings were conducted in 2008 to gather input from interested parties concerning new rates. The CRJs issued a ruling in 2009 to adopt the 2006 rates, which therefore remain in effect.[2]

---

**Tip:**  For updated royalty rates, including rates for digital phonorecord deliveries, i.e., downloads, subject to the statutory rate, visit http://www.copyright.gov/carp/m200a.pdf. See the "Digital Phonorecord Deliveries" section later in this chapter for a discussion of digital phonorecord deliveries.

---

Royalties must be paid on a monthly basis by the 20th day of each month and must include all royalties for the previous month. Monthly royalty statements accompanied by any applicable

**Table 5.1**   Statutory Mechanical Royalty Rates for Physical Phonorecords

| Year | Per-Song Rate | Per-Minute Rate |
|---|---|---|
| 1909 | 2 cents | None |
| 1976 | 2.75 cents | 5 cents |
| 1980 | 4 cents | 75 cents |
| 1984 | 4.5 cents | 8 cents |
| 1986 | 5 cents | 95 cents |
| 1988 | 5.25 cents | 1 cent |
| 1990 | 5.7 cents | 1.1 cents |
| 1992 | 6.25 cents | 1.2 cents |
| 1994 | 6.6 cents | 1.25 cents |
| 1996 | 6.95 cents | 1.3 cents |
| 1998 | 7.1 cents | 1.35 cents |
| 2000 | 7.55 cents | 1.45 cents |
| 2002 | 8 cents | 1.55 cents |
| 2004 | 8.5 cents | 1.65 cents |
| 2006 | 9.1 cents | 1.75 cents |

royalty payments must be made under oath, and in addition, an annual statement of account certified by a certified public accountant must be made. If you fail to make the required royalty payments or file the required monthly and annual statements of account, the copyright owner can send you notice of termination of the license. After termination, the making or distribution of all phonorecords for which the royalty has not been paid will be considered acts of infringement.

**Example 5.4**

Out-of-Tune Records obtains a compulsory license to record one song on an album. Out-of-Tune must pay the copyright owner(s) of that song 9.1 cents for each record made and distributed. If the album sells 100,000 units, Out-of-Tune would pay the copyright owner $9,100. If the same album sold 500,000 units, Out-of-Tune would pay the copyright owner $45,500. However, if the song was 5.3 minutes in length, Out-of-Tune would have to pay the per-minute rate (i.e., 9.275 cents) for each record because it would be a greater amount than the per-song rate. (Note: The copyright owner will often be a publishing company, which will normally be contractually obligated to pay the songwriters of the song half of what it receives.)

**Example 5.5**

If the album released by Out-of-Tune Records in the previous example contained 10 copyrighted songs (all under 5.3 minutes long) and Out-of-Tune obtained compulsory licenses for all of these songs, it would pay 91 cents in mechanical royalties for each album distributed to the copyright owners of the songs. If 100,000 albums were sold, Out-of-Tune would owe $91,000 in mechanical royalties. If one million albums were sold, Out-of-Tune would owe $910,000 in mechanical royalties.

## (2) Negotiated Mechanical Licenses

Despite the existence of the compulsory mechanical license, it is rarely used because its requirements are very strict and a bit impractical. For example, record companies do not want the administrative burden of accounting for and paying mechanical royalties on a monthly basis. Consequently, mechanical licenses are usually negotiated between the record company making the recording of a song and the copyright owner of the song to be recorded (usually a music publisher or an agency representing the music publisher, such as the Harry Fox Agency).[3]

Even though the compulsory license provision is rarely used, many of its terms are used in negotiated licenses. In practice, mechanical licensing is usually a simple process in which very little negotiation takes place. It is common in negotiated licenses for royalties to be paid on a quarterly rather than monthly basis with no annual accounting required. Royalty payments are usually required to be paid only on records sold rather than distributed, which allows record companies to hold a portion of royalties as a reserve against returns. Finally, the royalty paid under a negotiated mechanical license will be either the statutory rate or a reduced rate agreed upon by the publisher and record company. Reduced rates are usually specified as a percentage of the statutory rate, most commonly 75 percent of the statutory rate. Reduced rates are commonly granted for records sold through record clubs, records sold at less than normal prices, and for songs written by a songwriter who is subject to a controlled composition clause in a record contract.

**Controlled Composition Clauses**   Controlled composition clauses are commonly contained in record contracts between artists and record companies. Under such a clause, the artist guarantees the record company that it will be able to obtain mechanical licenses for any songs written, owned, or controlled by the artist at reduced rates.

**Example 5.6**

Mucho Music is the copyright owner of a song entitled "InnaGaddaLaVidaLoca." Mucho issues a negotiated mechanical license to LaBomba Records to use a song at a rate of 75 percent of the statutory rate. Mucho will receive 6.825 cents (75 percent of 9.1 cents) from LaBomba for each record sold. If an album containing this song sold 100,000 copies, Mucho would receive $6,825, half of which would typically be paid to the songwriter(s) of the song.

**Mechanical License Reform?** In 2004 and 2007, the Register of the United States Copyright Office testified before Congress that the compulsory mechanical license provision be repealed to allow copyright owners to negotiate mechanical licenses freely. In the interim periods between the Register's testimony, legislation to facilitate this recommendation was introduced in the House of Representatives as the Section 115 Reform Act (SIRA) in 2006.[1] The main goal of proposing that the compulsory mechanical license be eliminated is to make it easier to license musical compositions in new technological forms (digital downloads, etc.), for instance by blanket licensing similar to performance licenses issued by performing rights organizations. Although the parties that would be affected by the changes new legislation would bring (publishers, record companies, online music companies, etc.) seem to agree that the mechanical licensing system needs to be changed, they are not in agreement on how it should be changed. Consequently, the legislation did not pass. Online music companies are in favor of some type of blanket mechanical licensing that would allow them to license large numbers of songs collectively, but they would much rather keep some governmentally imposed rate rather than have to negotiate rates. Music publishers, on the other hand, have long objected to the fact that the compulsory mechanical license acts as an artificial limit on license rates.

### (3) Mechanical Royalty Licensing Agencies

Copyright owners of musical compositions may issue their own mechanical licenses or engage a publisher to do so. However, many publishers and copyright owners choose not to issue mechanical licenses themselves. Instead, they use a mechanical licensing agent to do so on their behalf. Many American publishers use the Harry Fox Agency to issue mechanical licenses and to collect mechanical royalty payments for them. The Harry Fox Agency charges licensors a commission rate of 6.75% of the licensor's royalties distributed for all categories of licensing (unless there is a special arrangement to the contrary).[4] Use of a licensing agent like the Harry Fox Agency is often a cost effective alternative for publishers because it would probably cost them more to issue licenses and collect mechanical royalties themselves. Another important benefit to publishers in using the Harry Fox Agency is that it periodically conducts audits of all of the major record companies and distributes any recovered monies among publishers in proportion to their earnings.

The Harry Fox Agency also provides a benefit to record companies because they don't have to request mechanical licenses from each individual publisher. Instead, when a record company is going to record an album, it merely sends mechanical license requests for the songs to be recorded to the Harry Fox Agency, which will issue mechanical licenses for all the songs except any songs not owned by a publisher affiliated with the Harry Fox Agency. The Harry Fox Agency also has agreements with foreign agencies that allow American publishers to monitor foreign mechanical royalties through the Harry Fox Agency. Some important limitations on Harry Fox Agency licenses are (1) It will only cover records manufactured and distributed in the United States; and (2) It will not give you the right to print song lyrics on album liner notes (you must obtain permission from the publisher that owns the song for this).

---

**Tip:** You can obtain mechanical license request forms from the Harry Fox Agency's website at http://www.harryfox.com. If you are going to make up to 2,500 recordings, you can obtain a license by filling out a form online at SongFile.com (you must be willing to pay the statutory royalty rate for 2,500 recordings by credit card in order to use this service).

---

### (4) Foreign Mechanical Royalty Rates

Mechanical royalty rates in virtually all countries other than the United States are based on either a percentage of the retail sales price or the wholesale price that records sell for. For instance, if the royalty rate is 8 percent of the retail sales price and a compact disc sold for $16, the mechanical royalties would be $1.28, which would be divided by the number of songs contained on the CD (if 10 songs, each would be allocated 12.8 cents).

An advantage that percentage-based systems of foreign countries have over the U.S. system is that the mechanical royalty will automatically adjust based on increases or decreases in the price of recordings. A potential disadvantage is that the total mechanical royalties per album will be the same regardless of the number of songs contained on the album. However, mechanical royalties tend to be higher in most major foreign countries than the U.S. statutory rate.

### (5) Digital Phonorecord Deliveries

Through the combination of digital technology and the Internet, it has become possible to reproduce musical works without copying the work onto a traditional physical object such as a compact disc. When a musical work is downloaded, the recording of the work is transmitted in digital form over the Internet. However, downloading music still involves reproduction of the musical work. Instead of being reproduced onto a compact disc, the music is reproduced onto a computer hard drive or other storage device.

The Digital Performance Right in Sound Recordings Act was passed by Congress in 1995 and amended Section 115(c) of the 1976 Copyright Act. This amendment states that the compulsory mechanical license is applicable to the distribution of phonorecords of musical works "by means of a digital transmission which constitutes a digital phonorecord delivery." The Copyright Act defines a "digital phonorecord delivery" as:

> *...each individual delivery of a phonorecord by digital transmission of a sound recording which results in a specifically identifiable reproduction by or for any transmission recipient of a phonorecord of that sound recording, regardless of whether the digital transmission is also a public performance of the sound recording or any nondramatic musical work embodied therein.*[5]

If you purchase music online from services such as iTunes, Napster, or Rhapsody, when you download the music, you have received a digital phonorecord delivery (DPD). The Digital Performance Right in Sound Recordings Act specifies a procedure for setting the royalty rate for digital phonorecord deliveries. Until the end of 1997, the rate was set at the same amount as the statutory mechanical royalty rate. Beginning in 1998, the rate was to be reached through negotiation between the music publishing and recording industry. A two-year agreement was negotiated that specified the rate would continue to remain the same as the statutory rate. It was also agreed that no royalties would be payable for digital phonorecord deliveries of music lasting for less than 30 seconds for promotional purposes.

The Copyright Office has issued regulations which identify different types of DPDs, for the purpose of ascertaining how to apply the statutory mechanical royalty rate to each. A permanent download is a digital phonorecord delivery that is distributed in the form of a download that may be retained and played on a permanent basis. The ringtones you may purchase for your cell phone are also considered DPDs. The regulations define a ringtone as "a phonorecord of a partial musical work distributed as a digital phonorecord delivery in a format to be made resident on a telecommunications device for use to announce the reception of an incoming telephone call or other communication or message or to alert the receiver to the fact that there is a communication or message."[6] Both permanent downloads and ringtones are subject to a mechanical license royalty rate. Permanent digital downloads currently bear the same statutory rate as physical phonorecord deliveries of 9.1 cents or 1.75 cents per minute of playing time or fraction thereof, whichever is larger. The statutory rate for ringtones is 24 cents per ringtone.[7]

Just as it is permissible for a mechanical license to make a physical recording to be negotiated and the terms of the compulsory license provision varied, it is also permissible to negotiate licenses for digital phonorecord deliveries. If the copyright owner of a musical work is willing to do so, it could license digital phonorecord deliveries at a rate lower than the rate that will be set by the CRJs.[8]

## B. Reproduction of Sound Recordings

In the United States, federal copyright law did not protect sound recordings until 1972, although sound recordings were protected under state laws. However, even though sound recordings are now protected under the Copyright Act, they still receive a lesser degree of protection than other types of copyrightable works.

### (1) The Dubbing Limitation

An important limitation on the reproduction right regarding sound recordings is that the right extends only to works "that directly or indirectly recapture the actual sounds fixed in the recording."[9] In other words, the copyright in a sound recording only protects against copying of the actual recorded sounds and not against imitation of those sounds. This limitation is sometimes referred to as the "dubbing limitation" because the reproduction right for sound recordings only prohibits dubbing (re-recording from an existing recording) and does not prevent making an independent recording of other sounds, even if those sounds imitate the sounds from a copyrighted sound recording.

### (2) Home Taping

The reproduction or copying of copyrighted works by people in their homes has been prevalent since home recording equipment first became available. It is a common practice for people to make copies of recordings on home audio recording equipment. Sometimes such copying is done in order to listen to a recording on different devices (e.g., copying a CD onto cassette to play in a car cassette deck). Other times, people make copies of recordings and give away or sell the copies. Obviously, this poses a problem for copyright owners of musical works and sound recordings because each home copy potentially displaces a sale.

With analog recording technology, a first generation copy made from an original recording would lose some degree of sound quality during the copying process, with the result being that the copy would not be quite as good as the original. Additionally, each successive generation of copying resulted in a further loss of sound quality. For instance, if you make a cassette copy of a CD, the sound quality of the cassette is not quite as good as the CD. If you then made a second cassette copy from the first cassette copy, the sound quality of the second copy will be a bit worse than the first copy.

Beginning in 1986, digital audio tape recording technology was introduced to the consumer marketplace. Digital audio tape (DAT) provided the ability to make copies of recordings with no loss of sound quality. Due to the preservation of sound quality from one copy to the next, digital audio technology also gave consumers the ability to make high-quality copies from copies (serial copying). Unlike analog recording technology, digital audio recording allows consumers to make nearly perfect copies and therefore poses a more serious threat to the music industry.

The music industry had tried on several occasions to secure some type of legal protection and compensation for the losses it incurred due to unauthorized home taping of copyrighted musical compositions and sound recordings. However, the consumer electronics industry strenuously resisted these efforts. Finally, after an attempted legislative solution stalled in 1990, a group of songwriters and music publishers brought a class-action lawsuit against Sony Corporation.

In *Cahn v. Sony Corp.*,[10] a group of songwriters and publishers alleged that manufacturers, importers, and distributors of digital audio tape recording equipment and blank digital audio tapes were guilty of contributory and vicarious copyright infringement. The alleged contributory and vicarious infringement resulted from the direct infringement by consumers who used the defendants' equipment to make unauthorized recordings of copyrighted works. This lawsuit could have resulted in an important legal decision because no United States court has ever ruled on whether unauthorized home audio taping is illegal.[11] However, no decision was made by the court because the parties reached a settlement that provided that the defendants would support legislation that would provide for royalties to compensate for losses incurred by copyright owners due to home taping. The contemplated legislation was passed as the Audio Home Recording Act of 1992.

### (3) The Audio Home Recording Act

The Audio Home Recording Act (AHRA) was designed to allow consumers to copy recordings of copyrighted music for private, noncommercial use while also compensating copyright owners for lost income due to such copying. The AHRA applies to "digital audio recording devices," which are defined as devices that are designed or marketed primarily for making digital audio recordings for private use. Devices that do not fit the definition of digital audio recording devices include professional recording equipment, analog recording equipment, audiovisual recording equipment, and computers. The AHRA contains three main sets of provisions.

*(a) Royalty System*

The AHRA established a royalty system under which manufacturers and distributors of digital audiotape recorders and digital audio tapes are required to pay a royalty on sales. The royalty is 3 percent of the transfer price of digital audio tape and 2 percent on the transfer price of digital recording equipment, with a minimum of $1.00 and a maximum of $8.00 for digital recording equipment. The royalties are collected by the Copyright Office and are distributed based on record sales and radio airplay. However, in order to be eligible to receive these royalties, one must file a claim with the Copyright Office.[12]

The royalties collected are divided into two funds. One-third goes to the "Musical Works Fund," which is split equally between songwriters and music publishers. The remaining two-thirds goes to the "Sound Recordings Fund." The Sound Recordings Fund is split, with 4 percent paid to nonfeatured performers (background musicians and vocalists). The remainder is split between featured performers, who receive 40 percent, and sound recording copyright owners (typically record companies), who receive 60 percent.

It is important to note that the royalty provisions of the Audio Home Recording Act only apply to digital recording equipment and tape. In contrast, many foreign countries, including Australia, Germany, and France, impose a royalty on analog as well as digital recording equipment and tape.

*(b) Copy Protection*

The AHRA also requires that manufacturers and importers of digital audio recording equipment must incorporate technology that prevents serial copying (i.e., making copies from copies).[13] A specific technological protection system called the serial copy management system (SCMS) is specified by the AHRA, although other systems may also be used.

**Example 5.7**

If a consumer buys a digital audio tape recorder equipped with SCMS and wants to copy a CD, the consumer could make an unlimited number of digital audio tape copies from the CD (first generation copies). The consumer could not, however, make additional copies from the digital audio tape copies (serial copies) because the SCMS would prevent this.

*(c) Infringement Exemption*

In return for the protections given to copyright owners by the AHRA, the Act exempts consumers from liability for direct copyright infringement for home taping of copyrighted works.[14] An important qualification for this exemption is that the home taping must be for a noncommercial use, although the AHRA neglects to define noncommercial use. Additionally, the exemption of liability applies under the AHRA only if the home recording is made using the types of digital audio recording devices covered by the AHRA. Since personal computers are not considered digital audio recording devices, the exemption would not apply to home taping using a computer.

When Congress passed the AHRA, it indicated that it only intended to allow consumers to copy authorized commercially released compact discs or other digital recordings.[15] Under this reasoning, it would not be permissible to make copies from copies or to make copies from unlawfully acquired recordings.

---

**Example 5.8**

---

Harry Hometaper, a high school student, receives a CD as a Christmas present. If Harry makes a copy of the CD in order to listen to it in his car, he is exempt from liability for copyright infringement under the AHRA. However, if Harry made copies of his CD and sold the copies to others, the home taping exemption would not apply because this is a commercial use. Even if Harry gave a copy to a friend, the home taping exemption might not apply because the potential displacement of a sale to the friend might be considered a commercial use.

---

### (d) The Diamond Rio Case

The AHRA was at the heart of one of the first highly publicized lawsuits involving digital music. On October 9, 1998, the Recording Industry Association of America (RIAA) filed a lawsuit against Diamond Multimedia, a company that made a portable MP3 player called the Rio.[16] The RIAA alleged that the Rio violated the AHRA because it did not contain SCMS copyright protection technology and because Diamond did not pay royalties on sales of the Rio.

The resolution of this dispute turned on two very technical definitions provided in the AHRA. A "digital audio recording" is defined as a material object upon which digital music is fixed, such as a compact disc or a digital audio tape (DAT). A "digital audio recording device" is defined as a device that creates digital musical recordings or copies of digital musical recordings such as a compact disc recorder (CD-R) or a DAT recorder.

Both the District Court and the Court of Appeals denied the RIAA's request to issue a preliminary injunction to prevent Diamond from selling the Rio. The Court of Appeals ruled that the Rio was not a digital audio recording device and was therefore not subject to the AHRA. The court based its decision on the fact that the Rio does not actually record anything directly but simply accepts the transfer of files from a computer's hard drive to make them portable. It is not possible to make a digital audio recording from a Rio because the Rio's output signal is analog. Because the Rio is incapable of creating digital audio recordings, it could not be considered a digital audio recording device. Further, when the AHRA was passed, the computer industry managed to get an exemption for copying from computer hard drives because their primary purpose is not to record digital audio. The RIAA argued that MP3 files did not qualify for this exemption because the exemption was not intended to exempt all files stored on a computer, but only computer programs with incidental audio files such as a computer game with audio sound effects. The court however disagreed with the RIAA, finding that the exemption applies to all files contained on a computer.

Although the court correctly applied the provisions of the AHRA, the result is probably not at all what Congress intended the AHRA to achieve. When the AHRA was enacted in 1992, it is unlikely that anyone expected computers to be used to copy music files to the extent that they are today. The exemption for computer hard drives has made the AHRA almost worthless because, once a music file is stored on a computer hard drive (regardless of where it came from or how it got there), it is exempt from the AHRA. The district court recognized the irony of this result, stating that the exemption for computers "would effectively eviscerate the Act" because:

> ...any recording device could evade regulation simply by passing the music through a computer and ensuring that the MP3 file resided momentarily on the hard drive. While this may be true, the Act seems to have been expressly designed to create this loophole.

### Example 5.9

Manufacturers of DAT recorders and digital audio recording tape must comply with the AHRA by using the SCMS copyright protection system and paying royalties on sales of the recorders and tape. This limits unauthorized copying and compensates for unauthorized copying that does occur. However, manufacturers of computers do not have to comply with the AHRA even though they are much more commonly used to make copies of illegal music files.

In the *Diamond* case, the court also concluded that although the Rio could be used to store and play illegal MP3 files, it could also be used for legitimate purposes. One such legitimate purpose was what the court referred to as "space-shifting," which involves copying a legally obtained music file from one medium (such as a computer hard drive) to another (such as a Rio player) to be able to listen to the music in other locations.

### Example 5.10

You may purchase and download an MP3 file and copy it onto a portable digital music player because the copying would be considered space-shifting, but you cannot legally resell or give away any copies of that file.

### (4) Sampling

In simple terms, the concept of sampling involves using part of an existing work in order to create a new work. Musicians and composers have always borrowed, at least to some degree, from prior works. For instance, some French composers in the 1940s developed a style of music called *musique concrete* that combined musical and nonmusical sounds into a collage by cutting, splicing, and manipulating pre-recorded tapes.

In the 1980s, sampling started to become much more prevalent in American music with the advent of digital technology, especially in rap and hip-hop music. Digital technology allows analog sound waves to be converted into digital code by breaking the waves into small bits represented by a digit. The digital code can then be electronically manipulated or combined with other digital recordings by using a machine with digital data memory capabilities, such as a computer or computerized synthesizer.

Two of the most successful songs in 1990 were based on sampled material. M.C. Hammer's "U Can't Touch This" contained a sample from the Rick James recording "Super Freak." Although the Rick James sample was licensed, many artists released recordings containing samples of copyrighted material without obtaining licenses. The 1990 hit "Ice Ice Baby" by Vanilla Ice sampled the melody line from a recording of the song "Under Pressure" by Queen and David Bowie. The sample was used without permission, but the subsequent threat of a copyright infringement suit prompted a settlement for an undisclosed amount of money.

---

**"Super Freak" Settlement**    Reportedly, M.C. Hammer agreed to split copyright ownership of the song 50/50 with Jobete Music, the publisher of "Super Freak." This might be viewed as a fair ownership split, since Hammer basically used the "Super Freak" music throughout his song, adding new rap lyrics. This is a bit similar to situations where entirely new songs are created with one person writing the music and another writing the lyrics; such co-authorship relationships commonly involve a 50/50 split of copyright in the song.

---

Up until the early 1990s, it was not totally certain that unauthorized sampling was illegal because there had not been any cases involving sampling. However, this uncertainty was resolved in 1991 by *Grand Upright Music Ltd. v. Warner Bros. Records.*[17] *Grand Upright* involved a copyright infringement suit brought against rap artist Biz Markie over a song on his album *I Need a Haircut*, which contained a sample from "Alone Again Naturally," written and recorded by Gilbert O'Sullivan. Biz Markie's song, "Alone Again," sampled the first eight bars and the three-word lyric phrase "alone again naturally," which comprised about 10 seconds of music. However, this relatively short sample was looped throughout the recording so that the same 10 seconds of music are heard repeatedly.

After recording the song but before its release, Biz Markie's attorney sent a copy of the recording to O'Sullivan's manager requesting permission to use the sample. Before receiving a response, Warner Brothers Records released Biz Markie's album. O'Sullivan's manager then responded with a letter demanding that the song be deleted from the album. Biz Markie's attorney sent a letter expressing Biz Markie's "sincere regrets that the new composition was released" without permission, but asserted that based on their previous negotiations, O'Sullivan had implicitly agreed that permission would be granted for a price to be agreed upon.

The court did not seem to be impressed with Biz Markie's implied license argument. Setting an ominous tone, the court began its written opinion by quoting the Seventh Commandment from the Old Testament, "Thou shalt not steal." To the court, sampling a copyrighted work without permission simply equaled theft, and because Biz Markie had admitted using the sample, he had admitted infringement.

The court issued a preliminary injunction ordering Warner Brothers to stop selling recordings containing the infringing song. Warner placed an ad in *Billboard* magazine asking retailers to return any copies of the Biz Markie album not yet sold and had the song deleted from subsequent pressings of the album. Two weeks after the court's decision, a confidential settlement was reached that reportedly included a substantial cash payment. Biz Markie's next album was appropriately entitled *All Samples Cleared*.

After *Grand Upright* was decided, record companies became much more stringent in making sure that samples were properly licensed. Although record contracts routinely provide that the recording artist is responsible for clearing samples, in practice, it is often the record company that obtains clearances. There are also several clearance agencies that specialize in obtaining sampling licenses for record companies and artists. The compensation a copyright owner receives for licensing the use of a sample ranges from a flat fee (i.e., $250–$10,000 and up) to a royalty (i.e., 1–5 cents per record sold), often with an advance, to an ownership interest in the new work. This ownership interest can be significant, as you will see in the following examples.

---

**Clearance Example**   Supposedly, the rap group 2 Live Crew paid about $100,000 to include sampled dialogue from the movie *Full Metal Jacket* in their single "Me So Horny."

---

It is important to realize that sampling usually involves the use of two separate copyrighted works: a sound recording and the underlying musical composition embodied in the sound recording. Consequently, an artist or record company wanting to use sampled material must normally negotiate two separate licenses with two different copyright owners (i.e., a record company and a music publisher).

**Some Other Sampling Disputes:** Many famous recording artists have had their music sampled. The following are just a few examples:

- Rappers Lord Tariq and Peter Gunz used a sample from Steely Dan's "Black Cow" on their song "DÉjÀ vu" without obtaining permission. After the threat of a copyright infringement lawsuit, the rappers' record company ended up paying $105,000 for the sample, which was more than three times the standard rate. If they had requested a license beforehand, they would likely have been much better off because Steely Dan has licensed samples of their music to other rap artists, including De La Soul's use of "Peg" in his song "Eye Know."

- Although De La Soul apparently knew better than to use unlicensed Steely Dan samples, they weren't so careful with their use of other artist's works. The trio was sued by the Turtles for the unauthorized use of a sample in "Transmitting Live from Mars." Reportedly, the suit was settled for an amount in the low five figures. De La Soul was also sued by Hall & Oates for their use of a sample from their song "Say No Go."

- Rap artist/producer Dr. Dre has been the target of several copyright infringement suits involving sampling. In one suit, a music publisher (Minder Music) sued Dre for using a sample from the Fatback Band's 1980 song "Backstrokin'" on his song "Let's Get High." Prior to using the sample, the doctor (Dre) had obtained a second opinion by consulting a musicologist, who believed that the sampled bassline was commonplace. Although the jury found that Dre's infringement was "innocent" because he relied on the musicologist's opinion, it awarded the publisher over $1.5 million (less than half of the amount sued for). Interestingly, the Fatback Band's music has been sampled over 80 times by artists such as Monica, Fatboy Slim (no relation), and Everlast. The moral of this case may be that using unauthorized samples from artists that are commonly sampled and used to licensing samples may be exceptionally risky even when you rely on the opinion of an expert.

- A Tribe Called Quest was forced to give Lou Reed 100 percent of the copyright of their song that incorporated an unauthorized sample from Reed's "Walk on the Wild Side." While it may be tempting to walk on the wild side, treading too boldly on a copyrighted work can result in harsh consequences.

Although using samples of copyrighted material without permission will normally be infringement, there are some defenses, such as fair use, that may allow very limited sampling in rare circumstances. Although it is risky to rely on, the fair use defense may apply to sampling in limited circumstances, especially if the sample is used for a transformative purpose (i.e., if significant original contributions were added to create a new work) and does not affect the market for the sampled work. Although copyright owners are generally willing to license the use of their works as long as the user is willing to pay appropriate compensation, sometimes copyright owners are unwilling to issue licenses for other reasons. For example, some copyright owners are hesitant to issue licenses to gangsta rappers who are known for profane, sexist, or violent lyrics.

---

**Example 5.11**

Music publisher Abilene Music sued rappers Ghostface Killah, Raekwon, and the Alchemist, alleging that they infringed its copyright in the song "What a Wonderful World," recorded by Louis Armstrong. The rappers altered the lyrics of "What a Wonderful World" to include the following slang references to marijuana:

I see buds that are green red roses too.

I see blunts, for me and you.

And I say to myself: What a wonderful world

In defense, the rappers argued that their adapted lyrics constituted a parody intended to criticize and make fun of the cheerful perspective of the original song and was therefore fair use. The court held that the rap song was a parody and a fair use of the original song, noting that while the lyrics of the original song "describe the beauty of nature, its 'trees' and 'roses' in 'bloom,' the rap reads more like an invitation to get high with the singer."

---

In addition to fair use, many people believe that if a sample is so small that it is unrecognizable, a license should not be required. Courts have occasionally held that a very small or brief use of a copyrighted work may be what is known as a "de minimis" use (i.e., too small to be important). However, there is no clear rule as to how much is de minimis. Arguably, a sample containing only a note or two might be de minimis. However, because most sampling artists want the samples to be recognizable, the de minimis defense will rarely be applicable. In 2004, a federal appeals court cast some doubt over whether sampling could ever be a de minimis use, holding that any sample, no matter how small, must be licensed.[18] This was a very controversial ruling because many people believe that the law should allow for some small degree of sampling, at least in certain circumstances. However, the court stated:

*Get a license or do not sample. We do not see this as stifling creativity in any significant way. It must be remembered that if an artist wants to incorporate a "riff" from another work in his or her recording, he is free to duplicate the sound of that "riff" in the studio. Second, the market will control the license price and keep it within bounds. The sound recording copyright holder cannot exact a license fee greater than what it would cost the person seeking the license to just duplicate the sample in the course of making the new recording. Third, sampling is never accidental. It is not like the case of a composer who has a melody in his head, perhaps not even realizing that the reason he hears this melody is that it is the work of another which he had heard before. When you sample a sound recording you know you are taking another's work product.*

The issue of de minimis copying remains a key issue in sampling. Because sampling often involves reproduction of only small amounts of a recording, it is sometimes difficult to convince a court that the amount copied was enough to constitute infringement, or to establish that what was copied was thematic and integral to the original recording. However, the Sixth Circuit Court of Appeals, which decided the *Bridgeport Music v. Dimension Films* case above, uses a slightly different approach to decide whether a sample is enough to infringe the copyright owner's rights. *Bridgeport Music, Inc. v. UMG Recordings* involved the use of the funk song "Atomic Dog." The song, written by George Clinton of the group Parliament-Funkadelic and his co-authors, was used by the group Public Announcement in the song "D.O.G. in Me." The court found that Public Announcement had sampled the phrase "Bow wow wow, yippie yo, yippie yea" and repeated conspicuous panting and the word "dog" in a specific rhythmic pattern that are all elements of "Atomic Dog," thereby infringing the copyright in "Atomic Dog." The court's reasoning is that if even a small fragment of a recording has been copied, an infringement occurs if that fragment is recognizable as an element of the original, i.e., if you can tell that the copy came from the original recording. Some courts have adopted this approach, while others prefer to use a more traditional substantial similarity test.[19]

# Endnotes

1.  The 2006 rates were still in effect as of 2011. For more information about the 2008 hearings see the Copyright Royalty Board's website at http://www.loc.gov/crb/proceedings/2006-3/index.html#trial. See also 74 FR 4510 January 26, 2009.
2.  The Copyright Act provides that copyright owners and licensees can vary the terms of mechanical licenses from the terms of the compulsory license provision. See 17 U.S.C. § 115(c)(3)(E).
3.  H.R. 5553 (2006).
4.  The Harry Fox Agency was established by the National Music Publisher's Association in 1927. http://www.nmpa.org/aboutnmpa/hfa.asp.
5.  17 U.S.C. § 115(d). It is important to note that the term "transmission" is used instead of "distribution" because distribution requires the transfer of a physical object, which does not occur in the context of digital downloads.
6.  37 CFR § 385.2; 37 CFR § 385.11. See these regulations for definitions of additional DPD categories subject to the mechanical license royalty rate. See also 37 CFR § 385.10 through § 385.17 for the formulas used to determine the license rates for these additional categories.
7.  37 CFR 385.3. The effective date of the royalty rate for ringtones has not been determined by the CRJs as of this writing.
8.  17 U.S.C. § 115(c)(3)(E)(i). An exception to the right to modify the rate for digital phonorecord deliveries applies in situations where reduced rates are specified by controlled

composition clauses in record contracts. In such situations, the copyright owner must be paid the full statutory rate unless: (1) the contract containing the controlled composition clause was entered into before June 22, 1995; or (2) the contract containing the controlled composition clause is entered into by an artist/songwriter who retains his music publishing rights and the contract is entered into after the songs have been recorded.

9.   17 U.S.C. § 114(b).

10.  No. 90 Civ. 4537 (S.D.N.Y. July 11, 1991).

11.  In 1984, the Supreme Court held that private home taping of television broadcasts for purposes of viewing the shows at a later time was a fair use. See *Sony Corp. v. Universal City Studios, Inc.*, 464 U.S. 417 (1984). However, that decision did not specifically address home audio taping.

12.  17 U.S.C. § 1007.

13.  17 U.S.C. § 1002.

14.  17 U.S.C. § 1008.

15.  S. Rep. No. 294, 102d Cong., 2d Sess. 18 (1992).

16.  *Recording Indus. Ass'n of Am. v. Diamond Multimedia Sys., Inc.*, 29 F. Supp. 2d 624 (C.D. Cal. 1998), aff'd, 180 F.3d 1072 (9th Cir. 1999).

17.  780 F. Supp. 182 (1991).

18.  *Bridgeport Music, Inc. v. Dimension Films*, 383 F.3d 390 (6th Cir. 2004).

19.  585 F.3d 267 (6th Cir. 2009). See Example 6.10 in Chapter 6 for a different judicial approach to sampling.

# 6 The Derivative and Distribution Rights

*"Only one thing is impossible to God, to find any sense in any copyright law on this planet."*

*–Mark Twain*

## I. The Derivative Right

The right to adapt or revise a copyrighted work, subject to certain limitations, belongs exclusively to the copyright owner of the work. However, copyright law prescribes the scope of protection for a derivative work, as well as the types of adaptations and derivative works subject to such protection.

### A. What Is a Derivative Work?

Section 106(2) of the Copyright Act gives copyright owners the exclusive right to prepare derivative works based upon a copyrighted work. A derivative work takes an existing work and adapts it in some way in order to create a new work. Consequently, the right to make derivative works is often referred to as the adaptation right. The Copyright Act defines a derivative work as:

> *...a work based upon one or more preexisting works, such as a translation, musical arrangement, dramatization, fictionalization, motion picture version, sound recording, art reproduction, abridgment, condensation, or any other form in which a work may be recast, transformed, or adapted.*[1]

Derivative works have not always received protection under copyright law. In the nineteenth century, English courts were unwilling to grant protection to derivative works based on music that was in the public domain. One English court decision stated that while an original work requires "genius for its construction, a mere mechanic in music can make the adaptation or accompaniment."[2] Courts in the United States have also been reluctant to recognize copyright in some derivative musical works.

---

**Example 6.1**

In 1885, Gilbert and Sullivan's *Mikado* was held to have entered the public domain in the United States.[3] British composers Gilbert and Sullivan owned the copyright to the opera in England and wanted copyright protection in the United States as well. Since the United States did not recognize foreign copyrights at the time, Gilbert and Sullivan hired an American musician, George Tracey, to create a piano arrangement from the original score. When an unauthorized performance of Tracey's arrangement took place, Tracey sued to enforce his copyright. The court, however, ruled that an arrangement could not be an original work because an arranger "originates nothing, composes no new notes or melodies, and simply culls the notes representing the melodies and their accompaniments."

---

The 1909 Copyright Act was the first United States copyright statute to allow for copyright in derivative works, and the 1976 Copyright Act continued the recognition of copyright in derivative works.

## B. Requirements for Derivative Works

An otherwise copyrightable work must satisfy two requirements to constitute a derivative work. First, the work must borrow from another work. Second, the work must recast, transform, or adapt the work upon which it is based.

---

**Example 6.2**

---

*Woods v. Bourne*[4] involved a dispute over different versions of the 1926 song "When the Red, Red Robin Comes Bob-Bob-Bobbin' Along." Bourne was a publisher who had acquired copyright ownership of the song from its composer, Harry Woods. Woods' heirs contended that they were entitled to royalty payments from several arrangements made by Bourne. Bourne argued that because Woods had only turned in a lead sheet (i.e., the melodic line with the lyrics written under it) to the original publisher in 1926, every version of the song published since then was a derivative work. The court disagreed, holding that the modifications to a work must be an original work of authorship in order for the resulting work to be a derivative. The court stated that: "In order therefore to qualify as a musically 'derivative work,' there must be present more than mere cocktail pianist variations of the piece that are standard fare in the music trade by any competent musician. There must be such things as unusual vocal treatment, additional lyrics of consequence, unusual altered harmonies, novel sequential uses of themes–something of substance added making the piece to some extent a new work with the old song embedded in it but from which the new has developed. It is not merely a stylized version of the original song where a major artist may take liberties with the lyrics or the tempo, the listener hearing basically the original tune. It is, in short, the addition of such new material as would entitle the creator to a copyright on the new material."

---

Derivative works are therefore created by taking existing material and adding new original expression to it, in the process transforming it into new work. If the existing material used to create a derivative work is protected by copyright, the author of the derivative work must obtain a license to use the existing work unless the derivative work is a fair use.

Like other copyrightable works, the Copyright Act requires derivative works to be fixed in a tangible medium of expression as a precondition to receiving copyright protection. However, a derivative work need not be fixed to infringe the work on which it is based. The legislative report to the 1976 Copyright Act echoed the conclusion of the prior legislative report of 1967, which stated that the derivative right:

> [O]verlaps the exclusive right of reproduction to some extent. It is broader than that right, however, in the sense that reproduction requires fixation in copies or phonorecords, whereas the preparation of a derivative work, such as a ballet, pantomime, or improvised performance, may be an infringement even though nothing is ever fixed in tangible form.[5]

---

**Example 6.3**

---

Jane Doe, a vocalist, wishes to create a gospel version of the song "I'm Every Woman," written by Nick Ashford and made popular by both Chaka Khan and Whitney Houston. Jane creates the adaptation during her live performance of the song, but the performance is not recorded or otherwise fixed. If a license is not obtained to create the derivative performance of the song, not only will the derivative work not be protected by copyright law since it is not fixed, the gospel adaptation may infringe the derivative rights in "I'm Every Woman."

## C. Types of Derivative Works

There are many different types of derivative works, some of the most common of which are as follows:

**Editorial Revisions:** A work that revises an earlier work.

---

**Example 6.4**

This book is a derivative work because it is a revision of the previous edition and includes new, original material not contained in the prior edition. If someone else wanted to use all or part of this book to create a derivative work, he would need to obtain permission unless his use would be considered a fair use. It is important to note that the derivative right does not prevent others from writing books or articles on copyright. It just prevents them from copying this particular expression.

---

**Fictionalizations:** The transformation of a preexisting nonfiction work into a fictional work such as a novel or screenplay.

**Dramatizations:** The transformation of a preexisting work into a work that can be performed on stage. Or the transformation of a novel into a dramatic screenplay, which could be transformed into a film.

---

**Example 6.5**

Andrew Lloyd Webber and Trevor Nunn composed the musical *Cats* based on poems contained in *Old Possum's Book of Practical Cats*. The preexisting material (the poems) was combined with music and used as the basis for the derivative dramatic work.

---

**Translations to New Language:** Although it may not seem that simply translating a work into another language creates a new work, translation typically involves some creative choices by the translator that enable the translation to make sense in the new language. These creative choices may satisfy the requirements of originality and expression necessary for a derivative work.

---

**Example 6.6**

In 2004, David Moser received an e-mail request from a graduate student in China to translate into Chinese an article he had written about online distribution of music. David gave him permission to do so and subsequently gave permission for the publication of the translated article in a Chinese journal. Although the only major change made to the original article is that it is written in Chinese rather than English, the translation is a derivative work. Similarly, translating an English language song into Chinese would also involve the creation of a derivative work. If someone translated David's article into Chinese without permission, it would generally constitute infringement under U.S. and Chinese copyright law. The expense of pursuing such an infringement in a foreign country such as China would greatly exceed the amount of compensation an author would likely receive in most circumstances, but authors tend to appreciate being asked for permission even when no financial compensation is involved.

**Translations to New Medium:** The transformation of a work from one medium into another medium.

**Example 6.7**

Virtually all sound recordings are derivative works because their creation typically involves transforming a song (or other copyrighted work such as a book) into a recorded medium.

**Abridgements and Condensations:** The transformation of an existing work into a shorter version (such as an abridged version of a novel).

## D. Degree of Protection in Derivative Works

Although derivative works can be copyrightable, it is important to understand that the copyright in a derivative work extends only to the original material contributed by the author of the derivative. According to Section 103(b) of the Copyright Act:

> *The copyright in a compilation or derivative work extends only to the material contributed by the author of such work, as distinguished from the preexisting material employed in the work, and does not imply any exclusive right in the preexisting material. The copyright in such work is independent of, and does not affect or enlarge the scope, duration, ownership, or subsistence of, any copyright protection in the preexisting material.*

The copyright in a derivative work does not affect the copyright in the original work upon which it is based. If an existing work is protected by copyright, it is still protected to the same extent after the creation of a derivative work. If an existing work is not protected by copyright, its public domain status will not be changed by the creation of a derivative work. Anyone is free to make derivative works based on works that are in the public domain and will own the copyright in the derivative work. However, if you want to make a derivative work based on a copyrighted work, you must obtain the copyright owner's permission. If you use a copyrighted work to create a new work without the copyright owner's permission, you will not have a copyrightable derivative work because copyright protection does not extend to any part of a derivative work in which preexisting material is used without permission.

**Example 6.8**

The song "Love Me Tender" is credited as being written by Elvis Presley and Vera Matson. It was derived from a public domain song called "Aura Lee" written in 1861. No permission was required to make a derivative work based on "Aura Lee" because it was in the public domain. Puff Daddy's song

"I'll Be Missing You" is a derivative musical composition based on Sting's "Every Breath You Take." Because "Every Breath You Take" is a copyrighted song, Puff Daddy had to obtain Sting's permission to use it. Sting consequently ended up owning part of the derivative as well as the original song and earning a lot more money from an already lucrative song.

## E. Derivative Musical Arrangements

Derivative works are generally held to a slightly higher standard of originality than works in general. This is particularly important in the case of musical arrangements. Commonly, when a recording artist is going to record a musical composition, an arrangement will be made of the composition to be recorded to fit the artist's performance style. Whether an arrangement is copyrightable as a derivative work depends on the amount of original expression that has been added by the arranger. Because musical composition is based on a fairly limited musical vocabulary, arrangements must contain substantial variations in order to be copyrightable as derivative works.

### Example 6.9

In *Shapiro, Bernstein & Co. v. Jerry Vogel Music Co.*, a court ruled that a derivative musical composition was not copyrightable because the only new elements added to the original work were a change in rhythm and accompaniment.[6] Similarly, in *McIntyre v. Double-A-Music Corp.*, a court refused to recognize copyright in an arrangement of a Bing Crosby song, stating that the arrangement involved merely "melodic and harmonic embellishments" that "are frequently improvised by any competent musician."[7]

Conversely, if an author makes substantial variations to an existing work, the resulting work will be a copyrightable derivative work.

### Example 6.10

In *Wood v. Boosey*,[8] a court ruled that a piano arrangement of an opera qualified as a derivative work. The court decided that the arrangement, by translating a score for many instruments into a piece for only piano, constituted a significant departure from the original and was therefore worthy of protection as a derivative work.

## F. Derivatives of Sound Recordings

Digital technology has spawned new ways to create products from preexisting works, including sound recordings. Accordingly, two digital art forms, remixes and mashups, began to appear during the early twenty-first century. However, remixes and mashups have long existed in one form or another through older technologies, such as multitrack recording of analog audiotapes. Therefore, these terms as used here refer to digital assemblages, arrangements, or collages of recorded sounds taken from a preexisting sound recording. A *remix* involves taking apart the sounds of a single recording and reassembling them to create a new recording of the original. A *mashup* is essentially a collage of multiple sound recordings combined to create a single recording. The popularity of both types of works has generated debate and questions concerning their legality. Section 114(b) of the Copyright Act describes the scope of rights that belong to copyright owners of sound recordings fixed after 1972 with respect to the creation of derivative works:

*The exclusive right of the owner of copyright in a sound recording under clause (2) of section 106 is limited to the right to prepare a derivative work in which the actual sounds fixed in the sound recording are rearranged, remixed, or otherwise altered in sequence or quality.*

---

**Mashup versus Remix**   The terms "mashup" and "remix" are commonly used to refer to modifications of both musical compositions and sound recordings. The distinction is made here to underscore the separate derivative works right for sound recordings and to highlight the language of the Copyright Act that specifically describes a remix as a type of derivative work for a sound recording.

---

According to this statutory provision, any "rearrangement, remixing, or alteration" of a sound recording as described in the law is a derivative work and can only be created by the copyright owner or with the copyright owner's permission. Therefore, remixes and mashups are generally derivative works when created in this way. However, whether a specific work is derivative or not and whether a particular derivative of a sound recording violates copyright law are subject to a court's analysis of the statute and of the particular adaptation in making such a determination.

**Example 6.11**

In *Saregama India, Ltd. v. Mosley*, a court ruled that a sound recording of the song "Put You on the Game" could not be deemed a derivative work based solely on the use of a "one-second snippet" (i.e., sample) of the original sound recording from which it was undisputedly taken. Rather, the court held that an interpretation of Section 114(b) did not negate the need to conduct an infringement analysis taking into account the degree of similarity between the original work and the derivative recording.[9]

## G. Arrangements Under the Compulsory Mechanical License

As discussed in Chapter 5, "The Reproduction Right," Section 115 of the Copyright Act provides for a compulsory license to record musical compositions and distribute those recordings without the copyright owner's permission. When an artist makes a recording of a musical composition, it will usually be necessary to make some changes to the composition in order to fit the artist's performance style. Accordingly, the compulsory license provision, in Section 115(a)(2), provides for a limited arrangement privilege, stating that:

*...the compulsory license includes the privilege of making a musical arrangement of the work to the extent necessary to conform it to the style or manner of interpretation of the performance involved.*

It is important to understand that this arrangement privilege is quite limited and allows only minor changes to be made. Under Section 115(a)(2), the "arrangement shall not change the basic melody or fundamental character of the work." Finally, Section 115(a)(2) provides that an arrangement:

*...shall not be subject to protection as a derivative work under this title, except with the express consent of the copyright owner.*

Although Section 115(a)(2) gives some general rules for the arrangement privilege under the compulsory mechanical license, applying these rules to specific situations can be problematic. Determining what changes are minor and thus permitted as opposed to changes that affect the basic melody or fundamental character of a composition is to some degree subjective. It is helpful, however, to keep the purpose of the limited arrangement privilege in mind in making such determinations. For instance, if an artist recorded a song in a different key from the key in which it was written, the change has probably been made to fit the artist's performance style and would be permitted. Similarly, if a male artist wanted to record a song written from a female perspective, it might be necessary to make some minor lyric changes, such as changing pronouns from feminine to masculine or vice versa (e.g. "I love him" to "I love her"). On the other hand, if an artist wanted to change more than a very minor portion of a song's lyrics, this would be likely to be considered a change in the fundamental character of the work and would not be permitted; the result would be a derivative work, which cannot be made without the copyright owner's permission.

### H. Copyrighting the Uncopyrightable

A copyrightable derivative work can be made based on a work in the public domain. A practice that is sometimes used by publishers who own valuable songs that are about to enter the public domain is to make a new copyrightable arrangement of the song. A publisher can then continue to commercially exploit the derivative arrangement after the copyright in the original song expires.

---

**Example 6.12**

Chappell Music, which owned the copyrights to some extremely valuable Gilbert and Sullivan works, had new arrangements of the works made shortly before the expiration of their copyrights in the 1970s. This did not prevent the original works from entering the public domain, but Warner-Chappell (which purchased Chappell) still earns money from licensing the copyrighted derivative arrangements.

---

## II. The Distribution Right

Another of the exclusive rights of a copyright owner is the right to distribute the work to the public. Section 106(3) of the Copyright Act provides that the copyright owner has the exclusive right to distribute and to authorize others to distribute "copies or phonorecords of the copyrighted work to the public by sale or other transfer of ownership, or by rental, lease, or lending." Section 106(3) covers not only the sale of a work, but all forms of transfer, including giving away or renting copies of phonorecords.

### A. Record Piracy

In 1972, the United States amended its copyright law to include sound recordings as a category of copyrightable works. The main reason for this amendment was to provide legal protection against record piracy. Record piracy involves reproducing copyrighted sound recordings and distributing the unauthorized phonorecords. Record piracy therefore always involves a violation of the copyright owner's reproduction and distribution rights.[10]

It is important to realize that the harm caused by piracy is not only to major record companies, but to all participants in the music industry and to some extent to the public. Piracy involves a violation not only of the rights of the sound recording copyright owner, but the copyright owners of any musical works contained on the sound recording as well. Consequently, recording artists, producers, songwriters, and music publishers, all of whom rely on royalties from the sale of legitimate recordings, are harmed. Consumers are also harmed because some of the income lost due to piracy as well as costs of fighting piracy is passed on to consumers in the form of increased prices for legitimate recordings. Piracy also has an economic effect on countries where pirated products are sold because, unlike legitimate record sales, sales of pirated recordings do not generate any tax revenues. Because a large portion of worldwide piracy is operated by organized crime, some of the income from piracy is used to fund other illegal activities such as drug trafficking, prostitution, and allegedly even terrorism.

---

**Piracy Doesn't Discriminate by Company Size**    Many people apparently believe that piracy of intellectual property (music, movies, books, computer software, etc.) only really harms big, rich companies. Based on my experience, this is a very misguided view. Although big companies like the major record labels are certainly harmed by piracy, the effect on smaller companies is often much greater. While huge multinational corporations are well diversified and can survive losses from piracy, many smaller companies cannot. To illustrate, several years ago David Moser received a Fulbright grant from the U.S. government to study piracy problems in the Philippines. During his three-month visit, he found that music is an extremely important part of Filipino life and culture. However, the Filipino record industry has been almost devastated by the high piracy rates, and very few Filipino musicians are able to earn a living in their home country. Filipino record companies have virtually no chance of competing with pirated sales of their recordings. Although a few major record companies have branch offices in the Philippines, they rarely invest in Filipino artists because the market for their recordings would be mostly local, and piracy rates are too high to make local releases profitable. This means that many artists lose out on the chance to have their music marketed to their audience on a wide scale. While the Philippines represents one example, it is by no means an isolated one. Other countries with very high piracy rates (e.g., Mexico and Spain) have also seen their local music and film industries devastated to near extinction.

---

### (1) Penalties for Record Piracy

In addition to civil awards for actual damages, lost profits, or statutory damages of up to $150,000 per infringement, record pirates can also be subject to penalties for criminal copyright infringement. The criminal penalties vary, depending on whether the infringing activity is for commercial advantage or private financial gain. Copyright law provides that financial gain includes bartering or trading anything of value, including sound recordings. If the infringing activity is for commercial advantage or private financial gain, infringers are subject to up to five years in prison and $250,000 in fines. Repeat offenders are subject to imprisonment for up to 10 years.

In addition to copyright law, other federal and state laws also prohibit record piracy. On the federal level, the Federal Anti-Bootlegging Statute[11] prohibits unauthorized recording, manufacture, distribution, or trafficking in sound recordings or videos of artists' live musical performances. Violators are subject to up to $250,000 in fines and five years imprisonment.

Additionally, the No Electronic Theft Act provides for criminal prosecutions even if no monetary profit or commercial gain is derived from the infringing activity. The No Electronic Theft Act has been applied to copyright infringement involving the trading of MP3 files over the Internet.

Most states have enacted statutes that prohibit the reproduction and distribution of sound recordings without authorization. Importantly, most of these state statutes apply to sound recordings created prior to 1972, when sound recordings were made a class of works subject to the Copyright Act.

### (2) Fighting Record Piracy

The Recording Industry Association of America (RIAA) in the United States and the International Federation of the Phonograph Industry (IFPI) on an international basis wage a continuous war against record piracy. The RIAA and IFPI work with law enforcement agencies to locate pirates and shut down their manufacturing and distribution facilities. Enforcement efforts are mainly directed at manufacturers and distributors of pirated recordings. The recording industry has been consistently concerned over piracy of recordings using compact disc recorders (CD-Rs). Consumers buy blank CD-Rs and, in many cases, use them to copy music files from CDs or download using file-sharing software. In addition to individuals copying music files from the Internet to CD-Rs, there has been an increase in the use of CD-R technology by large-scale record pirating operations.

The RIAA has also taken a very active role in enforcing the law against online piracy. The RIAA employs a team of Internet specialists and uses a 24-hour automated webcrawler to track down websites that offer illegal recordings. The RIAA, IFPI, and other organizations also attempt to deter piracy by educating the public about copyright law. The RIAA has published anti-piracy guidelines that provide suggestions for CD manufacturing plants to use in order to recognize pirated recordings. In addition, the RIAA's "CD-Reward" program provides monetary awards of up to $10,000 to people who provide information regarding CD manufacturers who are illegally producing RIAA member company sound recordings.

---

**Example 6.13**

In 1999, the RIAA settled a lawsuit it had brought against Americ Disc, a CD manufacturing plant. Americ Disc had been manufacturing pirated copies of CDs, including albums by virtually all of the world's most popular recording artists (Mariah Carey, Celine Dion, Madonna, etc.). The suit resulted in one of the largest copyright infringement settlements ever, with Americ Disc agreeing to pay $10 million plus an additional $500,000 for reimbursement of the RIAA's attorneys' fees and to help establish an anti-piracy program. Americ Disc also agreed to require its customers to supply copies of licenses for all copyrighted material to be reproduced.

---

While the Internet has served as a vehicle for digital piracy, it has also served as a viable means of legally and conveniently delivering music to consumers. These Internet sales have helped to displace some of the losses seen from piracy of both physical and digital media. According to IFPI, 2010 saw a decrease in sales of physical CDs due in part to piracy and to the closure of many brick-and-mortar retail record outlets. However, digital music revenues increased 1000% from 2004 to 2010, to $4.6 billion. When the impact of online piracy is compared to this increase, global music revenues overall have declined by 31% for the same period.[12] See Chapter 14, "Copyright and Digital Technology," for an additional discussion of the impact of music sales through digital distribution.

## B. Limitations on the Distribution Right

### (1) The First Sale Doctrine

Section 109(a) of the Copyright Act provides an important limitation on the distribution right by providing that:

> ...the owner of a particular copy or phonorecord lawfully made under this title, or any person authorized by such owner, is entitled, without the authority of the copyright owner, to sell or otherwise dispose of the possession of that copy or phonorecord.

This provision, commonly known as the first sale doctrine, means that once the copyright owner sells or gives away a copy or phonorecord, he has no further rights with respect to that particular copy or phonorecord. In other words, the copyright owner controls only the first public distribution of a copy or phonorecord of the work. People make use of the first sale doctrine on a daily basis when they rent videocassettes or DVDs or sell used CDs.

Under the first sale doctrine, the copyright owner gets to determine whether, when, and in what format copies or phonorecords of a work are to be published for the first time, but once that first distribution has been authorized, the copyright owner cannot control any future distribution. The first sale doctrine is based on the idea that ownership of a material object is distinct from ownership of copyright.

---

**Example 6.14**

If you bought (or otherwise lawfully acquired) the copy of the book you are now reading, you own this particular copy. As the owner of this copy, under the first sale doctrine, you can keep it (which we hope you will do), sell it (which we hope you won't want to do), or even destroy it (which we really hope you won't do unless you're going to buy another one to replace it). However, the first sale doctrine does not give you the right to make copies or adapt the copyrighted work embodied in the copy you own.

---

The first sale doctrine is not applicable if a copy or phonorecord is unlawfully made or if the first sale occurs outside of the United States. It also applies only to the owner of the particular copy or phonorecord, not to someone who possesses the copy or phonorecord but does not own it.

**Example 6.15**

If you stole the book you are now reading, you are a bad person and morally bankrupt. In addition to lacking a moral compass, you have no rights under the first sale doctrine because you possess an illegally acquired copy.

### (a) Used CDs

The first sale doctrine is responsible for the used CD business, which grew dramatically in the 1990s.[13] When a record company, which is the copyright owner of the sound recordings contained on a compact disc, sells compact discs to retailers, it loses all control over further distribution of those discs. The retailer is free to sell the compact discs it has purchased to consumers. The consumers then become the owners of the compact discs and are consequently free to redistribute them such as by selling them to used CD stores. The used CD stores can sell the discs to other consumers, who can in turn distribute them as they see fit, including reselling them to used CD stores, starting the process all over again. The record company has no control over any of these actions except for the first sale to the retailer.

The resale of recordings affects copyright owners in two ways. First, the record company does not receive any additional compensation for any distributions beyond the initial sale. Second, every resale potentially displaces a sale of a new CD from a retailer to a consumer.

Several potential solutions to issues posed by used CD sales have been considered, but none has been adopted. One solution would be to require a resale royalty on sales of copyrighted works. The rationale for this resale royalty is that music creators require a portion of the income generated by used CD sales because CDs retain their high sound quality and value well beyond their initial sale. The resale royalty is also based on an assumption that, given the choice between buying new and used compact discs, many consumers will buy used, denying the first sale of originals in a way that does not parallel other markets because most products depreciate over time. In order for a resale royalty to exist, Congress would have to enact legislation requiring used CD retailers to keep records of sales and pay royalties to record companies, which would be split with recording artists. The odds of this happening are remote because any such legislation would likely be met with strong resistance from retailers and consumers since the first sale doctrine is helpful to consumers and small businesses.

Legal distribution of music and other entertainment media via the Internet has become increasingly prevalent and therefore has interesting implications for the first sale doctrine. See Chapter 14 for a discussion of the first sale doctrine in the digital context.

### (b) Record Rental

Under the first sale doctrine, a compact disc purchaser is free to sell or rent a CD without the permission of the copyright owner and without paying any royalty. However, the Record Rental Amendment Act of 1984 imposes a limitation on the first sale doctrine. This Amendment, found in Section 109(b) of the Copyright Act, states that:

*Unless authorized by the owners of the copyright in the sound recording and musical works embodied therein, the owner of a particular phonorecord may not, for purposes of direct or indirect commercial advantage, dispose of, or authorize the disposal of, possession of that phonorecord by rental, lease, or lending.*

In other words, although people are free to sell or give away recordings that they own, they cannot rent them unless they have the permission of the copyright owners of the sound recording and songs contained on the recording. This provision was passed in response to the development of record rental outlets. The record industry convinced Congress that record rentals would displace sales, and record companies would be forced to spread their costs over the smaller number of records sold. Record companies would become more conservative and less likely to release records by unknown artists. The Record Rental Amendment Act applies to the rental of phonorecords, not copies, and therefore does not apply to the rental of movies. An exception to the prohibition against record rental exists for rentals by nonprofit libraries or nonprofit educational institutions.

### (2) Other Limitations on the Distribution Right

Many of the limitations on the reproduction right are also applicable to the distribution right. For example, Section 108's reproduction privileges for libraries and archives also allow for the distribution of copies made. Section 114(b)'s exemption for sound recordings included in educational television and radio programs applies to the reproduction, distribution, and derivative rights.

## Endnotes

1. 17 U.S.C. § 101.
2. *D'Almaine v. Boosey*, 160 Eng. Rep. at 123.
3. *Carte v. Duff*, 25 F. 183 (S.D.N.Y. 1885).
4. 841 F. Supp. 118 (1993).
5. H.R. Rep. No. 2236, 89th Cong., 2d Sess. 53 (1966); H.R. Rep. No. 83, 90th Cong., 1st Sess. 24 (1967), and repeated in H.R. Rep No. 1476, 94th Cong., 2d Sess. 62 (1976); S. Rep. No. 473, 94th Cong., 1st Sess. 58 (1975).
6. 73 F. Supp. 165, 167 (S.D.N.Y. 1947).
7. 166 F. Supp. 681 (S.D. Cal. 1958).
8. 3 L.R.-Q.B. 223, 229-30 (1868).
9. 687 F.Supp.2d 1325 (S.D. Fla. 2009). This court's holding represents a departure from the decision in *Bridgeport Music, Inc. v. Dimension Films*, 410 F.3d 792 (6th Cir. 2005), which is discussed in Chapter 5.
10. IFPI 2011 Digital Music Report, p. 14. http://www.ifpi.org/content/library/DMR2011.pdf.
11. 18 U.S.C. § 2319A.
12. IFPI 2011 Digital Music Report, p. 14. http://www.ifpi.org/content/library/DMR2011.pdf.
13. In 1993, several major record retailers (Wherehouse, Hastings, etc.) announced their intention to sell used CDs. The major record companies threatened to withdraw promotional allowances and refused to supply new releases of several well-known artists who objected to the practice. The record companies reversed their position on promotional allowances after being faced with a federal antitrust lawsuit. See *Wherehouse Entertainment, Inc. v. CEMA*, No. 93–4253 (C.D. Cal. filed Jul. 19, 1993).

# 7 Public Performance and Display Rights

*"For all songs I whistle while at work, I will be sure to get a license before I whistle."*

—Michael Robertson, CEO of MP3.com

## I. The Public Performance Right

Section 106(4) of the Copyright Act gives copyright owners the exclusive right to perform and to authorize others to perform their works publicly. Consequently, anyone who wants to publicly perform a copyrighted musical composition must obtain the copyright owner's permission. Like all of the other exclusive rights, the public performance right is not absolute and is subject to many limitations, the most important of which are discussed later in this chapter. However, one very important limitation to be aware of is that the public performance right of Section 106(4) does not apply to copyrighted sound recordings (see the "Sound Recordings and the Performance Right" section later in this chapter). Consequently, the discussion of the Section 106(4) performance right is limited to musical compositions.

---

**Note:** The entertainment industry consists of many works that are subject to the performance right besides musical compositions, e.g., films and electronic games. However, this book's focus is on musical works.

---

### A. What Is a Performance?

The term "perform" is defined very broadly by the Copyright Act and includes not only the initial rendition of a work but also any further act by which the rendition is transmitted or communicated. Section 101 provides that to perform a work means:

*...to recite, render, play, dance, or act it, either directly or by means of any device or process or, in the case of a motion picture or other audiovisual work, to show its images in any sequence or to make the sounds accompanying it audible.*

The performance right includes not only live performances but also recorded performances and transmitted performances. For instance, a band playing a song in a nightclub constitutes a live performance, while the nightclub's playing a compact disc or jukebox is a recorded performance.

Finally, a radio station's broadcast of either a live or recorded performance is a transmitted performance. In order to understand how the public performance right works, it is crucial to realize that public performances occur with not only the initial rendition of a work but also all further acts by which that rendition is transmitted to the public.

---

**Example 7.1**

If a vocalist sings a song, he has performed the song. If a radio or television station broadcasts his performance, that transmission by the radio station constitutes a second performance. If a person sitting at home with his radio tuned in to the radio station, that constitutes a third performance. Although all three performances are based on the same initial rendition (i.e., the vocalist's initial performance), the radio or television station's action and the home listener's action are further acts of performance, although they are not necessarily all public performances.

---

## B. What Is a Public Performance?

Not every performance requires the permission of the copyright owner of a work. This is because the copyright owner's exclusive right is limited to "public" performances. Anyone is free to perform copyrighted works in private.

---

**Example 7.2**

If an individual sings a copyrighted song at home, she has not infringed the performance right because this would be a private performance (unless she invites the public to join her). Similarly, when an individual plays a CD or turns on his television at home, these are performances that are private rather than public and do not require the copyright owner's permission. However, a television station's broadcast is a public performance, which requires permission because the broadcast is available to the public.

---

Sometimes it is not easy to determine whether a performance is public or private. In between the performances that are clearly public or private, there are many performances that occupy a middle ground, combining some characteristics of public performances and some characteristics of private performances. Under copyright law, there are four categories of performances that are classified as public performances:[1]

1. A public performance occurs anytime a work is performed at a place open to the public. A place that is open to the public is a place where the general public is free to go, regardless of how many people are actually present and regardless of whether an admission fee is charged. Some examples include concert venues, theaters, nightclubs, bars, restaurants, and retail stores.

2. A public performance occurs when a work is performed at a place where a substantial number of people other than family and friends are gathered. This includes what are commonly known as semipublic places such as private clubs, workplaces, and schools. Exactly how many people constitute a substantial number is not specified by the Copyright Act.

3. A public performance occurs when a work is transmitted to a place open to the public or where a substantial number of people other than family and friends are gathered. To transmit a work means to communicate it by any device that enables images or sounds to be received beyond the place where they originated. An example would be a radio broadcast of a copyrighted song that is received by a bar. Although the performance originates at the radio station, it is transmitted over the airwaves to a place open to the public.

4. A public performance occurs when a work is transmitted by a device, regardless of whether the public receives it in the same or separate places or at the same or different times. It is not necessary that anyone actually tune in as long as members of the public could have done so.

As technology continues to bring about new ways to make music available, the distinction between public and private places has become increasingly blurred. Modern technology has begun a trend towards distributing copyrighted works to private places such as people's homes rather than public places. For instance, are performances that originate from a website that allows visitors to listen to streamed files of copyrighted musical works public or private performances? On one hand, this might seem to be a private performance because the copyrighted work is being transmitted to one person at a time and generally to a private place such as a home. However, Congress has stated that a transmission may be considered to be made "to the public" when "the transmission is capable of reaching different recipients at different times, as in the case of sounds or images stored in an information system and capable of being performed or displayed at the initiative of individual members of the public."[2] In a way, the website that streams music is like a radio station in that it allows people to listen to performances of music without having to purchase the recordings.

Streaming, however, is different from downloading. When an individual downloads a music file, a reproduction, not a performance, occurs at the time of the download. This was the holding in the federal court decision in *United States v. American Society of Composers, Authors and Publishers.*[3] The court explained that a performance of downloaded music takes place only after the download is complete and the recipient takes the initiative to play, i.e., perform the song. The court described this initiated performance as a private one:

> [T]he Internet Companies transmit a copy of the work to the user, who then plays his unique copy of the song whenever he wants to hear it; because the performance is made by a unique reproduction of the song that was sold to the user, the ultimate performance of the song is not to the public."

The court reached this public vs. private performance distinction after first settling the question of whether downloads should be considered performances at all. Since downloads result from electronic transmissions, and transmissions are included in the Copyright Act's definition of a performance, the issue before the court was whether downloads are the types of transmissions that properly constitute a performance, a question arising from a dispute between ASCAP and two Internet companies, Yahoo! and RealNetworks, over whether Internet companies should have to pay a performance royalty for transmissions of music for download purposes. As the Court opinion states:

> In this case, the Internet Companies offer their customers the ability to download musical works over the Internet. It is undisputed that these downloads create copies of the musical works, for which the parties agree that copyright owners must be compensated. However, the parties dispute whether these downloads are also

*public performances of the musical works, for which the copyright owners must separately and additionally be compensated.*

In concluding that downloads of musical compositions are not public performances, the Court stated:

*Music is neither recited, rendered, nor played when a recording (electronic or otherwise) is simply delivered to a potential listener.... The downloads at issue... are not musical performances that are contemporaneously perceived by the listener. They are simply transfers of electronic files containing digital copies from an on-line server to a local hard drive.*

A key aspect of the Court's conclusion rested on whether the recipient could "contemporaneously perceive" the music, i.e., hear the music playing at the same time the transmission occurs. Where the song can only be heard later—after the transmission is complete—the result is a download, not a performance. Table 7.1 illustrates how royalty payments correspond to the distinction between performance vs. download (or other non-performance transmissions) of a musical composition.

## Table 7.1  Digital Transmission and Public Performance of Musical Compositions

| Comparison Factors for Digital Transmissions/ Performances (1) | Digital Transmission of Composition That = "Permanent" Reproduction of Phonorecord (DPD) (2) | Public Performance of Musical Composition via Digital Transmission (3) |
|---|---|---|
| Description | Recipient acquires (may purchase) digital phonorecord containing composition. | Recipient hears composition during transmission; may/may not pay a fee; may be interactive or non-interactive. |
| Type of Transmission/ Performance | Downloads, uploads, ripping, file-sharing, transfer of digital file from one network to another. | Subscription Internet radio (web-casting), satellite and cable sub-scription services; simulcast of traditional radio via Internet, on-demand streaming. |
| License Required? | Yes. | Yes. |
| Example of Licensee (sender of transmission) | iTunes, Napster. | SiriusXM radio, Music Choice, YouTube, Pandora, Spotify. |
| Type of License | § 115 Compulsory License. | Negotiated Performance License. |
| License Issuer(s) | Publisher, author, or Harry Fox Agency. | ASCAP/BMI/SESAC or publisher/ author. |
| Royalty Collection Agent | Publisher, author, or Harry Fox Agency. | ASCAP/BMI/SESAC or publisher/ author. |
| Royalty rates | Set by Copyright Office. | Set by performing rights organization. |
| Payees | Composers, authors, musical composition owners, publishers. | Composers, authors, musical composition owners, publishers. |

### C. Performing Rights Organizations

Performing rights organizations (PROs) play an important role in assisting composers, publishers, and songwriters in licensing and collecting royalties for public performances of their music.

### *(1) History of Performing Rights Organizations*

The public performance right was first made applicable to musical works under the 1909 Copyright Act. After 1909, although the performance right existed, there was no practical way to license and collect payments for public performances. Consider the amount of work that would be involved if a copyright owner had to negotiate individual licenses for performances of its music in every restaurant, bar, nightclub, concert venue, radio station, television station, and so forth throughout the world. The costs of tracking all of the performances of your music, not to mention licensing and collecting payments, would be much greater than the amount of money you would be able to collect.

This was the problem that existed for songwriters and publishers until 1914, when a group of popular composers including Irving Berlin, Victor Herbert, and John Philip Sousa decided that the only practical way they could get paid for public performances of their music was to form an organization to enforce the performance rights of composers and publishers. As a result, they formed the American Society of Composers, Authors and Publishers (ASCAP) to act as a clearinghouse for licensing performances and collecting license fees.

Initially, venues that allowed performances to take place were very resistant to paying for licenses, and ASCAP had to file lawsuits to enforce its members' rights. The 1909 Copyright Act provided that only for-profit performances had to be licensed, and some early court decisions held that there had to be a direct charge for music in order to constitute a for-profit performance. However, the Supreme Court set a crucial precedent regarding what constitutes a for-profit performance in the case of *Herbert v. Shanley*.[4] Composer Victor Herbert sued Shanley's Restaurant for allowing the performance of one of his compositions without a license. Shanley contended that the performances that occurred in its establishment were not for-profit because they didn't charge customers to listen to the music. The Supreme Court ruled that a direct charge to the customer for listening to music was not required. Instead, it is sufficient to show that music was used in the process of making a profit. The Court believed that music was a part of the total service for which the public pays, stating that:

> *If the rights under copyright law are only infringed by a performance where money is taken at the door, they are very imperfectly protected. Music is part of the total for which the public pays and the fact that the price of the whole is attributable to a particular item which those present are expected to order is not important. It is true that music is not the sole object, but neither is the food, which probably could be got cheaper elsewhere.*

The Supreme Court's view makes logical sense because businesses would not be likely to use music if they did not believe that music contributes to the atmosphere of the business, thereby increasing profitability. Although a bar or restaurant might not charge customers directly for the music it plays, it charges them indirectly in the price of food or drinks that it sells. In actuality, there are many things reflected in the price that a restaurant sells food for. For instance, most restaurants are decorated in some way, whether with high-class art or the movie memorabilia of

Planet Hollywood. Restaurants would have a difficult time convincing whomever they obtain such decorations from that they shouldn't have to pay for them because they don't directly charge their customers to look at them. Obviously, if a restaurant believes that music does not contribute to its profitability, it is free to let its customers eat in silence.

Although music certainly plays a role in the profitability of many types of businesses, businesses have always been very reluctant to pay for it, and there is a common perception among businesses (as well as many individuals) that having to pay for music is not justified. This is illustrated by the fact that the public performance right has been challenged in virtually every business context over the years since its establishment (live performance venues such as restaurants and nightclubs, radio broadcasters, television broadcasters, webcasters, etc.).

After the important precedent established by the *Shanley* decision, ASCAP began licensing restaurants, nightclubs, concert halls, and other venues where public performances took place. In the early 1920s, radio stations resisted obtaining licenses, contending that because they did not charge the public for their broadcasts, they did not have to obtain licenses. However, the Supreme Court once again sided with copyright owners, holding that radio broadcasts were for profit and had to be licensed.[5]

In 1931, a second performing rights organization began operating in the United States. The Society of European Stage Authors and Composers (SESAC) originally represented European composers and publishers. SESAC began to establish itself in the fields of country and gospel music and, although much smaller than ASCAP and BMI, is currently active in representing songwriters and publishers of all styles of music in the U.S. and abroad.

In the 1930s, ASCAP increased the license fees it charged to radio stations. Broadcasters claimed that ASCAP's practices constituted monopolistic price fixing and that radio airplay was a source of free advertising for sheet music and records. With ASCAP's licenses about to expire the next year, broadcasters formed their own organization, Broadcast Music Incorporated (BMI), in 1939. Broadcasters refused to agree to increased ASCAP license fees, and BMI began acquiring songs, sometimes luring songwriters by paying them advances on future royalty income. On January 1, 1941, the majority of radio stations stopped playing ASCAP music, instead playing mostly songs in the public domain. As a result, ASCAP eventually agreed to reduce its license fees. Since then, the three performing rights organizations (ASCAP, BMI, and SESAC) have co-existed in the United States, each licensing the music of different songwriters and publishers. Although having more than one performing rights organization benefits songwriters and publishers by providing a degree of competition, licensees are less than thrilled at having to obtain licenses from three organizations to play music that they would probably rather not pay for at all.

### (2) Operation of Performing Rights Organizations

The three American performing rights organizations as well as foreign performing rights organizations all operate in a similar manner. In order to get paid for performances of music, songwriters and publishers must join a performing rights organization. A songwriter or publisher who meets standards specified by the organization can join the organization. Although the exact requirements differ slightly among the different organizations, if you have songs that are being publicly performed on the radio or television, you are eligible to join. Upon joining, the songwriter or publisher transfers the nonexclusive right to license nondramatic public performances of its songs to the organization.

The performing rights organizations have three main responsibilities: (1) issuing licenses and collecting license fees; (2) monitoring public performances of music; and (3) paying songwriters and publishers based on the number of performances of their music.

The performing rights organizations issue licenses to businesses that allow public performances of music to occur, such as radio stations, television stations, websites, and live performance venues. Most of the licenses issued by the performing rights organizations are blanket licenses giving the licensee the right to publicly perform any music in the performing rights organization's repertory an unlimited number of times for a set fee. The amount of a blanket license fee depends on several factors but is essentially based upon the licensee's potential audience size, gross revenues, and the amount of music used. Each of the performing rights organizations has a fee schedule that specifies the fees for different types of licensees.

---

**Who Obtains Performance Licenses?** Performance licenses are obtained by the performance venue rather than by the performer. In other words, if a band plays copyrighted music at a bar, it is the bar's responsibility to obtain a performance license rather than the band's. Not only does the band not have to worry about obtaining a performance license, it doesn't even have to be concerned with what music it performs, because the performing rights organizations are responsible for this (even though they don't monitor performances of live music in the vast majority of live performance venues). Copyright law may impose legal liability on anyone who illegally participates in the performance of music. However, as a practical matter, businesses are generally the beneficiaries of having music performed in their establishments and are therefore held responsible for obtaining performance licenses.

*EMI April Music, Inc. v. White* provides an example of this principle in action. In this case, a defendant restaurant owner repeatedly failed to pay performance royalties based on his belief that the performers in his restaurant, rather than him, should be held responsible for paying the licensing fees. However, the court found the restaurant owner liable for non-payment of the fees.[6] In contrast, some foreign countries impose obligations on performers to keep track of the music they perform.

---

**Tip:** Performance rights organizations only license non-dramatic public performances of music. A license to use music in a dramatic performance such as a play must be obtained directly from the copyright owner.

---

Because there are millions of public performances of music taking place each day, it would be impractical for copyright owners to attempt to keep track of all performances. The costs of doing so would likely exceed the license fees collected. Instead, the performing rights organizations use sampling procedures to estimate the number of times songs are performed. The majority of performances sampled are radio and television broadcasts. Live performances, other than at major concert venues, are not sampled. Instead, the performing rights organizations assume that live performances are generally the same as broadcast performances. This assumption is a bit flawed because there are many live performances of music that is not performed on radio or television. This unfortunately results in some songwriters who perform their music in bars and other small venues not being paid royalties for these performances. However, the costs involved in sampling the huge number of live performances that take place in such venues would be disproportionate to the amount of income generated.

The performing rights organizations use formulas to assign a value or weight to different performances. Some of the factors taken into consideration by these formulas include the size of the potential audience (e.g., a network television performance would receive a greater weight than a local radio performance), the time of the performance (e.g., a performance at 5 p.m. would receive a greater weight than a performance at 2 a.m.), and the type of performance (e.g., a featured performance would receive a greater weight than a background performance). Based on these weights, different types of performances are assigned different values. For example, a radio broadcast that takes place at 5 p.m. might be worth five times the value of a broadcast that takes place at 2 a.m. (reflecting the size of the listening audience at the different times). The estimated number of performances of a song is then multiplied by the value of different types of performances to reach a dollar amount.

ASCAP and BMI are nonprofit organizations. From the total license fees collected, ASCAP and BMI first deduct their operating expenses and then distribute the remaining money among their songwriters and publishers. Operating expenses are generally about 15 percent of the total income collected, so songwriters and publishers receive 85 percent of the total income collected. SESAC, which is a for-profit organization, distributes over 50 percent of the income it collects to its songwriters and publishers, keeping the remaining income to cover its operating expenses and make a profit. Some songwriters assume that because SESAC pays only 50 percent of its collections to the publishers and songwriters, they will receive less money than from ASCAP or BMI. This is not necessarily true because SESAC is a for-profit organization and is not subject to many of the restrictions ASCAP and BMI are, such as government approval of their license fees.

---

**Tip:**  In order to be paid for performances of a song, you must inform your performing rights organization that you are the owner or writer of the song. This is accomplished by filing a registration or clearance form (separate from a copyright registration) for the song with your performing rights organization. Each of the performing rights organizations provides forms to do so.

---

The performing rights organizations pay 50 percent of the amount due for performances of a song to the publisher or publishers who own the copyright to the song and 50 percent to the songwriter or songwriters who wrote the song. The 50 percent of performance royalties paid to the publisher(s) is commonly known as the "publishers' share," and the 50 percent paid to the writer(s) is known as the "writers' share." Some writers choose to act as their own publisher, setting up an independent publishing company for that purpose. If a writer elects to do so, it is permissible to submit a separate membership application to the PRO to join as a publisher (as well as a writer) to receive the publisher's share, and to thereby receive 100 percent of the performance royalties. Given the administrative demands of acting as one's own publisher, this is a decision to be made knowledgeably.

**Example 7.3**

If a song composed by two authors, each of whom has a publishing contract with a separate music publisher, earns $10,000 in royalties, the performing rights organization will pay $2,500 to each of the publishers and songwriters. The publishers' share of income ($5,000) is split between the two publishers, and the writers' share of income ($5,000) is split between the two writers.

**Which PRO Should You Join?**   There is no easy way to determine which of the three performing rights organizations is the best for a particular songwriter or publisher to join. In the past, many people believed that the decision depended on the style of music involved (BMI was often presumed to be better than ASCAP for alternative rock, while ASCAP was presumed to be better for pop). These distinctions, if they were ever accurate, no longer carry much weight. We recommend that a writer or publisher contact all three organizations, research their sampling and payment systems, and choose the one that seems best. Often, the decision will come down to which one seems most interested in your music and which one you form the best personal relationship with. If you join one organization and later believe that another may be better, you can switch at the end of your contract.

## (3) Protecting PRO Members and Licensees: Consent Decrees

Today, the three American PROs coexist to facilitate a competitive choice between these licensing entities for authors and publishers wishing to affiliate with them. However, this economical environment has not always existed. PROs have the capacity to wield considerable power and influence over licensing terms and rates and to create licensing monopolies. Concerned about violations of the Sherman Antitrust Act—the law that governs inappropriate restraints on commerce—the U.S. government sued ASCAP in 1941 for failing to charge competitive rates to licensees for blanket licenses.[7] The case was settled when ASCAP agreed to sign a consent decree, an agreement that permits government oversight of ASCAP's licensing activities. For example, the decree requires ASCAP to maintain grievance procedures for authors, publishers, and licensees;[8] it also requires ASCAP to issue only non-exclusive licenses and to provide reasonable alternatives to blanket licenses and rates.[9] BMI was also sued in 1941 for antitrust violations and again in 1964; a new BMI consent decree was signed in 1966.[10] BMI's consent decree contains provisions similar to those in the ASCAP decree; however, one difference is that BMI does not have the grievance procedure requirements included in the ASCAP decree.[11] These consent decrees remain in effect and continue to be monitored and periodically amended in rate setting determinations when licensees and the PROs are unable to reach agreement on the applicable rates. SESAC is not a party to these consent decrees and is not bound by them.[12]

### (4) Foreign Performing Rights Organizations

Although ASCAP was the first performing rights organization in the United States, the idea to form a collection organization was not an original one. SACEM, the *Societe des Auteurs, Compositeurs et Editeurs de Musique*, had been in existence since 1851 in France. The formation of SACEM resulted from similar circumstances that led to the formation of ASCAP in the United States. In 1847, a French composer named Bourget got upset after hearing one of his songs played at a restaurant. While drinking a glass of wine, Bourget complained to the restaurant owner about the unauthorized performance and offered to accept the glass of wine free in return for the performance. The restaurant owner refused and later sued Bourget for not paying for his meal. Bourget successfully defended the lawsuit by contending that the restaurant infringed the copyright in his music.

Today, virtually every country in the world has a performing rights organization. Foreign performing rights organizations license performances and collect license fees for performances that take place in their country. The three American performing rights organizations have reciprocal agreements with these foreign organizations that provide a way for American songwriters and publishers to get paid for foreign performances of their music.

## D. Limitations on the Public Performance Right

Although a copyright owner has the right to publicly perform copyrighted works that it owns, this right is not absolute. Under the 1909 Copyright Act, copyright owners only had the right to control for-profit performances. This provision proved to be very problematic because distinguishing for-profit performances from nonprofit performances was not always easy. Instead of retaining this distinction, the 1976 Copyright Act provided for a broad performance right that applies regardless of whether a performance is for profit or not. However, Section 110 of the Copyright Act provides a number of exemptions from the performance right for certain types of uses. Most of these exemptions apply to certain nonprofit, educational, or charitable uses that Congress believed to be in the public interest or that would cause only minor loss of income to copyright owners. The following are a few of the exemptions specified.

### (1) Face-to-Face Teaching Activities

Section 110(1) exempts the performance of copyrighted works:

> ...*by instructors or pupils in the course of face-to-face teaching activities of a nonprofit educational institution, in a classroom or similar place devoted to instruction.*

This exemption allows teachers and students to read aloud from copyrighted books, to play or sing musical works, and to perform motion pictures. In order to fit within the Section 110(1) exemption, four conditions must be met. First, the performance can only be by students or teachers. If a band plays a concert in a school, the exemption will not apply. However, if a musician is brought into a class as a guest lecturer and performs copyrighted music as part of the lecture, the exemption will apply.

Second, the performance must be made in the course of face-to-face teaching activities and must be for teaching purposes rather than merely for entertainment. This means that the teacher and students must be in the same place. If a performance is broadcast (e.g., on radio or television) or transmitted (e.g., via the Internet) to a classroom, the exemption will not apply. Additionally, even if a teacher performs copyrighted music in a classroom, the purpose of the performance must be somehow related to what is being taught.

Third, the place where the teaching activities occur must be a nonprofit educational institution. A performance that takes place in a for-profit institution will not qualify for this exemption. For instance, a performance of copyrighted music in a dance studio or an aerobics class would not be exempt under Section 110(1).

Lastly, the performance must take place in a classroom or similar place devoted to instruction. This does not necessarily mean that the place where the performance occurs must be a full-time classroom. For instance, a performance that takes place in an auditorium would be exempt as long as there is an instructional purpose. In contrast, a performance in an auditorium during a school play or a performance in a school gym during a sporting event would not be exempt.

---

**Example 7.4**

If a copyright law instructor sings a copyrighted song in his class in order to illustrate that a performance that occurs in face-to-face teaching activities is covered by the Section 110(1) exemption and is therefore not an infringement of copyright, that performance would fit within the Section 110(1) exemption. However, if the instructor performed a copyrighted song just to entertain his students (though the entertainment value of such a performance other than for comedic purposes might be dubious if the instructor is not musically inclined), the Section 110(1) exemption would not be applicable.

---

### (2) The Teach Act

In November 2002, Congress passed the Technology, Education, and Copyright Harmonization Act (the "Teach Act"),[13] which amended the performance and display exemptions of the Copyright Act in order to allow for the educational use of copyrighted material in digital form in certain circumstances. The Teach Act is extremely important because distance education has become very common, with many universities offering online courses. Teachers ideally would like to have the same right to use copyrighted works in online education as they do in the traditional classroom environment. However, copyright owners are more concerned about the use of their works online because the risk of illegal reproduction and distribution of digital content is much greater. Consequently, the Teach Act attempts to strike a balance by giving educators some freedom to transmit performances and displays of copyrighted works but makes these transmissions subject to some conditions designed to limit the possibility of infringing use. Due to these complicated conditions, the Teach Act is more restrictive than the face-to-face teaching activities exemption discussed above.

**Tip:** It is possible that an educational use of copyrighted material that doesn't qualify as exempt under the Teach Act could be a fair use. However, because fair use analysis can be complicated and risky to rely on, educators should be cautious in exceeding uses allowed by the Teach Act.

The main conditions imposed by the Teach Act for teachers and students making digital transmissions of copyrighted works for educational purposes are these:

- The use must be made by an instructor or student in an accredited, nonprofit educational institution.

- The educational institution must have a policy concerning use of copyrighted works that promotes copyright compliance and must make information or resources about copyright available.

- Copyrighted works that are sold or licensed specifically for distance education may not be used.

- Illegal copies of works may not be used.

- If possible, the use should be limited to the amount and duration comparable to what would be displayed or performed in a physical classroom environment.

- The use of copyrighted material should be an integral part of the course for instructional purposes rather than for entertainment.

- Access to copyrighted material should be limited to students enrolled in the course, and technological tools should be used to prevent students from making copies or retaining copies for longer than necessary to achieve the instructional purpose.

- Students should be made aware that works are copyrighted and that any use beyond the course may violate the copyright owner's rights.

**Example 7.5**

The Teach Act would allow a music history teacher to make copyrighted recordings available to students in a similar manner to use of recordings in a physical classroom as long as access is restricted to students enrolled in the course, the music is used for instructional purposes, and the teacher uses legally obtained recordings. The Teach Act would not allow an instructor to make a textbook available in digital form.

### (3) Religious Services

Section 110(3) provides an exemption for performances of nondramatic literary or musical works and dramatic musical works of a religious nature "in the course of services at a place of worship or other religious assembly." Because this exemption includes dramatic as well as nondramatic works, performances of religious works such as masses and choral services may be exempt. In contrast, performances of secular dramatic works are not exempt even though they contain some religious subject matter.

---

**Example 7.6**

A performance of the musical *Jesus Christ Superstar* (a dramatic work) would not be exempt under Section 110(3) because, even though it is about Jesus, it is a secular work.

---

To fit within the religious services exemption, a performance must be made during the course of religious services. Performances that take place at a place of worship but are for social, educational, fund raising, or entertainment purposes would not be exempt. Additionally, a performance must take place "at a place of worship or other religious assembly." For instance, a performance at a person's home would not be exempt even if a religious service took place in the home.

---

**Example 7.7**

If a group of Satan worshippers play Beatles songs backwards during the religious services held at their church, the religious services exemption would be applicable. If, however, the Satan worshippers played Beatles songs backwards in order to raise money to help promote Satan worship, the performance would not be exempt because it would be for fund raising rather than a religious purpose.

---

### (4) Nonprofit Performances of Nondramatic Literary or Musical Works

Section 110(4) provides an exemption for certain nonprofit performances of nondramatic literary or musical works. There are four requirements that must be satisfied in order to fit within this exemption. First, the exemption does not include transmissions of performances and is therefore limited to performances made directly in the presence of an audience, whether by live performers or the playing of recorded music. It would not include radio or television broadcast performances because such performances constitute transmissions.

Second, the performance must be for nonprofit purposes. There cannot be any direct or indirect commercial purpose for the performance. The exemption is not applicable to any profit-making performances even if the public is not charged a fee to see or hear the performance.

Third, the performers, promoters, and organizers of the performance cannot receive any compensation. This requirement is intended to prevent the free use of copyrighted works under the guise of charity.

Fourth, there cannot be any direct or indirect admission charge unless the proceeds go solely to educational, religious, or charitable purposes. Section 110(4) gives copyright owners the right to prevent performances where there is an admission charge even if the proceeds are for educational, religious, or charitable purposes in order to allow copyright owners to prevent performances of their works in connection with charities they do not support. A copyright owner can give written objection stating the reasons for the objection at least seven days before the performance. The usefulness of this objection right is limited because a copyright owner will often not be aware that a charitable organization intends to perform its song in a fundraising event. However, it is also possible for performing rights organizations to give blanket objection notices to all potential users covering all performances of works within their repertories.

---

**Example 7.8**

Benefit concerts where admission fees are used to cover the costs of the event and where any excess goes to charity will generally fit the requirements of the Section 110(4) exemption. However, if a benefit concert was intended to raise money for abortion rights and a copyright owner of a song to be performed was a pro-life advocate, the copyright owner could prevent the use of its work by sending written notice stating its objection to the use.

---

### (5) The Homestyle Receiving Apparatus Exemption

One of the most problematic situations involving performance rights has involved performances that take place in business establishments. Many businesses cause public performances of music to take place, but not all businesses want to pay for those performances. Section 110(5) of the Copyright Act provides an exemption (sometimes referred to as the "small business exemption") for businesses who play radio or television broadcasts on standard radio or television equipment. There are three requirements necessary to fit within this exemption. First, the reception of the transmission containing the performance must be on a single receiving apparatus of a kind commonly used in private homes. Second, no direct charge can be made to see or hear the transmission. Finally, the transmission cannot be further transmitted to the public.

Many problems in applying the homestyle exemption resulted from the difficulty in determining what type of equipment constituted "a single receiving apparatus of a kind commonly used in private homes." The intention of this requirement was to apply to situations where a business plays music or television broadcasts over an ordinary receiving system commonly sold for in-home use. Factors that could be considered in order to determine whether a sound system was a homestyle or commercial sound system include size, physical arrangement, areas within the establishment where the transmissions take place, and the extent to which the receiving apparatus is altered or augmented to improve transmission quality for the audience. Many court cases have rendered decisions as to the extent of the homestyle exemption, with the results being inconsistent from one case to another.

---

**Example 7.9**

In *Cass County Music Co. v. Muedini*,[14] a restaurant used a Radio Shack receiver connected by concealed speaker wire to nine speakers that were recessed into a dropped acoustic tile ceiling to provide background music for its customers. Between 1985 and 1991, ASCAP sent letters and visited the restaurant in order to get the restaurant owner to obtain a performance license for $327. The owner repeatedly refused, and ASCAP sued. The court held that the restaurant did not qualify for the Section 110(5) exemption because the nine-speaker system used was not the type of sound system commonly used in a home.

---

---

**Example 7.10**

---

In *Springsteen v. Plaza Roller Dome, Inc.,*[15] the defendant operated a putt-putt golf course that received radio broadcasts of copyrighted songs. The receiving apparatus used by the golf course consisted of a radio receiver wired to six separate speakers mounted on light poles interspersed over the 7,500 square foot area of the course. The defendant argued that because its speakers were fairly poor quality, did not project well, and were inferior to many home systems, and the golf course was not of sufficient size to justify a subscription to a commercial background music system, it should be exempt. The court agreed and found that the golf course qualified for the Section 110(5) exemption. The court's decision seems to be based more on its belief that the golf course was too small to bother with rather than an interpretation of Section 110(5), because few people are likely to have six speakers mounted to light poles spread over 7,500 square feet in their homes. The court also mistakenly emphasized that the golf course generated very limited revenue; the Section 110(5) exemption is not conditioned on whether a business is profitable or not. It would be extremely unfair if businesses could avoid all of their financial obligations if they are unprofitable or only modestly profitable.

---

Due partly to the inconsistencies in interpreting the homestyle exemption and mostly to very strong lobbying by the National Restaurant Association, an amendment (the Fairness in Music Licensing Act) was passed to the Copyright Act in 1998 providing an additional exemption to many small businesses.

### (6) The Fairness in Music Licensing Act

In 1993, the National Restaurant Association began lobbying Congress to change the law, arguing that the homestyle exemption was too difficult to interpret and possibly because they did not want to have to continue paying performance license fees to play music in their businesses. From 1993 to 1998, music industry organizations successfully resisted these efforts. However, in a clever political move, the National Restaurant Association persuaded Congress to combine the Fairness in Music Licensing Act with another bill designed to add 20 years to the term of copyright. Due to the desire to pass the term extension bill, Congress passed the Fairness in Music Licensing Act in 1998.

The Fairness in Music Licensing Act provides a much broader exemption than the homestyle exemption. Under the Fairness in Music Licensing Act, certain businesses that perform music received from licensed radio, television, cable, and satellite broadcasts are exempt from having to obtain permission to publicly perform music in their establishments. Like the Homestyle Receiving Apparatus exemption, the Fairness in Music Licensing exemption does not apply to live performances.

There are three requirements that must be satisfied to fit within the exemption. First, the business cannot re-transmit a performance beyond its establishment. Second, no admission fee can be charged. Third, the business must meet certain size requirements. Specifically, restaurants and bars must be smaller than 3,750 square feet, while any other retail businesses must be smaller than 2,000 square feet. However, if a business exceeds the size limitations, it can still qualify for the exemption if it uses six or fewer speakers with no more than four speakers in any one room, or if it uses audiovisual equipment consisting of no more than four television sets with no more than one in each room and none having a diagonal screen size greater than 55 inches.

A business that claims to be subject to the exemption but that does not satisfy the requirements can be subject to damages (beyond those available for copyright infringement) of up to two times the amount of the license fee that should have been paid during the preceding three-year period when the business did not have reasonable grounds to believe it was exempt.

The Fairness in Music Licensing Act has put the United States in violation of two treaties, the Berne Convention and the TRIPS Agreement, both of which require that member countries provide performance rights not subject to arbitrary exceptions such as the Fairness in Music Licensing Act. In 2001, the World Trade Organization ruled that the Fairness in Music Licensing Act is in violation of these treaties and awarded a judgment of $1.1 million a year that the United States must pay to compensate European composers for income lost due to the Fairness in Music Licensing Act.[16]

### (7) Retail Record Sales

Section 110(7) provides an exemption for performances of nondramatic musical works in connection with the sale of phonorecords and/or sheet music that embody the works. This exemption is intended to allow stores that sell recordings to play them in order to promote sales. In order to qualify for this exemption, the store must: (1) be open to the public at large; (2) not receive any direct or indirect admission charge; (3) perform the records for the sole purpose of promoting record sales; and (4) not transmit the performance beyond the store. This exemption applies only to performances occurring in brick and mortar stores and does not apply to online previews of music sold through Internet music vendors.[17]

---

**Example 7.11**

A record store like FYE that plays recordings in-store would fit within the Section 110(7) exemption. Even though such performances serve as entertainment for customers, their primary purpose is at least arguably to interest customers in buying a copy of the record being performed.

---

### (8) Noncommercial Broadcasting

Although public broadcasters are not exempt from performance licensing, Section 118 of the Copyright Act provides for a compulsory license permitting the performance of published, nondramatic musical works. The rationale for this compulsory license is that public broadcasters should have easy access to copyrighted works. In order to obtain a compulsory license, the performance must be by public broadcasting entities or in the course of transmissions made by noncommercial, educational broadcast stations. Royalty rates under the compulsory license are significantly lower than those paid by commercial broadcasters. Section 118 also provides that the compulsory license provisions may be altered by voluntary licenses between the parties that must be filed with the Copyright Office.

## E. Sound Recordings and the Performance Right

The Copyright Act actually provides two separate performance rights. The public performance right discussed in this chapter up to this point involves the right set forth in Section 106(4) of the Act. As mentioned previously, the Section 106(4) public performance right applies to musical compositions (and other performable works, like films). However, the performance right of Section 106(4) does not apply to sound recordings. The Digital Performance Right in Sound Recordings Act of 1995 was enacted to provide a public performance right for sound recordings to remedy this gap. However, the law distinguished between the two performance rights to make it clear that Section 106(4) does not apply to sound recordings. Specifically, Section 114(a) of the Copyright Act provides that:

*The exclusive rights of the owner of copyright in a sound recording do not include any right of performance under Section 106(4).*

Because sound recordings were not added to the Copyright Act as a type of copyrightable work until 1972, the record industry has wanted to extend the Section 106(4) public performance right to sound recordings, but its attempts to do so have been unsuccessful due to resistance from the broadcasting industry. Broadcasters do not want to have to pay more than what they are already obligated to pay to copyright owners of musical works. Broadcasters also argue that free radio airplay of sound recordings benefits artists and record companies by promoting record sales and live performances. The practical result is that if a recording of a copyrighted song is broadcast over analog radio or television or performed in a live setting, the copyright owner of the song (typically a music publisher) and the songwriter will receive a royalty for the performance while the copyright owner of the sound recording (typically a record company) and the recording artist will not.

### Example 7.12

The song "I Don't Want to Miss a Thing" was written by Diane Warren and is owned by her publishing company, Realsongs. Aerosmith's recording of the song became their first number-one single. Another recording of the song became a number-one country single for Mark Chesnutt. Although both the Aerosmith and Mark Chesnutt recordings received substantial radio airplay, neither Aerosmith, Chesnutt, nor the record companies that released their records received any performance royalties from that airplay. However, Diane Warren and Realsongs earned a fortune in performance royalties as the songwriter and copyright owner of the song.

The lack of a comprehensive performance right in sound recordings creates several inequities. First, many foreign countries recognize a performance right in sound recordings. However, copyright owners of sound recordings in the United States do not receive royalties for performances of their recordings in these countries because international copyright treaties provide for reciprocal treatment. In other words, because U.S. copyright law doesn't provide for royalties to be paid for the performance of foreign copyrighted sound recordings in the United States, foreign countries do not pay for performances of U.S. copyrighted sound recordings. This has a serious adverse impact on the U.S. recording industry because U.S. recordings are performed on an international scale to a much greater degree than recordings from any other country.

Another problem is that because performance royalties earned by songwriters and copyright owners of songs contained on sound recordings can be a substantial source of income, many artists and producers are eager to record songs that they write even if their songs are not as good as many other songs available. An even more unfortunate result is that some artists and producers who are not songwriters insist on songwriting credit or partial song ownership as a condition to recording someone else's song so that they can receive part of the income earned by the song. This practice is commonly referred to as a "cut-in," which, despite potentially being unethical, occurs fairly commonly.

## F. The Digital Performance Right in Sound Recordings Act

For several decades, the recording industry had unsuccessfully tried to convince Congress to amend the Copyright Act to recognize a right of public performance for sound recordings under Section 106(4). By 1990, Congress began to be concerned with the impact that digital technology would have on the record industry. Over the next several years, Congress conducted hearings, supervised negotiations, and considered several bills to amend the Copyright Act to reflect these technological changes. Finally, in 1995, Congress amended the Copyright Act by enacting the Digital Performance Rights in Sound Recordings Act (DPRSRA), which granted a limited public performance right for sound recordings; this public performance right is set forth at Section 106(6) of the Copyright Act.

The DPRSRA is a very detailed and complicated piece of legislation.[18] Its complexity is primarily due to the competing interests of protecting sound recording copyright owners from losses caused by digital audio technology on one hand, while allowing digital technology to advance and flourish on the other. The DPRSRA made two basic changes to copyright law affecting the use of musical works, both of which have turned out to be very important in the context of music distribution over the Internet. First, the DPRSRA added a new exclusive right of public performance for sound recordings. Second, the DPRSRA expanded the compulsory mechanical license provision to include the reproduction and distribution of musical compositions in digital format (i.e., digital phonorecord deliveries), which was discussed in Chapter 5, "The Reproduction Right."

Although the DPRSRA was intended to provide sound recording copyright owners with protection in the digital environment, it failed to anticipate some of the developments that took place in connection with the digital transmission of music. For example, disagreements had developed between record companies and online music services over whether the music services were required to pay public performance royalties to record companies and recording artists under the DPRSRA. Consequently, the Digital Millennium Copyright Act (DMCA), which was passed in 1998, contains some provisions amending the DPRSRA, the most important of which extended the digital performance right to the practice of webcasting.[19]

The DPRSRA amended the list of exclusive rights, specifying in Section 106(6) of the Copyright Act that copyright owners of sound recordings shall have the exclusive right "to perform the copyrighted work publicly by means of a digital audio transmission," subject to certain conditions and limitations. A digital audio transmission is defined as a digital transmission "that embodies the transmission of a sound recording."

At the time of the DPRSRA's passage, the Internet was not in common use, and the main types of digital audio transmissions contemplated were transmissions made by cable and satellite. However, the definition of digital audio transmission is also broad enough to include transmissions made over the Internet such as webcasting, which is discussed in more detail in Chapter 14.

There are several basic limitations on the Section 106(6) performance right in sound recordings. First, the sound recording performance right applies only to performances made by "digital" audio transmission. This means that television performances of sound recordings are subject to Section 106(6) because these broadcasts are digital. However, analog performances of sound recordings, like those transmitted via terrestrial radio, are not subject to Section 106(6). Second, the right only applies to transmissions involving the communication of a performance where the recorded sounds are received beyond the place from which they are sent. It does not apply to performances that are not transmitted, such as live performances or playing recorded music in business establishments. Third, the right only applies to digital transmissions of sound recordings. It does not apply to digital transmissions of audiovisual works, because audiovisual works are subject to the performance right of Section 106(4). Fourth, the right only applies to digital audio transmissions that are "publicly" performed.

### Example 7.13

Referring back to Example 7.12, the performance of the Aerosmith or Mark Chesnutt recording of "I Don't Want to Miss a Thing" is not subject to the Section 106(6) performance right because the radio broadcasts are analog rather than digital. However, public performances of the same recordings over the Internet are subject to the Section 106(6) performance right because those performances are digital.

Legislative initiatives have attempted to expand the Section 106(6) right to include analog performances. In 2007, the Performance Rights Act was introduced in both houses of Congress to apply the Section 106(6) right to terrestrial broadcasts. Both bills were defeated by opposition from the broadcasting industry and were reintroduced in 2009 but were again defeated by the broadcasting lobby, which has successfully resisted a sound recording performance right for the past 50 years. Accordingly, as of this writing, these bills have not passed. However, the shift from analog to digital television broadcasting has lessened the severity of the limited scope of Section 106(6), and it seems reasonable to speculate that a similar shift will eventually occur with respect to analog radio, possibly in part through an increasing reliance on Internet radio or other Internet outlets.

In addition to the basic limitations discussed above, there are some additional limitations that are dependent upon the specific type of performance being made. These limitations are very technical in nature but are all motivated by a concern for protecting copyright owners of sound recordings from public performances of sound recordings that could be easily used by people to make high-quality, digital copies of the recorded music without having to pay for them.

The DPRSRA classifies digital audio transmissions into three categories that determine whether a license is required to publicly perform the sound recording and, if so, what type of license is required for the performance. The rationale for this classification is that certain types of transmissions are more likely than others to take the place of record sales. If there is very little likelihood of displacing record sales, the transmission is exempt from the digital public performance right, and a license is not required. If there is a high likelihood of displacing record sales, the transmitter must negotiate a license with the sound recording copyright owner. Finally, if there is only a moderate likelihood of displacing record sales, a compulsory license is available. Table 7.2 illustrates how royalty payments correspond to the statutory categories.

## Table 7.2  Digital Transmission and Public Performance of Sound Recordings

| Comparison Factors for Digital Transmissions/ Performances | Digital Transmission of Sound Recording That = "Permanent" Reproduction of Phonorecord (DPD) | Digital Performance of Sound Recording: Non-Interactive + Subscription | Digital Performance of Sound Recording: Interactive + Subscription | Digital Performance of Sound Recording: Non-Interactive + Non-Subscription |
|---|---|---|---|---|
| (1) | (2) | (3) | (4) | (5) |
| Description | Recipient acquires (may purchase) digital phonorecord | Recipient pays fee to hear transmission but cannot choose what to listen to | Recipient pays fee to hear transmission and determines what music will be transmitted; transmission by request | Recipient receives free music, like traditional free radio; anyone can listen; listener cannot choose what to listen to |
| Type of Transmission/ Performance | Downloads, uploads, ripping, file-sharing, transfer of digital file from one network to another | Subscription Internet radio (webcasting), satellite and cable subscription services, retransmissions and simulcasts of terrestrial radio broadcasts over Internet | On-demand streaming services | Terrestrial analog broadcasts |
| License Required? | Yes | Yes | Yes | No (Exempt) |
| Example of Licensee (sender of transmission) | iTunes, Napster | SiriusXM radio, Music Choice | Rhapsody, Pandora | FCC-licensed terrestrial broadcast stations |
| Type of License | Negotiated License | § 114 Compulsory License | Negotiated License | None |
| License Issuer(s) | Sound recording copyright owner (SRCO) | Sound Exchange (with notice to Copyright Office) | SRCO | N/A |
| Royalty Collection Agent | SRCO | Sound Exchange | SRCO | N/A |

**Table 7.2  Digital Transmission and Public Performance of Sound Recordings (*Continued*)**

| Comparison Factors for Digital Transmissions/ Performances | Digital Transmission of Sound Recording That = "Permanent" Reproduction of Phonorecord (DPD) | Digital Performance of Sound Recording: Non-Interactive + Subscription | Digital Performance of Sound Recording: Interactive + Subscription | Digital Performance of Sound Recording: Non-Interactive + Non-Subscription |
|---|---|---|---|---|
| (1) | (2) | (3) | (4) | (5) |
| Royalty Rates | Set by SRCO | Set by Copyright Office (SoundExchange.com); special rates for small webcasters and non-commercial broadcasters | Set by SRCO | N/A |
| Payees | SRCO; Artists—if contract with SRCO for these royalties | Featured artists, non-featured artists, SRCOs | SRCO; Artists—if contract with SRCO for these royalties | N/A |

### (1) Exempt Performances

Some digital audio transmissions of sound recordings are exempt from the digital public performance right, and licenses are not required for these types of transmissions. The reason these transmissions are exempt is that they are not likely to take the place of record sales; they do not give listeners advance notice of the recordings to be played and do not contain all of the songs from an artist's album.

The main type of exempt transmission is the "non-subscription broadcast transmission." Non-subscription broadcast transmissions are broadcasts of terrestrial radio stations that are licensed by the Federal Communications Commission that also broadcast over the Internet (and thereby broadcast in digital rather than analog form). When you listen to your favorite terrestrial radio station through your computer, you are listening to a non-subscription broadcast transmission. Just like terrestrial radio, listeners are not charged a subscription fee to hear these transmissions. Additionally, they are noninteractive which means that the radio station rather than the listeners decides what music is transmitted. Interactive services, on the other hand, transmit digital performances of music chosen by listeners.

Initially, under the DPRSRA, retransmissions of radio broadcasts (e.g., digitally transmitting an AM or FM radio broadcast over the Internet) were exempt. However, the Copyright Office issued a regulation stating that transmissions of an AM/FM broadcast signal over a digital communications network, such as the Internet, are subject to the sound recording copyright owner's digital public performance right. Consequently, radio stations that simulcast their broadcasts over the Internet must obtain compulsory licenses for the sound recordings to be transmitted.

(Alternatively, a radio station could negotiate individual licenses with the copyright owners of the sound recordings to be transmitted, because the law allows for negotiated licenses in place of compulsory licenses. However, it is unlikely that radio stations will want to negotiate licenses due to the great number of sound recordings they will be simulcasting.)

---

**Example 7.14**

WXYZ broadcasts its signal over-the-air and webcasts or simulcasts that broadcast over the Internet. WXYZ must obtain compulsory licenses and pay royalties for the right to publicly perform sound recordings over the Internet because these performances involve digital audio transmissions. However, WXYZ is not required to obtain any licenses for the right to broadcast its FM signal over-the-air because these performances are analog rather than digital in nature. Additionally, WXYZ must obtain licenses from the performing rights organizations allowing it to broadcast the various musical compositions contained on the sound recordings it broadcasts and webcasts.

---

### (2) Performances Subject to Compulsory Licenses

Some subscription transmissions (i.e., where customers pay subscription fees to hear the transmissions), although not exempt, are subject to a compulsory license because they are deemed as not likely to displace record sales. The types of services that make subscription transmissions available include satellite and cable companies, which offer digital performances to subscribers; webcasters, who transmit recordings over the Internet; and companies that transmit music to specially equipped automobiles, cell phones, and other devices. To be subject to the compulsory license, a subscription transmission must satisfy the following detailed requirements that exist primarily to prevent home taping of sound recordings:

**Non-Interactivity:** The transmission must be noninteractive meaning that it cannot allow listeners to choose what recordings they will hear.

**Sound Recording Performance Complement:** The transmission cannot, during any three-hour period, contain: (1) more than two consecutive songs or more than three songs in total from any individual sound recording; (2) more than three consecutive songs or more than four songs in total by the same recording artist.

**No Advance Notice:** The transmitter cannot publish advance notice of the recordings to be transmitted. It is permissible to specify what artists will be played in order to illustrate the types of music that will be available and to identify titles of songs immediately before they are performed.

**No Automatic Switching:** The transmitter cannot automatically switch listeners from one channel to another.

**Archived Programs:** Archived programs are programs posted on a website for listeners to hear repeatedly on demand. Archived programs cannot be less than five hours in duration. Additionally, archived programs cannot be posted for more than two weeks. The DMCA also prohibits merely changing a few songs in an archived program to avoid this condition.

**Looped Programs:** Programs performed continuously (i.e., repeated over and over) cannot be less than three hours in duration.

**Identifiable Programs:** Programs of less than one hour that contain performances of recordings in a predetermined order for which the transmission times have been announced in advance (identifiable programs) cannot be transmitted more than three times in a two-week period. Identifiable programs of more than one hour cannot be transmitted more than four times in a two-week period.

**Scanning Prevention:** The transmitter must cooperate with copyright owners to prevent listeners from using devices that scan transmissions for particular artists or recordings.

**Advertising Prohibition:** Transmitters are prohibited from falsely suggesting any connection between a song's copyright owner or recording artist with any products or services.

**Copy Prevention:** The transmitter cannot cause or aid listeners in making copies of transmitted recordings and must, when possible, use technology to prevent copying by listeners.

**No Bootlegs:** Bootleg recordings cannot be transmitted.

**Identifying Information:** The transmitter must identify, during but not before the time of the transmission, the title of songs performed, the recording artist, and the album title.

**Encoded Information:** The transmitter cannot interfere with any identifying information (i.e., title, name of artist, name of copyright owner, etc.) encoded in recordings. This differs from identifying information because encoded information is embedded in sound recordings to track use rather than to provide identifying information to listeners.

### (a) How Are Compulsory Licenses Obtained?

If you qualify for the compulsory license, you must file a notice of intent to obtain a compulsory license with the Copyright Office. The notice should specify your full legal name, address, phone number, fax number, and the date of first transmission. It must also be accompanied by a filing fee. You can then make ephemeral copies of sound recordings (i.e., copying selections from different sound recordings) that can only be used for Internet transmissions by means of streaming technology and must be destroyed within six months unless preserved solely for archival purposes.

### (b) What Will the Compulsory Royalty Rate Be?

Although the Digital Millennium Copyright Act provided for a compulsory license for digital transmissions of sound recordings, it neglected to establish royalty rates. Instead, it provided that rates should be negotiated by the parties, and if they could not reach an agreement, a Copyright Arbitration Royalty Panel (CARP) under the Library of Congress would determine rates. Webcasters and record companies spent over a year in contentious negotiations and were unable to reach any agreement, so a CARP ultimately recommended rates to the Librarian of Congress in 2002. However, neither webcasters nor record companies were satisfied with the rates proposed. The Librarian of Congress modified the rates proposed by the CARP, which resulted in royalty rates of $0.0007 (7 cents per 100 listeners) for commercial transmissions and $0.0002 for non-commercial transmissions, subject to a minimum $500 annual fee. In addition, webcasters must pay a fee of 8.8 percent for making ephemeral (temporary) copies of recordings needed to digitally transmit performances. Because the webcasting rates are subject to amendment, it is advisable to check with SoundExchange, a nonprofit organization that issues licenses and collects license fees for digital performances of sound recordings, or the Copyright Office for current applicable rates.

---

**Tip:**   Check with SoundExchange for currently applicable rates at www.soundexchange. com.

---

---

**Note:** The royalty rates went into effect as of September 1, 2002, but webcasters were required to pay royalties retroactively for all performances transmitted since October 28, 1998.

---

Although the Librarian of Congress lowered the rates proposed by the CARP, webcasters still believed they were too high and would cause many small webcasters to go out of business. In response to lobbying by the webcasting industry, Congress enacted the Small Webcasting Settlement Act of 2002, which authorized SoundExchange to negotiate rates with small webcasters based on a percentage of revenue or expenses (rather than a per performance royalty) subject to a minimum amount. The rates ultimately adopted for small webcasters are the greater of 10 percent of the first $250,000 in gross revenues and 12 percent of gross revenues exceeding $250,000 or 7 percent of annual expenses. These percentage rates are subject to a minimum annual fee of $2,000 for small webcasters with gross revenues of $50,000 or less and $5,000 for small webcasters with gross revenues over $50,000. Small webcasters are basically defined as those with less than $1.25 million annual gross revenues.

### (c) Who Gets the Money?

A nonprofit organization called SoundExchange issues licenses and collects license fees for digital performances of sound recordings. From the license fees it collects, SoundExchange deducts its administrative expenses and then pays the remaining amounts to sound recording copyright owners and recording artists in accordance with a formula established by law. After deducting its expenses, SoundExchange pays:[20]

*50% to the copyright owner of the sound recording (typically a record company)*

*45% to the featured recording artist*

*2.5% to non-featured musicians (backup musicians who are not part of the recording artist)*

*2.5% to non-featured vocalists*

**Tip:** In addition to the royalty rates discussed above for digital transmissions of sound recordings, webcasters must also obtain licenses for performances of the musical compositions performed by digital transmission. The performing rights organizations (ASCAP, BMI, and SESAC) offer various webcasting licenses that allow webcasters to digitally transmit all songs in their catalogs for an annual license fee. License fees are essentially based on some percentage of revenue, subject to a minimum annual payment. Check the performing rights organizations' websites for current applicable rate schedules.

The share paid to non-featured artists is distributed to unions representing background musicians and vocalists—2.5% to the American Federation of Musicians (AFM) and 2.5% to the American Federation of Television & Radio Artists (AFTRA)—and is distributed by these unions to their members. The share paid to featured artists is paid directly by SoundExchange to the artists and is therefore not subject to recoupment of any costs by record companies. The income collected by SoundExchange is likely to increase substantially as webcasting, satellite radio, and other digital music services (background music services such as Muzak, DMX, etc.) continue to flourish and grow.

### (3) Performances Subject to Negotiated Licenses

Some digital transmissions of sound recordings have a high likelihood of displacing record sales. Consequently, the only way such transmissions can be made is by negotiating licenses with the copyright owners. The types of transmissions for which licenses must be negotiated include interactive transmissions and subscription transmissions, which do not qualify for the compulsory license described earlier in this chapter.

Interactive transmissions allow listeners to choose the recordings they will hear and therefore have a relatively high potential to displace record sales. For instance, a consumer could choose all of the recordings by a particular artist rather than buying any of that artist's recordings. An artist or the artist's record company might choose not to negotiate licenses for all of the artist's recordings in order to avoid this potential scenario.

For webcasters, obtaining negotiated licenses is not a very practical option because they would have to negotiate with many different record companies for many different sound recordings. However, if a record company agreed to issue a license to a webcaster, the webcaster would pay the record company the agreed upon fee or royalty directly. The record company would then be responsible for paying the recording artist according to the royalty provisions of their recording contact.

### (4) Digital Transmissions of Sound Recordings vs. Public Performances of Sound Recordings

The DPRSRA, at Section 115(d) of the Copyright Act, defines a digital phonorecord delivery (discussed in Chapter 5 in relation to musical compositions) as:

> *...each individual delivery of a phonorecord by digital transmission of a sound recording which results in a specifically identifiable reproduction by or for any transmission recipient of a phonorecord of that sound*

*recording, regardless of whether the digital transmission is also a public performance of the sound recording... A digital phonorecord delivery does not result from a real-time, non-interactive subscription transmission of a sound recording where no reproduction of the sound recording... is made from the inception of the transmission through to its receipt by the transmission recipient in order to make the sound recording audible.*

The distinction between a download (or DPD) and a public performance of a musical composition is an important one with respect to sound recordings as well, as the licensing of DPDs differs from the licensing set forth in Section 114 of the Act (which defines public performances of sound recordings, as previously discussed). Table 7.2 illustrates these distinctions. Master use licenses for transmitting sound recordings for downloading must be contractually negotiated with the sound recording copyright owner (see Table 7.2). The importance of carefully drafting the contracting language for such licenses was illustrated in *F.B.T. Productions, LLC vs. Aftermath Records*.[21] The case involved a dispute between rap artist Eminem and several record companies concerning the percentage of royalties due to him and his production company for certain permanent downloads and mastertones. The core of the dispute was whether the royalty rate was established under the "Records Sold" provision of the agreement or under the "Masters Licensed" provision. The court opinion highlights the difference between the two provisions:

*The "Records Sold" provision of th[e] agreement provides that F.B.T. is to receive between 12% and 20% of the adjusted retail price of all "full price records sold in the United States... through normal retail channels." The agreement further provides that "[n]otwithstanding the foregoing," F.B.T. is to receive 50% of Aftermath's net receipts "[o]n masters licensed by us... to others for their manufacture and sale of records or for any other uses."*

The court found that the "Masters Licensed" provision was unambiguously applicable to rate setting for permanent downloads and mastertones of the sound recordings because third-party vendors (like Apple iTunes) who made the sound recordings available for download through agreements with Aftermath were deemed licensees.

## II. The Public Display Right

Section 106(5) gives copyright owners the exclusive right to display and to authorize others to display their copyrighted works publicly. This right is limited to the display of copyrighted works in copies and not phonorecords. The public display right is therefore not applicable to sound recordings. Although the public display right is applicable to musical works, it is arguably the least important of the music copyright owner's exclusive rights because musical works are generally performed rather than displayed. To display a work means:

*...to show a copy of it, either directly or by means of a film, slide, television image, or any other device or process or, in the case of a motion picture or other audiovisual work, to show individual images nonsequentially.*

The right to display a work includes showing the original work, either directly, such as exhibition in a museum, or indirectly, such as showing on television, as well as showings of reproductions of the work, such as by transmitting stored text from a database to a computer screen or by projecting individual images on a screen. The display right does not include the showing of images in sequence, which is instead covered by the performance right.

In order to infringe the display right, a display must be made in public. The display must therefore be made at a public place or must be transmitted or otherwise communicated to a public place.

---

**Example 7.15**

In *ABKCO Music, Inc. v. Stellar Records, Inc.*,[22] the defendant made a product called Compact Disc +Graphics (CD+Gs). CD+Gs are compact discs containing recordings of instrumental versions of popular songs for use in karaoke bars, where amateur singers sing along to the recording. In addition to the audio recording, the CD+Gs also allowed a song's lyrics to be shown on a television screen for the singer to read. The defendant had obtained compulsory mechanical licenses to record several songs by the Rolling Stones (e.g., "Satisfaction," "Jumpin' Jack Flash," etc.) on a CD+G. ABKCO, the publishing company that owns the copyrights to the Rolling Stones songs, sued for copyright infringement, claiming that the compulsory licenses did not include the right to display the song lyrics. The court agreed with ABKCO, holding that showing the lyrics implicated the display right in addition to the reproduction and distribution rights. Although the compulsory licenses covered the reproduction and distribution of the CD+Gs, it did not authorize the display of song lyrics.

---

## A. Limitations on the Public Display Right

Like the public performance right, the copyright owner's exclusive right to publicly display his work is limited.

### (1) Display of a Single Image at a Single Site

Section 109(c) allows the owner of a copy to display the copy publicly. However, the copy must have been lawfully made, and the display must be either a direct display or a display by the projection of no more than one image at a time to viewers present at the place where the copy is located.

---

**Example 7.16**

If you buy a compact disc, you are free to display the album cover artwork publicly. Similarly, if you buy a copy of a painting by Ringo Starr, you would be able to display it in a museum. However, you would not be able to display the painting on a website over the Internet because the display made pursuant to Section 109(c) can only be made to viewers present at the place where the copy is located.

---

### (2) Display in Situations Where Performance Is Exempted

Several of the exemptions discussed in connection with the public performance right also apply to the display right. Section 110 exempts displays for purposes of face-to-face teaching activities, instructional transmission, and religious services. Additionally, section 118's provisions for compulsory licensing of transmissions by noncommercial educational broadcasting stations apply to displays as well as performances.

**Example 7.17**

If the worship team of ABC Church wishes to create slides containing song lyrics for display to the congregation during worship services, the display right is implicated, as well as the reproduction right. The religious services exemption discussed earlier in this section may apply to the display of the lyrics; however, the church will still need a license to reproduce the song lyrics.

**Tip:**   Christian Copyright Licensing International (CCLI) assists churches with obtaining licenses for uses like those in Example 7.17. See their website at www.CCLI.com for additional information.

# Endnotes

1.  17 U.S.C. § 101.
2.  1967 House Report.
3.  627 F.3d 64 (2d Circuit 2010).
4.  242 U.S. 591 (1917).
5.  M. *Witmark & Sons v. L. Bamberger & Co.*, 291 F. 776 (D.N.J. 1923).
6.  618 F.Supp.2d 497 (E.D.Va.,2009). The court rendered a default judgment in the case.
7.  *United States v. Broadcast Music, Inc.*, 2000 WL 280034 (S.D.N.Y. 2000), Brief for the United States, pp. 11–12.
8.  William Krasilovsky and Sidney Shemel, *This Business of Music: The Definitive Guide to the Music Industry*, Eighth Edition, Billboard Books (2000), pp. 161–162.
9.  Noel L. Hillman, "Intractable Consent: A Legislative Solution to the Problem of Aging Consent Degrees in *United States v. ASCAP and United States v. BMI.*" *Fordham Intellectual Property, Media and Entertainment Law Journal*, Vol. 8:3, (1998):745.
10. See note 5, *supra*.
11. Hillman, p. 746, note 44. There are other differences between the two decrees as well.
12. In 2009 SESAC was sued by several broadcasting companies alleging SESAC's engagement in antitrust practices by failing to provide an alternative to the blanket license in *Meredith Corp. v. SESAC*, LLC, Sl. 2011 WL 856266 (S.D.N.Y. 2011). SESAC's motion to dismiss the suit was denied in 2011; therefore, the case is still pending as of this book's writing. Some industry observers view the lawsuit as an attempt to bring SESAC under a consent decree in line with BMI and ASCAP.
13. 17 U.S.C. §110(2).
14. 55 F.3d 265 (7th Cir. 1995).
15. 754 F. Supp. 1324 (N.D. Ill. 1990), aff'd, 949 F.2d 1482 (7th Cir. 1991).
16. Reportedly, the United States has refused to pay the $1.1 million annual penalty, apparently preferring to ignore its treaty obligations. Ironically, if the United States pays the

penalty, the American public will essentially be paying through tax dollars to subsidize businesses benefiting from the Fairness in Music Licensing Act.

17. *U.S. v. American Soc. of Composers, Authors and Publishers*, 599 F.Supp.2d 415, 433–434 (S.D.N.Y., 2009).

18. Senator Orrin Hatch, who co-sponsored the DPRSRA, remarked that it was a "complex" piece of legislation. An article reviewing the DPRSRA referred to Hatch's comment as an understatement, stating that "The Internal Revenue Code is 'complex'; the Digital Performance Right in Sound Recordings Act of 1995 is something else. 'Incomprehensible' perhaps, though 'You had to be there to appreciate it' may be fairer, because the convoluted language of the new Act appears to have been required by a number of very specific problems which the Act attempts to address with precision." Lionel S. Sobel, "A New Music Law for the Age of Digital Technology," Vol. 17, No. 6 *Entertainment Law Reporter* p. 3 (November 1995).

19. The webcasting regulations of the DMCA are contained in 17 U.S.C. §§ 112 and 114.

20. 17 U.S.C. 114(g)(2).

21. 621 F.3d 958 (9th Cir. 2010).

22. 96 F.3d 60, 40 U.S.P.Q.2d (BNA) 1052 (2d Cir. 1996).

# 8 Duration of Copyright

*"It is good that authors should be remunerated; and the least exceptionable way of remunerating them is by a monopoly. Yet monopoly is evil. For the sake of good we must submit to evil; but the evil ought not to last a day longer than is necessary for the purpose of securing the good."*

—*Lord Thomas Macaulay (British author, poet, and politician) in a speech delivered to the British House of Commons in 1866*

From the 1700s to the present, nothing has sparked a greater degree of debate and criticism of copyright than the question of how long copyright should last. Under the United States Constitution, copyright protection must be limited in duration. In other words, if Congress were to pass a law providing that copyright would last forever, that law would be unconstitutional. When the term of protection for a copyright ends or expires, the work enters the public domain. A work that is in the public domain cannot be owned by anyone, and anyone is free to use it.

While copyright can be very important to provide financial incentives for authors to create and for companies to invest in the production, distribution, and marketing of creative works, the public domain is also very important since it gives us a huge amount of creative works that can be freely used to create new works. For example, the song "Love Me Tender," which was recorded by Elvis Presley and became a number one hit in 1956, was based on an 1861 Civil War ballad entitled "Aura Lee." Since "Aura Lee" was in the public domain, it could freely be used as the basis for "Love Me Tender." Similarly, the popular musical *West Side Story* was based on the public domain work, *Romeo and Juliet,* written by William Shakespeare.

While it is often possible to use and adapt works protected by copyright to create new works, this usually requires permission from the copyright owner and payment for the use. In some circumstances, a copyright owner may not be willing to give permission. For example, a copyright owner might not license an adaptation of a work that the owner believes reflects negatively on the work or that might somehow lessen the author's reputation. Even if a copyright owner is willing to give permission, sometimes the fee to license a work will be unaffordable for a potential user. By limiting the term of copyright and allowing works to enter the public domain, we allow greater use of older works by creators of newer works.

**Tip:** While there is no comprehensive list of all public domain songs or other works in the public domain, a good source for finding public domain songs is The Public Domain Information Project website at http://www.pdinfo.com/.

The rules governing the duration, also referred to as the term, of copyright can be quite complex, primarily due to the fact that there are different terms of protection for different works. In order to determine which rules are applicable to a particular work, you must first know when the work was created. Works created and published before 1978 are governed by the provisions of the 1909 Copyright Act, while works created beginning in 1978 are governed by the provisions of the 1976 Copyright Act. However, the duration provisions of both the 1909 and 1976 Acts have been amended on several occasions, which makes things even more complicated.

# I. Evolution of Copyright Term

In order to understand the rules governing duration of copyright, it is helpful to understand how these rules evolved in the United States. After discussing this evolution, we will discuss the current rules for copyright duration.

## A. The 1909 Copyright Act

Until 1978, a dual system of copyright existed in the United States. Under the 1909 Copyright Act, federal copyright protection began upon publication of a work with proper copyright notice or on the date of copyright registration for certain unpublished works. Unpublished works were generally not protected under the 1909 Act and instead were protected by common law copyright until published. Common law copyright lasted until the work was published or registered as an unpublished work. If a work was never published or registered, it could be protected indefinitely under common law copyright.

Once a work was published or registered, it became subject to the 1909 Copyright Act. The 1909 Act provided for an initial term of 28 years of protection and a renewal term of an additional 28 years. Consequently, the maximum term of protection under the 1909 Copyright Act was 56 years. However, in order to receive protection during the renewal term, a renewal registration had to be made for the work. If a copyright was not renewed properly during the last year of the initial term, the copyright expired, and the work entered the public domain.

The distinction between common law copyright and federal copyright under the 1909 Act revolved around the concept of publication. Publication is defined as the distribution of copies or phonorecords to the public by sale or other transfer of ownership; by rental, lease, or lending; or the offer to distribute for purposes of further distribution. For example, if a record company distributes records to retailers, who offer them for sale to the public, publication has occurred. On the other hand, if the distribution is restricted as to who receives the work and the use to be made of it, publication would not have occurred. Also, the performance of a work does not constitute a publication.

The main reason for dividing the term of copyright into two periods (initial and renewal) was to protect authors. Often, authors transfer their rights upon or shortly after creation of a work, before the value of the work can be known. The renewal term was intended to protect authors from this situation. According to one court:

> *These provisions were introduced in response to the problem of unremunerative grants of copyright by authors. Because of the impossibility of predicting the commercial value of a work upon its creation and because of the weak bargaining position of authors, they sometimes assigned their copyrights in return for very little remuneration, such as small lump sum payments or inadequate royalty rates, and were thus prevented from sharing fairly, if at all, in the rewards from works that later became commercial successes. The termination provisions give authors an opportunity to renegotiate in the light of more knowledge as to the value of their works, and thereby obtain a fair share of the rewards from their works.*[1]

The renewal right belonged to the author of the work or the author's heirs as specified by the 1909 Copyright Act even if the author had previously transferred copyright ownership to someone else. Although the renewal requirement is no longer of practical importance, it is still helpful to have a basic understanding of the renewal provisions.

### (1) When to Renew?

Under the 1909 Copyright Act, a copyright owner could file a renewal application at any time during the last (28th) calendar year of the initial term. It was crucial that the renewal registration be made during the 28th year of the initial term because the failure to do so ejected the work into the public domain. Many copyrights expired at the end of the initial term due to the failure to renew. In fact, only about 20 percent of works published before 1978 were renewed.

The Copyright Renewal Act of 1992 amended the law and made renewal automatic for works created from 1964 to 1977. However, instead of totally eliminating the renewal system, the Copyright Renewal Act made it optional for these works. Under Section 304(a) of the 1976 Copyright Act, copyrights in works created from 1964 through 1977 automatically receive a 67-year renewal term. However, works published before 1964 still had to be renewed.

**Example 8.1**

A work published in 1963 had to be renewed in 1991 to receive the renewal term, while a work published in 1964 was automatically renewed.

Even though renewal was optional for works created beginning in 1964, there is an important benefit afforded to copyrights for which a renewal registration was filed. If a renewal registration was filed within one year of the expiration of the initial term, the registration certificate constitutes evidence of validity of the copyright and the facts stated in the renewal certificate during the renewal term.[2] This means that all of the facts stated in the renewal registration are deemed true without the need to prove them, if there is ever a dispute over ownership.

## (2) Assignment of Renewal Rights

The renewal provision ended up being largely ineffective at achieving its purpose because the United States Supreme Court held that authors could transfer their rights to the renewal term during the initial term. In *Fred Fisher Music Co. v. M. Witmark & Sons*,[3] the songwriters of "When Irish Eyes Are Smiling" transferred the copyright in the song as well as their renewal rights to a publisher. The Court held that the songwriters' assignment of their renewal rights was valid and that the publisher therefore had the right to renew. After this decision, it became a common practice in publishing contracts for publishers to require that authors assign their renewal right to them.

An author could make a promise to transfer his renewal rights at any time. However, transfers of renewal rights that were made before the time for renewal (i.e., in the 28th year of the initial term) were conditioned upon the author's surviving until the time for renewal. Similarly, an author's successors may also promise to transfer their renewal right, but their promises were also conditioned upon their surviving until the time for renewal. If an author or an author's successors promised to transfer their renewal rights but died before the 28th year of the initial term, the transferee did not have the right to renew. Instead, the renewal right belonged to the next succeeding successor specified by Section 304(a).

---

**Example 8.2**

A songwriter wrote a song in 1950 and transferred all of his rights to the song, including the renewal right, to a publisher. If the songwriter died before 1978, leaving a wife and children, the wife and children rather than the publisher would own the renewal right. The rationale for this result is that the songwriter's transfer of the renewal right was conditioned upon his living until the time for renewal.

---

## (3) Termination of Transfer of Renewal Term

An author or the author's heirs have the right to get back copyright ownership for the last 39 years of the copyright term by terminating any pre-1978 transfers of the renewal term. This termination right can be exercised during a five-year period beginning 56 years after first publication of the work or January 1, 1978, whichever comes later. The provisions for termination are otherwise essentially the same as the provisions for termination of transfer under section 203 of the 1976 Copyright Act (discussed in Chapter 4, "Ownership of Copyright").

---

**Tip:** Because the provisions for termination are somewhat complex, it is a good idea to consult with a copyright attorney no later than 54 years after the work's publication (earlier if possible) in order to ensure that the termination of pre-1978 works is carried out properly.

---

## B. The 1976 Copyright Act

Duration of copyright under the 1976 Copyright Act differs substantially from duration under the 1909 Act. Under the 1976 Act, copyright protection begins upon creation of the work and is not dependent upon publication. Creation occurs when an original work is fixed in tangible form.

Congress did away with the renewal term and instead decided to base copyright duration on the author's lifetime. The 1976 Act provided that copyright lasts for the life of the author plus an additional 50 years[4] (this period has since been increased to the life of the author plus 70 years). There were several reasons behind Congress' decision to make this change. First, due to increased life expectancies, the 1909 Act's maximum term of 56 years was not sufficient to compensate authors throughout their lives. Second, the renewal requirement often resulted in the inadvertent loss of copyright for many works due to the failure to file a renewal registration. Third, most foreign countries based their term of copyright on the author's lifetime plus a period after death. Finally, with a term based on the author's life, all works of an author enter the public domain at the same time.

---

**Tip:**   It is important to note that a copyrighted work's duration never changes regardless of any transfers of ownership in the work. The term is based on the original author's life regardless of who owns the copyright.

---

## II. Determining Copyright Duration

In order to determine how long copyright lasts for a particular work, it is helpful to divide works into three categories: (1) works created beginning in 1978; (2) works created but not published before 1978; and (3) works published before 1978. Table 8.1 summarizes the copyright duration rules for works created and published during these time periods.

### A. Works Created from 1978 to Present

For most works created on or after January 1, 1978 (other than anonymous works, pseudonymous works, and works made for hire), the term of copyright begins with the work's creation and ends 70 years after the death of the work's author.

**Example 8.3**

If a songwriter wrote a song in 1990 and died in 2000, the song's copyright will last through 2070 (i.e., 2000 plus 70 years).

If a work is created by two or more authors (i.e., joint authorship), the term of copyright will last for the life of the last surviving author plus 70 years after the last surviving author's death.[5]

**Example 8.4**

If two songwriters write a song in 1990, and one of the songwriters dies in 2000 while the other dies in 2010, the song's copyright will last through 2080.

**Table 8.1** Copyright Duration

| Date of Work | Protection Begins | Duration |
| --- | --- | --- |
| Created 1/1/78 and after | On date of fixation in tangible form | **General Rule:** Life of author plus 70 years. **Joint Works:** Life of last surviving author plus 70 years. **Works for Hire, Anonymous and Pseudonymous Works:** 95 years from publication or 120 years from creation, whichever is shorter. |
| Created before 1978, but published between 1/1/78 and 12/31/2002 | Upon creation under common law; 1/1/78 under 1976 Copyright Act | Life of author plus 70 years or 12/31/2047, whichever is longer. |
| Created before 1978, but not published | Upon creation under common law; 1/1/78 under 1976 Copyright Act | Life of author plus 70 years or 12/31/2002, whichever is longer. |
| Published from 1964 to 1977 | Upon publication with copyright notice (if published without notice, may be in public domain) | 28-year initial term plus 67-year automatic renewal term. |
| Published from 1923 to 1963 | Upon publication with copyright notice (if published without notice, may be in public domain) | 28-year initial term plus 67-year renewal term (if renewal registration filed during 28th year of initial term). |
| Published before 1923 | In public domain | Expired. |

## (1) Anonymous Works, Pseudonymous Works, and Works Made for Hire

There are three types of works involving authors who are either unknown or not an individual. An anonymous work is a work in which no natural person is identified as author on the copies or phonorecords of the work. A pseudonymous work is a work in which the author is identified under a fictitious name on the copies or phonorecords of the work. Works made for hire are created by an individual on behalf of an employer or hiring party. For these types of works, the term of copyright is not based upon the life of the author. Instead, the 1976 Copyright Act provides that copyright protection will last for 95 years from the work's first publication or 120 years from the work's creation, whichever expires first.[6] The rationale for having a dual period based on either creation or publication is to have a specific time period for all works, even if unpublished.

**Example 8.5**

A song written as a work made for hire is composed in 1995 and released on records (i.e., published) in 2000. The song's copyright will expire in 2095 (95 years from first publication). If, on the other hand, the song was not published until 2025, the copyright would expire in 2115 (120 years from creation).

In the case of anonymous works and pseudonymous works, the term of copyright can be converted to the life of the author plus 70 years by making the author's identity known to the Copyright Office before the expiration of the 95- or 120-year term.[7] Any person having an interest in a copyright may notify the Copyright Office of the actual author's identity in one of three ways: (1) registering under the author's true name; (2) filing a supplementary registration if the work has already been registered; or (3) recording a statement that specifies the name of the person filing the statement, the nature of that person's interest in the copyright, the title of the work, and the registration number if known.

---

**Pseudonyms for Copyright** If an author believes that he or she is not likely to live longer than 25 years, the author could register works under a pseudonym, thereby potentially receiving a longer term of copyright protection. For instance, if a chain-smoking, heavy-drinking, highly overweight 65-year-old author who does not expect to live to age 80 writes a song in 2000, he might choose to register the song under a pseudonym, and the copyright would quite possibly last longer than if the song were registered under the author's actual name. A similar result might also be accomplished if the author formed a corporation and wrote songs under work made for hire agreements with the corporation.

---

### (2) How Do You Know if a Copyright Owner Is Dead?

Because copyright duration is based upon the author's life under the 1976 Copyright Act, it is helpful to know whether an author is still living and, if not, the author's date of death. The Copyright Act provides for recordation in the Copyright Office of information concerning the lives and deaths of authors. Section 302(d) provides that:

> Any person having an interest in a copyright may at any time record in the Copyright Office a statement of the date of death of the author of the copyrighted work, or a statement that the author is still living on a particular date.

The Register of Copyrights is required to maintain current records on the deaths of authors of copyrighted works derived from statements recorded by copyright interest holders. There is also an incentive for copyright owners to provide the Copyright Office with statements allowed under Section 302(d). Under Section 302(e), if after 95 years from a work's first publication or 120 years from its creation, whichever expires first, a prospective user obtains a certified report from the Copyright Office that the Office records disclose nothing to indicate that the work's author is still living or died less than 70 years before, the prospective user is entitled to the benefit of a presumption that the author has been dead for at least 70 years. This creates a presumption that a work is in the public domain if the Copyright Office records show nothing indicating that the author is alive or has been alive during the past 95 years. A certified report can be obtained from the Copyright Office, and if a person relies on such a report in good faith, that reliance constitutes a complete defense to an action for copyright infringement. This defense will not be applicable if the copyright owner can prove that the user had notice that less than 70 years had elapsed from the year of the author's death.

---

**Tip:**   It is advisable for copyright owners of commercially valuable works to file statements regarding the author's status with the Copyright Office from time to time. For example, a copyright owner can file a statement saying that the author is still alive as of a certain date or giving the date of the author's death, thereby preventing people from relying on the presumption that a work is in the public domain.

---

### (3) Copyright Actually Lasts Longer than Life Plus 70 Years

Section 305 of the 1976 Copyright Act provides that all terms of copyright run to the end of the calendar year in which they expire. In other words, all copyrighted works will expire on December 31 of the year 70 years after the author's death.

**Example 8.6**

A song written on January 1 of any year would receive an actual copyright term of the author's life plus 70 years, 11 months, and 30 days because it would expire on December 31 of the year occurring 70 years after the author's death.

## B. Works Created but Not Published before 1978

Works that were created but had not been published prior to 1978 were protected by state common law copyright, which lasted indefinitely. The 1976 Copyright Act abolished common law copyright for works fixed in a tangible medium. Section 303 of the Copyright Act provides that works that were protected by common law copyright on the effective date of the 1976 Act (i.e., January 1, 1978) became subject to the term of protection specified by the 1976 Act (i.e., life plus 70 years) or until December 31, 2002, whichever expires later. The second potential expiration date (i.e., 12/31/02) protects works created by authors who have been deceased for more than 70 years by 1978 (which otherwise would not have received any federal copyright protection). Additionally, if such works are published before December 31, 2002, the copyright will not expire before December 31, 2047, thereby encouraging publication.

**Example 8.7**

Sally Songwriter wrote a song in 1950 that was not published. If Sally died in 1980, when does the copyright expire? The song was protected by common law copyright until 1978, at which time it became subject to federal copyright protection for Sally's life plus 70 years (i.e., 2050).

**Example 8.8**

Sammy Songwriter wrote a song in 1872 that was not published. If Sammy died in 1898, when does the copyright expire? The song was protected by common law copyright until 1978, at which time it became subject to federal copyright protection lasting until 12/31/2002 because that period is longer than Sammy's life plus 70 years (i.e., 1968). However, if Sammy's song is published before December 31, 2002, the copyright term would be extended to December 31, 2047.

As a result of the 1976 Copyright Act, the concept of common law copyright has lost most of its importance. There are, however, two categories of works that may still be protected under common law copyright. These are (1) works that have not been fixed in any tangible form, such as unrecorded improvisations; and (2) sound recordings fixed before February 15, 1972, which are protected until February 15, 2067.

## C. Works Published before 1978

The most confusing rules governing duration of copyright are for works that were published or registered prior to 1978. These works are governed by the 1909 Copyright Act, which provided for an initial term of 28 years from first publication with proper copyright notice. The 1909 Act also provided for a renewal term of an additional 28 years, resulting in a maximum term (initial plus renewal) of 56 years. In order to get the renewal term, a renewal registration had to be filed during the last year of the initial 28-year term.

---

**Example 8.9**

A song published in 1951 would have an initial term that expired in 1979. If the copyright to the song was renewed during 1979, it would have received an additional 28 years under the 1909 Act. The copyright would therefore have expired in 2007 (1951 plus 56 years). However, this result has changed with two subsequent amendments to the Copyright Act, which extended the length of the renewal term.

---

### (1) First Extension of Renewal Term

The 1976 Copyright Act extended the duration of the renewal term for an additional 19 years, making the total renewal term 47 years. With this extended renewal period, works published before 1978 received a maximum of 75 years of copyright protection. The rationale for this extension was to give copyrights existing under the 1909 Act a term of protection closer to that of copyrights under the 1976 Act.

---

**Example 8.10**

After the first extension of the renewal term, the copyright to the song from the previous example would have expired in 2026 rather than 2007 (1951 plus 75 years).

---

### (2) Second Extension of Renewal Term

The Sonny Bono Term Extension Act of 1998 amended the 1976 Copyright Act, extending the previous 47-year renewal term by an additional 20 years (as well as adding 20 years to works created beginning in 1978). Consequently, the renewal term now lasts for 67 years, and the maximum term for works in the initial or renewal term as of 1999 is 95 years (i.e., 28 plus 67 years) of copyright protection.

**Example 8.11**

After the second extension of the renewal term, the copyright to the song from the previous example would have expired in 2046 rather than 2026 (1951 plus 95 years).

The 1998 Term Extension Act was one of the most controversial amendments made to U.S. copyright law. It was passed largely at the instigation of copyright owners of some extremely valuable works that would have entered the public domain if the term had not been extended. Both the Disney Corporation and the Gershwin family estate lobbied vigorously for passage of the Term Extension Act, and its passage assured that copyrighted works such as the original Mickey Mouse character and "Rhapsody in Blue" by George Gershwin will continue to earn substantial income for the original copyright owners over the additional 20 years of protection. However, the Term Extension Act was also heavily lobbied against and was challenged shortly after its enactment by several publishers of public domain works, who contended that Congress exceeded its authority under the Constitution. Ultimately, the Supreme Court affirmed two lower court decisions upholding the term extension because the Constitution gives Congress the power to determine how long copyright protection should last, subject only to the restriction that it must be for "limited times."[8] Although the current term consisting of the author's lifetime plus 70 years is a long time, it is a limited time. The Supreme Court also concluded that Congress did not decide on the 20-year extension arbitrarily. Instead, Congress specified several reasons for doing so, including that some other countries had previously gone to a life-plus-70 term and that it did not make sense for the United States to have a lesser term of protection than what appeared to be emerging as the new international standard.

Critics of copyright term extension have made some valid points, most notably that the additional 20 years of copyright does little (if anything) to motivate authors to create and prevents works from entering the public domain for an additional 20 years. However, there is an alternative analysis of the criticisms of term extension that should be considered. First, critics' portrayals of the public domain as a free source of works for people to use and build upon are somewhat misleading. Although public domain works are not protected by copyright, this does not always mean they are free. In fact, there are publishing companies that specialize in selling public domain works. Shakespeare's plays and Beethoven's symphonies are certainly in the public domain, but if you want a copy of either, you'll likely have to pay for it. Ironically, copies of public domain works (e.g., books, sheet music, etc.) sometimes sell for about the same price as copyrighted works. The only difference is that none of the price is paid to the former copyright owner, the author, or the author's heirs. In fairness, there are some online publishers of free public domain works,[9] but these seem to be a minority compared to publishers that sell public domain works. In reality, whether a work is sold or made available for free often depends much more on economic considerations (whether there's a sizable enough market willing to pay for the work) than whether the work is in the public domain or not.

Another criticism of term extension is that the extra term of copyright protection only benefits big businesses that end up owning copyrights rather than benefiting authors. This criticism plays well in some academic circles and the media but is inaccurate. Although commercially valuable works often end up being owned by major entertainment or technology companies that acquire them from authors, unless created as works made for hire, they are subject to the author's termination rights.[10] Especially for highly valuable works, authors are very likely to exercise their right to terminate the initial transfer of copyright they made and regain ownership. In such situations, the author will clearly benefit from the extra 20 years of copyright. Even without considering termination rights, authors who transfer copyright do so according to some type of publishing contract that will almost always entitle the author to some type of royalty based on sales of the copyrighted work. In this situation, the author would not own the copyright for the 20 years of added protection but would still benefit financially from the copyright. Most works will have limited if any commercial value during the last 20 years of copyright protection, but for the few that do, the additional period of time certainly benefits the authors of these works or their heirs.

## D. Determining Whether a Work Is in the Public Domain

Because public domain works are free for all to use, anyone can freely copy them. However, it is often difficult to know whether a particular work is in the public domain. In order to determine whether a work is in the public domain, it is helpful to know when the work was first published. The date of first publication is usually specified in the copyright notice for copies or phonorecords of the work that have been distributed to the public. For works published prior to 1964, you will also need to know whether a renewal registration for the work was filed. To find out whether a renewal registration was filed, it is normally necessary to conduct a search of the Copyright Office records in one of the following ways:

1. Perform your own search by looking up the title of the work in the Catalog of Copyright Entries (CCE). The CCE is a series of annual catalogs listing and cross-referencing all registrations and renewals filed with the Copyright Office. The CCE is available at the Copyright Office as well as at certain libraries. Registrations and renewals made beginning with 1978 are also available online at the Copyright Office website at http://www .copyright.gov/records/. Although there is no charge to perform your own search, it may be advisable to use one of the following methods instead if you are not sure of what you are doing.

2. Have the Copyright Office search its records for you. The Copyright Office charges a per hour fee, and most simple searches will not take longer than one hour. Fill out a search request form and send it (along with a check) to Reference & Bibliography Section, LM-451, Copyright Office, Library of Congress, Washington, DC 20559. The only disadvantage to having the Copyright Office perform a search is that it might take a fairly long time to receive the search results (i.e., 1–3 months). For the current search fee, check the Copyright Office website at http://www.copyright.gov/docs/fees.html.

3. You could hire a professional search firm or a copyright attorney to conduct a search for you. This will likely be more expensive than having the Copyright Office perform a search, but you will obtain a quicker result (i.e, 1–5 days).

Many works that one might believe to be in the public domain are still protected by copyright. For instance, the song "Happy Birthday to You" was written in the 1890s. The copyright in a version with new lyrics was registered in 1935 by Warner-Chappell, a music publishing company. This copyright will not expire until 2030.

## E. Restoration of Copyright in Foreign Works

In general, once a work has entered the public domain, it remains in the public domain forever. However, there is an exception for certain foreign works. The copyrights in some foreign works that were published in the United States before 1964 entered the public domain in the United States due to the copyright owner's failure to file a renewal registration. Because most foreign copyright laws did not follow a renewal system, many foreign works lost protection in the United States, although they were still protected in their country of origin.

The General Agreement on Trade and Tariffs (GATT) remedied this situation by restoring the copyright in certain foreign works effective as of January 1, 1996. In order for copyright in a foreign work to be restored, the following three conditions must be satisfied:

1.  The work must have been created by an author who is a citizen or resident of a member country of the Berne Convention, World Trade Organization, or another copyright treaty with the United States.

2.  The work must have been first published in the foreign country and not published in the United States within 30 days after foreign publication.

3.  The work's copyright must not have expired under the foreign country's copyright law.

Restoration only applies to foreign works and is intended to compensate for the inadvertent loss of copyright due to failure to renew, which was not required under foreign copyright laws. Restored works receive the same term they would have received if a renewal registration had been filed.

---

**Example 8.12**

A song was published in Germany in 1949 and in the U.S. in 1950. If the copyright owner failed to file a renewal registration in 1978, the work entered the public domain in the United States in 1979, although it was still protected under German copyright law. Under GATT, the copyright is automatically restored as of January 1, 1996, and lasts through 2045.

---

The copyright owner of a restored work cannot recover for infringements that occurred before 1996 when the work was in the public domain. Additionally, the copyright owner must give notice to people who continued to use the work after 1996 before filing an infringement suit against them.

**Example 8.13**

If a record company released a recording of the song from the previous example in 1980, the copyright owner could not recover damages from the record company for any records sold from 1980 to 1996 in the United States because the song was in the public domain during that time period. The copyright owner could, however, provide notice to the record company that the copyright has been restored in the United States and then recover for any infringements that occur after the record company's receipt of the notice.

## F. Duration of Assignments

It is important to understand the difference between the term of copyright as specified by law and the term of copyright ownership under a contract. A contract may limit a person's ownership of a copyrighted work to a period less than the full term of copyright protection. If an assignment of copyright does not clearly indicate the term of its duration, it will be deemed effective for the remainder of the copyright term, subject to the author's termination rights.

**Example 8.14**

A contract between a songwriter and a music publisher provides that the songwriter assign the copyright in a song to the publisher for 10 years. At the end of the 10-year period, the ownership of the song reverts to the songwriter. The songwriter would then own the song for the remaining period of copyright protection or could assign it to someone else.

# III. Copyright Term in Other Countries

While the rules for determining the duration of copyright vary from country to country, most countries are now members of the Berne Convention, which requires a term of at least 50 years after the death of a work's author. This is, however, just the minimum required, and many countries have a longer term of protection. While this book is mainly focused on copyright in the United States, the following is a brief summary of the term of copyright in some (but by no means all) other parts of the world. See Chapter 13, "International Copyright Protection," for more information on international protection of copyrights.

## A. Canada

Under the Copyright Act of Canada, the basic copyright term is for the life of the author plus 50 years. Sound recordings are protected for 50 years from the end of the year in which the original recording was created. Canadian copyright law does not have a provision for works made for hire like that of the United States. Instead, Canadian law only recognizes a party that hires someone to create a copyrightable work as the author if there is an employment relationship between the parties. Since, in the entertainment industry, many works (e.g., sound recordings and films) are created under independent contractor rather than employment relationships, the lack of work for hire status can result in significant problems. The best way to avoid such problems and ensure that a work is owned by a hiring party rather than the actual creator or creators is to have written contracts with anyone who could potentially be considered an author clearly stating that such potential authors transfer any copyright interest they may have to the hiring party.

## B. The European Union

The European Union (EU) consists of 27 countries in Europe that have decided to standardize many of their laws, including laws dealing with copyright. Several EU nations have well developed music industries, including the United Kingdom, France, Germany, Spain, Italy, and Sweden. Although each EU country has its own copyright law, all EU countries' copyright laws follow some basic agreed-upon provisions, such as the term of copyright protection.

As in the United States, the general copyright term is for the life of the author plus 70 years. One important exception to the general term is for sound recordings, which have a term of 50 years from the date of first publication (or 50 years after creation for non-published recordings). For more information on the current status of sound recordings in the EU and the potential future extension in their term of protection, see Chapter 13.

## C. Australia

Until 2005, the term of protection for most copyrighted works in Australia was for the life of the author plus 50 years. However, beginning in 2005, the term was increased to the life of the author plus 70 years as part of an agreement under the U.S.-Australia Free Trade Agreement. This means that the term of protection for Australian copyrights is different, depending on the date of the author's death. For works published during the lifetime of an author who died in 1956 or earlier, the term was the author's life plus 50 years. For works published during the lifetime of an author who died after 1956, the term is the author's life plus 70 years. Works published after the author's death are protected for the author's life plus 70 years, and unpublished works can be protected indefinitely (unless eventually published). Sound recordings are protected for a term of 70 years from their first publication.

## D. Japan

Over the past several decades, Japan has developed a thriving entertainment industry that produces products popular throughout much of the world, including music, film, manga (comics), anime (animated cartoons), and computer games. For example, Japan is the second biggest market for sales of music recordings in the world after the United States. Accordingly, copyright protection has become an increasingly important issue for Japanese creators and businesses.

Japan's copyright law provides for a basic term of protection lasting for the life of the author plus 50 years. If a copyright is created as a work made for hire to be owned by a business entity, the term is for 50 years from publication (or 50 years from creation if the work is unpublished). Sound recordings have a term of 50 years from first publication.

There is an odd exception for certain foreign copyrights under Japanese copyright law, which is the result of Japan's defeat in World War II (WWII). Copyrighted works in existence at the beginning of WWII (December 7, 1941) or created or acquired up until the end of WWII (September 1945) owned by citizens of the countries that fought against Japan (the Allied Powers) get an extension of copyright for 3,794 days. So an American copyright that was in existence during WWII would be protected in Japan for the life of the American author plus 60.3 years instead of the usual life of the author plus 50 year term.

### E. China

China has a relatively small music market due largely to its high rate of piracy. However, as the world's second biggest economy, which is still developing rapidly, there is huge potential for growth despite the prevalence of piracy. Further, Hong Kong and Taiwan (the Republic of China) have long been important music industry centers in Asia, and the music industry in mainland China appears to be growing somewhat in recent years. China provides for a basic copyright term lasting for the life of the author plus 50 years. If a copyright is owned as a work made for hire by a business entity, the term lasts for 50 years from the work's first publication (or 50 years from creation if the work is unpublished). Sound recordings have a term of protection of 50 years from their first publication (or 50 years from creation if not published).

### F. South Korea

South Korea is another Asian country with a very modern, high-technology–oriented economy and a thriving music industry. Korean pop music (known as K-Pop) has become extremely popular throughout most of Asia and has even had some success in the West in recent years. Korean copyright law provides for a term consisting of the author's life plus 50 years. However, if a work is published 40 years after the death of its author but before 50 years after the author's death, the copyright is extended for 10 years after its publication date. Sound recordings are protected for 50 years from their first publication (or 50 years from creation if not published).

### G. Mexico

Mexico is a country that has a relatively high rate of copyright piracy and is often criticized for poor enforcement of its copyright laws by the United States. However, one way that Mexico provides more copyright protection than any other country in the world is with respect to the term of protection. Until 2003, Mexico's copyright law provided a term lasting for the life of the author plus 75 years. Although that was five years more than the copyright term for any other country at that time, Mexico extended its term to 100 years after the author's death beginning on July 23, 2003. This extension does not apply retroactively, so only works created on or after July 23, 2003, last for 100 years after the author's death. Sound recordings receive 75 years of protection from the date of creation.

## IV. The Rule of the Shorter Term

The Berne Convention requires that all member countries have a general minimum copyright term of the author's life plus 50 years. However, many countries protect copyrights for a longer term, most commonly for the author's life plus 70 years. Consequently, a copyrighted work can be protected for different periods of time in different countries. A work could also be in the public domain in one country and still protected by copyright in another country that has a longer term of protection.

While the Berne Convention requires that member countries give national treatment for foreign works, there is an important exception known as the rule of the shorter term. This rule allows countries that have a comparatively long copyright term the option of applying a shorter term to foreign works by using the term of the foreign work's country of origin. In other words, if Country A has a longer term of copyright than Country B, instead of protecting a foreign work from Country B for its own term (under the national treatment principle), Country A has the option of protecting the work for the term provided by Country B's copyright law (the shorter term).

---

**Example 8.15**

Jimin Kim, a South Korean singer-songwriter, writes and records a song that becomes popular in France after Ms. Kim dies in a tragic accident while touring in France in 2010. Although French copyright law provides for a term of the author's life plus 70 years, if France applies the rule of the shorter term, the song would only be protected until 2060, since South Korean copyright provides for a shorter term (life plus 50 years) than French copyright (life plus 70 years).

---

The rule of the shorter term can have a negative impact on American copyrights, especially with respect to works first published in the United States from 1923 to 1963 that were not renewed as required by the 1909 Copyright Act. Many such works were not renewed and therefore entered the public domain after 28 years of copyright. Although these works would still be protected under the laws of most other countries (which had no renewal requirement), most countries apply the rule of the shorter term (that of the United States in this situation), which results in these works being in the public domain in these countries.

Some countries, such as Brazil, China, Mexico, South Korea, and the United States, do not follow the rule of the shorter term. Other countries generally follow the rule but provide exceptions for U.S. copyrights under certain treaties or agreements with the United States. Canada, for example, does not apply the rule of the shorter term to U.S. works due to provisions of the North American Free Trade Agreement. Another important exception is that the United Kingdom does not apply the rule of the shorter term for works that were protected by copyright before July 1, 1996. Consequently, a work published in the U.S. between 1923 and 1963 that was not renewed (and is therefore in the public domain in the U.S.) could still be protected in the United Kingdom.

# Endnotes
1. *Harry Fox Agency, Inc. v. Mills Music, Inc.,* 543 F. Supp. 844 (1982).
2. 17 U.S.C. § 304(a)(4)(b).
3. 318 U.S. 643 (1943).

 4.  17 U.S.C. § 302(a).
 5.  17 U.S.C. § 302(b), as amended by the Copyright Term Extension Act of 1998.
 6.  17 U.S.C. § 302(c).
 7.  17 U.S.C. § 303(c).
 8.  *Eldred v. Ashcroft,* 537 U.S. 186 (2003).
 9.  For example, Eldritch Press (owned by Eric Eldred, who was the lead plaintiff in *Eldred v. Ashcroft*) is an online publisher of free public domain books. See http://www.eldritchpress .org/.
10.  See Chapter 4 for a discussion of termination rights.

# 9  Copyright Formalities

*"I didn't know anything about copyright laws or anything like that. I didn't have $2 a lot of times to have a copyright paper on a song sent into Congress."*

—*Willie Dixon*, I Am the Blues

Throughout most of the twentieth century, copyright protection in the United States had been conditioned upon compliance with certain formal requirements: copyright registration, deposit, and notice. Because of the 1976 Copyright Act's amendment by the Berne Convention Implementation Act of 1988, these formalities are no longer required as a condition to copyright protection, and registration and notice are both optional (although strongly recommended). However, these formalities still serve practical functions and continue to provide important benefits to copyright owners.

## I. The Copyright Office

Until 1870, copyright ownership claims were recorded by clerks of the United States District Courts. In 1870, the Library of Congress was given the responsibility of handling copyright registrations, and in 1897, the United States Copyright Office was formed as a department of the Library of Congress to handle this responsibility.

The Copyright Office processes registration applications and maintains records of copyright registrations and other recorded documents dealing with copyright ownership, such as assignments, wills, mortgages, and security interests.[1]

In addition to handling copyright registrations, the Copyright Office also performs some other important functions. Some of these functions are

- Advising Congress on anticipated changes in United States copyright law as well as compliance with international treaties.
- Analyzing and assisting in drafting copyright legislation.
- Conducting studies for Congress on copyright matters.
- Providing assistance to foreign countries in developing their copyright laws.

- Issuing regulations dealing with copyright in order to implement the provisions of the Copyright Act. After adoption, all regulations are listed in Volume 37 of the Code of Federal Regulations. Finally, all regulations are subject to court challenge if they are not consistent with the Copyright Act.

- Conducting searches of the Copyright Office indexes and records and assisting members of the public making their own searches.

- Providing the public with information about copyright law and about the Copyright Office's policies and practices. However, Copyright Office employees are not allowed to give specific legal advice regarding copyright issues such as infringement. The Copyright Office is also not authorized to refer members of the public to lawyers, publishers, or agents.

---

**The Copyright Office as a Resource** The Copyright Office is an excellent source of information on copyright law in general and copyright registration specifically. It provides easy-to-understand summaries on different subjects dealing with copyright (known as Information Circulars), forms and instructions for submitting registration applications, and summaries of recent and pending changes to copyright law. Much of this information is available from the Copyright Office website at www.copyright.gov. The Copyright Office is also open to the public from 8:30 a.m. to 5:00 p.m. on weekdays and is located at 101 Independence Avenue, S.E., Washington, D.C.

---

## A. Structure of the Copyright Office

The 1976 Copyright Act sets forth the rules governing the role and responsibilities of the Copyright Office. Under Section 701(a), the person responsible for the overall direction of the Copyright Office is the Register of Copyrights, who is appointed by the Librarian of Congress. The Register has the authority to carry out the Copyright Office's responsibilities by delegating those duties to specific divisions within the Copyright Office. Though the division titles may change over time, the primary functions of the Copyright Office are carried out through the following programmatic entities:

---

**Note:** In 2007 the Copyright Office implemented a major reengineering initiative to improve the efficiency of its operations, resulting in the introduction of electronic filing for copyright registrations and the reorganization of division titles and functions.

---

### (1) Receipt Analysis and Control Division

The Receipt Analysis and Control Division is responsible for receiving materials such as registration applications and transfer documents for recordation. It records and deposits payments for copyright fees. It also establishes and maintains deposit accounts, routes applications for registration, and handles incomplete claims. Finally, this division maintains files on all office correspondence cases, assigns copyright registration numbers, and creates and mails certificates of registration.

### (2) Registration Program

The Registration Program, consisting of three divisions—the Literary, Performing Arts, and Visual Arts Divisions—examines registration and renewal applications and any accompanying materials such as deposit copies. It typically registers over 600,000 applications a year.[2] The examination process consists of making sure that the application has been filled out correctly and that the material deposited constitutes copyrightable subject matter. It is important to understand that the Copyright Office makes no decision as to the validity of a registration applicant's ownership claim. In reality, the Copyright Office registers claims of copyright ownership rather than granting or issuing copyrights. If the materials submitted are in order, the Copyright Office will issue a certificate of registration. If any necessary information is missing, the examiner will contact the applicant by letter or phone to try to resolve any problems.

### (3) Information and Records Division

The Information and Records Division is responsible for educating the Copyright Office staff as well as the public. It prepares and distributes informational materials and responds to reference requests. Additionally, the Information and Records Division prepares search reports upon request for an hourly fee. This service can be extremely helpful if you want to find out information about a specific copyrighted work such as who is claiming ownership of the work and how that ownership has been obtained. The Information and Records Division also prepares certifications and other legal documents and processes recordation of transfer documents.

---

**Tip:**   Because Copyright Office fees are adjusted from time to time, check the Copyright Office's website for current search fees.

---

### (4) Licensing Division

The Licensing Division is responsible for carrying out compulsory license provisions of the Copyright Act such as the compulsory license for making and distributing phonorecords (discussed in Chapter 5, "The Reproduction Right") and for the distribution of digital audio recording devices or media (discussed in Chapter 14, "Copyright and Digital Technology").

### (5) Copyright Acquisitions Division

The Copyright Acquisitions Division administers the mandatory deposit provisions and issues demands for published works that have not been deposited.

---

**NewsNet**   The Copyright Office distributes a free electronic newsletter called NewsNet over the Internet. NewsNet alerts subscribers of proposed regulations, hearings, deadlines for public comments, new publications, and other information. You can subscribe to NewsNet at the Copyright Office website.

---

## B. Copyright Office Records

The Copyright Card Catalog consists of over 40 million individual cards and comprises an index for copyright registrations in the United States from 1870 to 1977. The Copyright Card Catalog and post-1977 automated files provide a comprehensive index to copyright registrations in the United States from 1870 to the present.

The Catalog of Copyright Entries consists of the Copyright Card Catalog in book form from July 1, 1891, to 1978 and in microfiche form from 1979 through 1982. From the Copyright Office website, you can search the online copyright catalog of public records to access records of copyright registrations from 1978 to present. Works registered prior to 1978 can only be found in the Copyright Card Catalog located in the Copyright Public Records Reading Room of the Copyright Office.

The Assignment and Related Documents Index can also be searched to investigate the ownership of a copyright. Assignment documents recorded after 1977 can be searched online at the Copyright Office website.

---

**Note:** The Copyright Office has implemented a digitization project to permit future online searching of pre-1977 records. The multi-year project was implemented as a pilot in fiscal year 2009 and continues as an ongoing initiative (no longer in pilot phase but as yet incomplete) as of this writing.

---

# II. Copyright Registration

Developing creative works represents an important investment of time, effort, and other valuable resources. Consequently, taking steps to secure your work is an important aspect of protecting your investment. Like installing an alarm system to protect your home, taking precautions to protect your intellectual property does not ensure that there will be no intruders. Rather, such precautions put the world on notice that you are asserting your right to protect what is yours. Likewise, copyright registration provides a way of staking your claim to protection of your creative works, positions you to enforce your rights in the event of infringement, and provides other important benefits.

## A. What Is Copyright Registration?

Many people have the mistaken belief that in order to own a copyright to a work, you have to register the work. In fact, copyright ownership arises automatically upon creation of a copyrightable work (see Chapter 3, "What Can Be Protected by Copyright?") and is not dependent upon registration. However, Section 408 of the Copyright Act provides for an optional registration system. Copyright registration essentially means that someone has made a claim of ownership to a work as of a certain date. Specifically, Section 408(a) of the Copyright Act states:

> [T]he owner of copyright or of any exclusive right in the work may obtain registration of the copyright claim by delivering to the Copyright Office the deposit specified by this section, together with the application and fee specified by sections 409 and 708. Such registration is not a condition of copyright protection.

However, the fact that someone has registered a work claiming to be the copyright owner does not absolutely guarantee that he is really the owner, because a registration can be contested in court. In other words, if you wrote a song and someone else registered the copyright claiming to be the owner, you can sue him, alleging that his ownership claim and registration are invalid. Of course, you would have to offer proof that you really are the owner, but assuming you could do so, the court (not the Copyright Office) would invalidate the other party's fraudulent registration.

## B. Why Should You Register?

Although registration is not required to own a copyright, there are important benefits that are gained by registering a work. In general, copyright registration can be thought of as a relatively cheap form of insurance. Although it doesn't guarantee that your work will never be infringed (i.e., violated), it makes it easier to prove that you own the work and to legally pursue infringements if they occur. The specific benefits afforded by registration are the following:

- **Registration creates a public record of your claim of copyright ownership.** Once a work has been registered, it is indexed in the Copyright Office records under the work's title and the author's name. Because the Copyright Office records are public records, anyone can search these records to determine who owns a work. This helps people find out who they need to obtain licenses from to use the work and helps to prevent fraudulent transfers of copyright ownership.

- **Registration provides what is legally known as *prima facie* (at first sight) evidence of ownership.** This means that if an ownership dispute ever arises, a court will presume that the registered claimant is the copyright owner unless the other party can disprove the registrant's ownership claim. Additionally, if you register within five years of a work's initial publication, a court will also assume that all of the information contained in the registration is valid. If a registration is made after five years of the work's publication, the amount of evidentiary weight given to the copyright certificate is up to the court.

- **Registration gives the copyright owner the ability to file suit.** Under Section 411(a), you must register a work before you can file a copyright infringement suit.[3] This requirement applies to works first published in the United States or simultaneously in the United States and another country. It does not apply if the copyright owner is not a U.S. citizen or resident and the work is first published in a foreign country that is a Berne Convention member. Although you could register a work immediately prior to filing an infringement suit, it is better to register earlier because you would either have to wait until your registration application is processed, which usually takes at least six months, or pay an additional fee for an expedited registration (see section G below).

---

**Tip:** At the time of this book's writing, the fee for expedited registration was $760, but because fees are subject to change, check the Copyright Office website for current fees.

---

- **Early registration entitles the copyright owner to attorneys' fees and statutory damages.** If a work is registered prior to its infringement or within three months after its first publication, the owner has the right to elect to receive statutory damages and attorneys' fees in a success-ful infringement claim (see Chapter 12, "Remedies for Copyright Infringement," for an explanation of the various remedies for copyright infringement). This can be extremely important because it is sometimes difficult to prove the actual monetary amount by which you are damaged due to an infringement. Further, the actual amount of damages may be comparatively small, while the cost of litigating an infringement claim can be quite high. Finally, an infringer who knows you have registered may be more willing to settle due to the possibility of being held liable for statutory damages and attorneys' fees.

- **Registration allows copyright owners to collect mechanical license royalties.** Copyright own-ers of musical compositions must register in order to be able to collect compulsory mechani-cal license royalties (discussed in Chapter 5).

- **Registration allows copyright owners to block importation of illegal copies.** Registration allows the copyright owner to record its ownership claim with the United States Customs Service in order to prevent the importation of infringing copies.

### C. Who Can Register?

Anyone who owns all or part of the exclusive rights to a copyrighted work (or their authorized agent) can register a work. This would normally include: (1) any of the work's authors; and (2) any party that acquires ownership of any of the exclusive rights. If only partial rights in a work are transferred, several parties may be entitled to register, although only one registration is needed to protect all owners, and normally only one registration should be made.

---

**Example 9.1**

If a songwriter transfers copyright ownership to a publisher, the publisher would have the right to register the song. The songwriter should make sure that the publisher does so, because even though the writer is no longer the song's owner, the writer will normally still have a royalty interest under its contract with the publisher in the song and will likely have termination rights as well if the song was not created as a work made for hire (see Chapter 4, "Ownership of Copyright," for an explanation of termination of transfers).

---

**Example 9.2**

If four members of a band co-write a song, any of them may register the copyright. However, it is not necessary for more than one of them to register because only one registration is required to protect all co-owners.

---

### D. When Should You Register?

A work can be registered at any time during its term of copyright. Ideally, however, you should register a work as soon as possible after its creation. It is also highly advantageous to register within three months after a work's initial publication in order to have the right to receive statu-tory damages and attorney's fees in an infringement action. Publication means a work has been made available to the public in some form (e.g., in print, in digital form online, etc.), either by sale, rental, or being given away.

Many copyright owners do not register their works immediately after they are created because they do not want to pay the $35 to $65 registration fee (depending on whether online or paper registration is chosen). For instance, a publisher that acquires ownership of many songs might not want to incur the registration fee for each song until it knows whether specific songs will generate any income.

---

**When to Register Copyrights** As a practical rule, we recommend that you register copyrights as soon as you know the work is going to be published (e.g., when a song is recorded by an artist or licensed for use in a movie) and at the latest, within three months after publication. Additionally, authors can register multiple unpublished works as a collection as discussed below.

---

## E. How to Register?

Generally, the registration process is very straightforward. You have the option of choosing one of two ways to apply for copyright registration, either by: (1) Filing an application with the Electronic Copyright Office (eCO) online system at the Copyright Office website; or, (2) Submitting a paper application form to the Copyright Office via regular surface mail. An explanation of each process follows. No matter which registration process you choose, an application must include three essential components: (a) A completed application form; (b) submission of a deposit—deposit refers to a copy of the work being registered, and is discussed in the following "Copyright Deposit" section; and, (c) payment of the appropriate application fee.

---

**Tip:** All application fees described below are the most current at the time of this writing; however, Copyright Office fees are subject to change; therefore it is always best to check www.copyright.gov for fee updates.

---

### (1) Applying through the Electronic Copyright Office Online System (eCO)

Electronic registration online is recommended as the fastest, least expensive method to submit your application form to the Copyright Office. Eighty percent of all registration applications are processed electronically, which has substantially increased the Copyright Office's timeliness since eCO was implemented in July 2008.[4] The average processing time for eCO applications is three (3) months, while the average processing time for paper applications is eleven (11) months. In addition to receiving faster processing times than paper applications, the fee for electronic applications is $35, which is the lowest application fee available for any of the registration processes. Additional advantages of using eCO include: 24-hour access to the system to track your application's status online; secure payment of the application fee through credit/debit card, electronic check, or deposit account; and the ability to upload certain types of deposits directly to eCO (instead of having to submit the deposit by mail).

A basic overview of the steps involved in applying online follows:

- Click on the eCO link at the Copyright Office website.

- You must have an e-mail address to use eCO.

- You must register with eCO to create a user ID and password. You will need to retain these to create and access your eCO application(s).

- Complete the online application using the prompts and instructions provided during the online process and using the suggestions provided below under "Filling Out the Application."

- Review all information you have entered carefully before clicking "Checkout" (which takes you to a payment screen). Use the navigation bar provided to go back and make corrections, if necessary.

- Pay the application fee. You must pay the application fee before you will be prompted to upload your deposit. After you have successfully submitted payment (the system will inform you as to whether your payment was received, and you will also receive an e-mail receipt), you will click "Continue" to proceed to selecting a method by which to submit your deposit.

- Submit your deposit. You may attach it to your online application by uploading it directly to eCO. If this method of submission is elected, the system will indicate whether your upload was successful. If you do not have an electronic copy of the work or if your electronic files do not meet eCO requirements for uploading (see www.copyright.gov/eco/help-file-types.html for a list of acceptable file types), you may still file the application via eCO to receive the $35 application fee, but can request a shipping label by clicking on the "Create Shipping Slip" link for submission of the deposit by mail. To meet the "best edition" requirement for deposit of published works, certain types of works may not be uploaded to eCO. See the following "What to Deposit" section for a definition of "best edition."

- If all deposit steps are completed correctly, the eCO will indicate that you have successfully filed your application(s), and a case number will be generated for each registration. An e-mail confirmation will also be forwarded to you using the e-mail address you provide during the application process. The confirmation e-mail should be retained for future reference, in the event you need to contact the Copyright Office concerning the application.

- Before logging off the system, you will have the opportunity to print a hard copy of your registration(s) for your records, if desired. You can return to eCO at any time in the future to track the status of an application using the case number provided.

---

**Tip:** An online tutorial with step-by-step instructions on how to register your work using the eCO is also available at www.copyright.gov and is recommended to supplement this basic overview. The tutorial includes details such as what types of works are suitable for eCO registration. For technical questions about eCO, you may contact the Copyright Technology Office at (202) 707-3002.

---

### (2) Applying with Paper Registration Forms

Although electronic application is the recommended method for filing an application to register a work, paper registration is still permitted by the Copyright Office if desired. Paper options include either use of Form CO, which is a bar-coded form, or use of the traditional paper forms that are specific to the type of work to be registered.

#### (a) Fill-In Form CO

Form CO is a paper alternative to electronic registration. This fill-in form can be used for all types of works, is easy to use, and contains 2-D barcode scanning technology that enables the Copyright Office to scan the form. At the time this book went to press, the Copyright Office was considering elimination of Form CO. If the form is eliminated, the forms referenced in the following "Traditional Paper Registration Forms" section would remain as the sole paper alternatives to electronic registration. However, it is important to note that even if Form CO is retained, studies by the Copyright Office have shown a high rate of user error, and it may be best to use the traditional paper registration forms. If Form CO is retained and you desire to use it, the instructions in this section may be used for its completion.

The form can be downloaded from the Copyright Office website at http://www.copyright.gov/forms and is available in Adobe Acrobat PDF format, so you will need the Adobe Acrobat Reader (the most current version is recommended and can be downloaded for free) to read and print the forms. The application fee for Form CO is $50 unless a faulty form is submitted. Faulty (incorrectly completed or spoiled) forms will be charged a fee of $65.[5] Form CO was originally intended to replace traditional Forms TX, VA, SR, PA, and SE. However, these forms are still accepted by the Copyright Office and are discussed in the following "Traditional Paper Registration Forms" section. Here is an overview of the steps involved in using Form CO.

---

Note:  Form CO cannot be used for group registrations.

---

■ Complete Form CO by checking the appropriate box to indicate the type of work being registered and by using the downloadable instructions available. (See also the suggestions provided in the following "Filling Out the Application" section.)

■ Even though use of Form CO is considered a paper application process, the form must be completed online and then printed; do not attempt to print a blank form for manual completion or to alter it with ink after online completion.

■ Print the form after completing it. The form will automatically print with a shipping label that must be used for mailing the application and deposit.

■ Form CO cannot be saved and reused since the barcode is unique to each work to be registered. Additionally, photocopies of the form cannot be used (unlike the traditional paper forms described in the following section).

■ Mail the application, deposit, and application fee using the form's instructions. See the suggestions provided in the following "Submitting the Application" section.

**Tip:** After printing, check to make sure your Form CO has a barcode on each page. Screen shots are not acceptable substitutes for the barcoded form. Additional tips for completing Form CO are available at www.copyright.gov/forms/notice.html.

*(b) Traditional Paper Registration Forms*

Electronic applications are recommended for seeking copyright registration. However, the Copyright Office permits registration through the use of several paper forms: TX, VA, SR, PA, and SE. In fact, some works can only be registered using the traditional paper forms. (For a list of these works, see http://www.copyright.gov/circs/circ01.pdf.) The filing fee for these forms is $65 per application, the most expensive application fee of all registration methods.

The traditional form names are based on the type of work to be registered (e.g., musical works, sound recordings, literary works), as described later in this section. The forms most commonly used in the music industry are Forms PA and SR, but Forms TX and VA are sometimes used as well.

**Form PA:** Works of the performing arts. This form should be used to register all works prepared to be performed directly before an audience. Form PA is used to register musical works (including accompanying words), dramatic works (including accompanying music), choreographic works, motion pictures and other audiovisual works, and multimedia works (works combining text with graphics, videos, and sounds).

**Form SR: Sound Recordings.** This form should be used to register sound recordings fixed on or after February 15, 1972 (sound recordings created before February 15, 1972, are not protected by federal copyright). Generally, Form SR covers only the series of sounds that make up the recording and not any musical, literary, or dramatic works contained on the recording. However, it is possible to use Form SR to register the underlying musical composition or album cover artwork as well as the sound recording in certain circumstances. In order to do so, the owner must be the same party, and you must specify that the application covers both works in the authorship statement in Space 2 of the form.

**Form TX: Nondramatic Literary Works.** This form is used to register written works such as books, poetry, magazine articles, etc. It can also be used to register song lyrics apart from music accompanying them.

**Form VA: Works of the Visual Arts.** This form is used to register pictorial, graphic, and sculptural works. Form VA can also be used for album cover art when the copyright owner is different than the copyright owner of the sound recording (when the copyright owner is the same, Form SR can be used for both).

The Copyright Office also has short forms available for the registration of certain works by their authors. The short forms are simplified versions of the full forms, consisting of one page rather than two, and are available for forms PA, TX, and VA. They can only be used if there is only one author and owner of the work, the work is not a work made for hire, the work is completely new, and the form is signed by the work's author.

Registration forms can be easily obtained from the Copyright Office in the following three ways:

**By Phone:** Call the Forms Hotline at 202-707-9100. This is an automated system that is available 24 hours a day. Leave your name and mailing address and specify the type of form and number of forms needed. The Copyright Office will send up to 10 copies of each form.

**By Mail:** Write to: Library of Congress, Copyright Office-COPUBS, 101 Independence Avenue S.E., Washington, D.C. 20559-6304.

**Online:** Forms can be downloaded from the Copyright Office's website at http://www.copyright. gov/forms/. The forms are available in Adobe Acrobat PDF format. You will need the Adobe Acrobat Reader (the most current version is recommended and can be downloaded for free) to read and print the forms. You can also request the forms online by filling out a request form at www.copyright.gov/forms/formrequest.html, and the forms will be mailed to you.

---

**Tip:**   You may use photocopies of the traditional paper forms (not Form CO), and the Copyright Office actually encourages doing so in order to save taxpayers paper and printing costs. Copies must be clear, on a good grade of white letter-size paper, and reproduced in two-sided copies with the top of the second page of the form at the same end as the top of the first page. Forms that do not satisfy these requirements will be returned.

---

### (3) Completing Registration Forms

Whether applying electronically or via paper application, the registration form should be completed carefully using the following suggestions that generally apply to all processes.

It is very important that you fill out registration forms clearly and accurately because it is possible that the form could be needed in court to prove your ownership claim. A person who intentionally lies on an application form is subject to a fine of up to $2,500. Copyright registration forms require the applicant to fill in information about the copyright claimant and the author of the work, information potentially required to determine the copyright's duration (i.e., creation date and author's death), and the basis of ownership for any parties other than the work's author. For purposes of illustration, the following describes how to supply these aspects of the registration for a musical work.

#### (a) Title Information

The applicant must supply information about the work's title in the "Title" space. The title you supply is used by the Copyright Office to index the work once it is registered. You should also supply any previous or alternative titles that identify the work. Finally, you must give a brief description of the nature of the work. This description is important because it is used by the examiner to determine whether the work is copyrightable. If the examiner finds the description to be insufficient or if it describes material not contained in your deposit, the examiner will usually send you a letter requesting that you correct and resubmit the application. Do not use the work's title as a description or merely specify the idea or concept that the work is based on.

Usually, a simple description of the work will suffice. For example, if the work is a song, you should specify "music and lyrics." If you are registering a sound recording, the description should generally be "performance and sound recording." If you also want to claim copyright ownership of any underlying works contained in a sound recording such as songs, artwork, photographs, or textual material (e.g., liner notes), you must clearly specify the material. However, if any of these underlying works were created by someone other than the author(s) of the sound recording, separate registration of those works will be required.

### (b) Author Information

You must give information about the author or authors of the work in the "Author" space. If a work has more than three authors use a Continuation Sheet (Form CON) for traditional paper registrations to list the additional authors and attach it to your registration form (do not staple or tape it to the form). Continuation Sheets are not needed for Form CO, as the PDF form contains online buttons to click on that will create additional space. The eCO form also contains an online button for entering additional authors' names.

A work's author is the person who created the work unless the work is a work made for hire, in which case the employer or commissioning party is the author. If the work is a work made for hire, you can include the name of the creator as well as the employer or commissioning party to make it part of the public record, although this is not required. You should specify the full legal name of the author, whether an individual or a business.

In addition to the authors' names, you must also fill in the authors' dates of birth and death (leave blank if the author is still living), the country of the authors' nationality, whether the work was made anonymously or under a pseudonym, and the nature of authorship.

If the author is anonymous, you can leave the author line blank or mark it N/A, write "anonymous" in the space, or state the author's name. However, if you specify the author's name, it will be part of the public record and can be discovered by anyone who searches the registration files.

If the author is using a pseudonym, you can leave the space blank, specify the pseudonym and identify it as such, or specify the author's actual name and the pseudonym.

An author's date of birth is not required to be filled in, but the date of death is required unless the author is anonymous or pseudonymous because it determines the work's expiration date. If the author is a corporation or other business entity, leave these spaces blank. The author's nationality or domicile is also mandatory. An author's domicile is the author's country of principal residence.

The "nature of authorship" description should identify the author's contribution to the work. If the work is a derivative work, you must specify only the new, original material added to the pre-existing work. Failure to do so can jeopardize your copyright registration.[6] If there is more than one author, specify the nature of each individual author's contributions.

**Example 9.3**

> If two authors co-wrote a song, with one writing the music and the other writing the lyrics, the nature of authorship descriptions would be "music" for the composer and "lyrics" for the lyricist. If both authors contributed music and lyrics, the description for each would be "music and lyrics."

### (c) Creation and Publication Dates

Specify the year in which the work was created in the "creation and publication dates" space. The creation date is the year in which the work was first fixed in tangible form. If the work has not been published, leave this space blank. If the work has been published, fill in the day, month, year, and country of publication. If you are not sure of the exact publication date, specify an approximate date as accurately as you can.

### (d) Copyright Claimant Information

Specify the name and address of the copyright claimants in the "claimant information" or "claimant" space. The claimants will be either the authors of the work or any parties that have acquired ownership of the work. If any copyright claimant is not an author of the work, you must also describe how that party acquired its ownership interest in this space. There are several ways in which ownership can be acquired, such as under a contract of transfer (commonly referred to as an "assignment of copyright"), by inheritance under a will or intestate succession, or by gift. If you don't have enough space to list all of the work's claimants, you can use Form CON for traditional paper forms.

**Example 9.4**

> If a music publisher is registering the copyright to a song it has acquired from a songwriter under contract, the publisher should state "by written contract" in the appropriate space. Please note that it is not necessary to include a copy of the contract with the registration application, and you should not do so because there may be confidential information in the contract, and copyright registrations are public records.

### (e) Previous Registration

If the work you are registering has never been registered before, simply indicate this in the "previous registration" space.

If any part of the work has been registered, this is referred to as "Limitation of Claim" when using eCO or Form CO, and the check-off boxes provided make entering this information very straightforward. For Forms TX, VA, PA, SR, and SE, mark the "Yes" box and check one of the three choices in Spaces 5(a)–(c). Choice (a) applies to a work that was previously registered as an unpublished work. Choice (b) applies if an author is registering a work previously registered with someone other than the author listed as claimant. For example, this applies if the work had previously been registered under a pseudonym and the author now wants to register in its legal name. Choice (c) applies to a previously registered work that has been changed in some manner (i.e., a derivative work).

You must also provide the previous registration number and year of registration. The registration number is found stamped on the work's certificate of registration and consists of a two-letter prefix (three letters if the work was unpublished) followed by a number (e.g., PA 098765).

### (f) Derivative Work or Compilation

If the work you are registering is a derivative work or a compilation, you must so indicate in the appropriate space. This information will be requested under "Limitation of Claim" when using eCO or Form CO. If using a traditional paper form, if the preexisting material used in your work has not been published or registered and is not in the public domain, simply mark "N/A." Otherwise, you must identify the preexisting material used in your work and distinguish it on the form from any new material added. Your description of new material added can usually be the same as the description of the nature of authorship.

Some examples of derivative sound recordings include recordings with additional material, remixed recordings, and recordings with substantial editorial revisions. Your description should specifically distinguish the new material from the material comprising the original work. In order for a derivative work to be copyrightable, the new material must be substantial rather than minor changes. For example, a remastered recording would probably not be a copyrightable derivative.

**Example 9.5**

If you are registering a song that is based on a preexisting poem, you would identify the poem in the space provided for the preexisting work and describe the new material (i.e., music) in the space allotted for indicating the new material.

Copyright in a compilation of musical compositions or recordings is separate from the copyright in the individual compositions or recordings. The compilation copyright covers the selection and arrangement of the individual compositions or recordings as long as that selection and arrangement are original.

### (g) Deposit Account

If you have a deposit account with the Copyright Office, you can charge the registration application fee to it by specifying the account name in the appropriate space on the form. You can also specify the name and phone number of the account holder that the Copyright Office can contact if it has any questions concerning the account. Generally, it is worth having a deposit account only if you will be registering more than 12 works a year.

### (h) Certification

The application must be signed. Additionally, the person signing the application must indicate the capacity in which she is signing in this space. For applications submitted electronically, the signature should be typewritten in this space by entering the signatory's name. A handwritten signature is required for Form CO and the traditional paper forms. The application may be signed by any of the following people:

**Author:** Only one author is required to sign even if there is more than one.

**Copyright claimant other than an author:** Anyone who is not an author of the work but has acquired ownership of all of the author's rights (such as a publisher).

**Owner of exclusive right(s):** Anyone who has acquired some but not all of the exclusive rights in the work (such as an exclusive licensee).

**Authorized agent:** Anyone who is an authorized representative of the author, claimant, or owner of exclusive rights (such as an officer or employee of a corporation or an attorney). You must also specify the name of the individual or organization on whose behalf you are signing.

---

**Tip:** If you are registering a published work, make sure that the date specified in the certification space is not earlier than the date of publication specified in the "date of publication" space.

---

### (4) Submitting the Registration Application

If submitting a paper application, you should mail the application and deposit a copy or copies along with a check or money order covering the registration fee in a single package after you have completed the application form. Your check or money order must be made payable to the "Register of Copyrights." Mail your package to Register of Copyrights, Copyright Office, Library of Congress, Washington, D.C. 20559. If you are submitting the registration electronically, eCO will guide you through each step for finalizing the application prior to submission, as described in the preceding "Applying Through the eCO" section.

---

**Keep a Copy and Track Your Package**  Before mailing a paper application to the Copyright Office, you should photocopy it and retain the copy for your records along with an exact copy of your deposit. Send paper registration applications by registered or certified mail, return receipt requested, in order to make sure that the Copyright Office receives your application package. Approximately three weeks after mailing your package for a paper application, you should receive a receipt card that specifies the date the package was received by the Copyright Office. If you have questions about registration, you may call the Copyright Office at 202-707-3000; an information specialist should be able to help you. A description of all the registration methods described here can be found at the "How to Register a Work" link at the Copyright Office homepage.

---

## F. Registering a Collection of Works

In certain circumstances, it is possible to register more than one work on one application form and pay only one fee.[7] This can be very beneficial, especially to prolific songwriters who would otherwise have to spend $35 to $65 for each song they register. Registration of a collection of works is not the same as registration of group works. For information on group works, see www.copyright.gov/forms/index.html#group.

You can register a collection of songs using one application and pay a single application fee, provided that the following five requirements are satisfied:

- The works to be registered must be unpublished.

- The same person or company must own all rights in the works and in the collection as a whole.

- The works must be by the same author, or if they are by different authors, at least one of the authors must have contributed copyrightable authorship to each work.

- The collection must be assembled in an orderly form. For example, if you are using a CD for your deposit, clearly specify the number of songs and the title of each song in the order that they are contained on the CD.

- The collection must be identified by a single title. For example, we could name a collection of our songs *Dave's and Cheryl's Greatest Hits*.

---

**Example 9.6**

In *Sylvestre v. Oswald*, two musicians sued Jani Lane of the glam rock band Warrant, alleging that his song "Heaven" was an infringement of their song of the same title. The musicians had obtained a registration for a collection of songs entitled *Cherry Bomb*. Although "Heaven" was included in the collection, it was not identified on the registration certificate. The issue decided by the court involved whether the registration for the *Cherry Bomb* collection extended to the individual song "Heaven." The court held that it did because "Heaven" was contained on the deposit tape submitted with the application.[8] The court denied Lane's motion to dismiss the suit, finding that the musicians had produced evidence of ownership and offered sufficient evidence of access and substantial similarity for a jury decision to be required. The evidence of access was that tapes of the song were distributed to musicians in the Los Angeles and San Francisco rock scene in 1985, that the song was performed at parties in Los Angeles from 1984 to 1987 (where Lane was present), and that the song was played at a Los Angeles studio where Lane worked. As far as substantial similarity, the court concluded that the melody, lyrics, and phrasing of the two songs were virtually identical, including the lyrics "heaven isn't too far away" being sung to eight identical notes. Because a jury trial never took place, it appears that the parties must have reached a settlement.

---

Even though the copyright in a collection of songs covers the individual songs contained in the collection, there is a small practical problem that can arise from registering works as a collection. When you register a group of works as a collection, only the title of the collection will be indexed in the Copyright Office records. Because the individual songs contained in the collection are not indexed in the Copyright Office Catalog of Entries, someone who searches the Copyright Office records to find out whether one of the songs has been registered will not find the song title. There is, however, a way to prevent this problem from occurring. After you receive a registration certificate for a collection, you can file a Form CA listing the individual titles of songs contained in the collection. Although filing Form CA involves an additional fee (currently $100), it will cause the Copyright Office to index each song title. If you have four or more songs, registering them as a collection and filing a Form CA listing the individual song titles will be less costly than registering each song individually.

## G. Expedited Registration

The registration process usually takes three to eleven months, depending on whether you are filing electronically or via paper submission. However, it is possible to request that the Copyright Office expedite your application in certain circumstances. An expedited registration application will usually be processed within five days. Expedited registration is available only if the registration is needed for litigation, to meet a contractual or publishing deadline, or for some other urgent need as determined by the Copyright Office.

In order to obtain an expedited registration, you should file online at eCO, which provides the option to indicate "Special Handling," i.e., a request for expedited processing, when you complete the registration application online. Or you may send a letter stating why special handling is needed. Whether requesting special handling online or via mail, you will need to indicate the compelling reason for your request, e.g., if needed for litigation, state whether a case has already been filed, who the parties are or will be, and the court hearing the case. In addition to the normal application fee, an additional fee, currently $760, is required for an expedited registration.

If submitting your request for special handling by mail, mail your letter, application form, deposit, and check or money order to: Special Handling, Copyright RAC Division, P.O. Box 71380, Washington, D.C. 20024-1380, or to Special Handling, Department 100, Washington, D.C. 20540 if your package is larger than 12" × 18" × 4".

## H. The Examination Process

After the Copyright Office receives your registration application, it will examine the registration form and deposit material and will usually issue a registration certificate if everything is filled out correctly and the material is copyrightable. It is important to note that the Copyright Office does not make any judgment as to the merit of your copyright claim. Its review of applications is limited to whether the work is copyrightable and whether the applicant has satisfied the registration requirements.[9] Accordingly, the Copyright Office does not resolve disputes concerning ownership of a work; such determinations can only be made by courts of law.

You should receive some type of response from the Copyright Office within six months after your application is received, although sometimes the process takes longer due to the Copyright Office's workload. If you haven't received any response within eight months, send a letter to the Copyright Office identifying yourself, the copyright owners, authors, date of application, and form used and briefly describe the work. If you have a canceled check for the application fee, include a copy of it as well.

If your application is approved, you should receive a registration certificate (a copy of your application with the Copyright Office's official seal and a registration number and date). The effective date of registration is the date on which the Copyright Office receives all of the required materials, rather than the date the registration is actually issued.

If your application contains any errors or omissions, the Copyright Office will return the application with a letter explaining what needs to be corrected. You must respond to a request for correction within 120 days, or you will have to submit a new application and pay another fee. Some common errors to avoid include the following:

- Failure to sign the application form.

- Failure to enclose the application fee.

- Failure to provide the required deposit.

- Failure to adequately describe the nature of authorship of the work.

- Checking the work for hire box, but failing to list the employer as the work's author or claimant.

- Failure to specify how ownership was transferred to a claimant.

- Failure to describe new material in a derivative work.

---

**Tip:**   One of the advantages of filing through the eCO is that you will not be permitted to submit the application without passing the system edits that detect and help to avoid many of these errors.

---

If the Copyright Office determines that a work can't be registered, it will deny the application. In practice, the Copyright Office rarely denies registration. Under what is known as the rule of doubt, the Copyright Office will usually grant registration even if it has a reasonable doubt about the copyrightability of a work. When the Copyright Office is not sure about the copyrightability of a work, it will usually send a letter informing the applicant that its ownership claim may not be valid even though a registration is issued. If a dispute ever arose over the work's copyrightability, a court would have to make the ultimate determination.

If your application is denied, you can make a written objection and request that the Copyright Office reconsider the application. If your first appeal is refused, you can make a second request for reconsideration, which will be reviewed by the Copyright Office Board of Appeals consisting of the Register of Copyrights, the general counsel, and the chief of the examining division. If your second appeal is refused, you can bring a legal action for a court to review the Copyright Office's decision.

## I. Correcting and Supplementing Registrations

Once a registration has been made for a work, it is generally not possible to make additional registrations for the same work. However, you can correct or supplement information supplied in a previous registration using Form CA. The main reason for correcting or supplementing a registration is that if you are ever involved in a legal dispute over the copyright, the registration certificate will be used as evidence in court. If your certificate contains errors or omissions, it could be detrimental to your case. Additionally, keeping your registration information accurate and current will make it easier for people searching the Copyright Office records to contact you for permission to use your work.

### (1) Correcting a Registration

Form CA can be used to correct significant errors made in a registration application. Some examples would include incorrectly identifying an author or copyright claimant, registering an unpublished work as published, or inaccurately stating the extent of a claim. It is not necessary to use Form CA to correct obvious errors that the Copyright Office should have caught; immaterial, inadvertent errors will not affect the status of your registration. Instead, simply send the Copyright Office a letter notifying them of the error and requesting that it be corrected. Although it is permissible to file a supplemental registration to correct or amplify information contained in the original registration, this does not mean that the type of corrections or amplifications that can be made is unlimited.

---

**Example 9.7**

An appeals court ruled that songwriters who had initially registered a musical composition as an "audiovisual work" (with a copy of a music video for deposit) could not file a supplemental registration to change the nature of the work registered to the "performance" of the song.[10] The court believed that the songwriters were trying to change the nature of the work rather than merely correct or amplify information contained in the original registration. The reason for the requested change was that the district court had dismissed the songwriters' copyright infringement suit against an advertising agency, holding that the advertising agency owned the copyright to the video.

---

### (2) Supplementing a Registration

You can also use Form CA to supplement the information contained in an existing registration. You can supplement a registration by providing additional information or by clarifying information provided in the registration. This would usually be done when there has been a change in some of the information that occurred after the registration was made. The supplementary registration must clearly identify the registration it refers to (include the registration number, title of the work, and date issued). Some examples of supplementary information include the following:

■ Change of address: It is not required that you supplement your registration when you change addresses, but it is a good idea to do so in order for potential licensees to contact you.

■ Change in the claimant's name other than due to ownership transfer.

■ Change in the title of a work.

■ An author or claimant was omitted from the original registration.

---

**Example 9.8**

John, Paul, George, and Ringo co-write a song together. Paul's publisher registers the copyright but inadvertently fails to list Ringo as an author of the song. A Form CA could be filed with the Copyright Office to supplement the previous registration by specifying that Ringo is also an author of the song.

---

A supplementary registration should not be made to reflect a change in ownership that occurred after the registration. Instead, the transfer of ownership can be recorded (see Chapter 4). Further, if changes are made in the content of a work, you should register the new work separately as a derivative work rather than supplementing the original work's registration.

### (3) Effect of Supplemental Registration

After the Copyright Office examines your supplemental registration, it will assign a new registration number and issue a certificate of supplementary registration. The supplementary registration augments the original registration rather than replacing it. The Copyright Office will place a note on the records of the original registration referencing the supplementary registration.

## J. Alternatives to Registration

Copyright registration is administered by the U. S. Copyright Office and carries certain statutory benefits available only through their application process. As such, it is a unique process that is not available outside the Copyright Office and cannot be duplicated or substituted. Over time, various practices have emerged that may appear to accomplish the same objectives as registration and have been erroneously considered to be alternatives to registration. However, an examination of such "alternatives" makes it clear that there are no valid alternatives or substitutes for federal registration with the Copyright Office.

### (1) The Myth of the Poor Man's Copyright

In order to save money on copyright registrations, some people utilize a procedure known as poor man's copyright, although the name is misleading because it is not part of copyright law. Poor man's copyright involves putting a copy or phonorecord of your work in an envelope, sealing it, and sending it to yourself by certified mail. When you receive the envelope in the mail, leave it sealed. The idea is that if you are ever involved in a dispute, the envelope can be opened in court, proving that you created the work no later than the date of the postmark stamped on the envelope.

Poor man's copyright, although it may be used as proof of existence of a work as of a certain date, is not a substitute for registration. First of all, the court must be convinced that the envelope has not been tampered with (i.e., opened and resealed). Secondly, since any individual could place a copy of a work in an envelope, including someone who is not its creator, it is not conclusive evidence of authorship. Additionally, poor man's copyright does not entitle you to any of the benefits provided by registration, such as the right to seek statutory damages and attorneys' fees in an infringement action. Consequently, poor man's copyright is of dubious value and is not recommended as a substitute for registration.

### (2) Registration Services

Some organizations, such as the Songwriters Guild of America, allow authors to register their claims to copyright ownership with the organization, e.g., with the Guild. There are also some online services that allow people to "register" copyright claims. For some of these services, registration simply means they will keep a record of the existence of your work. Be wary of these services because, unless they register your work with the U.S. Copyright Office, they are of very limited value. The only benefit of such registration is as a means of providing proof that a work was in existence as of a certain date. As with poor man's copyright, these services do not entitle you to any of the benefits provided by federal registration.

---

**Money-Saving Idea** If you do not want to spend $35 to $65 to register each song you write, you could wait until a song is about to be recorded or published and register at that time. Because unpublished songs are of no financial value, paying the application fee to register them may not be worthwhile unless you plan to submit demos of the song to a small number of entities for their consideration and desire registration as a precaution. As long as you register a work within three months after publication, you will not lose any of the benefits associated with registration. Many music publishers follow this procedure, registering songs only when they have secured a recording by an artist. You can also register a group of unpublished songs as a collective work as explained previously, which may be a cost-effective option for registering a number of unpublished works.

---

## K. Preregistration of Works

As set forth in Section 411 of the Copyright Act, one of two prerequisites must be met before a suit for copyright infringement may be initiated. As it states:

> No civil action for infringement of the copyright in any United States work shall be instituted until preregistration or registration of the copyright claim has been made.

Accordingly, in addition to registration, a work may be preregistered with the Copyright Office to permit litigation to proceed, provided certain very specific conditions are met. Before considering preregistration it is very important to understand its purpose and thereby recognize that preregistration is *not* a substitute for registration. Rather, registration of the work *must* take place within one month after the copyright owner learns of an infringement and no later than three months after the work is first published. If registration does not occur within these timeframes, any copyright lawsuit initiated pursuant to preregistration must be dismissed by the court in which the action was filed.[11]

Preregistration was instituted pursuant to the Artists' Rights and Theft Prevention Act of 2005, which recognizes, based on a determination by the Register of Copyrights, that certain types of works have a history of being infringed before they have been released commercially by the copyright owner. Consequently, preregistration is permitted only for these types of unpublished works:

- Motion pictures
- Sound recordings
- Musical compositions
- Literary works being prepared for publication in book form

- Computer programs (including videogames)
- Advertising or marketing photographs

In addition to requiring that the work be unpublished and in one of the categories listed above, the work must not have been commercially released but must be under preparation for commercial distribution. Therefore, preregistration is probably worthwhile for a minority of copyright owners since it is best suited to limited instances in which the copyright owner anticipates the possibility of unauthorized and potentially widespread distribution of its work before it is finished.

An application fee of $115 and an application for preregistration (available online only) must be filed with the Copyright Office; no deposit is required. To preregister, go to the "Preregister Your Work" link at www.copyright.gov, then click on the button labeled "Start Preregistration Process."

---

**Tip:** Make sure that you wish to preregister before starting this process. Do not mistakenly preregister when your intent is to register the work, or you will lose the preregistration application fee of $115 and will still not have registered your work.

---

# III. Copyright Deposit

Copyright registration is not complete until you have provided the Copyright Office with a copy of the work to be registered, referred to as a deposit. Since the U.S. Copyright Office is part of the Library of Congress, the deposit serves archival, recordkeeping purposes.

## A. Mandatory Deposit

Of the three copyright formalities, deposit is the only one that is still mandatory in the United States, even though it is arguably the least important. Section 407 of the 1976 Copyright Act provides for a mandatory deposit system for published works. The purpose of the deposit requirement is to enrich the resources of the Library of Congress. The law requires that two copies of the best edition of every copyrightable work published in the United States be deposited with the Copyright Office within three months of publication. Deposit should be made by the copyright owner or the owner of the exclusive right of publication and should be sent to: Library of Congress, Register of Copyrights, Attn: 407 Deposits, 101 Independence Avenue S.E., Washington, D.C. 20559-6600.

The mandatory deposit requirement is not applicable to unpublished works. Although unpublished works may be deposited by sending only one copy of the work, the Copyright Office does not encourage the deposit of unpublished works due to the additional workload that would result.

Although the deposit requirement is separate from the registration process, Section 408(b) provides for deposit in connection with registration. The copies or phonorecords deposited under Section 407 can be used to satisfy the deposit provisions of Section 408(b) if they are accompanied by the registration application form and filing fee.

### B. Penalties for Failure to Deposit

Although the deposit requirement is mandatory, many copyright owners do not make the required deposit unless they are also registering a work. There are no adverse consequences for failing to satisfy the deposit requirement. However, the Register of Copyrights may make a written demand for the deposit at any time after a work's publication, although generally only published works wanted for the Library of Congress' collections are demanded. If the deposit is not made within three months of this demand, the copyright owner can be fined up to $250 plus the retail price of the copies required for deposit. If a refusal to comply is willful or repeated, an additional fine of $2,500 may also be incurred.

### C. What Must Be Deposited

A deposit must contain two complete copies or phonorecords of the best edition of the work (if the work is unpublished, only one copy or phonorecord is required). The "best edition" is defined as the edition published in the United States at any time before the date of deposit that the Library of Congress determines to be most suitable. Generally, this means that if there is more than one edition of a work, the one of the highest quality should be used. For sound recordings, the deposit should include, in addition to two complete phonorecords (e.g., compact discs, cassettes, etc.) of the best edition, any text or pictorial matter published with the phonorecord. Textual material includes all packaging, record sleeves, and separate leaflets or booklets.

### D. Exemptions from the Deposit Requirement

Because some deposits are not suitable for addition to the Library of Congress, the Copyright Office has issued regulations to exempt certain categories of works from the mandatory deposit requirement. Currently, works that are published in the United States but are published in electronic form only, are available only online, and are not available in physical form are exempt from the deposit requirement until the Copyright Office issues a demand for a deposit of copies or phonorecords of such works.[12] Certain serials (such as newspapers or other periodicals) may also be exempted from the requirement by the Copyright Office. Exemption from the deposit requirement may also be requested. Such relief is granted solely at the discretion of the Copyright Office and is usually granted based on undue burden or cost to a copyright owner. To request exemption, you must write to the Copyright Office setting forth the specific reasons why special relief should be granted. If only mandatory deposit is to be made (as opposed to registration), the request should be forwarded to Library of Congress, Chief, Copyright Acquisitions Division, 101 Independence Avenue S.E., Washington, D.C. 20559-6600.

## IV. Copyright Notice

Copyright notice is a way of informing people that a work is protected by copyright and who it is owned by. Prior to March 1, 1989, placing notice of copyright on published copies of a work was required in order to have copyright protection in the United States.

Under the 1909 Copyright Act, the failure to use copyright notice had very harsh consequences. If notice was omitted or improperly placed on a work, the work automatically entered the public domain.

The 1976 Copyright Act maintained the notice requirement, but liberalized it by allowing for the correction of innocent errors or omissions of notice. However, if someone used a work that did not contain notice without knowledge that the work was protected by copyright, they could not be held liable for copies of the work sold prior to the copyright owner's correction and notification from the copyright owner.

Unlike the United States, the vast majority of foreign countries did not require copyright notice as a condition to copyright protection. In fact, the Berne Convention specifically states that copyright protection cannot be subject to any formality such as notice. Consequently, when the United States decided to join the Berne Convention, it had to eliminate the mandatory notice requirement. Under the Berne Convention Implementation Act of 1988, which became effective on March 1, 1989, notice is no longer required in order to have copyright protection. This did not change the law with respect to works created before March 1, 1989, which still require notice.

Although copyright notice is no longer required, it is still recommended, and there are some advantages to using it. One practical advantage is that placing the notice on copies of a work that are distributed makes it clear that the work is protected by copyright. It also makes it easier for people to identify the copyright owner in order to request a license to use the work. Another advantage is that someone who infringes a work that contains notice cannot claim innocent infringement (reducing the amount of damages they are liable for) even if they actually believed the work was in the public domain.

### A. What Should a Copyright Notice Contain?

There are three elements that a copyright notice should contain:

- The word "Copyright," the abbreviation "Copr.," or the copyright symbol "©." For sound recordings, the symbol "℗" should be used instead of the © symbol.

- The year of initial publication of the work or, if the work is unpublished, the year of creation.

- The copyright owner's name. This refers to the current owner rather than the author of the work. For example, the song credits on an album will specify the name of the music publisher that owns the copyright to the song rather than the songwriter, although songwriters may also be listed in the liner notes to give credit. If there is more than one copyright owner, specify all of their names in the copyright notice.

In addition to the three elements above, some copyright notices contain additional information. For instance, some notices will contain the phrase "all rights reserved," which is required in some Latin American countries under the Buenos Aires Convention. Sometimes notices will also contain some type of warning statement such as "Unauthorized reproduction is prohibited by law. Violators are subject to civil and criminal penalties." Such warnings are not required, but are used to deter potential infringers. Finally, when someone else's copyrighted material has been used, the notice might state "used by permission" to indicate that a license has been obtained.

### B. Where Should Copyright Notice Be Placed?

A copyright notice should be placed on every reproduction of a copyrighted work. According to the Copyright Act, notice should be placed "in such manner and location as to give reasonable notice of the claim of copyright."[13] For sound recordings, notice should be placed on the actual phonorecord (or its label) and on its container because the phonorecord can easily be separated from the container. Notice is usually placed on the back side of the album jacket and on the disc label. The notice for a sound recording in downloadable MP3 or other digital file format could likewise be placed on the label, images, or artwork accompanying the file.

In many situations, there is more than one copyrighted work embodied on a phonorecord (i.e., the sound recording itself, any underlying musical compositions, album cover artwork, and liner notes). In such situations, separate copyright notices can help distinguish between the owners of the various copyrighted works. At the least, there should be a notice on a phonorecord covering the sound recording and identifying its owner, which is normally a record company. If the copyright owner's name is not contained in the notice and the record producer's name is listed elsewhere on the label or container, the producer's name will be deemed part of notice. In many instances, the record company will also be the copyright owner of any artwork and textual material contained on phonorecords. In such situations, the sound recording notice covers both, although many record companies use both the ℗ and © symbols. If the record company is not the owner of the artwork or textual material, a separate notice should be placed near the artwork or textual material.

---

**Example 9.9**

Kramerica Records is the copyright owner of a sound recording entitled *Serenity Now* (consisting of performances by Jerry Seinfeld and George Costanza) as well as the accompanying artwork and liner notes. The copyright notice found on a phonorecord such as a compact disc of *Serenity Now* would appear as follows: "℗ © 2000 Kramerica Records." Alternatively, if the artwork and liner notes had been created by Elaine Benes as an employee of Pendant Publishing, the copyright notice for the sound recording would appear as "℗ 2000 Kramerica Records," while a separate copyright notice would appear near the artwork as "© 2000 Pendant Publishing."

---

# Endnotes

1. 37 C.F.R. 201.4(c) (1991).
2. Fiscal Year 2012 Budget Request, Statement of Maria Pallante, Register of Copyrights, before the Subcommittee of Legislative Branch Committee on Appropriations (March 31, 2011).
3. In *Reed Elsevier, Inc. v. Muchnick*, the Supreme Court of the United States held that the registration requirement set forth at Section 411 of the Copyright Act is not jurisdictional,

which could in effect permit federal courts to hear claims involving unregistered works (particularly those included in class actions), diluting and possibly eviscerating the statutory registration requirement. Specifically, the Court stated: "Section 411(a) imposes a precondition to filing a claim that is not clearly labeled jurisdictional, is not located in a jurisdiction-granting provision, and admits of congressionally authorized exceptions" (130 S.Ct. 1237, 1247, U.S. 2010). However, the Court did not directly address the question of whether registration is mandatory and appears to acknowledge it as "a precondition to filing a claim," albeit a potentially variable precondition. Therefore, the effect of the Court's holding on the registration requirement is uncertain and remains to be seen.

4. Fiscal Year 2012 Budget Request, Statement of Maria Pallante, Register of Copyrights, before the Subcommittee of Legislative Branch Committee on Appropriations (March 31, 2011).

5. This higher fee was made effective beginning August 1, 2011.

6. *Rich & Rich Partnership v. Poetman Records USA, Inc.*, 714 F.Supp. 657 (E.D. KY Central Division, 2010).

7. See 17 U.S.C. §408(c) and Copyright Office Regulation 37 C.F.R.§ 202.3(b)(3)(i)(B).

8. *Szabo v. Errisson.*

9. § 410(a) of the Copyright Act directs the Register of Copyrights to register any claim to copyright that constitutes copyrightable subject matter and meets the other legal and formal requirements of the Copyright Act.

10. *Racquel v. Education Management Corp.*, 98-3321 (Nov. 9, 1999).

11. 17 U.S.C. § 408(f).

12. This exemption was made effective February 24, 2010, via interim regulation. The interim regulation is subject to final adoption. 75 Federal Register 3863, January 25, 2010.

13. 17 U.S.C. § 401(c).

# 10 Infringement of Copyright

*"We were the biggest nickers in town; plagiarists extraordinaire."*

—*Paul McCartney*

The valuable nature of intellectual property is reinforced by the protections afforded through copyright law. Therefore, it is important to understand the enforcement parameters established within the law to address violation of the exclusive rights.

## I. What Is Copyright Infringement?

In the intangible property realm of copyright, infringement is the equivalent of stealing physical property. In general, infringement occurs whenever someone exercises any of the copyright owner's exclusive rights without permission to do so. As stated in Section 501(a) of the Copyright Act:

> *Anyone who violates any of the exclusive rights of the copyright owner as provided by sections 106 through 118, or who imports copies or phonorecords into the United States in violation of section 602, is an infringer of the copyright.*

A single act of infringement may violate one or more of the copyright owner's exclusive rights. For instance, someone who makes a recording of a copyrighted song without obtaining a license from the copyright owner of the song has infringed the reproduction right. If that person gives away or sells his recording, he has also violated the distribution right.

---

**Infringement Doesn't Hinge on Profit**   A fairly common response by someone accused of infringement is "but I didn't make any money from it." However, copyright infringement arises from the unauthorized exercise of a copyright owner's exclusive rights and is not dependent on any exchange of money or profit motive. A loose analogy would be if someone stole your car, it wouldn't help you if he merely stole it to drive himself rather than to sell to someone else. Even though, unlike a copyrighted work, a car is tangible property, the copyright owner (like the car owner) is still deprived of the use (or at least the licensing revenue from the use) of her property.

---

The key to winning an infringement claim is proving that the defendant copied the plaintiff's work. However, there are some circumstances where, even though the defendant has copied from the plaintiff's work, infringement will not result. This is because the copying must amount to an improper appropriation of the copyrighted work. In order to constitute improper appropriation, at least some of the elements copied must be copyrighted subject matter rather than uncopyrightable or public domain elements.

It is important to understand that just because another person's work is similar to yours does not necessarily mean that it is an infringement of your work. Many similarities can exist due simply to coincidence rather than by one person copying another person's work. In the field of music, where the creative vocabulary is quite limited, there will be many similarities among different works. Songs will routinely share notes, common chord progressions, common rhythmic patterns, and so forth.

Copyright infringement claims have become a commonplace occurrence, especially against highly popular recording artists. There are few highly successful artists who have escaped being sued by someone claiming to have written one of the artist's biggest hit songs. This trend began in the 1970s and has resulted in record companies and music publishers being much less receptive to listening to material submitted by new artists and songwriters. All of the major record companies have strict policies of not accepting any unsolicited material unless the material is submitted through an attorney or a known entity, partially due to the fear that accepting such materials will be used against them in a copyright infringement claim.

## II. What if You Believe Your Work Has Been Infringed?

Before initiating legal action against an infringer, a copyright owner will usually notify the alleged infringer and request that the infringer stop infringing. This is usually done by having a lawyer send the alleged infringer a letter known as a cease and desist letter. The copyright owner may also request payment for the unauthorized use that has been made. In some instances, the infringer may be willing to settle the claim by agreeing to pay the copyright owner some amount of money. Settlement agreements usually do not contain any admission of liability and are usually confidential, so the amount paid by the infringer is not known to the public.

---

**Example 10.1**

Billy Joel reportedly settled an infringement claim brought against him in 1980 in connection with his song "My Life" for about $50,000. Joel denied copying the song but may have decided that paying $50,000 was cheaper than defending an infringement lawsuit.

---

Many more copyright infringement claims are threatened than actually litigated. Consequently, if you send a cease and desist letter (especially one demanding money as opposed to merely stopping the infringement), it is possible that it will be ignored. In other words, threatening to sue as a bluff will often not work; if you're serious about enforcing your rights, you should be willing to file a lawsuit if necessary. Sometimes, just filing a lawsuit will make settlement much more likely because the other party knows you're serious and will have to go to the expense of defending the lawsuit.

If you cannot reach a settlement with an alleged infringer, your remaining option is to file and litigate a copyright infringement lawsuit. However, this is not always a practical option because infringement lawsuits can be very expensive and time consuming. Additionally, even if you win an infringement suit, the amount of money you can actually recover may not be enough to make it worthwhile. If you are considering filing an infringement suit, you should consult with a competent attorney who can advise you as to the validity of your claim, your chances of success, and the likely amount of money you may recover. Because copyright is a very specialized area of the law, most attorneys are not competent to give advice on infringement claims; hence, it is important that you find an experienced copyright attorney.

## III. How to Bring an Infringement Lawsuit

A plaintiff, as one who initiates a lawsuit, is responsible for understanding how and where to bring the case to court, as well as for proving the elements of her case. It is best to consult a lawyer concerning bringing an infringement lawsuit and to have a general sense of the issues and practical implications involved in litigating a case before making a final decision to sue someone for infringement.

### A. Who Can Sue for Infringement?

Generally, only the copyright owner or the exclusive licensee of a work can sue anyone who infringes upon the copyright owner's exclusive rights. Furthermore, the owner or the exclusive licensee can only sue for infringement of the particular right that he owns. For instance, if a songwriter transfers the rights of distribution and public performance of a song exclusively to a publisher but retains the right to create derivative works, then only the publisher could sue if someone performed the song at a stadium without a license, but only the songwriter could sue if the infringer created a derivative work but did not perform or distribute it.

Prior to the enactment of the 1976 Copyright Act, only the copyright owner of a work could sue for infringement because copyright ownership was indivisible. This meant that an exclusive licensee could not sue for infringement unless the copyright owner was also a party to the lawsuit. The 1976 Copyright Act changed this result by providing that any "legal or beneficial owner of an exclusive right" can sue for infringement of that right.[1] This rule reflects the concept of divisibility of copyright, which means that a copyright can be split up, and any of the exclusive rights can be owned separately.

---

**Example 10.2**

Most music publishers do not print sheet music of their songs. Instead, they license print rights to one of a few companies specializing in this area. If a publisher licensed a print company the exclusive right to print sheet music of a song and someone else began selling sheet music, the print company could sue the infringer as the song's exclusive print licensee without having to get the publisher to join as a party to the lawsuit.

---

**Example 10.3**

In the case of *In re Isbell Records, Inc.*,[2] the court found that a music publisher who transferred 50 percent of his copyright ownership in a musical composition did not lose his right to sue copyright infringers, even though the copyright assignment contained language assigning "all of the publisher's universe-wide right, title, and interest, including all claims for infringement of the copyrights whether now or hereafter existing, for the maximum terms of copyright." The court interpreted the assignment as granting him full copyright ownership for his remaining share, rather than a mere right to receive royalties or other forms of compensation that fall short of full copyright ownership. Accordingly, the divided copyright did not deprive the publisher of full ownership rights.

## B. Where to Bring a Copyright Infringement Lawsuit

Copyright infringement lawsuits must be filed in one of the federal district courts in the United States. This is because copyright law in the United States is derived from a federal statute, the 1976 Copyright Act, and only federal courts have jurisdiction over federal statutes.

Although any claims that deal with a copyright owner's rights under the Copyright Act such as infringement claims must be brought in federal courts, there are many types of disputes involving copyrights that do not actually involve any interpretation of the Copyright Act. For instance, disputes over copyright ownership or the right to receive royalties do not usually involve interpretations of the Copyright Act and would have to be filed in state rather than federal court.

**Example 10.4**

A songwriter signs a contract with a publishing company providing that the publisher will pay the songwriter royalties based on sales of records containing songs written by the songwriter. If the songwriter believes the publisher has not paid the proper amount of royalties, his claim is for breach of contract and should be brought in state court. Although the claim involves copyrighted works (i.e., songs), the dispute does not involve any interpretation of the Copyright Act. It merely requires that the court examine the situation in order to determine whether the provisions of the publishing contract have been complied with.

Sometimes a dispute will involve several different legal claims, some of which might involve an interpretation of copyright law and some of which do not. In such situations, the lawsuit will usually be filed in federal court in order to address the copyright claim. The district court will often decide any related claims, such as those involving a contractual dispute, as well.

**Example 10.5**

On January 1, 2009, a record company obtains a mechanical license from a publisher to record and distribute a song on records. Initially, the record company complies with all of the provisions of the license. However, after a year, the record company stops making accountings and royalty payments to the publisher. If the publisher believes that the record company had been underpaying royalties, it would have a claim for breach of contract for any royalties that should have been paid from 2009 to 2010 under the license. It would also have a claim for copyright infringement for any records sold after January 1, 2010, because the record company terminated the license when it stopped accounting.

Because the record company's continued use of the song after termination of the license is a copyright infringement claim, the lawsuit could be filed in federal court, and the court could decide the breach of contract claim as well as the infringement claim.

If you want to sue someone for copyright infringement, suit may be brought in any federal district where the defendant can be found. For instance, if an infringer lives in New York, you could sue him in a federal district court located in New York. Additionally, if the infringer has sufficient contacts with other jurisdictions, you could sue in one of these jurisdictions as well. For instance, if you want to sue a big corporation such as one of the major record companies for copyright infringement, you could probably bring suit in any state where the corporation does business. However, a court can transfer a suit to another district where the suit could have been filed if the court believes it will be more convenient for the parties and witnesses.

# IV. How Do You Prove Infringement?

Because the essence of a copyright infringement claim involves copying, a plaintiff must prove that he owns or is the exclusive licensee of the work that has been copied without permission. In order to prove an infringement claim, a plaintiff must prove two elements: (1) ownership of a valid copyright; and (2) copying of a copyrighted work. Copying is in turn established either by presenting direct evidence of copying or by proving two elements of circumstantial evidence: (1) access to the copyrighted work by the alleged infringer; and (2) substantial similarity between the copyrighted work and the alleged infringer's work.

## A. Ownership of a Valid Copyright

Obviously, in order for someone to have committed an infringement, he must have used part or all of a copyrighted work. As discussed in Chapter 3, "What Can Be Protected by Copyright?," in order for a work to be protected by copyright, it must be original, contain expression, and be fixed in tangible form.

The best way to prove ownership of copyright is to present a copyright registration certificate in court. If the registration was made within five years of the work's first publication, the court will presume that the copyright is valid and that all of the information contained in the registration application is true. The plaintiff will therefore not have to offer any other evidence that the work is original or that she is the owner. (If the plaintiff is the exclusive licensee, she will need to prove the existence of the license as well.) If the defendant believes that the copyright is not valid or that the plaintiff is not the owner, it is up to the defendant to offer evidence proving its beliefs, which will normally be very hard to do.

If the work was not registered within five years of its publication, the plaintiff will have to offer some other evidence of its ownership of copyright. For instance, the plaintiff could take the witness stand and testify as to when and how he acquired ownership. If the plaintiff is the author of the work, he would testify that he created the work and has not transferred it to anyone else. He could also have witnesses testify if they had direct knowledge of the plaintiff's ownership (e.g., someone who was present and witnessed a songwriter composing a song). If the plaintiff is someone other than the work's author, he would have to offer into evidence some written document under which ownership was acquired. The main disadvantage of using testimony rather than written documentation to prove ownership is that the judge or jury is allowed to decide whether or not to believe the testimony.

---

**Tip:**   A copyright registration obtained within five years of a work's publication is the best possible proof that you own a copyrighted work. If there is ever a dispute over copyright ownership, the registration fee is money well spent.

---

## B. Copying of a Copyrighted Work

After the plaintiff has established that he owns a copyrighted work, he must prove that the defendant copied protected parts of the work. It is important to understand that infringement cannot occur unless the defendant has copied the plaintiff's work. There are two common ways for copying to occur. First, an infringer may directly copy the copyrighted work by duplicating it in some form. For example, a record pirate who manufactures copyrighted sound recordings without authorization to do so directly copies the sound recordings as well as any underlying copyrighted musical compositions contained on the sound recordings. The other type of copying involves indirect copying of part of a copyrighted work. For example, if a songwriter composes a song by copying part of another copyrighted song—whether the copying is intentional or not—indirect copying has occurred.

Direct evidence of copying is rarely available, because a defendant will rarely admit copying a work. Additionally, finding witnesses who physically saw a defendant copy a work is not likely because most copying is done in private. Consequently, copying can be inferred from circumstantial (i.e., indirect) evidence. A plaintiff may prove copying through circumstantial evidence by offering proof of two elements: (1) access by the defendant to the copyrighted work; and (2) substantial similarity between the plaintiff's and the defendant's works.

### (1) Access

In order to copy a work, one must have access to the work copied. Without access, copying is not possible. Chapter 1, "What Is Copyright?," points out that it is possible for two people to create substantially similar works independently, and each own a copyright in their own work. But if you can prove that a defendant had access to your work and that the defendant's work is substantially similar to yours, a court can find infringement even if you have no direct evidence that the defendant copied your work. This is because it is impossible to copy (as opposed to independently create) a song you've never heard or a book you've never seen or read. In legal terms, "access" means that the defendant had a reasonable opportunity to view or hear the copyrighted work.

#### (a) Direct Evidence of Access

In the best of circumstances, a plaintiff will be able to present direct evidence of access. For example, a defendant might admit that she had access to the plaintiff's work. However, the fact that a defendant admits access does not necessarily mean that the defendant also admits copying the plaintiff's work.

---

**Example 10.6**

In *Bright Tunes Music Corp. v. Harrisongs Music, Ltd.*,[3] George Harrison's song "My Sweet Lord" was held to be an infringement of the Chiffons' hit song "He's So Fine." In this case, Harrison admitted hearing the Chiffons' song, although he did not admit copying it.

---

Additionally, if the plaintiff can find a witness who can testify that he saw the defendant listen to or view the plaintiff's work, this would also constitute direct evidence of access. Alternatively, if a witness heard the defendant admit he had heard the plaintiff's song, this testimony would also be direct evidence of access.

### (b) Circumstantial Evidence of Access

In most situations, a plaintiff will not be able to offer direct evidence that a defendant had access to her work. In such situations, the plaintiff will have to rely on circumstantial evidence instead. One type of circumstantial evidence of access involves showing that the plaintiff's work was very well known and widely available to the public. For instance, if the plaintiff's song was a major hit that received widespread exposure to the public through radio airplay or television broadcasts, it is reasonable to assume that the defendant heard it at some point. Alternatively, if the plaintiff's song has been widely disseminated through sales of sheet music or records, this might be circumstantial evidence of access. The more widely available and well known the work, the more likely access will be found.

---

**Example 10.7**

In the George Harrison case referred to in the previous example, although Harrison admitted hearing the Chiffon's song, access could also have been proven circumstantially based on the fact that "He's So Fine" was a number-one hit on the Billboard charts for five weeks and received substantial radio airplay. In contrast, in a case brought by an unknown composer named Ronald Selle, it was held that the Bee Gees song "How Deep Is Your Love" did not infringe Selle's song "Let It End."[4] The court's decision rested on the fact that Selle could not offer sufficient proof that the Bee Gees had access to his song. Selle offered evidence that "Let It End" was performed publicly two or three times in the Chicago area, but could not prove that the Bee Gees or anyone associated with them was in the area at the time of those performances.

---

Another type of circumstantial evidence of access involves showing that the plaintiff's work was available to the defendant. This usually results from the plaintiff proving that it distributed its work to the defendant or to some third party who is likely to have distributed it to the defendant, such as the defendant's record company or publisher. In one case, where the plaintiff had sent copies of her song to four individuals and two companies, all of which were returned, the court stated that:

> To support a finding of access there must be a reasonable possibility of access—not a bare possibility as we have in this case."[5]

Sometimes the link between the plaintiff's work and the defendant's will be quite tenuous. In a suit filed against Mariah Carey that was dropped before trial, a plaintiff alleged that Carey's song "Can't Let Go" infringed her song. As evidence of access, the plaintiff claimed that she gave a demo tape containing her song to Carey's hairstylist. It is unlikely that a court would consider this sufficient evidence of access unless the hairstylist testified that he gave the tape to Carey (which still would not conclusively prove that she listened to it).

In seeking to establish access to the plaintiff's work by the defendant, even plausible coincidences may not give rise to an inference of access.

---

**Example 10.8**

---

Recording artist Tim McGraw was sued for infringement by a plaintiff alleging that McGraw's song "Everywhere" copied plaintiff's song "Anytime, Anywhere Amanda" in *Martinez v. McGraw*.[6] Plaintiff Martinez alleged that McGraw had access to his song because he and McGraw used the same recording studio and personnel—namely Terri Clark, a country music artist—and that because both the studio and Ms. Clark had access to his song, McGraw had access to it as well. The plaintiff further alleged that his song was played within hearing range of Ms. Clark and her songwriters. However, the court did not find the allegations to be true, stating that:

*"Evidence that a third party with whom both the plaintiff and defendant were concurrently dealing had possession of plaintiff's work [may be] sufficient to establish access by the defendant, [however] access may not be inferred through mere speculation or conjecture."* Jones v. Blige, 558 F.3d 485, 491 (6th Cir. 2009) (quoting Murray Hill Publ'n, 361 F.3d at 316). *"Here, Plaintiff fails to provide facts that would show Ms. Clark had possession of Plaintiff's song at any point or that she, or people she worked with, made Plaintiff's song available to Defendants."*[7]

---

Other coincidences are present in the case, e.g., McGraw's *Everywhere* CD (which contains the allegedly infringing song) contains an additional song, "Hard on the Ticker," which plaintiff pointed out was similar in title to another of plaintiff's songs entitled "Easy on the Eyes, Hard on the Heart," which the court acknowledged was a unique phrase. Nevertheless, the court found that the plaintiff did not offer evidence "beyond mere speculation" as to how Ms. Clark received plaintiff's song, or how she put the song in the defendants' possession. Since the access element was unmet, the court declined a substantial similarity analysis stating that even if the two songs were similar, it would still be necessary to prove that the defendants had access to the song to facilitate copying it.

*Jones v. Blige*, cited above in *McGraw* and decided before it, is an important music access case concerning the role of third parties in granting access to alleged infringers. In *Jones*, a demo of plaintiff's song, "Party Ain't Crunk," was allegedly given to Universal Music Enterprise's senior vice president of A&R (McKaie) by plaintiff, which plaintiff asserted led to the creation of Blige's "Family Affair," allegedly copied from plaintiff's composition. The plaintiff sought to establish that Universal's mere receipt of the demo, when combined with Blige's ties to Universal through her record contract with them, was sufficient evidence of access. Despite the fact that the demo was hand-delivered to McKaie's office at Universal and the existence of Blige's contract with them, the court rejected these theories by focusing on the standard of proof required to establish access to an allegedly infringed work. While the court did not want to dismiss the difficulty of establishing a chain of custody of a work once received by a corporation, it rejected the "corporate receipt" doctrine in this case as requiring too much of a "quantum leap" since (1) there was no evidence that Ms. Blige knew McKaie or had any dealings with him; (2) even if she did, there was no proof that McKaie heard (a requirement for access) or passed on the demo to Blige; and (3) there was ample proof of independent creation of "Family Affair" by Blige. Accordingly, plaintiff's case failed, and no infringement was found. In the court's words, citing other access cases:

*"a bare possibility of access is not enough; rather a plaintiff must show that the defendant had a 'reasonable possibility' of [access]."*[8]

It was this reasoning in *Jones v. Blige* that guided the court in deciding the *McGraw* case. However, the *Jones* and *McGraw* decisions stand in contrast to the outcome in *Gaste v. Kaiserman*, described in Example 10.9 below.

---

**Example 10.9**

In *Gaste v. Kaiserman*,[9] composer of an obscure French song "Pour Toi" claimed that Morris Alpert's 1970s hit song "Feelings" was an infringement. Seventeen years before "Feelings" was written, Gaste had sent a recording of his song to Alpert's publishing company. Somewhat surprisingly, the jury held that Gaste's evidence of access was sufficient even though the publisher claimed it had never actually listened to Gaste's song. The court stated that "the lapse of time between the original publication of 'Pour Toi' and the alleged infringement and the distance between the locations of the two events may make copying less likely but not an unreasonable conclusion."

---

**No Unsolicited Material**   In order to reduce the possibility of being found guilty of copyright infringement, many famous recording artists as well as record companies and publishers have adopted policies of not accepting any unsolicited material. In other words, they will not accept demo recordings from anyone they don't know and trust; to do so could be used against them as evidence of access. Most courts (like those deciding *Jones v. Blige* and *Martinez v. McGraw*) would probably require more evidence of access than the *Gaste* court did, but this type of result explains why many artists, record companies, publishers, and movie companies refuse to accept material from anyone with whom they do not have a prior relationship or require submission through an attorney or reputable agent.

## (2) Substantial Similarity

Even if a plaintiff proves that the defendant had access to his work, this alone does not prove that the defendant copied his work. The plaintiff must also prove that there are substantial similarities between the plaintiff's and the defendant's works. The substantial similarity test is often a difficult one because it is hard to draw a clear line between substantial and insubstantial similarities. If the similarities between the defendant's and the plaintiff's works are so great that it is more likely than not that the defendant copied the plaintiff's work, they will be deemed substantial. However, there is no set number of notes or words that must be taken from a work in order to constitute substantial similarity.

Substantial similarity is a somewhat imprecise concept. Since the meaning of "substantial" is not defined in the Copyright Act, it is normally determined by what is known as the ordinary observer test. This test asks whether the defendant took from the plaintiff's work so much of what is pleasing to the ears of lay (i.e., ordinary) listeners, who comprise the audience for whom such music is composed, that the defendant wrongfully appropriated what belongs to the plaintiff. Even though substantial similarity is determined according to the ordinary observer standard, expert testimony will often be used to show the similarities between two works. A copyright owner will often hire an expert witness—someone with training in music composition and analysis, such as a musicologist—to point out all of the similarities in the defendant's work. This will help prove that the defendant could not have independently created the work and that similarities between highly unique elements indicate copying.

However, a defendant in a copyright infringement case may also hire an expert witness to point out that any similarities or dissimilarities are either public domain material or that alleged similarities also exist in other works created before the plaintiff's. Although experts can be used to testify about similarities between works and give their opinion as to whether similarities are the result of copying, their opinions are not binding on a court. Like any other witness, it is up to the judge or jury to decide how much credibility to give to their testimony.

---

**Expert Witnesses**    It is important to understand that experts are hired witnesses rather than neutral third parties. They are hired and paid to testify in a manner as favorable as possible to the party hiring them. Consequently, it is not uncommon to encounter situations where opinions of experts hired by opposing parties are completely contradictory. Additionally, a fairly common strategy of experts hired by defendants is to confuse the jury as much as possible in the hope that they will not be able to agree on whether infringement occurred or not. Although expert testimony can sometimes be very useful, this is why the decision as to whether infringement occurred or not is made by the judge or jury under the ordinary observer test.

---

The substantial similarity test is often especially difficult to apply to cases involving music because the elements of musical composition are much more limited than the elements of literary or dramatic composition. First of all, musical composition is limited by the 12 notes of the musical scale. Further, even though these 12 notes can be arranged in many ways, relatively few of these arrangements will be aesthetically pleasing. It is therefore quite possible that two songs may contain a great degree of similarity even though both songs are independently created. As stated by one court:

*It must be remembered that, while there are an enormous number of possible permutations of the musical notes of the scale, only a few are pleasing; and much fewer still suit the infantile demands of the popular ear. Recurrence is not therefore an inevitable badge of plagiarism."[10]*

Evidence of similarities between songs will usually focus primarily on similarities in the melodies of the songs because melody is usually the most memorable element of a song. However, rhythmic and harmonic similarities can also be examined.

It is also important to understand that not all of the similarities between two works will be applied in the substantial similarity analysis. In order to count, the similarities must be of copyrightable expression, rather than uncopyrightable elements. This is often referred to as "improper appropriation," which means that the defendant must appropriate elements of the work that are protected by copyright. If a defendant literally copied all of a plaintiff's song, this would clearly involve improper appropriation. However, many situations do not involve literal copying, and it then becomes necessary to dissect the two works in order to determine what elements are copyrightable expression as opposed to noncopyrightable ideas or public domain material.

It will often be permissible to copy a musical phrase from a copyrighted work. This would be true if the musical phrase copied is fairly simple and therefore not sufficiently original to merit copyright protection. If one could obtain copyright ownership over simple musical phrases or other compositional elements, this would have the effect of limiting musical composition because no one else could use such elements without permission. The most difficult question in analyzing issues of substantial similarity is how much copying is too much. Unfortunately, there are no bright-line rules, and the determination must be made on a case-by-case basis.

---

**The Six-Bar "Rule"**    A common misconception among musicians is that it is permissible to use up to six measures of music from a copyrighted song. This misconception has become widely known as the aforementioned "six-bar rule," which is really not a rule at all. In fact, there is no universally accepted minimum amount of music that may be freely copied. Courts have held that copying as few as two to four bars or even just six notes can constitute infringement.

---

## (3) Fragmented Similarity

Digital music sampling has challenged traditional conceptualizations of substantial similarity. As noted above, substantial similarity may be found where an integral aspect of a work has been copied when juxtaposing the work in its entirety against the thematic significance of the "fragment" copied. However, fragmented similarity may deem copying to have occurred when small portions of a work have been copied, even when those portions are insubstantial, whether quantitatively or qualitatively. Since sampling often involves only small portions of a musical work or sound recording, the fragmented similarity test was applied by the court in *Bridgeport Music, Inc. v. UMG Recordings, Inc.* The court distinguished its analysis as a departure from the usual substantial similarity test:

*We have previously held that the question for the jury in substantial-similarity cases is "whether a lay observer would consider the works as a whole substantially similar to one another."... However, as have several of our sister circuits, we have also noted that it is appropriate to modify this inquiry for situations in which a smaller fragment of a work has been copied literally, but not the overall theme or concept—an approach referred to in the literature as "fragmented literal similarity."... In such situations, even a small degree of copying may support a finding of substantial similarity, depending on the context.... Thus, the copying of a relatively small but qualitatively important or crucial element can be an appropriate basis upon which to find substantial similarity.[11]*

While the court's analysis in this *Bridgeport* decision seems to allow for a more traditional substantial similarity analysis than did the earlier *Bridgeport v. Dimension Films* decision discussed in Chapter 5, "The Reproduction Right," whether fragmented similarity is appropriate for sampling has been questioned by some courts and copyright scholars.

*But suppose the similarity, although literal, is not comprehensive—that is, the fundamental substance, skeleton, or overall scheme, of the plaintiff's work has not been copied; no more than a line, or a paragraph, or a page, or chapter of the copyrighted work has been appropriated. At what point does such fragmented similarity become substantial so as to constitute the borrowing an infringement?[12]*

*...[T]he practice of digitally sampling prior music to use in a new composition should not be subject to any special analysis: to the extent that the resulting product is substantially similar to the sampled original, liability should result.[13]*

## (4) Striking Similarity

In rare circumstances, a court may conclude that a defendant copied a work even if the plaintiff cannot prove that the defendant had access to the work. A court would do so only when it believes that the similarities between the two works are so striking that there is no reasonable possibility that the defendant independently created the work and that the similarities are coincidental. In other words, the only reasonable explanation for the similarities between the two works is that the defendant copied the plaintiff's work.

## (5) Presumption of Copying

If a copyright owner proves both access and substantial similarity, a court will presume that the defendant copied the plaintiff's work. The reason for this presumption is that there is no other reasonable explanation for the similarities other than copying. However, this presumption of copying can be countered or rebutted by the defendant.

A defendant can attempt to rebut the presumption that it copied the plaintiff's work in several ways. For instance, if the plaintiff offered evidence of access by proving that it submitted a demo tape to a record company, the record company could offer evidence that it had a policy of not listening to unsolicited demos or evidence proving that whoever the demo was submitted to at the record company had no contact with the artist.

To rebut evidence of similarities between two works, a defendant could offer evidence of the existence of other works containing the same similarities and showing that it was these other works rather than the plaintiff's that were copied. If the other works are in the public domain, they can be freely copied by anyone. Alternatively, a defendant could offer evidence that its work was created before the plaintiff's work. A defendant could also attempt to prove that regardless of any similarities, it created the work independently.

---

**Example 10.10**

In *Selle v. Gibb*,[14] the Bee Gees presented several witnesses who were present when the Bee Gees composed the song "How Deep Is Your Love." They also submitted into evidence a tape recording made during their song's creation that showed how ideas, notes, and lyrics were combined in order to create the song. The court believed that this evidence proved that the Bee Gees had independently created the song even though an expert witness for the plaintiff testified that "the two songs had such striking similarities that they could not have been written independent of one another." Although the plaintiff's expert witness believed the similarities were so striking as to preclude independent creation, the court obviously disagreed.

---

### C. Some Famous Music Infringement Cases

It is not uncommon for copyright infringement lawsuits to be brought by relatively unknown songwriters against the writers and owners of extremely successful hit songs. Although it is certainly possible that a hit song could be an infringement of a song by an amateur writer, when an infringement claim is made against a superstar artist over a hit song, it is possible that the amateur songwriter is merely attempting to extract a large cash settlement from the artist. In other situations, a songwriter will genuinely believe that his or her song has been infringed based on coincidental similarities rather than copying.

The following, although only a small sample, are some examples of interesting copyright infringement cases involving musical works.

#### (1) *The Song Is Mine*—Sanford v. Jackson

In 1984, Fred Sanford, an amateur musician from Illinois, sued Michael Jackson for $5 million, claiming that Jackson's song "The Girl Is Mine" infringed his song "Please Love Me Now." Sanford claimed that Jackson had access to his song because he gave a tape containing the song to an executive at CBS Records (Jackson's record label) in 1982. Sanford also alleged that at that time Jackson was behind schedule for his *Thriller* album and was looking for a duet to perform with Paul McCartney; Sanford's song was a duet.

Jackson claimed that he had never heard Sanford's song and that he composed "The Girl Is Mine" in 1981 while in London by singing the melody and other parts into a tape recorder. At trial, Jackson spent four hours on the witness stand demonstrating how he composed his song by clapping his hands, snapping his fingers, playing a work tape, and singing the melody over some of his other songs to show that it was part of his songwriting repertoire.

The jury reached a verdict in favor of Jackson after deliberating for over 21 hours. Sanford's attorney stated that he believed that his client would have won if it wasn't for Jackson's fame. Although this is debatable, it is certainly possible that an artist of Jackson's stature could have a prejudicial effect on a judge or jury. In fact, it was reported that the judge had Jackson come to his chambers to meet his 15-year-old daughter. Interestingly, CBS Records instituted a strict policy of not accepting any unsolicited material after this lawsuit was filed.

### (2) Being Famous Can Be Dangerous—Cartier v. Jackson[15]

In 1992, Crystal Cartier, an aspiring songwriter from Denver, sued Michael Jackson for $40 million, claiming that Jackson's song "Dangerous" infringed upon her song of the same title. Cartier claimed to have written her song in 1985 and registered it in 1991, while Jackson registered his song in 1992.

There were many problems with Cartier's claim, possibly reflected by the fact that she could not find any entertainment attorney willing to represent her. (Cartier maintained that everyone connected with the music industry was afraid to take her case.) Instead, she was represented by a small personal injury and real estate law firm that, during the trial, was frequently lectured by the judge on how to proceed with their case. It also became apparent that Cartier was obsessed with Jackson. She had written a novel that featured a vampire named Michael the Meek and wanted Jackson to co-star with her in a film based on the novel.

For proof of access, Cartier contended that she gave Jackson's road manager a copy of her demo tape backstage at a concert in 1988. She also claimed to have given a demo tape to an executive at Warner-Chappell Music, a publishing company that administered Jackson's publishing catalog. The executive claimed that he threw the tape away without listening to it. One of the many factors that hurt Cartier's claim was that she did not have a copy of the demo tape she allegedly distributed. She claimed that she had given all of her copies of the tape away and wasn't able to locate any of them. The court refused to allow her to submit a recording that allegedly re-created the original demo from Cartier's memory.

Jackson testified that he had never heard Cartier's song and that he had a strict policy of never accepting unsolicited tapes. He also stated that his "Dangerous" grew out of a song called "Streetwalker" that he had previously written in 1985. Supporting Jackson's explanation of how he composed the song, a co-writer of "Dangerous" testified that he had developed the song's musical structure by taking a bass line from "Streetwalker," after which Jackson wrote the melody and lyrics of the song.

Cartier used an expert witness to testify as to the similarities between the songs. The expert testified that both songs were in the key of D-minor, the rhythmic structures and melodies of the songs were identical, both recordings contained urban sound effects and rap passages, the bass and drum patterns were similar, and the word "dangerous" was repeated in the third measure of each song's chorus. The court gave little weight to the expert's opinion, partly due to the fact that he was employed as a construction worker (although he had formerly been an assistant to a producer for the Doors), and held that Cartier failed to prove access or substantial similarity.

### (3) Thieving Diva or Publicity-Hungry Plaintiff?—Selletti v. Carey[16]

Christopher Selletti brought a copyright infringement lawsuit against Mariah Carey and her co-writer in 1996, alleging that Carey appropriated a poem he had written in 1989 as the basis of her song "Hero," recorded in 1993 on her *Music Box* album.

Selletti's case was so weak that the judge stated that "I am firmly convinced that Selletti's allegation that defendants misappropriated the lyrics to 'Hero' from him is a complete fabrication." Selletti's only evidence of access was his testimony that he had worked for musician Sly Stone in 1989 as a personal assistant when he wrote his poem. He gave a copy of the poem to Stone shortly before being fired and never heard from Stone about the poem again.

The judge found it patently unbelievable that "two successful songwriters, including one who is a superstar of pop music, misappropriated his lyrics and published them as their own essentially without changing a word." The judge also stated that Selletti appeared to be more interested in "extorting potentially deep-pocket defendants" than in proving his claim. Selletti had repeatedly failed to comply with court orders to produce evidence while taking every opportunity to publicize his case in the media. For example, Selletti appeared on the NBC television show *Court TV: Inside America's Courts* in a segment that showed a photograph of Carey with the headline "Thieving Diva?" Selletti also contradicted himself repeatedly during the case, apparently changing his version of the facts as he thought up new ones.

On the other hand, Carey and co-writer Walter Afanasieff, who had previously written several hit songs together, presented strong evidence of their independent creation of "Hero." They submitted tape recordings of two writing sessions during which they worked on the song with Afanasieff playing the piano, Carey singing, and the two discussing different options.

Carey also submitted a notebook that she used to write down song ideas. The notebook included various versions of the lyrics to "Hero" in Carey's handwriting, with some words crossed out or added in a different color. Many of the pages were dated from 1992 to 1993.

Additionally, Carey introduced evidence that the producers of the movie *Hero* (starring Dustin Hoffman) approached Afanasieff about writing a song for the movie, and Afanasieff approached Carey about writing the song. Although the movie producers decided not to include the song in the movie, it appeared that it was written for the movie; the song and movie plot revolve around the same theme, that there is a potential hero inside even the most unlikely individuals.

### (4) Subconscious Songwriting—Bright Tunes Music Corp. v. Harrisongs Music, Ltd.[17]

Bright Tunes, a publishing company that owned the copyright to the song "He's So Fine," sued George Harrison, claiming that his song "My Sweet Lord" was an infringement. "He's So Fine" was recorded by the Chiffons in 1962 and became a number-one hit.

Proving access did not present a problem in this case because Harrison admitted having heard "He's So Fine" prior to writing "My Sweet Lord." Even without that admission, access could be inferred from the fact that "He's So Fine" was such a highly popular song that it received an abundance of radio airplay, providing access to the general public.

The court found Harrison guilty of infringement even though it believed that Harrison had not intentionally copied "He's So Fine." Instead, based on the fact that Harrison had access and that the songs were "virtually identical," the judge concluded that Harrison had subconsciously copied "He's So Fine," with the following explanation:

*I conclude that the composer, in seeking musical materials to clothe his thoughts, was working with various possibilities. As he tried this possibility and that, there came to the surface of his mind a particular combination that pleased him as being one he felt would be appealing to a prospective listener; in other words, that this combination of sounds would work. Why? Because his subconscious knew it already had worked in a song his conscious mind did not remember…. Did Harrison deliberately use the music of "He's So Fine?" I do not believe he did so deliberately. Nevertheless, it is clear that "My Sweet Lord" is the very same song as "He's So Fine" with different words, and Harrison had access to "He's So Fine." This is, under the law, infringement of copyright, and is no less so even though subconsciously accomplished.*

This case illustrates that you can be liable for infringement even if you are unaware that you are infringing. Harrison paid $587,000 in damages for his unintentional infringement. The idea of subconscious infringement has been criticized because it is based on knowledge of what is in a person's subconscious mind at the time a work is created. The next case presents an even more troubling example of subconscious infringement.

### (5) Infringement Isn't a Wonderful Thing—Three Boys Music Corporation v. Michael Bolton[18]

In a suit by the Isley Brothers against Michael Bolton, a jury concluded that Bolton's song "Love Is a Wonderful Thing" was an infringement of a 1966 Isley Brothers song by the same title. Bolton's defense relied on lack of access because he and his co-writer were only 15 years old when the Isley Brothers' song was released. Further, the Isley Brothers' song was not a hit and received only limited radio airplay. However, the song received some radio airplay in 1966 and 1967 in suburban Connecticut, where Bolton and his co-author grew up, and has had limited airplay on oldies radio stations since that time and has been performed at Isley Brothers concerts.

The court found Bolton guilty of infringement, noting that it may have been subconscious infringement. The court's decision is somewhat troubling because it relies on the assumption that Bolton subconsciously copied a 20-year-old song that was not a hit. The appeals court admitted that this case presented a much more attenuated case of access and subconscious copying than the Harrison case, but it did not believe that the evidence was so weak that it warranted a reversal of the jury verdict. The court stated that "[i]t is entirely plausible that two Connecticut teenagers obsessed with rhythm and blues music could remember an Isley Brothers song that was played on the radio and television for a few weeks and subconsciously copy it 20 years later."

### (6) I'm Not That Innocent (or Am I?)—Cottrill v. Spears[19]

Two songwriters claimed that Britney Spears infringed their song called "What You See Is What You Get," for which they obtained a copyright registration on December 1, 1999. After registering the copyright, they sent a copy of the song to an individual named Kahn, whom they hoped would give the song to an employee of Zomba Records, Britney Spears' record label. Kahn admitted receiving the song, but claimed he never gave it to anyone else because he didn't think it was any good. A copy of the song was also given to Lou Pearlman, the owner of a company responsible for teen pop groups the Backstreet Boys and *NSYNC as well as Spears, all of whom were signed to Zomba Records. A federal district court and appeals court both felt that there was not sufficient evidence of access by Spears to have copied the plaintiff's song. Although the songwriters could prove that the song reached individuals associated with Zomba, they had no evidence that these individuals made Spears aware of the song. Additionally, there was evidence that the melody of Spears' song (also called "What You See Is What You Get") was completed prior to the registration date of the plaintiff's song. Because they could not prove that Spears had an opportunity to view or copy the work, the case was dismissed.

### (7) Independent Infringement or Copyright Destiny—Toliver v. Sony Music Entertainment, Inc.[20]

A woman who wrote a song entitled "Independent Lady" sued Destiny's Child's record label, contending that their hugely popular recording of the song "Independent Women (Part I)" was an infringement. Although Sony admitted access to the plaintiff's song, it argued that "Independent Women" was independently created and not substantially similar to "Independent Lady." This case provides a good illustration of what portions of a song are protected by copyright and what portions are not. The plaintiff alleged that, even though there was no musical similarity, there was substantial similarity between the two songs in terms of format, narration, theme, subject matter, underlying idea, moral, incident, causal connection, structure, character, motivation, dominant psychological peculiarities, name, setting, peculiar arrangement of words, etc. Characterizing the plaintiff's claim as "off-key" and criticizing her attorney for encouraging her to bring an arguably frivolous claim, the court ruled that the only similarities were that the songs both had a female narrator and involved a theme of independence; the rest of the alleged similarities all involved uncopyrightable material. In this case, the court clearly believed that both songs were composed independently.

### (8) Fair Play by Coldplay? Satriani v. Christopher Martin, et al.[21]

In December 2008, guitarist Joe Satriani filed an infringement suit against English rock band Coldplay, alleging that Coldplay's "Viva la Vida" was based on Satriani's song "If I Could Fly." Double GRAMMY nominations of "Viva la Vida" that year helped focus attention on the lawsuit, sensationalized by reports that Coldplay's attempts to avoid being served with court papers might prompt Satriani's attorneys to serve them at the GRAMMY award show.[22] However, Coldplay responded definitively to the lawsuit, both by filing its answer in court in April 2009 and by posting a statement on its website. The website response stated:

> With the greatest possible respect to Joe Satriani, we have now unfortunately found it necessary to respond publicly to his allegations. If there are any similarities between our two pieces of music, they are entirely coincidental, and just as surprising to us as to him. Joe Satriani is a great musician, but he did not write the song "Viva la Vida." We respectfully ask him to accept our assurances of this and wish him well with all future endeavours."[23]

The sentiment of this public statement was echoed in their answer, which denied any infringement and asserted several affirmative defenses, including independent creation of "Viva la Vida" by Coldplay and an assertion that "If I Could Fly" lacked originality and was therefore not protectable under copyright law. Although "Viva la Vida" won two GRAMMYs for both the song and album on which it appeared, there were no winners or losers in the court case. The parties ultimately filed a joint stipulation for dismissal of the lawsuit, opting to settle their claims out of court in September 2009, yet the case sparked vigorous speculation and numerous analyses of the two songs during its pendency.

### (9) "Caught Up"... in a Losing Case—Pyatt v. Raymond, et al.[24]

Artist plaintiff Pyatt sued numerous well-known music industry defendants, including Usher, Alicia Keys, Sony Music Entertainment, La Face Records, Zomba Recording, EMI Music Publishing, Jermaine Dupre, and a number of other artists, music publishers, and record companies, alleging infringement of a song she wrote entitled "Caught Up," asserting that the defendants' song bearing the same title was copied from hers. The allegedly infringing song appears on recording artist Usher's album titled *Confessions*. Ms. Pyatt's association with the defendants began when she was signed to a record deal by MBK Entertainment (MBK), a record label and management company that scouted talent for Alicia Keys and Jeffrey Robinson (president of MBK). At MBK's request, Pyatt submitted handwritten lyrics, songs, and other materials to MBK, including her song titled "Caught Up." She was also asked by MBK to ghost write songs for Alicia Keys and other MBK artists and to release the rights to "Caught Up," all of which she declined. Her "Caught Up" album with MBK was suspended. In 2005, two years after she submitted her song to MBK, she heard Usher's "Caught Up" on the radio, prompting her to file an infringement suit to enforce her copyrights in two versions of song lyrics and a sound recording of "Caught Up." The court applied a "total concept and feel" substantial similarity test. After conducting a side-by-side comparison of the song lyrics, it concluded that although the songs shared a common theme, they had no other similarities. The court opined:

> The only similarity between the songs is the phrase "caught up," which also serves as the title of both songs and is spoken repeatedly by the narrator in both songs. The phrase "caught up," however, is used commonly in everyday speech.... Common phrases are not subject to copyright protection. Nor will substantial similarity be found if only a small, common phrase appears in both the accused and complaining songs; unless the reappearing phrase is especially unique or qualitatively important, there is no basis for inferring copying. ...Pyatt cannot claim that she coined the phrase "caught up" because it existed long before she included it in her song.

---

**Note:** The decision provides a brief description of each defendant, which aids in ascertaining the relationship of each to the song in dispute. Though these descriptions are not definitively clear in every instance, each defendant appears to either share in copyright ownership or was involved in the artistic development of the song at issue.

---

Likewise, the court found no similarity in the plaintiff's and defendants' sound recordings, noting differences between the lyrics and stylistic differences yielding a different "overall musical impression" of each work.

## V. Liability for Infringement

Once it has been decided that an infringement has occurred, it is often necessary to determine who is legally liable or responsible for the infringement. A person who actually commits an infringement will always be liable, and that type of liability is referred to as direct infringement.

However, copyright law also recognizes that third parties who aid, contribute to, participate in, or benefit from infringement may be held liable as well.

There are four types of copyright infringement: direct infringement, contributory infringement, vicarious infringement, and inducement infringement. Direct infringement applies to a person who actually commits the infringing act by violating the copyright owner's exclusive rights. However, in some cases, a direct infringer cannot easily be located or might be financially insolvent, which makes suing the direct infringer impractical. In such cases, copyright owners will often attempt to hold third parties liable, either in place of or in addition to any direct infringers, under three doctrines of secondary liability: (1) contributory, (2) vicarious, and (3) inducement infringement liability. Once parties have been found liable, it is permissible to recover any legal remedies due to the plaintiff from more than one liable party, known as joint and several liability.

## A. Contributory Infringement

Contributory copyright infringement occurs when a party has knowledge of the infringing activity and induces, causes, or materially contributes to the infringing conduct of another. In other words, if a business has control over its business operations and knows that infringing activity occurs when these operations take place, continued tolerance of the infringing activity contributes to the infringement, and the business may be liable for the infringement as well as the direct infringer.

**Example 10.11**

In *Gershwin Publishing Corp. v. Columbia Artists Management*,[25] the American Society of Composers, Authors and Publishers (ASCAP) sued Columbia Artists Management for copyright infringement. On January 9, 1965, concert artists managed by Columbia performed ASCAP songs for profit at a public concert. Although the performing artists rather than Columbia actually committed the infringing acts, Columbia knew that copyrighted music was being performed and that a license authorizing the performances had not been obtained. The court found Columbia liable for contributory infringement, holding that its participation in the formation, direction, and programming of the concert placed it in a position to police the conduct of the artists.

There are two requirements for contributory infringement. First, the defendant must have knowledge of the infringing activity. Second, the defendant must substantially participate in the infringing activity. Knowledge will often be proven by a copyright owner or its attorney sending a letter, known as a cease and desist letter, informing a business of infringing activity.

Substantial participation can include providing materials or facilities to commit the infringing activity. In one case,[26] an Internet bulletin board service was held liable for contributory infringement for downloading copyrighted video games over its service. The court held that the bulletin board service had knowledge of and encouraged the unauthorized uploading and downloading of the video games, "including provision of facilities, direction, knowledge, and encouragement," and that its participation in the infringement was therefore substantial. Another court ruled that a third party did not have to go so far as "expressly promoting or encouraging the sale of counter-feit products, or…protecting the identity of the infringers," and that simply "providing the site and facilities for known infringing activity" constituted substantial participation.[27]

## B. Vicarious Infringement

Vicarious infringement occurs when a defendant has the right and ability to control an infringer's activity and receives a direct financial benefit from the infringement. While contributory infringement requires knowledge of the infringing activity, vicarious liability can be imposed regardless of the defendant's knowledge or intention. Although it may seem strange to impose liability on someone who is not even aware of the infringement, vicarious liability is based in part on the third party's ability to supervise infringing conduct.

In *Shapiro, Bernstein & Co. v. H.L. Green Co.*,[28] a department store that leased floor space to a concessionaire who sold records was held liable for the sale of bootleg records, even though the department store was not aware that the records being sold were not legitimate. The court stated that:

> *When the right and ability to supervise coalesce with an obvious and direct financial interest in the exploitation of copyrighted materials, even in the absence of actual knowledge that the copyright monopoly is being impaired, the purposes of copyright law may be best effectuated by the imposition of liability upon the beneficiary of that exploitation.*

Because the store received a percentage of the revenue from record sales, it directly benefited from the infringing activity. Another important rationale for the court's decision was to discourage large department stores from using dummy concessions that would protect them from liability for copyright infringement while allowing them to benefit from infringement. This illustrates one of the underlying rationales for vicarious liability; businesses should not be able to escape liability by using others to actually commit infringing acts, while either pretending to be ignorant of or intentionally remaining ignorant of the infringing conduct.

One area where vicarious liability has often been found involves the public performance right. Many court decisions have held that a business that actively operates or supervises a place where unauthorized performances of music occur and receives a direct or indirect benefit from the performances will be liable as a vicarious infringer. Owners of bars and nightclubs have been found vicariously liable for infringements committed by performers at their premises because of their ability to supervise the music that is performed and because they receive a direct financial benefit from performances that bring customers into the club.

Some club owners have attempted to escape liability by arguing that they do not directly profit from the infringing performances when the club does not receive any cover charge for the performances. However, most courts have found that clubs still receive an indirect financial benefit because the performances are meant to attract customers, who spend money on drinks and food. Alternatively, club owners have argued that they do not have any control over whether performers play copyrighted music or not. However, courts have tended to view the control requirement fairly broadly, sometimes even holding clubs liable when they warned performers not to play any copyrighted works without a license.

---

**Example 10.12**

---

In *Dreamland Ballroom v. Shapiro, Bernstein & Co.,*[29] a dance hall hired an orchestra that chose all of the music it performed, including copyrighted compositions owned by the plaintiff. The dance hall was found liable for the infringement committed by the orchestra because it hired the orchestra and stood to make a profit from its performance. The court's decision was based solely on the dance hall's financial benefit from the performance and did not even mention whether the dance hall had any control over the performance.

---

---

**Example 10.13**

---

In *Fonovisa, Inc. v. Cherry Auction, Inc.,*[30] Cherry Auction ran a flea market where independent vendors set up booths to sell cassette tapes as well as other items. Fonovisa, a record company that specialized in Latin recordings, sued Cherry Auction, alleging that many of the tapes sold were unauthorized copies of its copyrighted sound recordings. Fonovisa also alleged that Cherry Auction knew that most of the tapes being sold were counterfeit because they were being sold for prices well below normal sales prices (for example, three tapes for $5). Although the vendors were direct infringers, Cherry Auction was found liable for both contributory and vicarious infringement. With respect to contributory infringement, the court found that Cherry Auction was clearly aware that massive quantities of counterfeited recordings were being sold and that Cherry Auction's provision of booth space, utilities, parking, advertising, plumbing, and customers materially contributed to the infringement. With respect to vicarious liability, the court found that Cherry Auction controlled and patrolled the vendors during the flea market and received substantial financial benefits from the infringing sales, including rental fees from vendors, admission fees from customers, and payments for parking, food, and other services.

---

Contributory infringement and vicarious liability are also extremely important in the context of infringements that occur over the Internet. Because there are many direct infringers, it is not practical for copyright owners to sue them all individually for infringement. Instead, copyright owners usually prefer to sue the Internet service provider that provides Internet access and other facilities that enable infringements to take place (see Chapter 15, "The Online Music War," for further discussion of contributory infringement and vicarious liability in the context of the Internet).

### C. Inducement Liability

*MGM v. Grokster,*[31] a Supreme Court case decided in 2005, is significant not only for its potential impact on online infringement through filesharing technology (see discussion in Chapter 15), but for its impact on interpretations of secondary liability. The *Grokster* decision imported the theory of inducement liability from patent law and applied it to copyright law in that case. Thus the court presented a new conceptualization of secondary liability, though one not wholly unfamiliar to copyright law, as inducement is considered one of the elements of contributory liability. An analysis of the court's approach in *Grokster* elucidates:

> *Justice Souter's majority opinion referred to contributory infringement this way: "One infringes contributorily by intentionally inducing or encouraging direct infringement ...." This passage evokes the classic formulation of contributory liability in copyright cases, predating Sony: "[O]ne who with knowledge of the*

*infringing activity, induces, causes or materially contributes to the infringing conduct of another, may be held liable as a 'contributory' infringer."*[32]

If inducement can subject a defendant to contributory liability, the question of whether inducement qualifies as a third category of secondary liability as an additional and separate cause of action with distinguishable elements was introduced, but not resolved, in *Grokster*. There the court set forth a description of inducement:

> Evidence of *"active steps...taken to encourage direct infringement,"* Oak Industries, Inc. v. Zenith Electronics Corp., 697 F. Supp. 988, 992 (N.D.Ill.1988), *such as advertising an infringing use or instructing how to engage in an infringing use, show an affirmative intent that the product be used to infringe....*[33]

It is not only that encouraging a particular consumer to infringe a copyright can give rise to secondary liability for the infringement that results. Inducement liability goes beyond that, and the distribution of a product can itself give rise to liability where evidence shows that the distributor intended and encouraged the product to be used to infringe. In such a case, the culpable act is not merely the encouragement of infringement but also the distribution of the tool intended for infringing use.[34] This description of inducement gives rise to a type of inducement inclusive of elements not found in traditional contributory theory, the element of intent, for example, and removes the knowledge element that would normally be required. Therefore, while inducement may be an aspect of contributory liability—which the court itself acknowledges—the ruling muddies these waters a bit. Moreover, the court explicitly declined to entertain a vicarious liability analysis but did not provide such a distinction for contributory liability.

Accordingly, the decision has yielded different interpretations of inducement liability. Some courts have found that inducement is not a third category of liability but is an aspect of contributory infringement, while others have not.[35] Most recently, in *Arista Records LLC v. Lime Group LLC, et al.,*[36] the U.S. District Court for the Southern District of New York found the LimeWire defendants, creators of the LimeWire filesharing service (see Chapter 15) liable for copyright infringement. LimeWire generated annual revenues "that grew from nearly $6 million to an estimated $20 million" between 2004 and 2006.[37] The court found liability under inducement liability, but not under contributory liability, upholding inducement theory as a third category of secondary liability. In setting forth its interpretation of the *Grokster* decision, the court stated:

> *In Grokster, the Supreme Court confirmed that inducement of copyright infringement constitutes a distinct cause of action.*[38]

The court went on to distinguish between the two types of liability, stating:

> *Unlike an inducement claim, a claim for contributory infringement does not require a showing that the defendant intended to foster infringement.*[39]

The court's rationale in upholding inducement as a third category of liability rested on its finding of evidence that LimeWire had "engaged in purposeful conduct that fostered infringement, with the intent to foster such infringement."[40] Though not all courts may choose to view inducement as a third category of liability, as the LimeWire court did, *Grokster* opened the door for recognition of inducement as a separate cause of action. (See Chapter 15 for further discussion of LimeWire.)

## D. Joint and Several Liability

If a copyright owner wins an infringement suit, all infringing parties (whether via direct, contributory, vicarious, or inducement theory) will be jointly and severally liable for the infringement. In other words, the copyright owner can try to collect its judgment from any of the losing parties. This is an important reason why copyright infringement lawsuits often include more than one defendant.

---

**Example 10.14**

If you believed that a song you own was stolen by a famous recording artist, you would sue not only the artist, but also the artist's record company and the publishing company that claims to own the artist's song. If you sue and win, you would then be able to collect your award from whomever you can get it from first. If the artist claims he is broke and files for bankruptcy, you would still be entitled to collect the full amount from the record company and the publisher.

---

# Endnotes

1. 17 U.S.C. § 501(b).
2. 586 F.3d 334 (C.A.5 (Tex.), 2009)
3. 420 F. Supp. 177 (SDNY 1976).
4. *Selle v. Gibb,* 567 F. Supp. 1173 (1983).
5. *Ferguson v. National Broadcasting Co.,* 584 F.2d 111, 113 (5th Cir. 1978).
6. 2010 WL 1493846 (M.D. Tenn. 2010).
7. *Id.* at 5.
8. 558 F.3d 485, 493 (6th Cir. 2009).
9. 863 F.2d 1061 (1988).
10. *Darrell v. Joe Morris Music Co.,* 113 F.2d 80 (2d Cir. 1940).
11. 585 F.3d 267, 275 (C.A.6 (Tenn.), 2009).
12. Melville B. Nimmer and David Nimmer, *Nimmer on Copyright* § 13.03(A)(2)(a) (Matthew Bender, Rev. Ed.).
13. *Id.* at 13.03(A)(2)(b).
14. 567 F. Supp. 1173 (1983).
15. 59 F.3d 1046 (1995).
16. 177 F.R.D. 189 (1998).
17. 420 F. Supp. 177 (1976).
18. 212 F.3d 477 (2000).
19. 2004 U.S. App. LEXIS 1440 (3d Cir. 2004).
20. 149 F. Supp. 2d 909 (2001).
21. Civ. No. 2:2008cv07987 (CCDA 2008).
22. Roger Friedman, "Gwyneth's Hubby: Viva La Lawsuit," FoxNews.com, February 4, 2009.
23. http://coldplay.com/newsdetail.php?id=242.
24. 2011 WL 2078531 (SDNY 2011).

25.  443 F.2d 1159 (2d Cir. 1971).
26.  *Sega Enters. Ltd v. MAPHIA*, 857 F. Supp. 679 (N.D. Cal. 1994).
27.  *Fonovisa, Inc., v. Cherry Auction, Inc.*, 76 F.3d 259 (9th Cir. 1996) (quoting *Fonovisa v. Cherry Auction, Inc.*, 847 F. Supp. 1492, 1496 (E.D. Cal. 1994)).
28.  316 F.2d 304 (2d Cir. 1963).
29.  36 F.2d 354 (7th Cir. 1929).
30.  76 F.3d 259 (9th Cir. 1996).
31.  545 U.S. 913, 125 S. Ct. 2764, (U.S., 2005).
32.  William Patry, *Patry on Copyright Law*, § 21:41. The "classic formulation" excerpted here by Patry is from *Gershwin Pub. Corp. v. Columbia Artists Management, Inc.*, 443 F.2d 1159 (C.A.N.Y. 1971).
33.  545 U.S. 913, 936, 125 S. Ct. 2764, 2779 (U.S., 2005).
34.  545 U.S. 913, 940, 125 S. Ct. 2764, 2782 (U.S., 2005).
35.  See, e.g., the "Perfect 10" cases, decided by the 9th circuit court of appeals: *Perfect 10, Inc. v. Visa Intern Ass'n*, 494 F. 3d 788, 800 (9th Cir. 2007); *Perfect 10, Inc. v. Amazon.com, Inc.*, 508 F.3d 1146 (9th Cir. 2007).
36.  2011 WL 1742029 (SDNY 2011).
37.  *Id.* at 19.
38.  *Id.* at 15.
39.  *Id.* at 21.
40.  *Id.* at 21.

# 11 Defenses to Infringement

*If nature has made one thing less susceptible than all others of exclusive property, it is the action of the thinking power called an idea, which an individual may exclusively possess as long as he keeps it to himself; but the moment it is divulged, it forces itself into the possession of everyone, and the receiver cannot dispossess himself of it... That ideas should freely spread from one to another over the globe, for the moral and mutual instruction of man, and improvement of his condition, seems to have been peculiarly and benevolently designed by nature, when she made them, like fire, expansible over all space, without lessening their density at any point, and like the air in which we breathe, move, and have our physical being, incapable of confinement or exclusive appropriation.*

—*Thomas Jefferson*

A copyright owner's exclusive rights are subject to various defenses. A defense is a defendant's assertion of a legal reason why the plaintiff's claim is not valid. In certain situations, even when someone has directly copied from a copyrighted work, the person may not be liable for copyright infringement if the otherwise infringing conduct is protected by a defense.

There are several general legal defenses that may apply to copyright infringement claims as well as certain specific defenses to copyright infringement claims. The most important of these defenses are discussed in this chapter.

## I. Statute of Limitations

Like most types of legal claims, copyright infringement claims are subject to a statute of limitations. A statute of limitations is a law that specifies a maximum time period during which a claim can be made. Statutes of limitations are intended to encourage people to act promptly to enforce their rights. In general, the longer you wait to bring a legal claim, the more difficult it is to resolve a dispute fairly because witnesses' memories fade over time, relevant documents may be lost, and witnesses may die or be unavailable to testify.

The 1976 Copyright Act provides that a claim for copyright infringement must be brought within three years from the date upon which the infringement should reasonably have been discovered.[1] When an infringement should have reasonably been discovered is a question that must be resolved by a court.

**Example 11.1**

In *Merchant v. Lymon*,[2] a court held that the three-year statute of limitations prevented the plaintiffs from recovering royalties from the hit song "Why Do Fools Fall in Love?" The plaintiffs—two members of the group Frankie Lymon and the Teenagers—claimed that the copyright registration for the song inaccurately attributed authorship credit and that they were co-authors of the song with Frankie Lymon. The song was recorded and released on Gee Records, which was owned by George Goldner. Goldner filed a copyright registration in 1956, listing himself and Lymon as sole co-authors. He later amended the registration to state that the actual authors were Lymon and Morris Levy, who had purchased Gee Records and Goldner's publishing company. Levy was reported to have ties to the Mafia, and although the plaintiffs alleged that the reason they had not brought their claim earlier was that Levy had threatened to have them killed, the court refused to suspend the statute of limitations. Because the plaintiffs took no formal legal action until bringing their lawsuit in 1987, the statute of limitations prohibited them from recovering royalties earned prior to three years before commencement of the lawsuit.

The three-year limitations period for copyright infringement claims begins to run from the moment the infringement begins. If the infringement is of a continuing nature, the limitations period begins to run from the date of the last act of infringement. Generally, if you win a suit for copyright infringement, you can only recover the damages or profits that were earned within three years before the suit.

In some circumstances, courts will decide to toll or delay the application of the statute of limitations. This is usually only done for what are called equitable reasons, if it would be unfair to apply the statute of limitations to the particular case. For instance, in cases where an infringer has concealed the infringing activity from the copyright owner, courts will almost always toll the statute of limitations. When deciding whether the statute of limitations should be tolled, courts will usually balance the degree to which the copyright owner was justifiably ignorant of the infringing conduct against the degree to which the infringer justifiably relied on the copyright owner's failure to sue within the limitations period. When the statute of limitations is tolled, it will not be applied until the copyright owner discovered or by reasonable diligence should have discovered the infringing activity.

**Example 11.2**

A recording artist in Australia records a song copyrighted in the United States without obtaining a license and without the copyright owner's knowledge. The record containing the artist's song is released solely in Australia in 1990. If the copyright owner doesn't find out about the record until 1999, a court might toll the statute of limitations and allow the copyright owner to recover damages for all of the record sales that occurred since 1990. However, if the record received radio airplay in the United States, a court would be much less likely to toll the statute of limitations because the copyright owner should have known of its existence. In this situation, the copyright owner would still be able to recover damages for infringements that occurred during the three years before the copyright owner files suit for infringement (1996–1999).

---

**Tip:** If you believe that a copyrighted work that you own is being infringed, contact a copyright attorney promptly to avoid potential statute of limitations problems. The longer you wait to enforce your rights, the greater the risk that you will lose your rights.

---

# II. Abandonment of Copyright

A copyright owner can abandon its copyright by committing some act that clearly indicates an intent to surrender rights in the copyrighted work and to allow the public to copy it. Abandoning a copyright essentially means donating a work to the public domain so that it can be freely used by others. For instance, a copyright owner may declare its intent to abandon the copyright to a work by placing a statement on copies of the work indicating that the work is free to be reproduced, performed, or displayed. Prior to March 1, 1989 (the effective date of the Berne Implementation Amendment), abandonment could occur due to the copyright owner's distribution of a work without copyright notice. However, the Copyright Act does not specify how copyrights can be abandoned, so courts have had to address this issue at times. The basic test that courts have come up with is that a copyright owner must intend to abandon his or her rights in the copyrighted work and must manifest this intent through some overt act.[3]

The best way for a copyright owner to manifest an intent to abandon a copyright is to make a clear statement indicating such intent in writing. For example, a copyright owner could include a statement on copies of the work such as "This work is donated to the public domain and is not protected by copyright." It might also be advisable to include a date in such a statement if the work has previously been protected by copyright. A signed document abandoning copyright can also be recorded with the U.S. Copyright Office to make it clear that the copyright has been abandoned (although this is not required).[4]

It is also possible for a copyright to be abandoned without any written document if a copyright owner's actions clearly show an intent to abandon the work.

---

**Example 11.3**

Folk singer Pete Seeger used a song he learned from a woman who had added new material to a folk hymn. To ensure the song's use, the woman gave Seeger permission to publish it and agreed that she would not receive any authorship credit, ownership, or payment for the new material she had added to the original folk hymn.[5] In this situation, the woman's actions clearly showed her intent to abandon any ownership claim she had to the contribution she had made to the song.

---

Abandonment of copyright does not occur very often and will not be implied by actions such as the failure to prosecute copyright infringements or to promote the copyrighted work. For example, the fact that a formerly published work becomes unpublished, in and of itself, does not constitute abandonment.[6] While abandonment of copyright is not frequent, it has become a bit more common in recent years for copyright owners to allow some degree of free use of their works through new types of licenses such as those provided by the Creative Commons organization.

Under these licenses, copyright owners generally retain copyright ownership of their works but allow certain uses without the need to obtain permission or pay any fees or royalties (see the Creative Commons website at http://creativecommons.org/licenses/ for more information).

# III. Independent Creation

If a defendant in a copyright infringement lawsuit can prove that it created its work independently, rather than having copied it from the plaintiff's work, the defendant will not be liable for infringement. This makes sense because the essence of copyright infringement is copying, and if the defendant did not copy the plaintiff's work, there could not possibly be an infringement.

In order to prove independent creation, the defendant would have to prove that any similarities between its work and the plaintiff's work are coincidental. If the defendant can prove that its work was created before the plaintiff's work, it will be clear that its work was independently created because it obviously could not have copied a work that didn't exist. In such a situation, if the defendant had registered its work shortly after its creation, the registration certificate would be proof of independent creation. If the work was not registered or was registered after creation of the plaintiff's work, the defendant would have to offer some other form of proof of when it created the work, such as witnesses who observed the defendant creating the work or dated notes or recordings evidencing independent creation.

---

**Example 11.4**

In some copyright infringement trials, the artist being sued will actually perform songs or portions of songs in order to show how they were created. In a suit over her song "9 to 5," Dolly Parton sang the Ray Charles song "I Can't Stop Loving You" in the same style as "9 to 5" in order to show how you can make one song sound like another. In 1999, during an infringement trial in Canada, Sarah McLachlan spent a considerable amount of time performing portions of her songs to illustrate her songwriting process. These examples are attempts to prove independent creation and can often be helpful in influencing a jury.

---

**Tip:** Songwriters should keep any written notes (lyric sheets, etc.) or computer files created during the songwriting process or record their songwriting sessions. Mark any notes, files, or recordings with the titles of the songs worked on, the names of the writers, and the date or dates during which the songwriting activity took place. This kind of documentation can be extremely useful if you are ever sued for copyright infringement (as well as in disputes between co-authors) because the notes or recordings can be used as evidence of independent creation.

---

# IV. Fair Use

The defense of fair use is one of the broadest and most confusing doctrines in copyright law. Basically, fair use means that although certain uses of copyrighted works would otherwise be infringements of copyright, these uses should be allowed due to some public benefit derived from them.

## A. What Is Fair Use?

Fair use can be defined as a privilege that allows someone other than the copyright owner to use a copyrighted work in a reasonable manner without the owner's consent.[7] One purpose of fair use is to help accomplish copyright law's primary goal of providing wide access to creative works. It also allows for the right of free speech guaranteed by the First Amendment. The fair use doctrine is intended to allow certain uses of copyrighted works that encourage the advancement of learning and knowledge. As stated by the Supreme Court, fair use:

> [A] llows courts to avoid the rigid application of the copyright statute when, on occasion, it would stifle the very creativity which that law is designed to foster.[8]

---

**Example 11.5**

A music reviewer's quotation of lyrics from a copyrighted song in a review of the song or the album containing the song would be fair use.

---

It is important to understand that fair use is a legal defense rather than an affirmative right. Consequently, the only way to know for sure whether a particular use is fair is if the copyright owner sues for infringement and the court upholds the fair use defense. Although many people use copyrighted works on the assumption that their use is fair, this assumption can be risky because no use is technically a fair use until a court says so. There is no way to be absolutely certain in advance whether a use will be considered fair. You cannot prevent being sued for copyright infringement by claiming fair use.

---

**What Is Fair?**  Some people have misconceptions about the fair use doctrine, often believing that it allows them to use copyrighted works as long as they think it is fair to do so. Fair use, however, depends on whether *a court* thinks your use is fair. Even if you believe that your use qualifies as fair use, it can be very costly to prove that in court. Consequently, it is often advisable to request permission for the use of copyrighted works and pay the customary fee or royalty even if you think the use may be fair. The amount you pay under a license to use a work will almost always be less than the amount you will spend in defending a copyright infringement claim.

---

**Credit Does Not Equal Fair Use**  Some people mistakenly believe that it is fair use to use a copyrighted work as long as you give credit to the author or copyright owner of the work used. There is no such rule, and crediting the author is not likely to be helpful in proving fair use. Others believe that any use of a copyrighted work is fair as long as the user does not profit financially from the use. These misconceptions can be costly if you are sued for infringing a copyrighted work.

---

## B. Origins of Fair Use

Unfortunately, courts have applied the fair use defense inconsistently over the years. The fair use doctrine developed through court decisions in England and the United States and was made a part of the Copyright Act of 1976. The first case to apply the fair use doctrine, *Folsom v. Marsh*,[9] involved an infringement suit brought in 1841 by the copyright owner of a 12-volume historical work on George Washington against a defendant who had made a condensed version of the plaintiff's work. In doing so, the defendant copied 353 pages of the plaintiff's work. The Court stated that to determine whether a particular use of a copyrighted work is fair, the court should examine:

> [The] nature and objects of the selections made, the quantity and value of materials used, and the degree in which the use may prejudice the sale, or diminish the profits, or supersede the objects, of the original work.

Applying these criteria, the court found that the defendant's use was not fair because it would unduly reduce the economic incentive of authors to produce. The court also relied on the fact that the defendant did not really create a new work, but merely edited an existing work into a shorter version. The factors put forth in *Folsom* to evaluate fair use became the basis for every subsequent fair use case in the United States and for the fair use provision of the 1976 Copyright Act. In essence, fair use involves a balancing test between the social benefit that the public derives from the unauthorized use against the interest of the copyright owner.

## C. Fair Use Under the 1976 Copyright Act

The 1976 Copyright Act recognized the fair use doctrine that had developed through case law. However, the Copyright Act does not actually define fair use. In fact, the legislative history to the Copyright Act stated that the fair use doctrine is "an equitable rule of reason" and, as such, is not susceptible to any "generally applicable definition."[10] Instead of providing a definition, the Copyright Act lists several illustrative examples of the types of use that are likely to be fair use and specifies a four-factor test to be used to determine whether a specific use is fair. The fair use provision of the Copyright Act is contained in Section 107, which provides that:

> Notwithstanding the provisions of sections 106 and 106A, the fair use of a copyrighted work, including such use by reproduction in copies or phonorecords or by any other means specified by that section, for purposes such as criticism, comment, news reporting, teaching (including multiple copies for classroom use), scholarship, or research, is not an infringement of copyright. In determining whether the use made of a work in any particular case is a fair use the factors to be considered shall include: (1) the purpose and character of the use, including whether such use is of a commercial nature or is for nonprofit educational purposes; (2) the nature of the copyrighted work; (3) the amount and substantiality of the portion used in relation to the copyrighted work as a whole; and (4) the effect of the use upon the potential market for or value of the copyrighted work.

The first part of Section 107 gives some examples of the types of uses that may be fair use (i.e., criticism, comment, news reporting, teaching, scholarship, and research). It is important to note that these examples are not exhaustive, and there may be other types of uses that will be considered fair use as well. Further, the fact that a use fits one of these categories will not guarantee a finding of fair use. Instead, a determination of whether a use is fair or not depends on the specific circumstances of the use and the application of the Copyright Act's four-factor test to those circumstances.

The second part of Section 107 lists the four factors that must be considered in evaluating a fair use question. To determine whether a particular use is fair, a court must evaluate each of the four factors and weigh them. Although Section 107 does not specify what weight should be given to each of the four factors, courts usually give the greatest weight to the first and fourth factors. A court may also consider any additional factors that it believes are relevant.

### (1) The Purpose and Character of the Use

The analysis of the first factor of the fair use test involves determining the purpose for which the use is being made. There are several considerations that are normally involved in analyzing the purpose of the use, such as whether the use is for a commercial or noncommercial purpose and whether the use is for an educational or some other socially valuable purpose.

One important consideration under the first factor is whether the use is for a commercial or a nonprofit purpose. In general, commercial use will weigh against fair use while nonprofit use will weigh toward fair use. However, not all commercial use will be unfair, and not all nonprofit use will be fair. In reality, most uses are commercial to some extent. According to the Supreme Court:

> [T]he crux of the profit/nonprofit distinction is not whether the sole motive of the use is monetary gain but whether the user stands to profit from exploitation of the copyrighted material without paying the customary price.[11]

Even a commercial use can qualify as fair use if the public will receive some benefit from the defendant's use. In fact, the majority of cases finding fair use have involved commercial uses. As stated by the Supreme Court:

> If, indeed, commerciality carried presumptive force against a finding of fairness, the presumption would swallow nearly all of the illustrative uses listed in the preamble paragraph of Section 107, including news reporting, comment, criticism, teaching, scholarship, and research, because these activities are generally conducted for profit in this country.[12]

The public generally benefits from uses that provide information (i.e., criticism, comment, and news reporting) and uses related to education (i.e., teaching, scholarship, and research). These types of use are therefore more likely to be fair than uses that do not fall within these categories. Additionally, a use that has a productive or transformative purpose is more likely to be fair than a use that merely replaces the original work. If a use changes an original work in some way to create something new, its transformative character may outweigh its commercial purpose.

---

**Example 11.6**

In a 1962 case,[13] Austris Wihtol, who owned the copyright to a musical composition entitled "My God and I," sued Nelson Crow, a high school music teacher who used the composition without permission. Crow copied the composition and used it in a choir arrangement, of which he made 48 photocopies. Crow credited the work as "arranged Nelson E. Crow" and failed to credit Wihtol as the original composer. The District Court ruled that Crow's use was fair, focusing incorrectly on his innocent intent. The Court of Appeals reversed the decision, noting that "whatever may be the breadth of the doctrine of 'fair use', it is not conceivable to us that the copying of all, or substantially all, of a copyrighted song can be held to be a 'fair use' merely because the infringer had no intent to infringe." This example shows that a use made for an educational purpose will not automatically be considered fair.

In certain situations, the character of a use may be incidental. For instance, if a copyrighted work is used incidentally and as background in a different type of work, the use might be fair because it does not compete with the copyrighted work.

### Example 11.7

A television broadcast of a parade that included a band playing a copyrighted song was held to be a fair use. The use was described as an "incidental and fortuitous reproduction, in a newsreel or broadcast, of a work located in the scene of the event being reported."[14] Similarly, the use of 15 seconds of a copyrighted song as part of a political campaign advertisement was held to be fair use when the song was in the background of an opposing politician's radio commercial.[15]

Courts have also considered a defendant's bad faith as weighing against a fair use finding and a defendant's good faith weighing in favor of a fair use finding. Although a defendant's good faith is relevant in fair use analysis, the failure to obtain the copyright owner's permission to use a copyrighted work does not constitute bad faith.

### Example 11.8

In *Campbell v. Acuff-Rose Music, Inc.*[16] (discussed in detail later in this chapter), the court stated that 2 Live Crew's failure to obtain permission to use the song "Oh, Pretty Woman" in a parody did not evidence bad faith. Instead, the Court believed that 2 Live Crew's license request may have been a good faith effort to avoid litigation, showing that they were willing to pay the customary price for their use.

## (2) The Nature of the Copyrighted Work

The second factor to be considered under Section 107 is "the nature of the copyrighted work." This factor is concerned with the copyrighted work itself rather than the use made of the copyrighted work. The use of an unpublished work is less likely to be fair than that of a published work because the copyright owner may have decided for some reason (such as privacy) not to make the work available to the public. Additionally, the use of a factual work is more likely to be fair use than the use of a creative work because facts should be free for everyone to use. Because musical works such as songs and sound recordings are virtually always creative in nature, this factor will normally weigh against fair use. However, this is also usually viewed as the least important of the four factors.

## (3) The Amount and Substantiality of the Portion Used

The third factor involves the amount and substantiality of the portion of the copyrighted work used compared to the copyrighted work as a whole. In general, the greater the amount of a copyrighted work used, the less likely that a use will be fair. In evaluating this factor, it is important to consider only the amount of copyrightable material that has been copied, rather than uncopyrightable ideas or other unprotected material that may be contained in the copyrighted work. It is also important to realize that there are no absolute rules as to how much of a copyrighted work may be copied and still be considered fair use.

---

**Example 11.9**

In a 1978 case,[17] a candidate for political office used 15 seconds of his opponent's copyrighted campaign song in a political ad. The court found that this was a fair use because the song was part of a political message and the portion copied was relatively brief. However, if a more substantial portion of a song was used under similar circumstances, the result could be different. It is not uncommon for songwriters and performers of popular songs to object to the use of their songs by political candidates, especially when they don't share the candidate's political views. In 1984, Bruce Springsteen objected to Ronald Reagan's use of his hit song "Born in the USA" in Reagan's presidential campaign. More recently, in 2011, Tom Petty's music publisher requested that Republican presidential hopeful Michele Bachmann stop using Petty's "American Girl" in her campaign events, and former Florida governor Charlie Crist issued a video apology (posted on YouTube) to David Byrne for his use of the Talking Heads' hit song, "Road to Nowhere" in his 2010 Senate campaign. In 2008, Republican presidential candidate John McCain apologized for his campaign's unauthorized use of the Jackson Browne song "Running on Empty," which was used to criticize his opponent, Barack Obama. Obama, however, was not immune to a copyright owner's objection to the unauthorized use of music when his campaign agreed to stop using "Hold On, I'm Coming" by Sam Moore (half of the Sam & Dave duo that released it in 1966).

---

In addition to the quantity of material copied, the quality of that material must also be considered. In other words, even if only a small portion of a copyrighted work is used, if the portion used is an essential part of the copyrighted work, it will weigh against fair use. Courts often make numeric comparisons (i.e., of words, musical notes, measures, etc.) between the total length of the plaintiff's work and the amount copied by the defendant. For instance, in *Fisher v. Dees*,[18] a court held that the use of the first six bars of a 38-bar song was a fair use. However, more emphasis is normally placed on the quality of the amount copied. Even if only a very small part of a work is copied, the use will not usually be fair if the part taken is of critical importance to the work as a whole. Especially in the case of musical composition, the use of even a very small amount of a copyrighted work may be considered substantial.

---

**Example 11.10**

If someone were to copy the four-note theme from Beethoven's Fifth Symphony, most people would recognize that theme. Even though the copying would only involve four notes and would be quantitatively insubstantial, it would be qualitatively substantial because those four notes constitute the most recognizable part of the work. In this situation, however, there would be no risk of copyright infringement because Beethoven's Fifth Symphony is in the public domain and can therefore be freely copied.

---

**Music Snippets and Fair Use**   Many uses of music, even if only a small portion is used, will probably not be fair unless they are noncommercial and for purposes of criticism, comment, education, or news reporting. In most circumstances, it is advisable to obtain a license rather than rely on fair use. For example, when music is previewed over the Internet, the duration of the preview is generally 10 to 30 seconds. This has apparently led to a mistaken belief that uses of copyrighted works that do not exceed 30 seconds are permitted or may be considered a fair use. However, in *United States v. American Society of Composers, Authors and Publishers,*[19] the court applied the fair use factors to previews of cell phone ringtones or ringbacks of copyrighted musical compositions—whereby customers listen to a shortened version of the composition in order to make a purchasing decision regarding the ringtone/ringback containing the composition—and found that such previews are not fair uses of the copyrighted works.

## (4) The Effect of the Use upon the Potential Market for or Value of the Copyrighted Work

Under the fourth factor, an analysis must be made of how the defendant's use will affect the value of the copyrighted work. This factor is generally viewed as the most important of the four. In the broadest sense, every fair use involves some degree of harm to the copyright owner, because fair uses are not licensed and do not produce income for the copyright owner. However, some degree of harm to the copyright owner is tolerated in certain circumstances due to the public benefit derived from the use of the work.

**Example 11.11**

If a movie producer uses copyrighted music as part of the soundtrack for a movie without obtaining a license, this will usually not be a fair use. Obviously, such a use negatively impacts the market for the copyrighted work because this type of use is normally licensed and is one of the ways copyright owners earn income.

The analysis of the fourth factor must include consideration not only of any actual harm to the market for the work, but also any harm to potential markets for the work. In other words, you have to consider not only what uses of the work the copyright owner has made, but also any future uses the copyright owner might make. Some courts will only consider the impact of the use on traditional or reasonable markets. If the defendant's use produces a work that competes with the plaintiff's work or reduces the potential market for the work, it is likely that there will be an adverse effect on that work and that the use will not be fair. Using a work that is no longer available to the public (i.e., out of print) will be likely to be fair because the use will not impair the market for the original work.

**Example 11.12**

Since the advent of filesharing to download music and other copyrighted works, some people have assumed that downloading is fair use. They may believe that since no money is being charged, copyright owners are not being harmed by such use. However, all courts that have addressed this issue in the United States (as well as most other countries where the question has arisen) have ruled that unauthorized downloading does not qualify as fair use. For example, in *BMG Music v. Gonzalez,*[20] a woman was sued for illegally downloading 30 songs. She asserted the fair use defense on the grounds that she downloaded the songs to determine whether to buy them later. The court found that her use was not fair, relying largely on the fourth fair use factor. Since there were numerous websites that legally allowed users to listen to samples of songs to determine whether to purchase downloads, the court found the sampling fair use argument disingenuous. Downloading entire songs without permission is much more likely to substitute for legal downloads or other legal forms of access. While some people might do so in order to determine whether to purchase a legal copy, many downloaders do so to avoid paying for a legal copy. Further, while it is true no money is charged by file-sharing websites, many of these websites make money through advertising. This does harm copyright owners since these websites do not generally pay any portion of their advertising income to license the copyrighted works that are being used to draw visitors to their websites and create advertising revenue.

When a use is commercial, an adverse impact on the market for the copyrighted work will often be presumed, and the copyright owner will only have to prove that if the use were to become widespread, it would harm potential markets for the work. On the other hand, if the use is transformative, an adverse impact on potential markets for the work will not be presumed.

**Example 11.13**

A magazine publishes a record review that contains part of the lyrics of a song. This use will very likely be fair because the purpose of the use is comment or criticism (a transformative purpose), and it does not adversely affect the market for the original work. Even so, magazine publishers often obtain permission to quote lyrics; music publishers are normally glad to give permission, provided that copyright notice and the phrase "used by permission" accompany the use.

### (5) Parody as Fair Use

Parody is one type of use that will often qualify as fair. One court defined parody as "a literary or artistic work that imitates the characteristic style of an author or a work for comic effect or ridicule."[21] In order for a parody to be protected as fair use, the work copied to make the parody must, at least in part, be the object of the parody. In other words, a parody must comment upon or criticize the original work. The legal definition of parody is different from what is commonly known as satire. Parody involves the use of a copyrighted work in order to criticize or make fun of the work. Satire involves the use of a copyrighted work in order to comment on or make fun of something other than the copyrighted work, such as society in general. Satire, unlike parody, is not as likely to be fair use because it is not necessary to use a copyrighted work to comment upon something other than the copyrighted work.

Although parodies will often be considered to be fair use, there is no rule that all parodies will qualify as fair use. As with any other fair use determination, the specific facts must be analyzed under the four-factor test of Section 107.

#### (a) The 2 Live Crew "Pretty Woman" Case

In order to illustrate how the four-factor fair use test is applied to parody, it is helpful to examine how the Supreme Court utilized this test in an actual case. In 1994, the Supreme Court decided a case that clarified some of the confusion and inconsistency of prior case law applying the fair use doctrine to parody. In *Campbell v. Acuff-Rose Music, Inc.*,[22] a music publisher, Acuff-Rose, sued Luther Campbell of the rap group 2 Live Crew for infringing its copyrighted song "Oh, Pretty Woman," written by Roy Orbison and William Dees. 2 Live Crew had recorded a song called "Pretty Woman" that copied parts of the music and lyrics from "Oh, Pretty Woman." 2 Live Crew had requested a license to use the song from Acuff-Rose, but Acuff-Rose denied the request, and 2 Live Crew released their version of the song anyway.

2 Live Crew asserted that their song was a parody that should be protected under the fair use doctrine. The District Court agreed, holding that 2 Live Crew's "Pretty Woman" was a fair use parody of the Orbison song. Acuff-Rose appealed the decision, and the Court of Appeals reversed, holding that the "blatantly commercial purpose" of 2 Live Crew's parody prevented it from being a fair use. 2 Live Crew appealed this decision, and the Supreme Court agreed to review the case.

The Supreme Court first addressed whether 2 Live Crew's song constituted a legal parody of the Orbison song. The Orbison song involves a 1960s romance and begins with a man who notices a beautiful woman walking down the street. He pleads with her to spend the night with him, but she rejects his advances and walks on by. However, in the last verse, she walks back to him. 2 Live Crew's song also involves a man who notices a woman walking down the street. However, it's a different time period (the 1990s) and a different street (in the hood), where the idealism of the Orbison song no longer exists. According to the Court, 2 Live Crew's version of the song "derisively demonstrates how bland and banal the Orbison song seems to them," stating that:

> *Although the parody starts out with the same lyrics as the original, it quickly degenerates into a play on words, substituting predictable lyrics with shocking ones ... The physical attributes of the subject woman deviate from a pleasing image of femininity to bald-headed, hairy, and generally repugnant. To complete the thematic twist, at the end of the parody, the "two-timin'" woman turns out to be pregnant.*

Under its analysis of the first factor, the Court rejected the idea that the commercial purpose of a use automatically makes the use unfair.[23] Instead, the Court found the transformative nature of the use to be more important. Parody is by definition a transformative use. The value of transformative works is that, rather than merely copying the original work, they also add something new, thereby creating a new work with a different purpose or character. As explained by the Supreme Court:

> *The central purpose of this investigation is to see whether the new work merely supersedes the objects of the original creation or instead adds something new, with a further purpose or different character, altering the first with new expression, meaning or message; it asks, in other words, whether and to what extent the new work is "transformative." Although a transformative use is not necessary for a finding of fair use, the more transformative the new work, the less will be the significance of other factors, such as commercialism, that may weigh against a finding of fair use.*

The Court held that the second factor, the nature of the copyrighted work, weighed against fair use due to the creative nature of the Orbison song. However, the Court didn't place too much weight on this factor because the vast majority of parodies are based upon creative works.

Under the third factor, the amount and substantiality of the portion used in relation to the copyrighted work as a whole, the Supreme Court expanded the degree to which a parodist may copy from an existing work. Earlier cases had held that a parodist is allowed to recall or conjure up the original work. In other words, a parodist could copy enough of a work to make the work recognizable as the object of the parody. Acuff-Rose argued that the 2 Live Crew had taken more of "Oh, Pretty Woman" than was necessary to make it recognizable; 2 Live Crew used almost identical music throughout their parody. The Supreme Court, however, held that parody allows for greater use of a copyrighted work than other types of use because a song is difficult to parody effectively without exact or nearly exact copying. Certainly, a song parody would not be as effective if the music of the original song was not used throughout the parody. As to exactly how much a parodist can copy, the Court related the third factor to the first and third factors, stating that:

*Once enough has been taken to assure identification, how much more is reasonable will depend, say, on the extent to which the song's overriding purpose and character is to parody the original or, in contrast, the likelihood that the parody may serve as a market substitute for the original.*

The Court also stated that in order for a parody to be effective, it must utilize the heart of the original work because:

*It is true, of course, that 2 Live Crew copied the characteristic opening bass riff (or musical phrase) of the original, and true that the words of the first line copy the Orbison lyrics. But if quotation of the opening riff and the first line may be said to go to the "heart" of the original, the heart is also what most readily conjures up the song for parody, and it is the heart at which parody takes aim. Copying does not become excessive in relation to parodic purposes merely because the portion taken was the original's heart. If 2 Live Crew had copied a significantly less memorable part of the original, it is difficult to see how its parodic character would have come through.*

Finally, the Court also mentioned that the amount copied must be balanced against the amount of original material contributed by the parodist. In this case, the Court found that 2 Live Crew had contributed substantial new material (i.e., new lyrics and certain musical effects). The Court remanded to the trial court the issue of whether 2 Live Crew's use of the famous bass line throughout its song was excessive (although the case was subsequently settled so this issue was never resolved).

In analyzing the fourth factor, the effect of the use upon the potential market for or value of the copyrighted work, the Court began by stating that a use that has no demonstrable effect upon the potential market for, or the value of, the copyrighted work need not be prohibited in order to protect the author's incentive to create. Parodies normally will be held to be fair use when the parody is unlike any use the copyright owner could reasonably be expected to make of the work.

In terms of direct competition, the 2 Live Crew song would not seem to have much effect on the market for the Orbison song. In other words, a person desiring the Orbison song is not likely to be satisfied with the 2 Live Crew song. However, licensing harm and harm to the market for potential derivative works must also be considered. Noting that the 2 Live Crew song is not only a parody, but also a rap song, the Court determined that the market for derivative rap versions of "Oh, Pretty Woman" should be considered and remanded this issue to the trial court.

The Court also noted that a parody may harm the original work by criticizing it, thereby potentially reducing its demand. However, such critical impact should not be considered under fair use analysis because parody's primary function is to criticize. The Court stated that:

*...parody may quite legitimately aim at garroting the original, destroying it commercially as well as artistically.*

Although the Court remanded two issues in the 2 Live Crew case for determination by the district court, these two issues were never actually resolved. Apparently, both Acuff-Rose and 2 Live Crew decided they had spent enough time and money fighting over "Pretty Woman" and settled the dispute in 1996 with Acuff-Rose issuing a mechanical license for the 2 Live Crew song.

The Supreme Court's decision in the 2 Live Crew case has been misinterpreted by some people as setting forth a strict rule that all parodies are fair use. In reality, the Supreme Court merely ruled that parodies are likely to qualify as fair use but are subject to evaluation under the four-factor test of Section 107. The Supreme Court did indicate that the two most important factors in analyzing whether a particular parody is a fair use are whether the use is transformative and the effect of the use on the potential market for the original work.

---

**Tip:** Because fair use is never guaranteed, it is often advisable to obtain permission to make a new version of a copyrighted work. For example, Weird Al Yankovic obtains licenses for his derivative versions of popular songs such as "Eat It" (Michael Jackson's "Beat It"), "Like a Surgeon" (Madonna's "Like a Virgin"), "Pretty Fly for a Rabbi" (The Offspring's "Pretty Fly for a White Guy"), and "Perform This Way" (Lady Gaga's "Born This Way"). Legally, Weird Al's recordings might not be considered parodies at all because they typically poke fun at the singer and society at large rather than the song itself, so his derivative works, humorous as they may be, might not qualify as fair use.

---

### (b) Other Parody Cases

There have been a number of copyright lawsuits involving parodies over the years, many of which are very interesting and entertaining. The following are several notable parody cases involving musical works:

1. *Fisher v. Dees:*[24] Disc jockey Rick Dees recorded a parody song entitled "When Sonny Sniffs Glue," which used the music from the 1950s hit song "When Sunny Gets Blue," recorded and made popular by Johnny Mathis. The parody was determined to be a fair use because it did not unfairly diminish the value of the parodied work (i.e., no one interested in hearing a romantic ballad would be satisfied to hear the "silly parody" instead). Although the plaintiff had argued that the parody reflected negatively on the original song and therefore affected its marketability, the court stated that "the economic effect of a parody with which we are concerned is not its potential to destroy or diminish the market for the original—any bad review can have that effect—but whether it fulfills the demand for the original... Parodists will seldom get permission from those whose works are parodied. Self-esteem is seldom strong enough to permit the granting of permission even in exchange for a reasonable fee." In other words, a parody's critical impact on the market for the parodied work is not relevant to the fair use analysis.

2. *Berlin v. E.C. Publications:*[25] Mad Magazine published an issue that contained various parody lyrics (i.e., lyrics that were to be sung to the tune of popular songs). One example involved Irving Berlin's "A Pretty Girl Is Like a Melody." The song was turned into

"Louella Schwartz Describes Her Malady," in which Berlin's tribute to feminine beauty became a parody of a hypochondriac. The parody was held fair use because the use had neither the intent nor the effect of fulfilling the demand for the original songs.

3. *Elsmere Music, Inc. v. NBC:*[26] The television show *Saturday Night Live* did a skit making fun of New York City's public relations campaign, with actors singing a song called "I Love Sodom" to the tune of "I Love New York." The only parts of the original song copied were the words "I love" and four musical notes, but the court held this to be qualitatively substantial. The court ruled it to be a fair use, primarily relying on the fourth factor ("the defendant's version of the jingle did not compete with or detract from the plaintiff's work").

4. *Walt Disney Productions v. Mature Pictures Corp.:*[27] Mature Pictures produced a movie entitled *The Life and Times of the Happy Hooker* that contained a scene in which three teenagers sing part of the lyrics of "The Mickey Mouse March," after which the song is played as background music while the three young men have a sexual encounter with the heroine. Held not to be fair use because the use was not legally a parody; it did not comment or criticize "The Mickey Mouse March." Further, the defendants used the original work without changing or adding anything, so their use was not transformative.

5. *MCA v. Wilson:*[28] A musical play called *Let My People Come,* which was billed as an "erotic nude show," contained a song entitled "Cunnilingus Champion of Company C" sung to the tune of the Andrews Sisters' "Boogie Woogie Bugle Boy of Company B." It was held not fair use because it did not comment on the original work. The court stated that "[w]e are not prepared to hold that a commercial composer can plagiarize a competitor's copyrighted song, substitute dirty lyrics of his own, perform it for commercial gain, and then escape liability by calling the end result a parody or satire on the mores of society."

6. *Bridgeport Music, Inc. v. UMG Recordings, Inc.:*[29] Bridgeport Music, the copyright owner of a 1982 hit song entitled "Atomic Dog," written by George Clinton (leader of the popular funk band Parliament-Funkadelic), sued hip-hop group Public Announcement and its record company, UMG Music. Bridgeport claimed Public Announcement's 1998 song "D.O.G. in Me" infringed the copyright to "Atomic Dog" by copying the phrase "Bow wow wow, yippie yo, yippie yea" and using a repetition of the word "dog" in a low tone of voice at regular intervals throughout the song accompanied by a rhythmic panting sound. Public Announcement admitted that it copied from "Atomic Dog" but argued that the parts copied were insignificant and commonplace and should therefore not be protected by copyright or, even if protected, its use should be considered fair. The jury disagreed and concluded that Public Announcement had infringed. UMG appealed, contending that the jury was improperly instructed on the fair use defense and therefore didn't give it proper consideration. UMG claimed that the use of parts of Atomic Dog was intended to be an homage, or tribute, to George Clinton and his music, which should be treated as fair use. The court believed that the use was transformative under the first

factor, "having a different theme, mood, and tone from 'Atomic Dog.'" Discussing the third factor, the court stated that although the elements copied were relatively small, they were the most distinctive and recognizable parts of "Atomic Dog." The fourth factor also weighed against fair use, since there is loss to the market for derivative works; specifically, there is a licensing market for the use of samples in the music industry. Since "Atomic Dog" is a commonly sampled song, Bridgeport could lose licensing substantial revenue if fair use could simply be based on the assertion that a sample was used as an homage to the song or artist who recorded it. Further, there was no evidence that established that the sample from "Atomic Dog" was intended as an homage to George Clinton, such as some acknowledgment in the credits or liner notes of the Public Announcement album.

Although fair use questions are decided on a case-by-case basis, and there is no way to guarantee that a use is fair, in order to get an idea of whether a use is likely to be fair, ask yourself the following questions:

1. Are you just copying from someone else's work or adding substantial original material in order to transform it into a new work? The more transformative your work, the more likely it will be a fair use.

2. Will your use compete with the work you are copying from? If your use harms or even potentially harms the market for the original work or any derivatives of the original work, it will not likely be fair. Since copyrighted works often derive the majority of their revenue from various forms of licensing, it is important to consider not only whether your use directly competes with the copyrighted work but also whether the market for any type of licensing could be adversely affected.

3. How much copyrighted material have you copied? The more you have copied, the less likely your use will be fair. Also, even if you copied a relatively small portion of a copyrighted work, if the portion copied is very distinctive or recognizable, your use is less likely to be fair.

4. How important is the part of the work you have copied to the original work? The more important the material copied (even if only a small portion), the less likely your use will be fair.

---

**Tip:** Although most countries recognize some degree of fair use, the extent and application of fair use differs. For example, fair use is more limited in some other countries (e.g., United Kingdom) than it is under U.S. copyright law.

---

# V. De Minimis Copying

In some circumstances, a court might decide that, although material from a copyrighted work was copied, the amount copied is insubstantial and inconsequential, or *de minimis*. For example, it is possible that if a recording artist incorporated a sample of a very small, unrecognizable portion of a copyrighted sound recording in a new sound recording, the use might be excused as *de minimis*. However, it is risky to rely on this defense because there are no clear legal rules on how much can be copied, and courts tend to be quite conservative in applying the *de minimis* defense.

---

**Example 11.14**

---

In a controversial 2005 case,[30] the Sixth Circuit Court of Appeals ruled that any sampling of a copyrighted sound recording, regardless of how small a portion, cannot be considered *de minimis*, effectively eliminating the *de minimis* defense for cases involving sampling of sound recordings in the Sixth Circuit's jurisdiction (Kentucky, Michigan, Ohio, and Tennessee). The case involved the use of a two-second guitar sample from the Funkadelic song, "Get Off Your Ass and Jam," which was looped throughout rap group N.W.A's song "100 Miles and Runnin'." Although a district court felt that the sampling was so small that the *de minimis* defense should apply, the Sixth Circuit Appeals Court reversed this decision. The court disagreed with many critics of this decision (who believe that very small samples of copyrighted works should be allowed without copyright owners' permission in order to encourage creativity), advising people considering using samples of copyrighted recordings to: "Get a license or do not sample. We do not see this as stifling creativity in any significant way."

---

# VI. Innocent Intent

The fact that a person does not realize that his actions constitute copyright infringement is not a defense to copyright infringement. A person who infringes a copyrighted work unintentionally, even without reason to believe that he is infringing, is liable for infringement. Innocent infringement can occur when an infringer believes that a copyrighted work is in the public domain. It can also occur when a music publisher, record company, or record distributor relies on a songwriter's promise that an infringing song was written by the songwriter when it was actually copied from someone else's copyrighted work. The primary reason for not allowing innocence as a defense is the belief that, as between the copyright owner and the infringer, it is fairer to put the burden on the infringer to guard against infringing.

Although innocent intent is not a defense to copyright infringement, it will often limit the extent of liability for infringement. Under Section 504(c)(2) of the Copyright Act, if an infringer proves that he or she "was not aware and had no reason to believe that his or her acts constituted an infringement of copyright," the court may reduce an award of statutory damages from the generally applicable minimum of $500 to not less than $200.

---

**Example 11.15**

---

In *Bright Tunes Music Corp. v. Harrisongs Music, Ltd.*,[31] George Harrison was found to have subconsciously infringed the song "He's So Fine." In other words, the court found that when Harrison composed his song "My Sweet Lord," he thought he was composing it solely from his own imagination and did not realize that he was copying "He's So Fine." The court held that although Harrison was liable for the infringement, he had innocent intent. This resulted in a considerably lower award of damages than he would otherwise have been liable for.

---

# Endnotes

1. 17 U.S.C. § 507.
2. 828 F. Supp. 1048 (1993).
3. *National Comics Publications, Inc. v. Fawcett Publications, Inc.*, 191 F.2d 594 (2d Cir. 2004).
4. United States Copyright Office, *Compendium II of Copyright Office Practices*, § 1507.14.
5. *Sanga Music, Inc. v. EMI Blackwood Music, Inc.*, 55 F.3d 756, 761 (2d Cir. 1995).
6. *Dodd, Mead & Co., Inc. v. Lilienthal*, 514 F. Supp. 105 (S.D.N.Y. 1981).
7. *Black's Law Dictionary* 415 (6th ed. 1991).
8. *Stewart v. Abend*, 495 U.S. 207 (1990).
9. 9 F. Cas. 342 (C.C.D. Mass. 1841).
10. H.R. Rep. No. 94-1476, 94th Cong., 2d Sess. at 65 (1976).
11. *Harper & Row Publishers, Inc. v. Nation Enterprises*, 471 U.S. 539, 562 (1985).
12. *Luther R. Campbell aka Luke Skyywalker v. Acuff-Rose Music, Inc.*, 510 U.S. 569 (1994).
13. *Wihtol v. Crow*, 309 F.2d 777 (8th Cir. 1962).
14. *Italian Book Corporation v. American Broadcasting Companies, Inc.*, 485 F. Supp. 65 (1978).
15. *Keep Thompson Governor Committee v. Citizens for Gallen Committee*, 457 F. Supp. 957 (D.N.H. 1978).
16. *Luther R. Campbell aka Luke Skyywalker v. Acuff-Rose Music, Inc.*, 510 U.S. 569 (1994).
17. *Keep Thompson Governor Committee v. Citizens for Gallen Committee*, 457 F. Supp. 957 (D.N.H. 1978).
18. 794 F.2d 432 (9th Cir. 1986).
19. 599 F.Supp.2d 415 (S.D.N.Y. 2009).
20. 430 F.3d 888 (7th Cir. 2005).
21. *Luther R. Campbell aka Luke Skyywalker v. Acuff-Rose Music, Inc.*, 510 U.S. 569 (1994).
22. *Id.*
23. The Court of Appeals had relied on the presumption that a use for any commercial purpose is unfair. This presumption originated in a previous case, *Sony Corp. v. Universal City Studios, Inc.*, 464 U.S. 417, 451 (1984). However, the Supreme Court in *Campbell* held that the Court of Appeals had placed too much emphasis on the commercial purpose and failed to take into account the transformative character of the use.
24. 794 F.2d 432 (9th Cir. 1986).
25. 329 F.2d 541 (2nd Cir. 1964).
26. 482 F. Supp 741 (S.D.N.Y. 1980).
27. 581 F.2d 751 (9th Cir.).
28. 425 F.Supp. 443 (S.D.N.Y. 1976).
29. 585 F.3d 267, 6th Cir. (2009).
30. *Bridgeport Music, Inc. v. Dimension Films*, 410 F.3d 792 (6th Cir. 2005).
31. 420 F. Supp. 177 (1976).

# 12 Remedies for Copyright Infringement

*Creative work is to be encouraged and rewarded, but private motivation must ultimately serve the cause of promoting broad public availability of literature, music, and the other arts.*

—*U.S. Supreme Court in* Sony Corp. of America v. Universal City Studios, Inc. *464 U.S. 417 (1984)*

If you win a copyright infringement lawsuit, there are several different legal remedies to which you may be entitled. Some of these remedies are coercive in nature and are designed to prevent further infringement, while others are compensatory and therefore are designed to compensate the copyright owners for losses incurred as a result of the infringement. Finally, some copyright infringements are subject to criminal prosecution as well as civil liability.

## I. Coercive Remedies

While receiving compensation for infringement is often an important factor for copyright owners who choose to sue for infringement, it is not always the only important factor. Often, copyright owners also want to stop the infringing act from continuing. The Copyright Act therefore provides several coercive remedies that are intended to prevent infringement from continuing.

### A. Injunction

Courts have the authority under Section 502(a) of the Copyright Act to grant injunctions on terms that the court believes reasonable to prevent or restrain infringement. An injunction is a court order telling someone to do or stop doing something. In a copyright infringement lawsuit, a court might grant an injunction ordering the defendant to stop its infringing conduct.

---

**Example 12.1**

In a 1991 case,[1] rap artist Biz Markie used an unauthorized sample from the song "Alone Again (Naturally)" on an album released by Warner Bros. Records. The court issued an injunction ordering Warner Bros. to stop selling the album containing the infringing song. Warner Bros. consequently had to discontinue sales of the album and take back unsold copies from retailers and distributors.

---

An injunction may be temporary (pending resolution of the suit) or final. A judge will usually order a preliminary injunction when it seems likely (based on evidence submitted before trial) that the plaintiff will be successful in proving infringement and the plaintiff would be irreparably harmed if the injunction is not issued. In copyright infringement claims, irreparable harm (harm that cannot be cured otherwise) is normally presumed to exist. An exception might be when an infringement involves a defendant's recording of a musical work. In this situation, irreparable harm would not be presumed; the defendant's use would be subject to compulsory mechanical licensing under the Copyright Act and therefore would be fully compensated by a monetary award in the amount of the mechanical license fees that would have been paid if a license had been obtained.

In some cases where a preliminary injunction is issued, the court also orders the plaintiff to post a bond as a form of security. If the plaintiff loses its suit, the defendant will be allowed to collect the damages incurred as a result of the injunction from the bond. If a defendant continues the infringing conduct after an injunction has been issued, the defendant is subject to fines and potential imprisonment.

## B. Impoundment

In addition to an injunction, a court may also order the impoundment of allegedly infringing articles. Section 503(a) of the Copyright Act provides that a court may:

> ...order the impounding, on such terms as it may deem reasonable, of all copies or phonorecords claimed to have been made or used in violation of the copyright owner's exclusive rights, and of all plates, molds, matrices, masters, tapes, film negatives, or other articles by means of which such copies or phonorecords may be reproduced.

Under an impoundment order, all infringing goods, as well as equipment and materials used to make such goods, are collected and held until the court makes a final judgment on the infringement claim. After a plaintiff files an affidavit identifying the number, value, and location of the alleged infringing copies or devices and a bond, the court can order a federal marshal to seize and hold the materials identified in the affidavit. The defendant has the right to ask the court to order the return of impounded articles by filing an affidavit showing that the articles are not infringing.

### Example 12.2

In a copyright infringement action involving unauthorized manufacturing and distribution of compact discs containing copyrighted songs and sound recordings, a court could order the impoundment of not only the allegedly infringing recordings, but also any recording equipment, including computers, blank tapes and discs, labels, and packaging materials used to manufacture the infringing recordings.

## C. Destruction

If a court finds a defendant guilty of infringement, it may order the destruction of infringing articles. Courts have some flexibility in ordering the disposition of infringing articles because

Section 503(b) allows, as an alternative to destruction, other reasonable disposition of infringing articles. A court could therefore order that the infringing articles be sold, given away, or delivered to the plaintiff.

# II. Compensatory Remedies

Many copyright owners who want to sue someone for copyright infringement have overly optimistic expectations of the amount of money they can recover. In reality, you cannot just pick an amount of money to sue for out of thin air, no matter how much you might believe you are entitled to, because the monetary damages you can sue for are specified by the Copyright Act. Unfortunately for songwriters and other copyright owners, copyright law does not allow you to recover for the emotional distress or mental anguish that may have resulted from having your creation infringed.

The Copyright Act allows a plaintiff who wins a copyright infringement action to recover several different types of monetary remedies. Some of these remedies are designed to compensate the copyright owner for losses incurred due to the infringement and expenses incurred in connection with the infringement action, while others are also designed to deter copyright infringers.

### A. Actual Damages and Profits

Under Section 504(b) of the Copyright Act, a successful copyright plaintiff may recover:

> … the actual damages suffered by him or her as a result of the infringement, and any profits of the infringer that are attributable to the infringement and are not taken into account in computing the actual damages.

Actual damages are intended to compensate the copyright owner for the losses incurred as a result of the infringement. Allowing the plaintiff to recover the defendant's profits, in addition to actual damages, is intended to prevent the defendant from profiting from the infringement and to act as a deterrent to infringement.

In order to be awarded actual damages, the copyright owner must prove the amount of money it has lost because of the infringement. In other words, actual damages refers to the amount of money the copyright owner would have made if the infringing use had been authorized by the copyright owner. Generally, actual damages will be equal to the fair market value of the use made by the infringer. In many situations, the fair market value would be the amount that a copyright owner would normally charge for a license to use the copyrighted work. For instance, if someone made and distributed unauthorized recordings of a copyrighted song, the amount of actual damages might be fairly easy to determine. You would simply multiply the number of recordings distributed by the statutory mechanical license rate provided by Section 115 of the Copyright Act. However, if the song was released as a single from an album, determining its fair market value might be a bit more difficult. Because a single promotes sales of the album, its fair market value may be higher than other songs on the same album that are not singles.

**Example 12.3**

In a copyright infringement lawsuit brought by the Isley Brothers against Michael Bolton,[2] the jury decided that the Isleys were entitled to 66 percent of the profits from Bolton's song as well as 28 percent of Bolton's profits from the album it was contained on. This amounted to $5.4 million at that time because Bolton's album had sold over seven million copies, and the song was a huge radio hit. Reportedly, the Isleys had been willing to settle for about $500,000, but Bolton refused. Sony Music, Bolton's record company, came out the worst as a result of this decision, owing $4.2 million of the $5.4 million damage award. Bolton was ordered to pay $932,924, his co-writer $220,000, and their publishing companies $75,900.

In other situations, proving the amount of actual damages can be more difficult. For example, if a copyrighted song was used in a national television commercial without authorization, the plaintiff would have to prove the amount of money it lost due to defendant's use of the song. If the plaintiff could prove that a synchronization license for this type of use would have cost $100,000 (by offering evidence of licenses issued for similar uses or expert testimony), a court would probably award actual damages of $100,000. Finally, there may be situations where proving the amount of actual damages is very difficult or impossible. One such situation involves uploading copyrighted works to Internet websites, from which they can be downloaded by others. If this type of use was authorized, there might be a small royalty payment made to the copyright owner for each download. However, in most cases where such use is unauthorized, there is probably no way to know how many times the work has been downloaded, so there may not be any way to reasonably estimate the copyright owner's actual damages (in such situations, statutory damages, discussed in the next section of this chapter, may provide an alternative).

In addition to actual damages, a copyright owner is allowed to recover the profits of the infringer that are attributable to the infringement and are not taken into account in computing the actual damages. The copyright owner must prove the amount of the infringer's gross profits resulting from the infringement. It would do so in the discovery period before trial by requesting financial documents from the defendant or taking the defendant's deposition. The infringer can then offer proof of any expenses that should be deducted from these gross profits. Deductible expenses would include any expenses that are directly attributable to the production, distribution, performance, or display of the copyrighted work. Additionally, the infringer may offer proof of any elements of profit attributable to factors other than the copyrighted work, which would also be deducted from gross profits.

**Example 12.4**

In a case involving the unauthorized use of compositions contained on a record company's release of a five-record album of Scott Joplin compositions,[3] the court awarded the copyright owner one-half of the profits earned from sales, even though the infringed works occupied only one side of the five-record set. The defendant argued that, on a strictly proportional basis, the plaintiff should receive only 10 percent of its profits, but the court held that the inclusion of the infringing compositions allowed the defendant to advertise the album as the only complete set of Joplin's works and that the defendant had failed to produce evidence disputing the contributions of the infringing compositions to the album's marketability.

In addition to profits earned directly from infringing conduct, a copyright owner may also be able to recover profits that the infringer earned indirectly as a result of its infringement. However, because indirect profits are often difficult to quantify, courts will often be hesitant to award them.

---

**Example 12.5**

In one case,[4] the defendant used the plaintiff's musical compositions in a musical revue performed at its hotel without permission. In addition to holding the defendant liable for direct profits, the court also awarded the plaintiff a portion of the indirect profits from the defendant's hotel and casino revenues that may have resulted from increased patronage generated by the infringing show. This portion of indirect profits was found to be $699,963.10, while the direct profits were $551,884.54.

---

## B. Statutory Damages

In many situations, it is difficult to prove the amount of actual damages and the defendant's profits from an infringement. Further, in many instances, actual damages and profits may be a very small amount of money. For example, if someone makes a recording of a song without a license, the amount of actual damages would be the statutory mechanical royalty rate multiplied by the number of records sold. If only 1,000 records were sold, the amount of actual damages would only be $85, which would often have to be split among several publishers and songwriters. Even if 100,000 records were sold (a sales figure that only a small percentage of recordings achieve), the actual damages would only be $8,500, which would be unlikely to cover the copyright owner's costs and attorneys' fees incurred in connection with an infringement suit.

In order to make it potentially worthwhile to sue for infringement in situations where actual damages and profits are hard to determine or a relatively small amount, the Copyright Act allows a copyright owner to elect to receive monetary damages within a specified range (known as "statutory damages") instead of actual damages and profits.

Unlike actual damages and profits, a copyright owner who chooses to receive statutory damages does not have to prove the amount of its losses or the defendant's profits from the infringement. A copyright owner may elect to receive statutory damages at any time before the court makes its final judgment of liability in the case. However, in order to be eligible to elect statutory damages, the copyrighted work must have been registered either before the infringement began or within three months after the work's initial publication.

Under Section 504(c), the general range of statutory damages is from $750 to $30,000. However, in cases where a court finds that the infringement was committed willfully (i.e., the defendant knew, had reason to know, or recklessly disregarded the fact that its conduct constituted infringement), a court can increase the award of statutory damages up to a maximum of $150,000. Alternatively, in cases where a court finds that the infringement was committed innocently (i.e., the defendant was not aware and had no reason to believe that its acts constituted infringement), the court may reduce the award of statutory damages to $200 and may even decide not to award any statutory damages at all in certain cases where the defendant reasonably believed that its use of a work was a fair use.

---

**Note:** The statutory damages minimum and maximum amounts were increased by the Digital Theft Deterrence and Copyright Damages Improvement Act, which became effective on December 9, 1999. Prior to that date, the statutory damages range was $500 to $20,000.

---

Within the statutorily prescribed range, courts have discretion as to the actual amount to be awarded. Most courts will try to approximate actual damages and profits when possible; in cases where a plaintiff suffered little or no actual damages and the defendant made little or no profits, courts will usually award the minimum statutory amount. When actual damages and profits cannot be easily estimated, courts tend to rely on the rationale for statutory damages—sustaining copyright incentives while deterring infringement. Statutory damage awards will normally be at the low end of the range when the infringement was technical rather than substantive. However, awards will usually be higher when the defendant's conduct indicates that a greater deterrent is necessary. For example, courts tend to make relatively high statutory damage awards in the following types of situations:

- A defendant continues the infringing conduct after a copyright owner's objection and request that the defendant obtain a license.

- A defendant continues selling allegedly infringing goods after being served with process in a copyright infringement suit.

- A defendant fails to cooperate with the plaintiff's discovery efforts intended to determine actual damages (e.g., failing to provide documentation of record sales containing the infringing work).

- A defendant is a repeat offender.

An award of statutory damages covers all infringements that occur with respect to any single work.[5] For instance, an infringer who sells a recording containing one unlicensed song is liable for one statutory damages award regardless of how many records were actually sold, although the number of sales might affect the court's determination of the actual amount of the award within the statutory range (e.g., sales of a million records would probably result in a greater single award than sales of 100 records). However, if the infringing recording contained 10 unlicensed songs, the infringer is liable for 10 statutory damage awards (one for each work infringed).

### Example 12.6

Although courts have substantial discretion over the range of statutory damages, they will sometimes award only the minimum amount when the court believes the claim involves a relatively minor infringement and the copyright owner should have settled the dispute. In one case,[6] famous musical theater composer Jerome Kern was sued for copying part of an *ostinato* (i.e., an eight-note repeated pattern) in a song's background. Because the ostinato was not an important part of the song and the plaintiff was unable to prove any actual damages, the judge awarded the plaintiff only the $250 minimum statutory damage amount, stating that: "This controversy is a mere point of honor of scarcely more than irritation, involving no substantial interest. Except that it raises an interesting point of law, it would be a waste of time for everyone concerned."

### (1) Illegal File Sharing and Statutory Damages

The impact of statutory damages is aptly illustrated in the context of copyright infringement lawsuits against individuals accused of illegal file sharing of copyrighted works. Over several years, the Recording Industry Association of America (RIAA) brought copyright infringement lawsuits against thousands of individuals for using file sharing software to illegally upload and download copyrighted sound recordings (see Chapter 15, "The Online Music War," for a discussion of illegal file sharing). The RIAA generally targeted its lawsuits at people it considered to be large-scale infringers (i.e., people who made 1,000 or more copyrighted recordings available for downloading by others). Most of the people sued chose to pay settlement fees averaging around $3,000 to $5,000.

In these file sharing lawsuits, the RIAA has elected to sue for statutory damages rather than actual damages and profits, mainly because proving the amount of actual damages and profits incurred due to this type of infringement would be extremely difficult. Statutory damages, on the other hand, provide a much easier alternative for copyright owners in this type of situation, since a court would have to award an amount between $750 and $30,000 (or $150,000 for willful infringement) for each copyrighted work infringed. If 1,000 works were infringed, the minimum amount of statutory damages would be $750,000 (1,000 times $750). While that's enough to put most people into bankruptcy, the maximum amount would be $150,000,000 (1,000 times $150,000). By contrast, the $3,000 to $5,000 average settlement the RIAA had been offering seems like a bargain, even compared to an award of statutory damages at the minimum amount possible.

While the vast majority of file sharing cases have been settled without a trial, the few that have reached a trial decision have resulted in very high statutory damage awards. This has not only brought to light the risk of serious financial liability for online copyright infringement, but has also brought into question the appropriateness of statutory damages in such situations.

In the first file sharing lawsuit to reach a jury decision, Jammie Thomas was found to have willfully infringed the copyrights in 24 sound recordings.[7] In October 2007, the jury awarded statutory damages of $222,000 ($9,250 for each of the 24 recordings). However, the judge ordered a retrial due to a potential mistake in his instructions to the jury. After the retrial in mid-2009, a new jury also found Thomas liable for willful infringement and awarded statutory damages of $1.92 million ($80,000 for each copyright infringed). Thomas filed a motion requesting another retrial, alleging that the amount of statutory damages was so disproportionate to actual damages that it should be held unconstitutional. Thomas claimed that the amount of statutory damages should be reduced to zero or, at most, the minimum of $750 per copyright infringed. In early 2010, the judge reduced the statutory damage award to $54,000, referring to the previous $1.92 million jury award as "monstrous and shocking." Both Thomas and the RIAA indicated that they would appeal the judge's ruling, but before doing so the RIAA offered a $25,000 settlement, which Thomas refused. In late 2010, a third trial was held, and another jury decided that Thomas was liable for $1.5 million ($62,500 for each copyright infringed). In response, Thomas again requested that the judge reduce the amount to zero or to an amount the court believes constitutional, reiterating her claim that such a high amount is unconstitutional. The judge refused Thomas' request, so it is likely that an appellate court will end up reviewing the lower court decision.

In another file sharing case, Joel Tenenbaum was found to have willfully infringed 30 copyrights, and a jury awarded statutory damages of $675,000 ($22,500 per copyright infringed).[8] However, as in the *Thomas* case, the judge decided to reduce this award to a lower amount of $67,500 ($2,250 per infringement). Tenenbaum was not satisfied with the reduction and believes that he shouldn't have to pay anything. In September 2011, a federal appeals court reinstated the original $675,000 jury award against Tenenbaum, ruling that the judge improperly reduced the award without following the proper procedure (which would require a judge to set a lower amount that the RIAA would agree to or have a new trial to determine an appropriate amount). The appeals court did, however, reject Tenenbaum's argument that he is not liable for copyright infringement since he did not intend to profit from his unauthorized use of copyrighted works. Consequently, the *Tenenbaum* as well as the *Thomas* case are still subject to further court proceedings on the issue of the determination of statutory damages at the time of this book's writing.

Since the *Thomas* and *Tenenbaum* decisions, there has been some criticism of such high statutory damage awards for file sharing. Tenenbaum's attorney, Charles Nesson, contends that the record companies' damages should be limited to a maximum of $21.00, since the works infringed could be purchased for 99 cents each from iTunes. However, this greatly oversimplifies the determination of actual damages and ignores much of the rationale for statutory damages. Actual damages should not be limited to the amount a person would have paid to legally download the work, but should also include any amounts lost due to other file sharers downloading from the copy that person "shared" through a file sharing network. A single file containing a copyrighted work made available through file sharing networks such as KaZaa (used by both Thomas and Tenenbaum) is made available to millions of other users. While it is probably impossible to know how many people made copies by downloading from Thomas' or Tenenbaum's infringing copies, it could certainly be more than one and might be much more, especially in the case of very popular works. Statutory damages are particularly appropriate in this type of situation where proving the amount of actual damages is not feasible or possible and the potential for large-scale infringement is significant.

Additionally, unlike actual damages, statutory damages are not only intended to compensate copyright owners for income lost due to infringement. Another purpose of statutory damages is to deter future infringement. If infringers' liability were to be limited to the amount they would have paid if they hadn't infringed, this would actually encourage infringement instead of providing a deterrent.

While many people may believe that the statutory damage awards in the *Thomas* and *Tenenbaum* cases are too high, restricting statutory damage awards to the approximate amount of actual damages would defeat much of the purpose for statutory damages and leave copyright owners in many circumstances with no viable monetary remedy when their works are infringed. It is important to note that, in both cases, juries found that the defendants had willfully infringed copyrights, lied about their conduct, and concealed evidence. Tenenbaum also ignored several warnings to stop his illegal activities, not only by the RIAA, but also by his college and his father. These factors can all be considered by a jury in determining the amount of statutory damages and arguably justify awarding an amount significantly higher than the minimum. It is also worth noting that even the highest awards in these two cases were much less than the maximum amount of $150,000 per copyright infringed.

## C. Costs and Attorneys' Fees

Under Section 505 of the Copyright Act, a court may award reasonable attorneys' fees to the prevailing party as well as the costs or expenses incurred in connection with an infringement lawsuit. The right to recover attorneys' fees can be very important because many copyright infringement suits involve long, expensive trials that may result in relatively small amounts of money being awarded.

Costs that may be awarded include court filing fees, expert witness fees (which can often be very costly), photocopying and postage expenses, and transcription costs for witness depositions. As an incentive to encourage copyright owners to register their works, the Copyright Act requires that in order to be entitled to attorneys' fees, the copyrighted work must have been registered before the infringement began or within three months of the work's publication.

The rationale for allowing a plaintiff to recover its attorneys' fees and costs is to deter potential infringers and to encourage copyright owners to bring infringement suits even when actual damages and profits or statutory damages may not sufficiently cover the expenses of litigation. The rationale for allowing an award of attorney's fees and costs to prevailing defendants is to encourage them to defend against claims they believe to be invalid (rather than settling solely to avoid litigation expenses) and to discourage copyright owners from bringing frivolous claims.

It is important to note that the authority to award attorneys' fees is discretionary, and courts are therefore not required to do so. Until a few years ago, there was some disagreement among courts on the factors to be considered in determining whether to award attorneys' fees. Further, some courts applied a different standard to prevailing plaintiffs and defendants in deciding whether to award attorneys' fees. These courts generally required prevailing defendants to prove that the plaintiffs acted in bad faith or that their claim was frivolous. In *Fogerty v. Fantasy*, an appeal of a decision by a court awarding $1,374,519 in attorneys' fees to musician John Fogerty, the Supreme Court held that courts must treat prevailing plaintiffs and prevailing defendants alike.[9] The lower court's ruling held that successful copyright defendants had to prove that the suit was frivolous or in bad faith in order to recover attorneys' fees. The Supreme Court's ruling may make prospective plaintiffs give more thought to bringing infringement claims and to settling their claims because, if they lose, they may have to pay substantial attorneys' fees to the defendant.

When deciding whether or not to award attorneys' fees to the prevailing party, courts will normally consider the losing party's frivolousness, motivation, and good or bad faith, as well as general considerations of compensation and deterrence. Bad faith generally occurs when a defendant willfully infringed the copyrighted work, unnecessarily delayed the litigation, or refused a reasonable settlement offer. Similarly, a court may find that a plaintiff has acted in bad faith when its infringement claim clearly lacked merit, when its real motive is to harass the defendant, or when it has rejected a reasonable settlement offer. One court, for instance, held that a plaintiff had acted in bad faith when its claim "rested ultimately on alleged showings of similarities which ranged from the patently erroneous to the ridiculous or involved palpable trivialities."[10] Making a misrepresentation in an application for copyright registration may also constitute bad faith, justifying an award of attorneys' fees against the plaintiff.[11]

Because Section 505 provides that a court may award a "reasonable" attorney's fee, the question arises as to what a reasonable fee is. A court may decide to award attorneys' fees but decline to award the full amount of attorneys' fees actually incurred. Some factors that courts tend to consider in determining how much to award are the time and labor required for the services performed, the customary fee, the amount of monetary damages involved, the results obtained, and the experience and reputation of the attorney. In one case, a court awarded the plaintiff its actual attorneys' fees of $22,000 even though the plaintiff had only been awarded $250 in statutory damages.[12] Although the statutory damage award was quite low, the plaintiff also received an injunction preventing any further infringement, and the court therefore felt that the amount of attorneys' fees was reasonable.

---

**Enforcing Copyright Judgments**   It is important to understand that even if you go through the considerable time and expense of successfully suing someone for copyright infringement and are awarded a substantial amount of money, there is no guarantee that you will be able to actually collect the amount awarded. A court merely issues a judgment specifying the amount of damages awarded, but it is up to the copyright owner to collect from the infringer. Many people will not pay voluntarily, and the copyright owner will then have to go back to court to obtain an order to enforce the judgment. There are legal procedures to collect (e.g., obtaining a lien on assets, garnishing wages, etc.), but if the person you're trying to collect from doesn't have the money or sufficient assets, you're out of luck. Also, if your judgment is for an amount greater than the value of the infringer's assets, the infringer will likely file for bankruptcy, and your judgment will be treated as an unsecured debt, which usually means you will ultimately receive a very small portion of the judgment amount. Usually, if you obtain a judgment for infringement of a song, you can get the court to order any royalty collection agents (e.g., performing rights organizations, Harry Fox Agency, etc.) to pay royalties to you, but unless the song is still earning substantial amounts, it may take a long time to collect the full amount of your judgment. When considering suing someone for copyright infringement, these are some practical issues that should be considered in addition to the legal validity and strength of your case.

---

# III. Criminal Copyright Infringement

The vast majority of copyright infringements are civil in nature and are not subject to any criminal penalties. Congress has historically been hesitant to impose criminal liability for copyright infringement in fear of deterring technological progress and due to the ease with which any individual can violate a copyright. Consequently, in the past, criminal liability has usually only applied to situations of large-scale piracy of copyrighted works. More recently, however, Congress has increased the scope of criminal copyright liability in response to lobbying by the entertainment and computer software industries. Congress realized that with the widespread availability of copying technology and the resulting ability to make perfect reproductions, anyone can now commit large-scale copyright infringement.

## A. The 1976 Copyright Act

The criminal provisions of the 1909 Copyright Act did not apply to sound recordings. Due to estimates that record piracy was costing the recording industry over $100 million annually, the

1976 Copyright Act made certain instances of infringement of sound recordings subject to criminal penalties. If an infringement is made willfully and for purposes of commercial advantage or private financial gain, the infringer may be subject to criminal liability. For an infringement to be considered willful, the government must prove that the defendant knew that its acts constituted copyright infringement or, at least, knew that there was a high probability that its acts constituted copyright infringement. In order to prove that the defendant's conduct was for purposes of commercial advantage or private financial gain, the defendant does not have to actually make a profit, but only hope or intend to make a profit.

Under Section 506(a) of the Copyright Act, criminal copyright infringement of any of the copyright owner's exclusive rights is a misdemeanor, punishable by imprisonment for up to one year, a fine of up to $100,000, or both. However, criminal infringement of the reproduction or distribution rights may also be punishable as a felony if the defendant reproduced or distributed at least 10 copies or phonorecords of one or more copyrighted works with a retail value of more than $2,500 during any 180-day period. Felony copyright infringement is punishable by imprisonment for up to five years (and up to 10 years for subsequent offenses), a fine of up to $250,000, or both.

In criminal cases, infringing articles as well as any equipment used in the manufacture of infringing articles can be impounded and destroyed. Under Section 506(b), impoundment and destruction in criminal cases is mandatory.

Under Section 506(c) of the Copyright Act, criminal liability may also be imposed upon anyone who knowingly puts false information on a copyright notice with fraudulent intent. It is also a crime to remove or alter a copyright notice on a copy containing a copyrighted work with fraudulent intent. Finally, Section 506(e) makes it a crime to knowingly make a false representation of a material fact in an application for copyright registration or in any written statement filed in connection with the application. All of these actions are punishable by a fine of up to $2,500.

> **Example 12.7**
>
> In 2010, Julius Chow Lieh Liu was convicted of criminal copyright infringement by a California jury.[13] He was arrested in 2006 after a three-year FBI investigation and ultimately sentenced to four years imprisonment. Liu had operated a business that made and sold thousands of copies of copyrighted music CDs, movie DVDs, and computer software for several years.

## B. The No Electronic Theft Act

In 1997, the No Electronic Theft ("NET") Act was signed into law.[14] The NET Act expanded the applicability of criminal penalties for copyright infringement to situations where an infringer acts without direct financial motivation. Congress stated the reasoning for passing this legislation as follows:

*What we are essentially saying is if you trash somebody else's property, even if you are not doing it for money but you are just doing it because you want to show how smart you are and because you are seriously maladjusted and cannot make an impression on anybody in any other way, it is as criminal as if you stole.*[15]

The NET Act's passage was in response to a legal loophole that was brought to light in *United States v. LaMacchia*.[16] In *LaMacchia*, David LaMacchia operated a website bulletin board that allowed subscribers to upload and download copies of computer software without authorization of the copyright owners. LaMacchia not only encouraged people to upload and download copyrighted software using his bulletin board, but also warned his subscribers to act cautiously in order to avoid detection. Even though the unauthorized reproduction and transmission of software facilitated by LaMacchia resulted in more than $1 million in potential lost revenue to copyright owners, the court found that LaMacchia was not subject to criminal liability due to a loophole in then existing copyright law.

Section 506(a) of the Copyright Act requires that in order to be guilty of criminal copyright infringement, the infringing conduct must be "for purposes of commercial advantage or private financial gain." Because the government did not have any evidence that LaMacchia had received any financial gain from his infringing conduct, he could not be convicted of criminal copyright infringement, although he would clearly have been liable for civil copyright infringement if any of the software copyright owners sued him.

Despite its ruling, the *LaMacchia* court encouraged Congress to reexamine the state of criminal copyright law and suggested that criminal penalties should be applicable to blatantly willful, large-scale infringements, even in the absence of a financial incentive. Congress took the court's advice and passed the NET Act, which expanded the Copyright Act's definition of "financial gain" to include the "receipt, or expectation of receipt, of anything of value, including the receipt of other copyrighted works." It provides for criminal penalties for the "reproduction or distribution, including by electronic means, during any 180-day period, of one or more copies or phonorecords of one or more copyrighted works, which have a total retail value of more than $1,000." If an offense involves 10 or more copies of one or more copyrighted works that have a retail value of $2,500, the maximum penalty is three years in prison, a fine of $250,000, or both. Although the NET Act may provide some degree of deterrence for online piracy, criminal prosecutions are not too common, since copyright infringement has historically not been one of the FBI's or U.S. Attorney's main concerns. This may be changing somewhat as federal government law enforcement agencies have been a bit more active in pursuing copyright infringement in recent years.

**Example 12.8**

In 1999, Jeffrey Levy, a 22-year-old college student at the University of Oregon, became the first person convicted under the NET Act. Levy pled guilty to criminal infringement of copyright in violation of the NET Act and the Copyright Act.[17] He admitted that he illegally posted thousands of MP3 files of copyrighted musical recordings, as well as computer software and digitally recorded movies, on his website, allowing the general public to download and copy these copyrighted works. The University of Oregon brought the matter to the attention of the Oregon State Police after it noted a very large amount of bandwidth traffic being generated from Levy's website on its server. The Oregon State Police and the FBI investigated and confirmed that thousands of music recordings, software programs, and movies were available for download from the site. Levy was fined $2,500, the minimum amount under the NET Act, and placed on two years' probation.

## C. Pre-Release Piracy

Another relatively new area of criminal copyright infringement involves what is known as pre-release piracy. Record companies (as well as film companies) usually pick a specific date on which to release a new product (e.g., single, album, or film) to the public. This is done in order to generate publicity before the release date, coordinate marketing activities before and after the release date, and ensure that no retailer gains an unfair advantage over its competitors. By 2005, it had become a fairly common practice for some people to make copies of copyrighted works available online prior to their official release. This "pre-release piracy" became a major problem for the entertainment industry because film production companies, record companies, and computer software companies often make huge investments in the creation and marketing of their works. Often, the biggest sales occur relatively shortly after release, and if a work is illegally available before its release, this can result in significant losses in revenue.

In response, Congress passed the Family Entertainment and Copyright Act of 2005 (FECA), an amendment to the 1976 Copyright Act, which makes it a criminal offense to make copyrighted works available to the public before they are officially released.[18] It also makes it a criminal offense to record movies in theaters, which is one of the sources for digital copies of movies that end up being illegally made available online. Violators are subject to up to three years in jail but up to five years if they received any financial gain, and repeat offenders can get up to 10 years if they received any financial gain from the offense.

---

**Example 12.9**

In late 2005, shortly after passage of the FECA, one of this book's authors received a phone call from a man who was worried about a visit he had received early that morning from two FBI investigators. The man was a music reviewer for newspapers and magazines who had received an advance copy of a new CD by Ryan Adams entitled "Jacksonville City Nights." Advance copies are given to reviewers before a CD's release date to generate publicity. After listening to the CD, the reviewer gave it to a friend who copied some of the recordings. These copies were passed along to Jared Bowser, who then sent the recordings to Robert Thomas, who posted them to a website about a month before the CD's release. After learning of the leaked release, Adam's record company contacted the FBI. Bowser and Thomas were eventually indicted and pled guilty to charges of criminal copyright infringement. Both of them admitted that they hoped people who downloaded the Adams recordings would in turn provide them with other free copyrighted music (which constitutes financial gain under the FECA). In return for pleading guilty, the U.S. Attorney reduced the charges from felony to misdemeanor level, which resulted in sentences of house arrest for eight weeks and probation. According to U.S. Attorney Jim Vines:

"Any perception that copyright violations are victimless crimes is just plain wrong. Whether stolen intellectual property is given away or sold by thieves for a profit, the rightful owners of such property are still hurt. Many individual and corporate victims of copyright crimes live, work, and create here in the Middle District of Tennessee, and persons who knowingly violate federal copyright law face serious consequences whether or not they intend to harm anyone."[19]

---

In another pre-release piracy case, three men were convicted of criminal copyright infringement and sentenced to prison terms.[20] The men were members of a pre-release piracy group known as Apocalypse Crew, which acquired digital copies of recordings before their commercial release and posted them to various computer servers. From these computer servers, the recordings were made available for downloading worldwide through file sharing networks. One of the men received a 6-month house arrest sentence, while another was sentenced to six months in prison and six months house arrest, and the third received a 15-month prison sentence because it was his second offense.

### D. The Digital Millennium Copyright Act

In 1998, Congress passed another piece of legislation that increased the penalties for criminal copyright infringement, the Digital Millennium Copyright Act (the "DMCA"). The DMCA, discussed further in Chapter 14, "Copyright and Digital Technology," provides criminal penalties for circumventing copyright protection systems and tampering with copyright management information. If the circumvention is willful and for commercial advantage or private financial gain, an infringer is subject to a fine up to $500,000, imprisonment of up to five years, or both. Further, the penalty may be increased to a fine of up to $1,000,000, imprisonment of up to 10 years, or both for repeat offenders.

# Endnotes

1.  *Grand Upright Music Limited v. Warner Brothers Records, Inc.*, 780 F. Supp. 182 (1991).
2.  *Three Boys Music Corp. v. Michael Bolton*, 212 F.3d 477 (9th Cir. 2000).
3.  *The Lottie Joplin Thomas Trust v. Crown Publishers, Inc.*, 592 F.2d 651 (9th Cir. 1978).
4.  *Frank Music Corp. v. Metro-Goldwyn-Mayer, Inc.*, 886 F.2d 1545 (9th Cir. 1989).
5.  17 U.S.C. §504(c)(1).
6.  *Fred Fisher, Inc. v. Dillingham*, 298 F.145 (S.D.N.Y 1924).
7.  *Capitol Records, Inc. v. Thomas*, 579 F. Supp. 2d (D. Minn. 2008).
8.  *Sony BMG Music Entertainment, et al v. Joel Tenenbaum*, 721 F. Supp. 2D 85 (D. Mass. 2009).
9.  *Fogerty v. Fantasy, Inc.*, 510 U.S. 517 (1994).
10. *Burnett v. Lambino*, 206 F. Supp., 517 (S.D.N.Y 1962).
11. *Whimsicality, Inc. v. Maison Joseph Battat, Ltd*, 27 F. Supp. 2d 456 (U.S.P.Q. 1998).
12. *Rockford Map Publishers, Inc. v. Directory Service Company of Colorado, Inc.*, 768 F.2d 145 (1985).
13. "El Cerrito Man Sentenced to 48 Months for Criminal Copyright Infringement," U.S. Dept. of Justice press release, available at http://www.justice.gov/usao/can/press/2010/ 2010_12_14_liu.sentenced.press.html.
14. Criminal Copyright Improvement Act of 1997, S. 1004, 105th Cong. (1997).
15. Quoting 143 Cong. Rec. H9885 (daily ed. Nov. 4, 1997).
16. 871 F. Supp. 535 (D. Mass. 1994).
17. "Defendant Sentenced for First Criminal Copyright Conviction Under the No Electronic Theft (NET) Act for Unlawful Distribution of Software on the Internet," U.S. Dept. of Justice press release, available at http://www.cybercrime.gov/levy2rls.htm.
18. For more information on the FECA, see the Copyright Office website at http://www. copyright.gov/legislation/pl109-9.html.
19. "Feds Bust Fans for Pirated Ryan Adams Tunes," *Billboard*, March 11, 2006, available at http://www.billboard.com/bbcom/news/article_display.jsp?vnu_content_id=1002156838.
20. "Three Defendants Sentenced in Federal Internet Music Piracy Crackdown," U.S. Dept. of Justice, May 19, 2006, available at http://www.cybercrime.gov/borchardtSent.htm.

# 13 International Copyright Protection

*"We take copyright violations very seriously, but when it comes to copying a disk, most Chinese people don't see what's wrong."[1]*

—Xu Guoji, Shanghai Industrial and Commercial Administration

*"Building a copyright system is like building a house... You can have the house structure all set up, very beautiful. But then, you need electricity and water pipes. That takes more time."[2]*

—Li Changxu, head of China United Intellectual Property Investigation Center

Over the past several decades, advances in technology have created an increasingly global economy. Especially in the Internet age, national borders have little meaning for copyrighted works, which can be distributed and transmitted worldwide easily and almost instantaneously. Doing business abroad and protecting intellectual property rights in foreign countries have consequently become increasingly important to many countries that produce a lot of intellectual property–based creations. Worldwide protection of intellectual property has correspondingly gained increasing importance in the United States, because intellectual property is one of the most positive trade areas in the American economy (i.e., exports exceed imports). In 2007, foreign exports of intellectual property products (music, films, software, etc.) totaled about $125.6 billion, more than any other major industry sector, including agriculture and automobiles.[3] Although the United States is the largest producer of intellectual property, other countries have also developed industries highly dependent on protection of intellectual property rights, including Japan, many European nations, South Korea, and India. Even for less technologically developed countries, intellectual property protection is needed in order to foster the development of local entertainment and technology industries and to encourage foreign investment.

American music is popular throughout most of the world, and as the worldwide economy and international trade have grown, it has become crucial that copyrights be protected on an international basis. However, protecting anything on an international basis poses substantial problems because each country operates independently with its own laws. There is no such thing as an international copyright law that provides copyright protection on a worldwide basis. Instead, most countries have their own copyright laws, which are not applicable outside of their borders. The United States Copyright Act, for instance, has no effect in any country other than the United

States; if a work copyrighted under U.S. copyright law is infringed in another country, the United States has no jurisdiction over that infringement.

Does this mean that copyrighted works can be infringed at will outside of the United States? Fortunately not. Because it is crucial that copyrighted works be protected on a worldwide basis, a system of treaties has developed under which countries agree to give protection to other countries' copyrighted works. In fact, the vast majority of nations in the world are members of one or more copyright treaties, thus providing some degree of international protection for copyrighted works. In essence, the various treaties between countries are like a network of copyright laws. As international protection and enforcement of copyright have become more important, a trend toward harmonization of copyright law in different countries has started to emerge and is likely to continue in the future.

# I. History of U.S. Attempts at International Protection

The United States has become a strong advocate for strengthening international copyright protection only over the past several decades. Previously, the United States took a much more isolationist position. According to former Register of Copyrights, Barbara Ringer:

> Until the second World War the United States had little reason to take pride in its international copyright relations; in fact it had a great deal to be ashamed of. With few exceptions its role in international copyright was marked by short-sightedness, political isolationism, and narrow self-interest."[4]

In fact, the United States did not grant protection to foreign works at all until 1891, over 100 years after the passage of the nation's first copyright statute. Although the United States is currently one of the strongest advocates for international copyright enforcement and routinely criticizes other countries for inadequate protection and enforcement of copyrights, the United States itself was the most notorious pirate country over a century ago. At that time, many British works were legally used in the United States without any compensation to their authors. Charles Dickens, for one, was very vocal about how Americans unfairly used his works and, during a trip to the United States in 1842, spoke out publicly against what he viewed as copyright piracy in America. Dickens claimed that, if American publishers had paid Sir Walter Scott (a popular early nineteenth-century Scottish novelist and poet) royalties for copies of his books sold in the United States, Scott would not have faced bankruptcy and died at the age of 61, "broken in body and mind by years of financial difficulties, and unjustly deprived of his rightful income."[5] Dickens had good reason to complain since, as soon as his books such as *The Pickwick Papers* and *Oliver Twist* were published in England, they were printed and sold in the United States without permission from or any payment to Dickens. While Dickens might have assumed that his pleas for fairness would be taken seriously in the relatively new nation founded on principles of justice and equality, the reaction in America was quite the opposite. The American press scorned Dickens, justifying their free use of foreign copyrighted works with arguments that literature should not be regulated by law and that a developing nation such as the United States must have inexpensive access to information and entertainment. Ironically, these are the same arguments that developing nations currently use when the United States complains about high rates of piracy and poor enforcement of copyright law.

## A. Bilateral Treaties

In 1891, an amendment to the United States Copyright Act known as the Chace Act allowed the president to extend copyright protection by proclamation to works originating in foreign countries if they in turn provided protection for American works. As a result, the United States gradually entered into bilateral treaties (treaties between two countries) concerning copyright. The United States has many bilateral treaties with foreign countries dealing with copyright, although many of these treaties have been superseded by multinational treaties such as the Berne Convention. However, a few countries are not members of any of the multinational treaties. In order for copyrighted works to be protected in these countries, the United States has bilateral treaties with some of them.

## B. Multinational Treaties

By the 1950s, it had become more important that the United States ensure the protection of copyrighted works abroad. The growth in foreign markets for American goods and the piracy of copyrighted works abroad were important reasons for doing so. Additionally, some foreign countries believed that the United States was not really committed to international protection due to its historical reluctance to protect foreign works. As a result, the United States eventually joined several multinational treaties.

### (1) The Berne Convention

The first international copyright convention was held in Berne, Switzerland, in 1886 and resulted in an agreement called the Berne Convention for the Protection of Literary and Artistic Works (commonly known as the Berne Convention). Before the Berne Convention, copyright laws applied only to works created within a country (not to foreign works). Since its inception in 1886, most of the major countries in the world have gradually become members of the Berne Convention. Because it also provides for the greatest degree of copyright protection of any multinational treaty, it has consequently become the most important international copyright treaty. The Berne Convention is administered by the World Intellectual Property Organization (WIPO), an agency of the United Nations based in Geneva, Switzerland.

---

**Note:**  The Berne Convention has been revised seven times since its origin in 1886. The most recent revision is the Paris Act of 1971, of which the United States is a member.

---

---

**Note:**  As of the writing of this book, the Berne Convention had been signed by 136 nations.

---

The Berne Convention applies to "literary and artistic works which shall include every production in the literary and artistic domain, whatever may be the mode or form of its expression."[6] The Berne Convention, however, does not include sound recordings as protected works due to the fairly common belief that performers are not equivalent to authors.

### (a) The National Treatment Principle

The Berne Convention is based on the principle of national treatment. This principle realizes that it would be impossible to implement a uniform international copyright law, applicable to every country. Under the national treatment principle, each country agrees to give citizens of foreign countries the same degree of copyright protection that it gives to its own citizens. Consequently, when an American copyright owner sues for an infringement occurring in a foreign country that is a member of the Berne Convention, the foreign country's copyright law will be applied.

The Berne Convention became effective in the United States on March 1, 1989. Any copyrighted works created after that date are entitled to national treatment by all other Berne Convention members. The Berne Convention was not applicable to works published in the United States prior to March 1, 1989, unless the work was simultaneously published in a Berne member country before that date. Before March 1, 1989, some American book publishers published their books simultaneously in the United States and Canada in order to be eligible for protection under the Berne Convention, a practice that became known as "the back door to Berne."

### (b) Minimal Standards of Protection

In addition to national treatment, the Berne Convention also imposes certain minimum standards of protection that all member countries must guarantee. Two of the most important of these minimum standards are:

- The duration of copyright protection must be at least for the life of the author plus 50 years. The United States and many other countries provide a longer term of protection (life of the author plus 70 years). A few countries provide an even longer term, life plus 75 years in Guatemala and Honduras, life plus 80 years in Colombia, and life plus 100 years in Mexico. Berne member countries are free to provide greater protection but cannot provide a shorter period of protection.

- Each member country's laws must provide for some fair use of copyrighted works for purposes such as education and news reporting (such as Section 107 of the U.S. Copyright Act, discussed in Chapter 11, "Defenses to Infringement").

### (c) Formalities

Under Article 5(2) of the Berne Convention, formalities such as copyright registration and notice cannot be required as a condition to copyright protection. However, some countries provide greater copyright protection conditioned upon compliance with certain formalities. For example, in countries such as the United States and Japan, registration, although not required, gives copyright owners important enforcement rights (see Chapter 9, "Copyright Formalities").

### (d) Exclusive Rights

The exclusive rights required to be protected under the Berne Convention are similar to those specified by Section 106 of the 1976 Copyright Act. These rights include reproduction,[7] translation,[8] adaptation,[9] and public performance.[10] Berne, however, does not mention any rights of distribution or public display. Berne also requires the recognition of the moral rights of attribution and integrity, stating that:

*...the author shall have the right to claim authorship of the work and to object to any distortion, mutilation or other modification of, or other derogatory action in relation to, the said work, which would be prejudicial to his honor or reputation.[11]*

The Berne Convention also encourages its members to recognize new authors' rights and authorizes members to provide higher levels of protection in their own copyright laws.[12]   Article 10 of the Berne Convention specifies some important limitations on copyright, such as exceptions for fair quotation from copyrighted works and exemptions for educational uses of copyrighted works. Article 10 also authorizes limitations on the recording of musical works, such as the compulsory license provision of Section 115 of the 1976 Copyright Act.

### (e) U.S. Membership in Berne

While the United States has historically lagged behind many European countries in the protection of foreign copyrights, it finally became a member of the Berne Convention on March 1, 1989, due mostly to its interest in combating piracy of American copyrights on an international basis. In order to join Berne, Congress passed the Berne Convention Implementation Act of 1988, which added certain amendments to the 1976 Copyright Act, including the following: (1) Copyright notice was made optional rather than mandatory for works published after March 1, 1989; and (2) Copyright transfers no longer have to be recorded in order to file a copyright infringement suit.

In some respects, the Berne Convention Implementation Act is a cautious approach by the United States regarding the provisions of the Berne Convention. For example, the Berne Convention Implementation Act refused to recognize moral rights required by Berne as part of American copyright law. Instead, Congress stated that legal protection under other types of law such as unfair competition, defamation, privacy, and contract law were sufficient to protect moral rights. This, however, is debatable, as some recent court decisions indicate that U.S. law does not protect moral rights as required by the Berne Convention. For example, authors of most types of works have no right to receive credit (the right to claim authorship as referred to in the Berne Convention) under U.S. copyright law. The United States claims that this right, even though not expressly provided by the Copyright Act, is protected under contract law. However, it is questionable whether any affirmative right actually exists, since contract law would allow an author to negotiate to be credited as a work's author but would not guarantee any right to claim authorship.

### (f) Protection of Foreign Copyrighted Works

For foreign works that are owned by citizens of Berne member countries and were first created or published after March 1, 1989, full protection is afforded under U.S. copyright law.

---

**Example 13.1**

Wolfgang, a German citizen, composes a symphony in 1998. Because Germany is a member of the Berne Convention, Wolfgang's symphony is protected in the United States under U.S. copyright law to the same extent as works of American citizens (for the author's life plus 70 years). If, however, the symphony had been composed and published before March 1, 1989, it would not be protected in the United States under the Berne Convention.

---

## (2) The Universal Copyright Convention

Another multinational treaty is the Universal Copyright Convention (UCC), which the United States joined on September 16, 1955. The main goal of the UCC was to bring the United States into the international copyright community.

The UCC is similar to the Berne Convention, with the exception that it allows member countries to require some formalities as conditions to copyright protection. However, the copyright owner of a work published in one UCC member country can avoid complying with the formalities required by another UCC member country by placing copyright notice on all published copies of the work.

The UCC, like the Berne Convention, requires its members to give foreign copyrights national treatment. It also requires certain minimum levels of protection, such as a term of at least the life of the author plus 25 years. The UCC, like the Berne Convention, does not provide any protection for sound recordings.

Many countries are members of both the UCC and the Berne Convention. In these countries, the Berne Convention takes priority over the UCC. When the United States signed the Berne Convention on March 1, 1989, the UCC's relevance to American works was limited to: (1) countries that are UCC members but not Berne members; and (2) works published in the United States prior to March 1, 1989, that were not simultaneously published in a Berne member country.

---

**Example 13.2**

---

If Wolfgang's symphony from the previous example had been published in the United States prior to March 1, 1989, although it would not be protected under the Berne Convention, it would be protected in the United States under the Universal Copyright Convention.

---

## (3) The Geneva and Rome Conventions

Many countries, including the United States until 1972, have been hesitant to recognize creators of sound recordings as authors under copyright law. This hesitancy is based on the belief that sound recordings, as recordings of performances of other works such as songs, are more the result of a mechanical process than of creative authorship. Consequently, ownership rights in sound recordings have historically been protected by several neighboring or related rights treaties that are not technically part of copyright law. The concept of neighboring rights recognizes that, even if sound recordings are not the type of creation that merits protection under copyright law, they are closely related, and their creators contribute artistic expression, technical skill, and/or participate in distribution or transmission, all of which deserve some type of protection. Neighboring rights, where recognized, are usually provided to performers, broadcasters, phonograph producers, and electronic transmitters of copyrighted works.

The Convention for the Protection of Producers of Phonograms Against Unauthorized Duplication of Their Phonograms (the "Geneva Convention") was passed in 1971 and became effective in the United States on March 10, 1974. The Geneva Convention is designed to provide international protection against record piracy by recognizing the rights of reproduction, distribution, and importation of sound recordings. Another treaty, the International Convention for the Protection of Performers, Producers of Phonograms and Broadcasting Organizations (the "Rome Convention"), provides a higher level of protection than the Geneva Convention. However, the United States has not joined the Rome Convention. Both of these treaties provide protection to performers and producers of sound recordings (musicians who perform and record companies that pay for, produce, and distribute the recordings). The protection provided is very similar to that provided by the Berne Convention for copyrighted works, including national treatment and minimum levels of protection.

The main practical difference between countries that protect sound recordings under copyright law and countries that protect them under neighboring rights involves international protection. If a country protects sound recordings through neighboring rights, the minimum standards and national treatment provisions of the Berne Convention will not apply. Instead, any protection for such sound recordings will be subject to the international standards imposed by the Geneva and Rome Conventions if the country is a party to one or both of these treaties.

### (4) The North American Free Trade Agreement

Starting in the 1980s, the United States began to link intellectual property protection more closely to international trade by incorporating copyright provisions into multinational trade–based agreements. This rests on the assumption that the failure to adequately protect intellectual property on an international basis is an unfair trade practice.

The North American Free Trade Agreement (NAFTA) was entered into in 1992 by the United States, Canada, and Mexico. NAFTA requires copyright protection for computer programs, data compilations, and sound recordings; recognition of rental rights for sound recordings; limitations on compulsory licensing; and recognition of rights against unauthorized importation of copies of protected works for NAFTA member countries.

NAFTA contains detailed provisions providing for the protection of sound recordings.[13] Producers of sound recordings can authorize or prohibit a recording's direct or indirect reproduction, importation of unauthorized copies, first public distribution, and commercial rental.[14] NAFTA also provides for a minimum copyright term of 50 years for sound recordings.[15]

### (5) The General Agreement on Trade and Tariffs

The General Agreement on Trade and Tariffs (GATT) is a multinational treaty that is designed to encourage free international trade. GATT includes an agreement on intellectual property called the Trade Related Aspects of Intellectual Property Rights (TRIPS). Under TRIPS, member countries must agree to enact copyright laws that give effect to the substantive provisions of the Berne Convention. TRIPS incorporates most of the minimum standards specified by the Berne Convention.[16] However, due primarily to pressure by the United States, TRIPS does not require recognition of moral rights.

TRIPS incorporates the Berne Convention's requirement of a minimum term of copyright protection lasting for the life of the author plus 50 years. If a work's term is not based on the life of a natural person, the term must be at least 50 years from either the year of publication or, if the work has not been published, within 50 years of its creation.

Quite possibly the most important part of TRIPS is that it provides for a practical international enforcement system for intellectual property rights, the lack of which has been a major weakness among all of the other multinational treaties. Under the Berne Convention, disputes could be adjudicated by the International Court of Justice. However, the International Court of Justice's enforcement power is severely limited because a judgment cannot be enforced unless the country that the judgment is to be enforced against agrees to it. TRIPS, however, provides for a much more practical enforcement system that includes provisions for injunctions and damages, seizure and interdiction at the border, and criminal penalties. TRIPS also provides for international panels to hear complaints about copyright violations.

### (a) Neighboring Rights

In order to implement the obligations imposed by TRIPS, the United States passed the Uruguay Round Agreements Act (URAA) in 1994. The URAA added a new Chapter 11 to the United States Code (not technically a part of the Copyright Act) that provides for protection for performers against the unauthorized fixation of performances and reproduction of such fixation.[17] It also provides performers with a right to prevent the unauthorized broadcast or communication to the public of a live performance.[18] TRIPS similarly gives broadcasting organizations the right to prevent unauthorized fixation of broadcasts, the reproduction of such fixations, the rebroadcasting of such broadcasts by wireless means, and the communication to the public of television broadcasts.[19] TRIPS provides for a term of protection for performers and producers of phonograms of 50 years from the date of the performance or fixation and 20 years for broadcasts from the year in which the broadcast took place.[20] Violations of these provisions are subject to criminal penalties and seizure and forfeiture of copies of unauthorized fixations.[21]

### (b) Restoration of Foreign Copyrights

One of the main features of copyright law is that once the term of a copyright expires, the work enters the public domain. In general, once a work has entered the public domain, it can never be brought back under copyright protection. However, in the United States this rule is subject to some exceptions that apply solely to certain foreign works.

The Uruguay Round Agreements Act amended Section 104(a) of the 1976 Copyright Act, providing for automatic restoration of copyright for certain foreign works that previously entered the public domain in the United States due to publication without copyright notice (a requirement under U.S. law that did not exist in other countries). In order to qualify for restoration, a work must not be in the public domain in its source country but in the public domain in the United States for one of the following reasons: (1) failure to comply with U.S. copyright formalities; (2) lack of subject matter protection if the work is a sound recording fixed before February 15, 1972; or (3) lack of national eligibility if the work's source country had no copyright relations with the United States at the time of publication.[22]

The restoration provisions are subject to a limitation that applies to parties who previously relied on foreign works that had fallen into the public domain (known as "reliance parties"). This limitation provides that any party who committed any infringing act with respect to a public domain work before the work's restoration is immune from infringement claims for one year from date of restoration.[23] If a copyright owner of a restored work intends to enforce the copyright against a reliance party, it must provide a notice of intent to enforce the copyright to the reliance party or must file a notice with the U.S. Copyright Office.

### (6) The WIPO Treaties

The World Intellectual Property Organization (WIPO) is an agency of the United Nations that works for increasing international legal protection for copyright and other intellectual property. In 1998, WIPO drafted two treaties designed to balance the interests of creators and owners of copyrighted works with the interests of users and distributors of such works in digital media. The WIPO treaties require member countries to provide protection to certain works from other member countries that must be no less favorable than the protection provided for domestic works. Both WIPO treaties contain provisions requiring the protection of copyright management information against tampering and circumvention of technical safeguards (see Chapter 14, "Copyright and Digital Technology," for more information). The United States ratified these treaties by passing the Digital Millennium Copyright Act in 1998.

#### (a) The WIPO Copyright Treaty

The WIPO Copyright Treaty updates the Berne Convention with respect to technological developments. Most importantly, it clarifies that the reproduction right under Article 9 of the Berne Convention applies in the digital environment by providing that the storage of a work in a digital or electronic medium is a reproduction. For example, digitally downloading a recording from a website would constitute reproduction.

#### (b) The WIPO Performances and Phonograms Treaty

The WIPO Performances and Phonograms Treaty is the first international treaty that specifically provides protection for sound recordings distributed digitally over computer networks such as the Internet. The treaty requires that member countries provide at least 50 years of protection after the first fixation of a recording. It also gives sound recording copyright owners the exclusive right to authorize others to make their recordings available by interactive Internet communications, including by wire or wireless means, in such a way that members of the public can access the recordings from places and at times individually chosen by them.

Under the Performances and Phonograms Treaty, performers receive greater protection than under TRIPS. In addition to economic rights, the treaty also provides for moral rights for performers of live audio performances fixed in phonorecords.

## C. Differences in Copyright Term for Sound Recordings

One problem with the treaty system that exists for the protection of copyrights is inconsistency of protection in different countries. For example, U.S. copyright law recognizes the same term of protection for sound recordings as for other types of works. However, many countries (such as the European Union nations) only protect sound recordings for 50 years, the minimum term required by the WIPO Performances and Phonograms Treaty. A few countries (e.g., Australia, Singapore, Turkey) have a longer term of protection than the United States. The result of this inconsistency is that record companies and artists will lose income from sales and licensing in the European Union of older recordings that are still commercially viable and protected by copyright in the United States and some other countries. It is important to realize that this does not mean that these recordings will necessarily be freely available in the European Union, although they will be in the public domain. Instead, they can be sold by anyone without any payment to the artists, producers, and record companies that created and marketed them. The United States as well as European music industry organizations are obviously not happy about this and have been putting pressure on the European Commission, the executive body of the European Union, to increase the term of protection for sound recordings.

In 2009, the European Parliament approved a proposal that would extend the term of protection for sound recordings from 50 to 70 years from the date of first release. In September 2009, the fate of this term extension proposal was approved by the EU Council of Ministers despite strong opposition by several European nations on the grounds that the additional 20 years of copyright result in little practical benefit for most sound recordings. The proposal will need to be enacted into law by EU member nations, which might take several years. For current information on the EU term extension proposal see the European Commission website at ec.europa.eu/internal_market/copyright/term-protection/term-protection_en.htm.

Even with the EU term extension, the term of protection of sound recordings in EU member countries will still be less than that of the United States. Opponents of sound recording term extension claim that an extra 20 years of copyright will not matter for most recordings because they will have very little commercial value 50 to 70 years after their initial release. While that is true, it is also true that some of the most commercially successful recordings will be adversely affected. For example, some recordings by Elvis Presley (one of the best-selling recording artists of all time) are already in the public domain in the UK (and other nations with a 50-year term for sound recordings). Without the EU term extension, recordings by the Beatles (the best-selling recording artist of all time) would start entering the public domain in the UK beginning in 2013 (although such recordings will receive an additional 20 years of protection, assuming the UK enacts the EU term extension). These recordings will still be protected in countries such as the United States, which recognize a longer term of protection. Further, it is important to understand that the copyright in the songs recorded will still be protected even in the EU because copyrights in works other than sound recordings generally last for the author's life plus 70 years.

## II. Countries That Have No Copyright Relations with the United States

There are a few countries that do not have any copyright relations with the United States because they are not members of any of the multinational treaties and are not parties to a bilateral treaty with the United States. In these countries, American copyrighted works are not given any protection. These countries include Afghanistan, Ethiopia, Iran, and Iraq.

## III. Piracy and the Use of Economic Pressure to Enforce Copyright

Piracy of copyrighted works is widespread throughout most of the world and poses a serious problem for copyright owners. Pirated goods are sold at much lower prices than legitimate products but are often much more profitable because the pirates do not incur most of the costs incurred by legitimate producers. These costs include production costs, marketing costs, and royalty payments to artists, producers, and songwriters. While it is an exaggeration to say that each pirated copy sold displaces a legitimate sale, it is also unrealistic to suggest that pirated copies have no negative effect on legitimate sales. Although piracy hurts the major entertainment companies, it often hurts small companies and entrepreneurs even more. Especially in countries with a local or regional entertainment industry, the effect can be devastating. Pirated copies of popular motion pictures and recordings displace sales of locally produced entertainment products and can cripple these smaller, much less diversified companies.

---

**Example 13.3**

The damage caused by piracy can best be seen in countries with high piracy rates such as the Philippines, where despite an enormous love of music, the local record industry has a hard time surviving. Although a few of the major international record companies have regional offices there, they generally do not invest in Filipino artists because the high piracy rate eliminates any reasonable chance of earning a profit. Instead, major record companies are mostly limited to marketing popular recordings from other countries.

---

Although the United States currently has copyright relations with virtually all of the major countries in the world, problems can still arise over enforcement of copyright protection. During the past several decades, the United States has resorted to threatening and, in some instances, actually using economic pressure against foreign countries to encourage them to strengthen their copyright laws and enforcement efforts. For example, the United States may impose trade sanctions against countries that allow widespread copyright violations.

Under Section 301 of the Trade Act of 1974,[24] Congress has authorized the U.S. Trade Representative (USTR) to identify and investigate countries that fail to adequately enforce or protect copyrights and to recommend retaliatory trade measures if the offending countries refuse to take steps to increase copyright protection. Each year, the USTR identifies certain foreign countries that it believes lack sufficient intellectual property protection, and the United States then puts pressure on these countries to increase their level of protection.

The best example of the use of economic pressure by the United States involves the People's Republic of China. China has a piracy rate of approximately 90%, according to the USTR. Considering that China is the most populous country in the world, with more than 1.3 billion people, potential income lost due to piracy is enormous. While China has made significant progress in enacting laws to protect copyrights over the past few decades, the USTR as well as many American and European companies believe that China's enforcement is still insufficient, considering the very high piracy rate that still exists.

In 1995, the United States threatened to impose 100% import duties on Chinese products in retaliation for China's alleged lack of effective intellectual property enforcement. United States Trade Representative Mickey Kantor stated that the main reason for the threatened sanctions was annual losses of $1 billion to Chinese intellectual property piracy.

Although much of the concern was due to piracy of computer software, piracy of American music and sound recordings was also a major concern. For example, China had allowed 29 manufacturing plants to operate that produced 75 million pirated compact discs a year. After strong pressure from the United States, China enacted new laws to protect intellectual property, although the United States continues to criticize China for its lack of effective enforcement. Although piracy in some Asian nations as well as other countries is still a major problem, economic pressure by the United States has resulted in the enactment and enforcement of intellectual property laws that may help to reduce international piracy, at least to some extent.

---

**Note:** China became a member of the Berne Convention in 1992 after amending its copyright laws to bring them in line with international standards.

---

## IV. What to Do if Your Work Is Infringed in a Foreign Country

If you own a copyrighted work that is infringed in a foreign country, there are several issues that should be considered. First of all, it is necessary to determine to what treaties, if any, the foreign country belongs. If the foreign country is a member of a treaty to which the United States is also a member, you can pursue legal action against the infringer. However, you should also consider whether it is practically worthwhile to take such action because it can be very complicated, costly, and time consuming to do so.

In some circumstances when a copyrighted work is infringed abroad, you can sue the infringer in the United States. However, the U.S. court will apply the copyright law of the foreign country where the infringement occurred. In other circumstances, you would have to sue the infringer in the foreign country. Either way, it is important to understand that the foreign country's copyright laws will govern and that you will be entitled to the same protection that a citizen of the foreign country would receive. Consequently, it is very important to determine what remedies are available if you are successful under the law that will be applied before pursuing legal action.

While this book deals primarily with United States law, copyright law in most countries is similar in many respects, largely due to the effect of the Berne Convention, which most countries have joined. However, if you would like to find more specific information on copyright law in other countries, the following are some useful online sources:

■ **Database of International Copyright Law:** digital.lampdev.columbia.edu/cmc—This database provided by Columbia University Libraries allows you to search copyright laws by country and compare certain copyright law provisions of up to three countries at a time.

- **WIPO Lex:** www.wipo.int/wipolex/en/—This page is part of the World Intellectual Property Organization's website, which allows you to search for intellectual property laws and treaties of many countries as well as providing news about updates and changes to intellectual property laws. WIPO also provides a list of Intellectual Property offices for many countries at www.wipo.int/directory/en/urls.jsp.

- **Copyright Watch:** www.copyright-watch.org—This website allows you to search by country or continent to find copyright laws, as well as reports and links to experts monitoring copyright laws of various countries.

Please note that while we have tried to provide online sources that provide accurate and up-to-date information, the authors cannot vouch for the information obtained from these websites or guarantee that links to or from these websites will remain valid.

## Endnotes

1. Seth Faison, "China Turns Blind Eye to Pirated Disks," N.Y. Times, Mar. 28, 1998, at D1 (quoting Xu Guoji, senior official in Shanghai's Industrial and Commercial Administration).
2. Marcus W. Brauchli & Joseph Kahn, "Intellectual Property: China Moves Against Piracy as U.S. Trade Battle Looms," Asian Wall St. J., Jan. 6, 1995, at 1 (quoting Li Changxu, head of China United Intellectual Property Investigation Center).
3. *Copyright Industries in the U.S. Economy: The 2003–2007 Report*, by Stephen E. Siwek of Economists Incorporated, prepared for the International Intellectual Property Alliance (IIPA), June 2009, available at www.iipa.com.
4. Ringer, "The Role of the U.S. in International Copyright - Past, Present & Future," 56 Geo. L.J. 1050, 1051 (1968).
5. Ackroyd, Peter. *Dickens.* London: Sinclair-Stevenson, 1990. p. 350.
6. Berne Convention, Art. 2(1).
7. Berne Convention, Art. 9(1).
8. Berne Convention, Art. 8(1).
9. Berne Convention, Art. 12.
10. Berne Convention, Art. 11.
11. Berne Convention, Art. 6.
12. Berne Convention, Art. 19.
13. Article 1706.
14. Article 1706(1)(a)–(d).
15. Article 1706(2).
16. Articles 1–21 of the 1971 Act of the Berne Convention with the exception of Art. 6, which deals with moral rights.
17. 17 U.S.C. 1101(a)(1) (1995).
18. TRIPS, Article 14(1).
19. TRIPS, Article 14(3).
20. TRIPS, Article 14(5).

21.  18 U.S.C. 2319A (1995).
22.  Pub. L. No. 103-465, 514, 108 Stat. 4809, 4980 (codified at 17 U.S.C. 104A(h)(6)(A)–(C) (1995)).
23.  17 U.S.C. 104A(d)(2)(A)-(B) (1995). See Section 104A(d)(2) for the specific provisions dealing with enforcing copyright in restored works against reliance parties.
24.  19 U.S.C. § 2242(a)(1)(A).

# 14 Copyright and Digital Technology

*"The only way to discover the limits of the possible is to go beyond them into the impossible."*

—Arthur C. Clarke, "Technology and the Future"

*"Technology is dominated by those who manage what they do not understand."*

—Murphy's Law

*"No manufacturer would ship his or her goods on a highway if his trucks were routinely hijacked."*

—U.S. Senator Orrin Hatch

The music industry has played a pivotal role in shaping public perceptions of copyright law and the law itself. Over the past several years, copyright has received more public attention than ever before, largely due to filesharing lawsuits against consumers and filesharing companies (discussed in Chapter 15, "The Online Music War"), and other infringement lawsuits in the digital realm. Some of the media coverage has contributed to a public view of copyright as a tool of the entertainment industries to maintain control of music and other creative works. Although the law has sometimes been used as such, it is not intended for such purposes and usually fulfills its intended purpose of providing incentives to authors to create new works of art while assuring the public of access to those works.

Yet this balance of interests creates what may be a natural tension: Advocates for a less restrictive, less content owner–driven version of copyright law may tend to oversimplify or take a broad view of the issues that copyright law seeks to resolve. Using slogans such as "information wants to be free" and "the genie is out of the bottle" and relying on ideas of "free speech" and "fair use," these causes may avoid the difficult balance that copyright law attempts to strike between providing access to creative works while providing authors with incentives to create such works. Instead, they attempt to convince the courts, the legislature, and the public that use of creative works without permission from or compensation to the owners of these works is a desirable legal framework or encourage consideration of new models of providing access to works. On the other hand, content owners have often been aggressive in seeking to enforce rights in the most absolute sense, e.g., in seeking monetary damages from consumers that far exceed the cost of the work produced and in seeking court decisions that would not only preserve rights in the case being litigated but set precedents that could arguably chill the access to works and creativity that copyright law was designed to encourage.

# I. Copyright Law in the Internet Age

Some people believe that we have reached the end of the copyright era and that intellectual property should be free to all in the Internet age. According to John Perry Barlow, a former lyricist for the Grateful Dead and current copyright critic:

> Intellectual property law cannot be patched, retrofitted, or expanded to contain digitized expression any more than real estate law might be revised to cover the allocation of broadcasting spectrum (which, in fact, rather resembles what is being attempted here). We will need to develop an entirely new set of methods as befits this entirely new set of circumstances.[1]

Barlow's analogy may disregard the fact that copyright has always been an evolving body of law. Just because expression can be stored in digitized form does not mean that copyright has outlived its usefulness. If all laws were thrown out when any new set of circumstances challenged their application, society would be in a constant state of chaos. Certainly, there are new circumstances to which copyright law must adapt, but copyright has been adapting for over two centuries and will almost certainly continue to do so.

Digital technology is still relatively new and very innovative, particularly in the ways we are finding to use it. It has revolutionized most art forms, particularly music in the ways it can be created, stored, played, and copied. Entire orchestral arrangements can now be scored with a few keystrokes, reducing what was once a substantial expense for developing and recording music. That same music can be compacted and transferred at lightning speed without losing sound quality through the Internet,[4] a digital phenomenon to which existing laws such as copyright must be applied. Music in digital form that is copied and distributed using computers and the Internet is generally protected by the same provisions of copyright law that apply to music in more traditional formats such as compact discs. The Copyright Act specifically recognizes that technological advances will alter the media in which works are fixed in tangible form, and the Copyright Act was specifically intended to include works fixed in digital form in such media as computer files, compact discs, etc.[2]

In recent years many amendments to the United States Copyright Act have been proposed, although very few have been enacted. Copyright owners try to convince Congress that greater protection is required, while new industries that use copyrighted works attempt to limit copyright law's application and obtain exemptions favorable to them. Some copyright scholars are also worried that some recent amendments have gone too far and unfairly limit the rights of individuals to build upon existing works, thereby stifling rather than promoting creativity. In the authors' opinions, passing legislation in response to every technological change is likely to be a self-defeating prophecy. Although some amendments to copyright law will be required, too much legislation (especially as the result of lobbying by affected industries) could actually further the tension between competing interests[3] and result in the creation of complicated, impractical laws, many of which may become obsolete as technology continues to evolve.

# II. New Technologies

Technological developments have always provided a challenge to copyright law. In fact, copyright law initially developed as a response to the invention of the printing press. Innovations in technology have led to new ways to reproduce and distribute copyrighted works and have consistently expanded the boundaries of copyright.

New technologies provide both threats and opportunities for copyright owners. Initially, the threats must be dealt with, but in the long run, copyright owners have benefited greatly from technological advances. After the invention of the photocopy machine, the print publishing industry worried that its business would be ruined by people photocopying rather than buying print publications. However, many books, newspapers, magazines, and other print publications continue to be sold. Similarly, the motion picture industry originally believed that the VCR would destroy the movie business. In fact, people continue to pay to watch movies in theaters, and renting copies of movies to consumers on physical media or via streaming services such as Netflix has provided motion picture companies with a revenue stream that now surpasses their theatrical receipts.

The music industry has also been no stranger to technological advances. Since Thomas Edison invented the gramophone in 1877, advances in recording technology have challenged copyright law and forced it to adapt. The gramophone was followed by inventions like the phonograph, eight-track, analog cassette, compact disc, digital audiotape, and MP3. In the early years of radio, many felt that it would destroy the record business and several decades later worried that music videos would supplant radio. Generally, each new invention has been an improvement over its predecessors and has changed the way people listen to music.

It is important to note that none of the new technologies mentioned above have destroyed their respective industries. In fact, some products such as the VCR and the compact disc at the time actually rejuvenated their industries, bringing in huge new sources of revenues. However, the concern of the various entertainment industries when a major new technology is introduced is not totally misplaced. The mistake is to focus the concern on the technology itself rather than on the use of technology. No technology is inherently bad. Instead, it is the illegal and unethical use of technology that poses the real threat to copyrighted works; likewise the use of copyright law can pose a threat to new technologies.

The evolution of copyright law has not always been smooth, but it has managed to work reasonably well overall. Copyright law was designed to be fairly flexible. In fact, some provisions of copyright law may seem to be too broad. This is often because these provisions were designed to apply not only to existing technologies, but also to technologies that had not yet been invented. Even so, it has been necessary to revise and update certain provisions of the law from time to time in order to accommodate technological advances.

In the early part of the twenty-first century, the greatest challenge to copyright and the music industry is the combination of digital technology and the Internet. These technologies have changed the way people listen to music. Through these technologies, copyrighted works are much more easily accessed than in the past. This also means that copyrighted works can be much more easily infringed than in the past. When new technologies are invented, businesses develop that intend to profit from the use of these technologies. These businesses, which are frequently based on the idea of providing access to copyrighted content in some form, often find themselves at odds with the owners of the copyright in that content over the use of the content and how (or whether) the copyright owners should be compensated for such uses.

### A. Digital Technology

Digital technology involves converting information such as sounds into mathematical bits that are represented by a series of 0s and 1s. With analog recording, each successive copy results in a decrease in sound quality. The main advantage of digital audio technology is that there is virtually no loss of sound quality regardless of how many generations of copies are made. Additionally, digitization provides an easy and inexpensive way to reproduce and distribute an unlimited number of copies.

### B. The Internet

The Internet is a worldwide network of various types of computers and servers. It allows computers and their users to share data and communicate with each other. Users access the Internet in various ways: through digital cable modems, DSL lines, analog dial-up lines, and robust network connections like T3 lines.

## III. How Music Is Used on the Internet

In order to understand how copyright law applies to the Internet, it is necessary to examine how the copyright owner's exclusive rights are commonly exercised in the Internet medium. There are two primary ways music is distributed over the Internet: digital downloading and streaming. Both of these technologies allow music to be transmitted over the Internet to users' computers.

### A. Streaming

Streaming technology allows for the continuous transmission of music over the Internet in real time so that listeners hear the music as it is transmitted to them from a website or other source, e.g., "cloud" storage systems. Streaming can facilitate a type of Internet radio but can also provide for "on demand" services, where the user can choose a song to stream with the click of a mouse. No permanent copy of the music transmitted is made on the listener's computer because the audio is merely "streaming" through the computer on its way to speakers connected to the computer. Many radio stations transmit their broadcasts over the Internet through websites, a process known as "webcasting." In order to play the webcasted music, you need software, which can often be downloaded for free. One disadvantage of streaming is that the listener generally must be online to hear the music, although some music services have begun offering "offline streaming" by permitting users to play files that have been "cached" in a web browser even if the user does not have an Internet connection. Additionally, the music is usually of lesser sound quality than downloaded files because it has to be heavily compressed in order to flow through typical modems, although as broadband Internet connections increase, this will be less of an issue.

Many record companies use streaming technology to allow consumers to preview recordings and videos. There are also online subscription services that offer large amounts of music that can be accessed online and listened to at any time, but not downloaded.

## B. Downloading

Digital downloading allows people to make (or download) copies of digital music files from the Internet. Downloaded files can be stored on a computer hard drive or other storage device and played on demand. In order to play a downloaded file, you need to have a software program that can read the particular file type; such programs can usually be downloaded for free. In order to play the downloaded file away from the computer, you need a hardware device like an iPod that can play that particular type of file.

When uncompressed audio files are copied to a computer hard drive, they take up a lot of the computer's memory. Consequently, audio files must be compressed in some manner in order to transmit and store them effectively. Compression involves taking digital data such as a recording and representing it with a smaller number of data or bits. Compression algorithms delete redundant parts of a digital file as well as parts of the file that are inaudible to the human ear. The result is a smaller or compressed file, which reduces the amount of bandwidth necessary to transmit a file over the Internet and the amount of space needed to store a file on a computer. MPEG Layer 3 (MP3) is a compression format that reduces the size of digital audio files by a ratio of 11 to 1 without much loss of sound quality.[4] Whereas a typical four-minute music file in uncompressed format takes up about 40 megabytes of hard drive space, the same recording in MP3 format takes up only 3.5 megabytes. The MP3 compression format has been around for more than a decade now. It is not owned by anyone and has become one of the most commonly used compression formats for music files. Newer compression formats, such as Windows Media (used by Microsoft's Windows Media Player), AAC (used by iTunes), and Ogg Vorbis, accomplish virtually the same thing as MP3 files, often with better sound quality at small data rates.

MP3 files can be downloaded from many websites to the downloader's computer. You can then play the MP3 file using software known as an MP3 player. You can also create MP3 files from compact discs. To do so, you must use a software program called a "ripper" that extracts music tracks from the compact disc while it is loaded in the computer's CD or DVD drive. The extracted tracks can then be saved on the computer's hard drive and converted to a compressed format. Most of the modern software programs that play music files, such as iTunes, Windows Media Player, and RealPlayer, accomplish ripping, converting, and indexing of compressed files in one step.

Once you have a music file stored on your computer in MP3 format, you can play the music using your computer (equipped with a sound card and speakers) or record or "burn" it onto compact discs. You can make an infinite number of copies, which if made from a lawfully acquired file and used solely for your own personal use may constitute a fair use for this purpose. However, you cannot legally give away, sell, or upload copies to websites without the copyright owners' permission.

There is nothing inherently illegal about MP3 or other compression formats. However, they are often used illegally. Uploading and downloading an MP3 file containing a copyrighted work is legal when the copyright owner gives the uploader or downloader permission to do so. However, if you upload or download an MP3 file containing a copyrighted work without the copyright owner's permission, you will generally be infringing upon the copyright owner's exclusive rights.[5]

The use of MP3 software for the distribution of music has generated considerable fear in the music industry. Many individuals have reportedly ripped MP3 files of their entire CD collections, and the trading of illegal MP3 files over the Internet using file sharing software has become rampant. Worsening the problem, compact disc recorders can be used to burn and sell CDs of illegally acquired music files or to make counterfeit copies of music that was initially acquired lawfully. You can find illegal and pirated CDs available for sale all over the world, many of which contain MP3 files.

---

**Example 14.1**

The Philippines is one of many countries with a high physical piracy rate. You can find pirated CDs as well as movies and computer software in virtually all major shopping areas. Most of the illegal CDs contain MP3 files that have either been burned from CDs or downloaded illegally. Rather than merely including all of the songs on a legitimate recording, many of these pirated CDs contain all of the songs recorded by an artist, since the compressed nature of MP3 files allows many more audio tracks to be recorded onto a single CD than the typical 10 to 12 songs on a commercially released CD. For instance, you can buy a CD containing all recordings of artists such as the Beatles, Elton John, and the Eagles for about $1.50. While it is admittedly tempting to buy CDs at prices so much lower than those of legitimate CDs, it is important to keep in mind that not only is it illegal to purchase such pirated copies, but the people and organizations selling them don't have to incur any of the costs that legitimate businesses do (e.g., production, marketing, etc.) and do not pay royalties to the recording artists, songwriters, producers, music publishers, or anyone else who has contributed to the creation of the recordings.

---

# IV. How Does Copyright Apply to the Internet?

One of the main problems for businesses attempting to legally offer music over the Internet is the complexity involved in licensing music. This can be a complicated process because most uses will involve two separate copyrighted works—a musical composition and a sound recording—which are usually owned by different parties (though independent artists who are also writers may own both the song and the recording). Another difficulty that can affect the legitimate availability of music on the Internet concerns the negotiation of licenses with content owners who are not always interested in negotiating a license that will allow the business to provide music at a cost that is economical for all parties involved: the content owners, the services providing the music, and the consumers. Additionally, the separate but related copyrights in the musical composition and the sound recording include different rights and limitations.

The preceding chapters discuss the statutory parameters for the copyright owner's exclusive rights, which we now examine in the context of the Internet.

## A. The Reproduction Right

Copyright owners of musical works and sound recordings have the exclusive right to reproduce or make copies of their works. The reproduction right is exercised continuously by Internet users, often without users even being aware of it. Whenever someone receives an e-mail containing copyrighted material or visits a website, a copy of the computer file accessed is made on the computer user's hard drive. Reproduction occurs when a work is entered into a computer for more than a temporary period. For instance, a reproduction occurs in each of the following situations:[6]

- A work is copied to a computer file, whether on the computer's hard drive, a floppy disk, CD-ROM, or other storage medium. This includes "ripping" an MP3 file from a compact disc; it also includes the automatic copying of a webpage when the user visits that page.

- A digitized file is uploaded from a computer to a website.

- A digitized file is downloaded from a website.

- One person's computer is used to access a file on another computer, such as through the use of file-sharing software.

- A file is transferred from one computer on a network to another.

If you operate a website that allows digital downloads of files containing copyrighted sound recordings and musical compositions, you need to obtain licenses from the copyright owners or their agents. Licenses to reproduce copyrighted sound recordings are obtained directly from the record company or artist that owns the sound recording. In some instances, relatively unknown artists may be willing to license the right to reproduce their sound recordings for free to promote themselves and build a fan base. Record companies and well-known artists, on the other hand, are generally less likely to be willing to license the right to download their recordings for free because this generally limits their ability to make money by selling recordings. However, artists Radiohead and Nine Inch Nails rocked industry headlines in 2008 with album donation programs that demonstrated that it is possible to use free downloads to extend a fan base and to successfully experiment with new business models the Internet makes possible.[7]

In addition to the license for a sound recording, a mechanical license is also required for any copyrighted musical compositions contained on a sound recording. Artists cannot grant this right unless they also happen to be the songwriter and copyright owner of the musical compositions. Licenses to reproduce musical compositions can be obtained either from the songwriter or music publisher that owns the copyright or from a licensing agent authorized by the copyright owner (such as the Harry Fox Agency, which represents many music publishers in the United States).

## B. The Public Performance Right

A copyright owner has the exclusive right to publicly perform a copyrighted work directly or through a means of communication or transmission. The transmission of music over the Internet can constitute a public performance. When you listen to streamed music over the Internet, the music is certainly being performed, but it may not seem that the performance is a "public" one. However, if the same file is being accessed by multiple users, the fact that a performance occurs at different times for different users does not prevent it from being a public performance. Downloads, by contrast, do not implicate a public performance right, as discussed in Chapter 7, "Public Performance and Display Rights."

Licensing of the public performance right for musical compositions is handled predominantly by performing rights organizations (such as ASCAP, BMI, and SESAC in the United States). All three of these organizations offer licenses that authorize performances of musical compositions over the Internet. It is also important to realize that under the Digital Performance Right in Sound Recordings Act of 1995 (see Chapter 7), sound recordings transmitted over the Internet are also subject to a performance right. Licensing of the performance right for sound recordings is handled by an organization called SoundExchange.

## C. The Reproduction/Performance Controversy

Before the digital distribution of music over the Internet, the difference between a reproduction and a performance of music was usually clear. Unfortunately, music transmitted over the Internet does not always fit within these distinct categories. Often, both rights are potentially involved.

Resolving this controversy has not been easy, in great part due to the turf war between reproduction rights licensing agents and performance rights agents and between content owners (music publishers, who receive performance income from performances, versus recording companies, who receive reproduction income for sound recordings), none of whom wants to give up a potentially lucrative source of income from royalties. The transmission of music over the Internet makes the act of copying automatic because the digital representation of the music is copied into the computer's random access memory (RAM) so that it can be played. Consequently, recording companies and reproduction rights agents like the Harry Fox Agency have traditionally believed that virtually all transmissions of music involve a reproduction. At the same time, music publishers and performance rights agents (ASCAP, BMI, and SESAC) want to collect public performance royalties on as many types of transmissions as possible. Some of these issues have been resolved (see discussion of *United States v. American Society of Composers, Authors and Publishers* in Chapter 7), so a website wanting to make music available by digital transmission over the Internet may need to obtain several licenses for the right to transmit musical compositions, as well as separate licenses to transmit sound recordings.

---

**Example 14.2**

A website that allows users to download from a choice of many copyrighted musical compositions and sound recordings would have to obtain at least the following licenses: mechanical licenses for the reproduction of musical compositions from the Harry Fox Agency or individual publishers and licenses for the reproduction and performance of the sound recordings from SoundExchange and the sound recording copyright owners (see Tables 7.1 and 7.2 in Chapter 7).

---

## D. The Distribution Right

Another complication brought about by the transmission of music over the Internet involves the copyright owner's exclusive right to distribute a copyrighted work. Under the first sale doctrine, once someone has legally acquired a copy or phonorecord containing a copyrighted work (e.g., a compact disc, cassette, etc.), he can sell or otherwise distribute that copy or phonorecord without the copyright owner's consent.[8] The first sale doctrine applies to the material object containing a copyrighted work and is limited to that material object. For example, someone who has lawfully acquired a compact disc is free to distribute that compact disc to someone else. However, the compact disc owner is not free to make and distribute copies of the copyrighted works contained on that compact disc.

In the online environment, the concept of distribution becomes a bit fuzzy. When a copyrighted work such as a sound recording is transmitted over the Internet, it seems like a distribution has taken place. However, this is not technically true because such a transmission does not involve the transfer of a material object. Instead, the owner of the copy or phonorecord transmitted still possesses that copy or phonorecord. Instead of a distribution, what has taken place is really a reproduction of the original work that results in a new copy being created. Because a reproduction rather than a distribution has taken place, the first sale doctrine does not apply (because the first sale doctrine is limited solely to the distribution right). The new copy resulting from a digital transmission would therefore be an infringement unless made with the copyright owner's permission.

Some critics have argued that the first sale doctrine should be extended to reproduction to the extent necessary to allow the digital transmission of a work by the owner of a legally made copy of the work as long as the owner of the copy destroys his or her copy after making the transmission. The Copyright Office has recommended that Congress refrain from expanding the first sale doctrine, basing its recommendation on the inherent differences between physical copies and digitally transmitted copies. Physical copies of works (especially those in analog formats) degrade over time, making used copies less desirable than new ones. However, digitally transmitted copies do not degrade over time regardless of how much they are used. Additionally, with an Internet connection, digital copies can be transmitted almost instantaneously to an infinite number of people worldwide. The Copyright Office Report states that:

> The need to transport physical copies of works, which acts as a natural brake on the effect of resales on the copyright owner's market, no longer exists in the realm of digital transmissions. The ability of such "used" copies to compete for market share with new copies is thus far greater in the digital world.[9]

The issue of whether the first sale doctrine applies in the Internet context is tied to how the distribution right operates on the Internet. Thus far, courts have held that simply making copies of a work available through Internet transmission does not constitute the making of a distribution. The issue has been raised in filesharing cases where plaintiffs have attempted to hold defendants liable not only for violating the reproduction right through illegal downloads, but for violating the distribution right as well through sharing the illegal file with others, who may in turn transmit it to others, creating a perpetual "distribution." It should be noted that even if making a work available constituted a distribution, the first sale doctrine would only apply to distribution of legally made copies of the original work. Therefore, it would not be available as a defense to illegal downloaders or filesharers. However, on the question of whether the "sharing" aspect of filesharing constitutes distribution, courts have held that distribution does not occur in these retransmissions. This is the primary inquiry in *Atlantic v. Howell*, where the court focused on whether defendants' use of the KaZaA filesharing network to share songs with others constituted a distribution. The court did not find violation of the distribution right, stating:

> The court agrees with the great weight of authority that Section 106(3) is not violated unless the defendant has actually distributed an unauthorized copy of the work to a member of the public. The statute provides copyright holders with the exclusive right to distribute "copies" of their works to the public "by sale or other transfer of ownership, or by rental, lease, or lending." 17 U.S.C. § 106(3). Unless a copy of the work changes hands in one of the designated ways, a "distribution" under Section 106(3) has not taken place. Merely making an unauthorized copy of a copyrighted work available to the public does not violate a copyright holder's exclusive right of distribution.[10]

When record company plaintiffs attempted to use the "making available" argument derived from patent law in *Capitol Records v. Thomas* (discussed in Chapter 15), the court reached the same conclusion as the court in *Atlantic v. Howell*:

> The Court's examination of the use of the term "distribution" in other provisions of the Copyright Act, as well as the evolution of liability for offers to sell in the analogous Patent Act, lead to the conclusion that the plain meaning of the term "distribution" does not including [sic] making available and, instead, requires actual dissemination.[11]

# V. The Digital Millennium Copyright Act

The Digital Millennium Copyright Act (DMCA) is an amendment to the 1976 Copyright Act that was signed into law in 1998. The DMCA's enactment was prompted by advances in technology and the exponential growth of the Internet as a communications medium. Before its passage, a considerable amount of lobbying took place; consequently, many of its provisions reflect legislative compromises. The end result is a very detailed and complicated piece of legislation. The three most important issues addressed by the DMCA relevant to the music industry are anti-piracy provisions, limitation on liability for online service providers, and rules for webcasters (discussed in Chapter 7).

## A. Anti-Piracy Provisions

Digital technology can be used to facilitate widespread copying and unauthorized access to works in unprecedented ways. The DMCA anticipates and addresses this possibility through its anti-piracy provisions.

### (1) Anti-Circumvention

Due to the threat of widespread infringement of works in digital format over computer networks, copyright owners have begun to use several technological devices to make their works more difficult to infringe. For instance, a digital computer file can be transmitted in encrypted form, requiring someone who receives the file to have a software code to be able to read or listen to the file. However, no protection technology is infallible, and there are people (commonly referred to as hackers) who will attempt to deactivate technologies used by copyright owners. The DMCA makes it illegal to manufacture, import, distribute, or provide products or services that are primarily designed or produced for the purpose of circumventing technological measures used by copyright owners to protect their works. Circumvention of technological measures means descrambling a scrambled work, decrypting an encrypted work, or otherwise bypassing, removing, deactivating, or impairing technological measures without the authority of the copyright owner.

One major criticism of the DMCA is that it makes some conduct that does not constitute copyright infringement illegal. For instance, a person who circumvents copyright protection technology for a lawful purpose like making a fair use of the work is still violating the DMCA.

---

**Example 14.3**

A court held that the distribution of software that enables users to defeat copy protection technology encoded into DVD movies violates the anti-circumvention provisions of the DMCA.[12] Movies released in DVD format are protected by encryption software called the Contents Scramble System (CSS), which can only be decrypted and viewed on a DVD player that has a licensed CSS key (DeCSS). Computers using the Windows and Macintosh operating systems that come with DVD players have the DeCSS key built in, but computers using the free Linux operating system do not have the decryption key and cannot view DVD movies. The defendant posted the DeCSS software on his website, where it could be downloaded by Linux users. The movie studios alleged that DeCSS is a piracy tool and that without the anti-circumvention protection afforded by the DMCA, copyright owners would be reluctant to make encrypted works available. The defendant claimed that DeCSS is merely a way to help Linux users watch DVD movies they already own, contending that DeCSS has legitimate uses. The court agreed with the movie studios, issuing an order banning the defendant from posting, linking to, or otherwise trafficking in the DeCSS code.

---

Every three years the Librarian of Congress is required by the anti-circumvention provisions in Section 1201(a) of the Copyright Act to evaluate whether there are classes of works that should be exempted from the prohibition on anti-circumvention. The purpose of doing so is:

[T]o "determine whether the prohibition on circumvention of technological measures that control access to copyrighted works is causing or is likely to cause adverse effects on the ability of users of any particular classes of copyrighted works to make noninfringing uses of those works."[13]

The proceeding referenced is the rulemaking process conducted by the Register of Copyrights. The Register invites comments and conducts hearings through the process, and if such works are identified, the Librarian (through the Register) may promulgate regulations to implement such exemptions. Accordingly, in 2010 regulations were issued exempting six classes of works from Section 1201(a)(1):[14]

1.  Motion pictures on DVDs that are lawfully made and acquired and that are protected by the Content Scrambling System when circumvention is accomplished solely in order to accomplish the incorporation of short portions of motion pictures into new works for the purpose of criticism or comment, and where the person engaging in circumvention believes and has reasonable grounds for believing that circumvention is necessary to fulfill the purpose of the use in the following instances:

    (i)   Educational uses by college and university professors and by college and university film and media studies students

    (ii)    Documentary filmmaking

    (iii)   Noncommercial videos

2.  Computer programs that enable wireless telephone handsets to execute software applications, where circumvention is accomplished for the sole purpose of enabling interoperability of such applications, when they have been lawfully obtained, with computer programs on the telephone handset.

3.  Computer programs, in the form of firmware or software, that enable used wireless telephone handsets to connect to a wireless telecommunications network, when circumvention is initiated by the owner of the copy of the computer program solely in order to connect to a wireless telecommunications network and access to the network is authorized by the operator of the network.

4.  Video games accessible on personal computers and protected by technological protection measures that control access to lawfully obtained works, when circumvention is accomplished solely for the purpose of good faith testing for, investigating, or correcting security flaws or vulnerabilities, if:

    (i)    The information derived from the security testing is used primarily to promote the security of the owner or operator of a computer, computer system, or computer network; and

    (ii)   The information derived from the security testing is used or maintained in a manner that does not facilitate copyright infringement or a violation of applicable law.

5.  Computer programs protected by dongles[15] that prevent access due to malfunction or damage and are obsolete. A dongle shall be considered obsolete if it is no longer manufactured or if a replacement or repair is no longer reasonably available in the commercial marketplace.

6.  Literary works distributed in e-book format when all existing e-book editions of the work (including digital text editions made available by authorized entities) contain access controls that prevent the enabling either of the book's read-aloud function or of screen readers that render the text into a specialized format.

The effect of these exemptions on the music industry remains to be seen, though they are consumer friendly in nature and may indicate an interest on the part of the Copyright Office in smoothing the road to accessing copyrighted works for content users.

### (2) Protection of Copyright Management Information

In addition to prohibiting circumvention of technological measures, the DMCA also provides for protection of copyright management information. Copyright management information is information embedded into a digital file that identifies the work such as the author, the copyright owner, the performer, and the terms and conditions for the use of the work. Copyright management information can be embedded so that it remains in a file regardless of where the file is transmitted, allowing the copyright owner to detect unauthorized uses and track royalty payments.

The DMCA prohibits the falsification, alteration, or removal of copyright management information or trafficking in copies of works that are linked with copyright management information that has been falsified, altered, or removed, if the offending party knew or should have known that its actions would facilitate infringement.[16]

## B. Online Service Provider Liability

One of the problems in applying copyright law to the Internet involves determining who is responsible for infringements. People who, without permission, upload copyrighted music to the Internet or download it from the Internet are direct infringers. However, copyright owners face several problems in enforcing their copyrights against such individuals. First, it can be difficult to determine the identity of individual infringers in some circumstances. Second, it is often not economically practical to sue individuals for copyright infringement because copyright owners would have to sue thousands or millions of people, often for relatively small amounts of money. Third, copyright owners are often afraid of the negative publicity that will result from suing individual consumers.

Fortunately for copyright owners, in addition to direct infringers, the law also imposes liability on third parties who aid in infringement (contributory infringement), financially benefit from infringement (vicarious liability), or induce (promote and encourage) infringement (see Chapter 10, "Infringement of Copyright"). This allows copyright owners to sue websites and online service providers for infringements by individuals who use their services to commit infringements. Prior to the enactment of the DMCA, several courts had indicated that online service providers may be contributorily liable for copyright infringement by website operators.[17] The fear of liability resulted in heavy lobbying by service providers, which led to the enactment of Title II of the DMCA, the Online Copyright Infringement Limitation on Liability Act (OCILLA).

The DMCA creates limitations on the liability of online service providers for copyright infringement. An online service provider is defined as "a provider of online services or network access, or the operator of facilities therefore."[18] The DMCA does not completely immunize online service providers from liability. Instead, it limits the remedies available against online service providers in certain circumstances and provides a procedure to aid in limiting online infringement.

The DMCA specifies four types of conduct for which an online service provider is not subject to damages or other monetary relief. In order to fit any of the four categories, a service provider must satisfy two general conditions: (1) It must adopt and reasonably implement a policy of terminating the accounts of subscribers who are repeat infringers. (2) It must accommodate and not interfere with technical measures that copyright owners use to identify or protect copyrighted works, such as watermarks and encryption. In addition, there are specific conditions applicable to each of the four categories of conduct.

## (1) Transitory Communications

Section 512(a) limits the liability of service providers for copyright infringements of third parties (i.e., their users). In other words, this section limits the liability of service providers that act merely as data conduits, transmitting digital information from one point on a network to another at the request of users. A service provider must satisfy the following conditions to qualify for this limitation: (1) The transmission must be initiated by a person other than the service provider; (2) The transmission must be carried out by an automatic technical process without selection of material by the service provider; (3) The service provider must not determine the recipients of the material; (4) Any intermediate copies must not be accessible to anyone other than anticipated recipients and must not be retained for longer than necessary; and (5) The material must be transmitted with no modification to its content.

## (2) System Caching

Section 512(b) limits the liability of service providers for system caching. System caching refers to the process by which a service provider retains a temporary copy of frequently accessed Internet material for a limited time so that subsequent requests for the material can be fulfilled by transmitting the retained copy instead of retrieving the material again from the original source. This reduces the waiting time on subsequent requests for the same material. This limitation is subject to the following conditions:

- The content of the retained material must not be modified.

- The service provider must comply with rules about updating material and replacing retained copies of material with material from the original location, when specified in accordance with accepted industry standards.

- The service provider must not interfere with technology that returns hit information to the person who posted the material.

- The provider must limit users' access to the material in accordance with conditions on access (e.g., password protection or access fees) imposed by the person who posted the material.

- Any material posted without the copyright owner's authorization must be removed or blocked promptly once the service provider has been notified of its existence.

## (3) Hosting at the Direction of Users

Section 512(c) limits the liability of service providers for infringing material on websites hosted on their systems. To be eligible for this limitation, the following conditions must be satisfied:

- The service provider must not have actual knowledge of infringing activity, must not be aware of facts or circumstances from which infringing activity is apparent, or upon gaining knowledge or awareness, must respond expeditiously to take the material down or block access to it.

- If the service provider has the right and ability to control the infringing activity, it must not receive a financial benefit directly attributable to the infringing activity.

- Upon receiving proper notification of any claimed infringement, the service provider must promptly take down or block access to the material. The service provider must file a designation of an agent to receive notifications of claimed infringement with the Copyright Office and must make contact information available through its websites in an accessible location.

The DMCA creates a notice and takedown procedure, allowing a copyright owner to submit a notice of claimed infringement to the service provider's designated agent. If the service provider promptly removes or blocks access to the material identified in the notice after receiving it, the service provider will be exempt from monetary liability. The service provider will also be protected against liability to any person due to its having taken down the material, provided that it notifies the subscriber that it has removed or disabled access to the material. The subscriber can then file a counter notice including a statement that the material was removed or disabled through mistake or misidentification. It is then up to the copyright owner to file an action seeking a court order against the subscriber. If the copyright owner neglects to do so, the service provider must put the material back up within 10–14 business days after receiving the counter notice.

This safe harbor for service providers represents one of the DMCA's most controversial provisions. Since the DMCA was enacted when the Internet was in its early infancy, the purpose of the safe harbors was to facilitate the growth of the Internet by making it "safe" to introduce innovations, like websites offering music or other content in fresh ways. Yet the fairness, utility, and practicality of Section 512(c) has been met with skepticism. From the perspective of a service provider, the notice and takedown procedures are potentially burdensome requirements to meet to qualify for the safe harbor. If an Internet service provider falls short of meeting the requirements, liability might ensue. Accordingly, the provision should ideally be clear enough and easy enough to follow that online service providers can take advantage of the intended statutory refuge. For content owners like artists, composers, and recording and production companies, the notice and take down procedures are likewise potentially onerous. Content owners have asserted that the provision essentially permits ISPs to infringe their works or facilitate such infringement. From the perspective of content users, the Internet has opened up a whole world of access to copyrighted works in new and interesting ways. And though the requirements of the DMCA are transparent to most consumers and users of works, it is safe to speculate that few desire to live in a world that makes such works unavailable or too inconvenient to access.

### (a) Testing the Bounds of Safe Harbors
As the Internet has matured, website operators have provided the kind of innovation ripe for testing the boundaries of Section 512(c). For example, YouTube provides both User Generated Content (UGC) and copyright-protected content capable of a wide range of uses, from entertainment to academic research. Consequently, services such as YouTube and Veoh Networks, which allow users to search for and watch UGC and copyright-protected movies and television productions, have been challenged by content owners seeking to protect their works from potential abuses by service providers, who in turn have looked to the safe harbor to shield them from liability. The result was two important test cases: *UMG Recordings v. Veoh Networks,*[19] and *Viacom Intl. v. YouTube.*[20] Both cases commenced in 2007. *Veoh* was decided first and was persuasive for the court in the *Viacom* case. Both share key similarities.

- Both Veoh Networks (Veoh) and YouTube permitted users to upload copyrighted music (owned by the plaintiffs) to their websites, although Veoh is described as a video sharing service.

- In both cases the courts validated the website operators' efforts to identify repeat infringers (with their use of filtering software) and to comply with the takedown procedures required under Section 512(c).

- A key aspect of both cases centered on the knowledge requirement of Section 512(c), as both cases were expected to clarify the extent of knowledge of infringing activity a service provider must have to be secondarily liable, whether actual or constructive knowledge or a general awareness of infringing materials on their sites. The *Veoh* court rejected the idea of Veoh being charged with actual knowledge:

> UMG *first asserts that Veoh had actual knowledge of infringement because it "knew that it was hosting an entire category of content—music—that was subject to copyright protection." If merely hosting user-contributed material capable of copyright protection were enough to impute actual knowledge to a service provider, the section 512(c) safe harbor would be a dead letter because vast portions of content on the internet are eligible for copyright protection.*[21]

Likewise, in *Viacom*, general awareness of infringing materials was not required of the service provider to impute liability:

> [I]f *a service provider knows (from notice from the owner, or a "red flag") of specific instances of infringement, the provider must promptly remove the infringing material. If not, the burden is on the owner to identify the infringement. General knowledge that infringement is "ubiquitous" does not impose a duty on the service provider to monitor or search its service for infringements.*[22]

- In *Viacom*, inducement liability, introduced in *MGM v. Grokster,* was held not to apply to YouTube, since the court held that *Grokster* applied to peer-to-peer filesharing networks not covered by Section 512(c);

Both Veoh and YouTube were found to fit within the safe harbor provisions, and neither was found directly or secondarily liable for copyright infringment or inducement liability. Appeal is expected in *Viacom v. YouTube*, but as of this writing these services are legally entitled to continue operating on the Internet.

### (b) Clouds and Music Lockers

*Viacom* and *Veoh* serve as important precedents for similar services. As new ways of experiencing copyrighted content on the Internet continue to evolve, the applicability of the DMCA safe harbors to new types of service providers is important to the future of innovative content services and to the Internet.

*Capitol Records v. MP3Tunes*[23] considered whether providers of Internet music lockers, a type of cloud computing, are eligible for the DMCA safe harbors. The case involved MP3tunes.com, which provides users with the ability to upload to their lockers MP3 files stored on their personal hard drives and to transfer music files stored on third-party servers connected to the Internet. MP3Tunes, LLC, also owns a second website, sideload.com, which allows users to search for free song files on the Internet, and "if the user has a locker on MP3tunes.com, sideload.com displays a link that if clicked will 'sideload' (i.e., download) the song from the third-party website and save it" to the user's locker.

The plaintiffs alleged that defendant MP3Tunes did not comply with the DMCA takedown procedures and therefore did not qualify for the DMCA safe harbor protection. Plaintiffs also sought to hold the defendant contributorily liable for storing material at the direction of its users. The court found the defendant contributorily liable because "MP3Tunes continued to provide locker services to its users even though it knew they had unlawfully downloaded EMI's protected material."[24] Nevertheless, the court's decision is a favorable one for music locker service providers, as the court found that MP3Tunes qualified for the DMCA's safe harbors. Often citing the *Veoh* and *Viacom* decisions, the *MP3Tunes* court upheld those court findings concerning the degree of knowledge required to qualify a service provider for DMCA protection and placing the responsibility for identifying infringed works on the copyright owner of the work. The court held:

> [T]he DMCA does not place the burden of investigation on the internet service provider...The DMCA is explicit that safe harbor shall not be conditioned on "a service provider monitoring its service or affirmatively seeking facts indicating infringing activity."[25]

In support of DMCA protections for Internet music lockers and the type of services provided through the sideload.com site, the court stated:

> If enabling a party to download infringing material was sufficient to create liability, then even search engines like Google or Yahoo! would be without DMCA protection. In that case, the DMCA's purpose—innovation and growth of internet services—would be undermined.[26]

### (4) Information Location Tools

Section 512(d) limits the liability of service providers that link users to websites (through hyperlinks, directories, search engines, etc.) containing infringing material. The conditions for this exemption are the same as those required for the Section 512(c) exemption specified in the preceding section of this chapter.

# VI. Balance or Battleground?

The ability to distribute copyrighted works in digital form over the Internet provides exciting opportunities but also poses serious challenges. However, potential challenges are not limited to protection of copyrighted works, but also include protection of the Internet itself as a viable medium for such distribution, as well as protection of users of the Internet. It is not inconceivable that the zeal to protect music or other creative works could usher in changes to the Internet that have far-reaching consequences that may help the cause of rights protection but damage the present operability of the Internet and unnecessarily restrict its uses.

## A. Net Neutrality

Today we think of the Internet as being free and open. To the extent that a user does not violate existing law, individuals may market, inform, persuade, entertain, or otherwise freely contribute to and access Internet content. However, as the Internet matures, so do new possibilities for limiting those freedoms. The following analysis is excerpted from an article titled "Meet the New Internet: Cause for Concern or Celebration in the Entertainment Industry?" It describes some of the pertinent issues.

> In 2007, a group of Comcast subscribers discovered that Comcast was limiting their access to BitTorrent peer-to-peer filesharing services that consumed large amounts of bandwidth. Subsequently, two consumer organizations—Public Knowledge and Free Press—filed a complaint with the Federal Communications Commission (FCC), as well as a petition for a declaratory ruling, to halt Comcast's practices and to declare their conduct a violation of FCC policy and unreasonable network management. The FCC issued an order which prohibited Comcast from blocking the traffic in question, and Comcast responded by filing a petition with the U.S. Court of Appeals for the District of Columbia Circuit to review the FCC's order in Comcast Corporation v. Federal Communications Commission (600 F.3d 642 (2010).
>
> Comcast prevailed. The D.C. Circuit ruled that the authority the FCC relied upon for its power to regulate internet services, i.e., certain policy statements the FCC derived from sections of the Communications Act of 1934 and the Telecommunications Act of 1996, actually provided no direct authority to do so.
>
> Despite the D.C. Circuit decision, the FCC does not foresee precluding its regulation of internet service providers. Rather, in May 2010 the FCC announced its intent to identify a specific regulatory scheme, which it has said may involve either reclassification of internet services to bring them within their statutorily mandated authority, or continuing to rely on the policy statements ruled invalid by the Court. In the meantime, in order to reach a consensus on the best regulatory approach, they initiated a series of private meetings with stakeholders. Accordingly, certain Internet service providers are seizing the opportunity created by the Court ruling to consider new Internet directions. In an August 2010 article, the New York Times reported on developments in an agreement between Google and Verizon that "could allow Verizon to speed some online content to Internet users more quickly if the content's creators are willing to pay for the privilege." ("Google and Verizon Near Deal on Web Pay Tiers," New York Times, Aug. 4, 2010).[27]

No tiered payment systems have gone into effect as of this writing. However, the absence of FCC authority to regulate the Internet declared in the *Comcast* decision has left open that possibility, as well as room for private and legislative initiatives. In 2009, the House of Representatives introduced the Internet Freedom Preservation Act (originally introduced in the Senate in 2006) "to establish a national broadband policy, safeguard consumer rights, [and] spur investment and innovation...."[28] The music industry has some discomfort with this bill and has voiced concern that Net Neutrality will make it more difficult to combat piracy if a user's bandwidth access is legally protected, regardless of the legality of the content the user is accessing.[29] Although the fate of Net Neutrality is not yet known, it is likely to affect the future of copyright law on the Internet.

## B. The Future of Protecting Intellectual Property on the Net

The global possibilities of the Internet make it ripe for creating both private and legislative initiatives to strengthen protection of intellectual property.

### (1) Copyright Alert System

As noted earlier in this chapter, it was efforts to limit BitTorrent peer-to-peer filesharing through an Internet service provider that spawned the series of events leading to *Comcast v. FCC*. Likewise, efforts to utilize Internet service providers like Comcast to enforce copyrights have found new and unprecedented vigor under the Copyright Alert System. Led by the entertainment industry in partnership with Internet service providers like Comcast and Verizon, these entities have formed the Center for Copyright Information, which will oversee the alert system. The system will provide a series of alerts to Internet users who are suspected of downloading illegally or otherwise violating copyright law. The system will be comprised of six progressive alerts, each intended to discourage suspected activity. If suspected activity (the steps do not indicate an attempt to confirm actual content theft; rather, the language in each step is if the subscriber's account "appears to have been used for content theft") continues after a fifth alert:

> [T]he ISP may take one of several steps, specified in its published policies, reasonably calculated to stop future content theft. These steps, referred to as "Mitigation Measures," may include, for example: temporary reductions of Internet speeds, redirection to a landing page until the subscriber contacts the ISP to discuss the matter or reviews and responds to some educational information about copyright, or other measures that the ISP may deem necessary to help resolve the matter. ISPs are not obligated to impose any Mitigation Measure that would disable or be reasonably likely to disable the subscriber's voice telephone service (including the ability to call 911), e-mail account, or any security or health service (such as home security or medical monitoring). The use of the mitigation measure is waivable by the ISP at this point.[30]

The sixth step implements the Mitigation Measure. Subscribers who believe their account has been identified in error have the opportunity to request an independent review and maintain their rights to challenge in court, although this is a prohibitive option for the average individual because of the potential costs of litigation. For recording companies, media conglomerates, and other music copyright holders, this system may provide needed incentives to stem the tide of music theft. However, for the Internet user who does not infringe, the implications are uncertain and possibly adverse.

### (2) Protect IP Act of 2011

For content owners, the advantage of the Copyright Alert System previously described is that it is simply a private agreement between copyright owners and Internet service providers and requires no legislative permission to implement. Additionally, since the FCC appears to have no authority to regulate the kind of Internet activity the agreement prescribes, the alert system can go forward, unless challenged in court by a subscriber. Legislative initiatives to stop online infringement have surfaced nonetheless. The Combating Online Infringement and Counterfeits Act (COICA) (S. 3804) never became law and was reintroduced in the Senate as the PROTECT IP Act, short for Preventing Real Online Threats to Economic Creativity and Theft of Intellectual Property. This version of the bill, which is less aggressive than its predecessor, would allow Internet service providers to refuse to recognize Internet domains (i.e., shut down a website as a practical matter) that a court considers "dedicated to infringing activities," but does not require a determination of whether the site is actually infringing prior to applying the penalty. The legislation, among other provisions, would also require credit card companies, search engines, and others to refuse to deal with the owners of such sites.[31]

### (3) Toward a "Copyright Ecosystem"

Initiatives to curtail illegal copyright activity are appropriate because copyright owners and their works are fully entitled to the protection the law provides. Yet parameters exist within the law, because the law endeavors to strike a balance to protect the innocently accused and the structure of democracy. Copyright law is no less subject to the need for balance. The dialogue about enforcing copyrights on the Internet is sometimes metaphorically framed as a battleground, a war on infringement. But in fact there are many legitimate Internet uses and users that warrant the same protection as copyrighted works. In addition to the Recording Industry Association of America[32] and the National Music Publishers Association,[33] other voices in the dialogue that help stimulate balance in the "copyright ecosystem"[34] include the Electronic Frontier Foundation—a non-profit organization that "defend[s] free speech, privacy, innovation, and consumer rights,"[35] and Creative Commons—a non-profit organization that "develops, supports, and stewards legal and technical infrastructure that maximizes digital creativity, sharing, and innovation."[36]

While the law should provide protection for copyrighted works, it should also allow for the development of new, innovative technologies. If used legally and ethically, technology can provide consumers with a wide variety of ways to enjoy music and other artistic works, while also allowing creators and owners of copyrighted works to market, expand, and be compensated for their creativity and investment.

## Endnotes

1. "The Economy of Ideas," *Wired*, Mar. 1994, at 84, 85.
2. See H.R. Rep. No. 1476, 94th Cong., 2d Sess. 47 at 52 (1976).
3. See Ben Depoorter, "Technology and Uncertainty: Shaping the Effect on Copyright Law," 157 *University of Pennsylvania Law Review* 1831–1868 (2008–2009).
4. Some audiophiles would disagree as to the loss of sound quality when music is compressed in MP3 format. However, to most casual listeners, the reduction in sound quality is minor and possibly unnoticeable. The m4a file format, developed by Apple, Inc., and used by the iPod, is considered a "lossless" format that loses no quality, according to m4a.com.
5. The word "generally" is used here because, in limited circumstances, uploading or downloading a copyrighted work without the copyright owner's consent may not constitute copyright infringement if the defense of fair use is applicable. See Chapter 12 for a discussion of fair use.
6. See Final Report of the National Commission on New Technological Uses of Copyrighted Works (1978) at 40.
7. Radiohead's "In Rainbows" album charted at No. 1 in the UK and sold 3 million copies when Radiohead allowed consumers to choose the album payment amount (see Daniel Kreps, "Radio Publishers Reveal 'In Rainbows' Numbers," *Rolling Stone*, October 15, 2008), while Nine Inch Nails followed their lead and employed a similar promotion, earning $1.6 million in the first week of selling their *Ghosts I–IV* album on nin.com and an additional $1 million on Amazon.com. See Jennifer Netherby, "Two Kinds of Free," *Billboard*, March 22, 2008, Vol. 5, p. 3.
8. 17 U.S.C. §109.
9. Digital Millennium Copyright Act of 1998, Section 104 Report, August 2001, pp. 82–83.
10. *Atlantic Recording Corp. v. Howell* 554 F.Supp.2d 976, 983 (D.Ariz., 2008).

11. *Capitol Records, Inc. v. Thomas* 579 F.Supp.2d 1210, 1218–1219 (D.Minn., 2008).

12. *Universal City Studios Inc. v. Reimerdes*, 82 F. Supp. 2d 211 (S.D.N.Y. 2000).

13. Statement of James H. Billington, Librarian of Congress, July 26, 2010. http://www.copyright.gov/1201/2010/Librarian-of-Congress-1201-Statement.html.

14. See 75 Federal Register 43825, 143, 839–40, July 27, 2010, and "Apple Loses Big in DRM Ruling: Jailbreaks Are Fair Use," Nate Anderson, *Ars Technica*, July 29, 2010.

15. A dongle is a device attached to a laptop or desktop computer that makes it possible to access secured software. The term can also apply to any hardware attached to a computer. [Wikipedia.org].

16. 17 U.S.C. §1202.

17. See *Religious Technology Center v. NetCom Online Communications Services, Inc.*, 907 F.Supp. 1361 (N.D. Cal. 1995); *Marobie-FL, Inc. v. Nat. Assn. of Fire Equipment Distributors*, 983 F. Supp. 1167 (N.D. Ill. 1997).

18. 17 U.S.C. § 512(k)(l)(B).

19. 665 F. Supp. 2d 1099 (C.D. Cal. 2009).

20. 718 F.Supp.2d 514 (S.D.N.Y. 2010).

21. 665 F.Supp.2d 1099, 1108 -1109 (C.D.Cal., 2009).

22. 718 F.Supp.2d 514, 525 (S.D.N.Y., 2010).

23. 2011 WL 3667335 (S.D.N.Y. 2011).

24. *Id.* at p. 15.

25. *Id.* at p. 10.

26. *Id.* at p. 12.

27. Cheryl L. Slay, "Meet the New Internet: Cause for Celebration or Concern in the Entertainment Industry?," Music and Entertainment Industry Educators Association *eZine*, September 12, 2010.

28. H.R. 3458, Internet Freedom Preservation Act of 2009.

29. Anne Broache, "RIAA: Don't Let Net Neutrality Hurt Piracy Fight," CNET News, cnet.com, May 6, 2008.

30. Excerpted from Center for Copyright Information and Copyright Alert System Fact Sheet. http://www.copyrightinformation.org/alerts.

31. The complete bill text is available at copyright.gov or at http://www.scribd.com/doc/55156515/ProtectIPActof2011.

32. http://riaa.com/.

33. http://nmpa.org/home/index.asp.

34. The authors' term to indicate a state of balance and the supports needed to achieve it, such as the proliferation of perspectives that recognize the interests of copyright owners, technology innovators, and consumers and users of copyrighted content. We lay no claim to the term "ecosystem," which we clearly did not coin but do find descriptive of the ideals described here when applied to copyright.

35. http://www.eff.org/about.

36. http://creativecommons.org/.

# 15 The Online Music War

*"The record industry's priority now is to license music—to as many services, for as many consumers, on as many formats and devices for use in as many places and countries as it can. The straightforward conditions are that the business must be legitimate, the music must be correctly licensed, and record companies and other rights holders must get properly paid."*

—John Kennedy, Chairman, International Federation of the Phonograph Industry

*"[I]f I were to say that in the name of promoting innovation, we should allow suicidal monsters to figure out how to build worse chemical and biological weapons because that's new technology and innovation, you'd laugh. I mean, prohibiting technology for illegal purposes is very different than being anti-technology."*

—Rep. Howard Berman, D-Calif. (July 9, 2005, interview in Billboard shortly after the Supreme Court's Grokster ruling)

The Internet has dramatically changed the way people access and enjoy music in the twenty-first century. Like most innovative technologies, there have been positive and negative consequences. The use of digital technology and the Internet have certainly enabled much wider availability of music worldwide than ever before. However, the same technologies pose huge challenges to the music industry because a large amount of the music available online is made available illegally, without permission of copyright owners. The dawn of the twenty-first century began an era in which infringing copyrights is much easier for many more people and on a far greater scale than ever before. The music industry has fought back against this widespread unauthorized use of their copyrighted works by suing filesharing companies such as Napster, Grokster, and Limewire and suing individual filesharers. Despite winning (or settling) most of the lawsuits, illegal filesharing has not significantly subsided, and it is estimated that only one out of 20 music downloads worldwide is from a legal online music service.[1] There has, however, been some progress; a variety of new legal online music services have developed (although many struggle to achieve profitability), and the record industry is now trying to gain cooperation from Internet service providers in order to reduce illegal downloading. (See Chapter 14 for an explanation of the Copyright Alert System introduced in 2011, also briefly discussed in this chapter.) This chapter describes how copyright law has been challenged, applied, and adapted in the context of online filesharing of music.

The music industry's troubles with online music began in 1999 when a college student named Shawn Fanning created a computer program called Napster that allowed people to share digital music files online. Napster quickly became tremendously popular, and before long, people were

271

freely downloading millions of music files each day. While Napster seemed like a blessing to music fans, who could now get virtually any music they wanted without paying for it, Napster was more of a curse to copyright owners. For more than 20 years prior to the introduction of Napster, record sales had generally increased on an annual basis. However, in 1999, annual sales began declining at a dramatic rate. Over the next 10 years, income from sales of recorded music in the United States declined by over 50 percent, from $14.6 billion in 1999 to $6.3 billion in 2009.[2] As a result, major record companies have laid off large numbers of their employees, and many music retailers, including the once-famous Tower Records, have gone out of business.

Many filesharing proponents argue that factors other than filesharing—such as the maturation of the market for CDs and competing entertainment options—have caused the decrease in record sales.[3] However, most of these factors existed prior to 1999, and while they may have had some effect, it is not likely that any one or any combination of them could result in the sudden and dramatic decline experienced since 1999. Worried about the dramatic decline in their revenues, the recording industry initiated an aggressive legal campaign against illegal filesharing, first taking aim at Napster, followed by other filesharing software providers and then at illegal downloaders.

---

**Note:** Not all filesharing is illegal. For instance, it is legal to share files containing public domain music. Further, some artists have authorized filesharing of their works, usually for promotional purposes and to build a fan base.

---

# I. Legal Enforcement

Rights under copyright law, like any legal rights, are worth little on a practical basis if they are not enforced. Especially in an area of law such as copyright, which many people are unaware of or do not understand, it is sometimes necessary for copyright owners to assert and enforce their rights. Consequently, one of the ways that the music industry enforces its rights is by taking legal action against copyright infringers.

In addition to copyright infringement lawsuits filed by individual copyright owners, several music industry organizations bring lawsuits on behalf of their members. For instance, the Recording Industry Association of America (RIAA) brings lawsuits on behalf of its member record companies. Similarly, the performing rights organizations (ASCAP, BMI, and SESAC) bring lawsuits on behalf of their publisher and songwriter members.

While copyright owners are certainly free to enforce their legal rights, they should also be sure to make their works legally available in ways that consumers want them. Although the recording industry was initially hesitant to make recordings legally available online, which may have contributed to the early adoption of illegal filesharing, music is currently being licensed for various types of online distribution, as illustrated by the quote at the beginning of this chapter.

## A. What Is Filesharing?

The controversy over distributing music online primarily involves a technology known as peer-to-peer (P2P) filesharing, which started to become popular in the late 1990s. Filesharing software makes it possible for individual computers connected over the Internet to communicate with each other, allowing people to search for and transfer files from one computer to others. Peer-to-peer filesharing networks allow many different computers to be connected to each other without any centralized computer (a server) storing files. Unlike visiting a website making music files available for download, P2P networks allow people to connect directly to other users' computers and download files stored on those computers. Filesharing software allows users to connect their computers to a network and to search for and download files stored on other network members' computers. Although this can be a very convenient and useful technology, it has raised serious problems for copyright owners because the vast majority of files traded contain copyrighted works that have not been authorized to be made available in this manner. When filesharing software first became widely used by the general public, it was used almost exclusively to share music, but as high-speed Internet connections have become more common, files containing movies, computer software, and videogames are also commonly shared.

Courts thus far in the United States and a number of other countries have concluded that people who use filesharing software to trade copyrighted works without the authorization of the copyright owners are committing copyright infringement. For example, court decisions in cases involving filesharing companies such as Napster, Aimster, Grokster, Limewire, and The Pirate Bay have all agreed that people who use filesharing software to download copyrighted works without permission are committing direct copyright infringement. Downloading a file using filesharing software involves making a copy of the file on a computer hard drive or other storage device; this is consequently an exercise of the copyright owner's reproduction right under Section 106 of the Copyright Act. A more difficult legal question for the courts is whether companies that provide filesharing software can also be held liable for infringements committed by users of their software and, if so, under what circumstances. That question has largely been answered in the United States (as well as some other countries) by a series of lengthy, complicated lawsuits beginning in late 1999.

## B. The War Begins: *A&M Records v. Napster*[4]

The first major battle in the music industry's war on illegal filesharing began on December 7, 1999, when the RIAA, on behalf of its member record companies, sued filesharing company Napster, claiming that Napster should be held liable for copyright infringement because it allowed users of its software to trade copyrighted sound recordings without permission.

Napster was a company that developed software that it gave away for free and that allowed its users to trade MP3 music files using their computers. People who downloaded the Napster software could log on to Napster and share MP3 files with other Napster users. MP3 music files were stored on Napster users' computer hard drives, and the Napster software sent a list of songs on each user's hard drive to Napster's computer servers, resulting in a searchable database of all MP3 files on each user's computer.

At the time the lawsuit was initiated, it was estimated that approximately 10,000 music files were being traded every second using Napster. The vast majority of the files traded contained copyrighted songs and sound recordings; neither Napster nor its users had permission to reproduce and distribute these copyrighted works, nor did they pay any compensation to the copyright owners and creators of the works. After filing suit, the RIAA asked the district court to issue an injunction preventing Napster from continuing to assist in the infringement of copyrighted music.

## (1) The Ruling

The District Court began its written ruling by stating that:

> The matter before the court concerns the boundary between sharing and theft, personal use and the unauthorized worldwide distribution of copyrighted music and sound recordings.

The District Court issued a preliminary injunction ordering Napster to stop:

> ...engaging in or facilitating others in copying, downloading, uploading, transmitting, or distributing plaintiffs' copyrighted musical compositions and sound recordings...without express permission of the rights owner.

The injunction did not, as was commonly reported, order Napster to shut down. Rather, it required Napster to take steps to monitor its service in order to prevent the massive copyright infringements that had been occurring. Napster appealed, but the appeals court agreed that Napster could be held liable for copyright infringement and upheld the injunction order.

---

**Note:** A trial was never held in the Napster case because, shortly after the appeals court's ruling that required Napster to use filtering technology to prevent the infringements being committed by users of its software, Napster filed for bankruptcy in order to avoid the potentially astronomical judgment that it would likely have been liable for after a trial decision.

---

## (2) Napster's Arguments

Napster put forth several legal arguments asserting why it should not be held liable for copyright infringement. All of these arguments were rejected by both the district and appeals courts. First, Napster argued that it had not committed any infringements because the files traded, instead of being stored on Napster's computer servers, were stored on individual users' computers. Napster claimed that, even if its users were trading copyrighted files, it had no way of knowing they were doing so and could not do anything to prevent it.

In order for Napster to be contributorily or vicariously liable for copyright infringement (see Chapter 10, "Infringement of Copyright," for a discussion of contributory and vicarious copyright infringement), the court first needed to determine that Napster users were directly infringing. The court found that Napster users commonly infringed upon copyright owners' reproduction rights because users downloaded copyrighted music files to their hard drives, which resulted in unauthorized reproduction.

In order to be liable for contributory infringement, a defendant must: (1) have actual knowledge of the infringing activity; and (2) cause or materially contribute to the infringing conduct of another. The District Court believed that there was sufficient evidence that Napster had actual knowledge that its service was being used to commit infringement. In fact, Napster admitted that it knew this on several occasions. For instance, several documents written by one of Napster's co-founders made incriminating statements such as "Napster was created to facilitate unlawful copying," "we are not just making pirated music available but also pushing demand," and that it was important for Napster to remain ignorant of its users' real names and Internet addresses "because they are exchanging pirated music." The court found that these statements proved that facilitating copyright infringement was an important part of Napster's business strategy. There was also evidence that Napster promoted its service with web ads listing infringing files.

The court also concluded that Napster materially contributed to the infringing conduct because it provided the software, search engine, and computer servers used to infringe and enabled users to access each other's computer hard drives. Without these contributions by Napster, its users would not have been able to infringe.

A defendant can also be vicariously liable for the infringing conduct of others if the defendant has the right and ability to supervise infringing activity and has a direct financial interest in the infringing activity. Napster argued that it was not technologically possible for it to distinguish between infringing and non-infringing activity. However, at the time of the preliminary injunction hearing, Napster was clearly doing so because it had begun blocking the access of some infringing users. The court also found Napster's assertion that it did not have a direct financial interest in the infringing conduct of its users to be disingenuous. Although Napster had not yet made any money or even decided on a business model, it had always been a for-profit company that intended to develop a business model—whether based on subscriptions, advertising, etc.—by taking advantage of its large user base. The court found that Napster's value was primarily based on the number of Napster users and that the ability to download many popular music files without payment was the main factor that attracted users.

Napster also claimed that even if its users were trading copyrighted music, they were protected by the fair use defense (see Chapter 11, "Defenses to Infringement," for an explanation of fair use). The District Court applied the fair use test specified by Section 107 of the Copyright Act and concluded that all four factors weighed against a fair use finding. The purpose and character of the use was commercial because "Napster users get for free something they would ordinarily have to buy." The nature of the use also weighed against fair use because the copyrighted musical compositions and sound recordings at issue were creative rather than factual in nature. Because Napster users copied entire works, the amount and substantiality of use weighed against fair use. Finally, Napster was found to harm the market for copyrighted music in at least two ways. First, a survey introduced into evidence indicated that Napster use reduced CD sales among college students. Second, Napster adversely affected the ability of the plaintiffs to enter the market for digital downloading of music. The major record companies had expended considerable funds and effort to begin offering digital downloads. However, having digital downloads available for free through filesharing networks such as Napster necessarily harms the copyright holders' efforts to charge for music download services.

Napster's fair use defense relied heavily on a Supreme Court decision holding that a technology with substantial non-infringing uses is protected under the fair use doctrine even if that technology is also used for infringing purposes. In *Sony Corporation of America v. Universal Studios*,[5] two major movie companies (Universal City Studios and Walt Disney Productions) claimed that Sony was committing contributory copyright infringement by manufacturing and selling Betamax home videotape recorders. Consumers used the recorders to record television programs for later viewing. The Supreme Court ruled that home videotaping for private viewing at a more convenient time (referred to as "time-shifting") was fair use because it was primarily nonprofit and noncommercial.

Napster compared its filesharing software to the Betamax recorder, arguing that its software had substantial non-infringing uses. Although the substantial non-infringing use defense had at least some potential merit, both courts recognized that Napster's situation was different from Sony's in several important respects. For example, while much of the copying by Betamax users was fair use, the vast majority of filesharing of copyrighted music by Napster users was not. Further, while Napster claimed to have significant non-infringing uses, it also claimed that the preliminary injunction would put it out of business, thereby indicating that uses other than infringing ones were not very substantial. Ironically, one of the substantial non-infringing uses Napster asserted was that its service was used to promote new artists. However, the court realized that Napster's "New Artist Program" was only started after Napster was sued and that earlier versions of the Napster website advertised the ease with which users could find their favorite music without "wading through page after page of unknown artists."

### (3) The Aftermath

After the appeals court upheld the preliminary injunction against Napster, Napster began implementing a filtering system designed to block access to infringing files identified by the plaintiffs. Ultimately, however, Napster decided that the risk of going to trial was too great because the courts' preliminary injunction decision made it extremely likely that Napster would lose and be subject to an extremely large damage award for the millions of infringements involved. Napster filed for bankruptcy, and its main asset, its name, was purchased by a company that, in 2003, introduced a new legal online service selling downloadable music.

Shortly after the *Napster* decision, the music industry won several more legal battles against similar filesharing companies. Several of these companies settled or went out of business after being sued. The music industry also scored another legal victory against a filesharing company called Aimster in 2001.[6] Although the recording industry was winning the legal battle, this didn't seem to deter people, because filesharing continued to increase as new, decentralized filesharing networks like Grokster and Kazaa replaced Napster.

### C. *Grokster,* Parts One and Two: The Music Industry Suffers Its First Legal Losses

After the *Napster* court decision, new filesharing software programs were developed that were designed to attempt to avoid legal liability on the part of companies distributing the software. Two such companies, Grokster and Streamcast, were sued by the RIAA and MPAA (the Motion Picture Association of America) on essentially the same grounds as were alleged in the *Napster* lawsuit. Unlike the Napster filesharing network, which operated through central computer servers that listed files available on the computers of Napster users, the Grokster and Streamcast filesharing systems were decentralized. In other words, instead of using central computer servers to index the files, the Grokster and Streamcast software allowed files to be transmitted directly between users of the software without passing through any computer servers operated by Grokster or Streamcast. Consequently, Grokster and Streamcast argued that they were unable to exercise any control over the files being shared by users of their software.

In 2003, a federal district court held that although individuals who used the Grokster and Streamcast software to download copyrighted works without permission committed direct infringement, Grokster and Streamcast were not contributorily liable for these infringements.[7] This decision was upheld by an appeals court in 2004.[8] In addition to the decentralized nature of the filesharing networks, these courts relied on the aforementioned Supreme Court precedent established 20 years earlier in *Sony Corp. of America v. Universal City Studios, Inc.*[9] Similar to the Betamax videotape recorder in that case, although the Grokster and Streamcast filesharing software was primarily used by people to trade copyrighted works, it was also capable of non-infringing use like trading public domain material and works authorized by the copyright owners. The courts reasoned that because the filesharing software was capable of non-infringing use, Grokster and Streamcast were not contributory infringers because they were not directly involved in and had no actual knowledge of the direct infringements by users of their software.

The *Grokster* decision was hailed by the filesharing community and mistakenly perceived by many people as validating filesharing of copyrighted works. In reality, the courts merely found that the filesharing companies were not liable for infringements committed by users of their software even though individuals actually sharing files were infringing. Needless to say, the music and movie industries were not happy with this result, so the RIAA and MPAA appealed the case to the U.S. Supreme Court.

## D. *RIAA v. The People*

The *Grokster* decision put the music and film industries in a difficult position. Until that time, they had fought illegal filesharing by suing the companies distributing the most popular filesharing software. However, based on the district and appeals courts' decisions in the *Grokster* case, that was no longer an option. Instead, the only legal enforcement option left was to sue individual filesharers for directly infringing copyrights using filesharing software. The decision to sue potential consumers could not have been an easy one, but with the district and appeals court rulings in *Grokster* relieving the filesharing companies of liability for infringement by their users, the exponential growth of illegal filesharing, and an educational campaign that had been largely ignored, the music and film industries didn't have much choice other than letting millions of people infringe their copyrights on an unprecedented basis.

---

**A Proposed Resolution?**   Although not widely reported, prior to its legal campaign against filesharers, the RIAA indicated that it would be likely to refrain from suing filesharers if filesharing companies agreed to: (1) adopt policies clearly disclosing to their users that unauthorized uploading and downloading of copyrighted works is illegal; (2) use available technology to filter and block illegal filesharing; and (3) change default settings of their software so that users were not unknowingly making files available. (The default settings for filesharing programs are set so that users automatically make files stored on their computer available to others.)

In mid-2003, the RIAA filed the first round of lawsuits against filesharers. Not surprisingly, the public and media did not react with any sympathy for the record industry. Copyright critics and the media vilified the RIAA for suing 12-year-old children and grandparents. In reality, the RIAA cannot really target any particular group of people, because they don't know who they are suing until after a lawsuit is filed and a court issues a subpoena ordering the applicable Internet service provider to identify the individual sued. The process used to gather evidence against filesharers and initiate lawsuits worked essentially as follows:

- The RIAA (or an agent on its behalf) uses software programs to search the Internet for files containing copyrighted music.

- When the software locates files available for sharing on someone's computer, a copy is downloaded to determine whether it contains a copyrighted recording.

- The RIAA takes a computer screenshot (a digital picture) of a list of files made available for filesharing.

- The RIAA's monitoring software records the Internet address of the computer that is making files available for sharing. The software also checks files for digital watermarks encoded on digital music files, which indicate the source of the files.

- The RIAA files a John Doe lawsuit (a lawsuit against an unknown defendant) requesting the court to issue a subpoena compelling an Internet service provider to provide the name and address of the subscriber whose Internet connection corresponds to the Internet address identified.[10]

---

**Suing Children and the Elderly?** Among the lawsuits most publicized were those filed against a 12-year-old girl who lived in a New York housing project and a 71-year-old grandfather in Texas whose teenage grandchildren downloaded music onto his computer while visiting his home. Whether parents or grandparents are liable for illegal filesharing by their children is not clear. If they have knowledge or reason to know of the illegal activity, they could be liable for contributory infringement. Alternatively, the RIAA could amend lawsuits against parents to include the child as a defendant, in which case their parents may be responsible for any damage awards against the child.

---

By 2008, the RIAA had filed over 18,000 lawsuits. These lawsuits primarily targeted what the RIAA considers to be "major offenders" who were usually making over 1,000 copyrighted works available for sharing. The vast majority of people sued chose not to contest the infringement allegations by going to trial. Instead, most of the lawsuits have been settled, with the alleged infringers paying settlement fees of $3,000 to $5,000 and promising not to continue infringing. In December 2008, the RIAA ended its massive systemic practice of filing lawsuits against individual infringers, although it has by no means abandoned its right to enforce its members' copyrights against infringement.

---

**Example 15.1**

In one of the few filesharing cases that was not settled, a woman admitted downloading 30 songs without permission, but she claimed that her conduct constituted fair use because she was just sampling music to determine whether to buy it, and her actions did not cause any financial harm.[11] The court found her fair use arguments to be "without merit" because a prior court decision (i.e., the *Napster* case discussed earlier in this chapter) held that sampling is not a valid excuse for filesharing. The court also believed that "the cumulative effect of direct infringers...harms the recording industry by reducing sales and 'raising barriers' to the recording industry's entry into the market for digital downloading of music" (quoting the *Napster* decision). The record company plaintiffs were awarded a $22,500 judgment (the minimum statutory damages amount of $750 multiplied by the 30 infringements).

---

Because many millions of people use filesharing software, even in the heyday of the RIAA's lawsuit campaign, the odds of being sued were quite small. However, laws that are not enforced at all tend to be ignored. For instance, many people drive in excess of speed limits. Most of the time, you won't get caught for speeding, but the more you do so, the more likely you'll eventually get pulled over and given a ticket. If you receive enough tickets, you'll probably slow down eventually. Further, the possibility of getting a speeding ticket makes many people more cautious about speeding than they would otherwise be. The RIAA and other music industry organizations hoped that the legal campaign against illegal filesharing provided a similar deterrent. Although the RIAA could not possibly sue everyone who illegally downloads a file containing copyrighted music, the lawsuits were intended to make it clear that it is illegal to use filesharing software to upload or download copyrighted works without the copyright owner's permission and to deter people from doing so. While some people will continue to download illegally, they might at least think twice about it if they realize the possibility that they could be sued and it would cost them at least $3,000 to $5,000 to settle the claim.

While there have been no new filesharing lawsuits brought by the RIAA against individuals since December 2008, the lawsuits that had been filed previously and not settled have continued. As of mid-2011, two of these lawsuits have made it through trial decisions that resulted in very large and controversial statutory damage awards.

### (1) Virgin Records America, Inc. v. Thomas[12]
The first filesharing case to reach a trial decision has so far lasted over five years. In August 2005, the RIAA sent Jammie Thomas a letter notifying her that they had evidence of her use of the Kazaa filesharing network to illegally download and share copyrighted recordings. The RIAA offered to settle, but Thomas refused and was subsequently sued in April 2006 for illegally downloading and making available 24 copyrighted sound recordings. The Thomas case has been

highly unusual in that there have been three jury trials due not to any question over Thomas' liability but to how much money should be awarded to the plaintiff copyright owners under the Copyright Act's statutory damages provision (this aspect of the case is discussed in more detail in Chapter 12, "Remedies for Copyright Infringement"). On the other hand, deciding whether Thomas had committed infringement was relatively easy.

During the trial, the RIAA presented evidence that there were about 1,700 music files (including 24 recordings at issue) stored in a file folder on Thomas' computer that were made available to other users of the Kazaa filesharing software. Thomas denied that she downloaded the recordings despite evidence that these recordings were downloaded by someone using the Kazaa filesharing software with the username "tereastarr," which was also a name Thomas used for an email address. Additionally, Thomas repeatedly contradicted herself during her testimony. After being contacted by the RIAA, Thomas replaced her computer hard drive in an effort to destroy evidence of her filesharing activity. In court, she lied about the date she had the hard drive replaced and denied being given back the replaced drive, contradicting testimony from the store that replaced the drive for her. Both the judge and jury found Thomas' testimony not credible since it was clearly contradicted by substantial evidence, the judge stating that Thomas "lied on the witness stand by denying responsibility for her infringing acts and instead, blamed others, including her children, for her actions." On October 4, 2007, the jury unanimously found that Thomas willfully committed copyright infringement and awarded statutory damages of $9,250 for each infringement (for a total of $222,000). However, the judge later vacated this award and ordered a new trial, stating that he might have made an error in instructing the jury that making sound recordings available through a filesharing network constitutes distribution under the Copyright Act (at least traditionally, distribution under copyright law involved physical distribution of a copy). While this issue has yet to be fully resolved (see Chapter 14 for discussion of the distribution and the first sale doctrine on the Internet), it is important to note that, even if Thomas was found not to have distributed copies of recordings, she would still be liable for violating the reproduction right by downloading copyrighted recordings.

In June 2009, a second trial was held and another jury found Thomas liable for copyright infringement. This jury also found that Thomas' infringement was willful and awarded statutory damages of $1.92 million ($80,000 per recording infringed). Thomas asserted that the statutory damage award was highly disproportionate to actual damages and therefore unconstitutional and announced that she would appeal the decision. The judge agreed with Thomas that the amount was excessive and reduced the award to $54,000 ($2,250 per recording infringed). A few days later, the RIAA offered to settle for $25,000, but Thomas again refused.

In November 2010, a third trial was held, solely to review the amount of damages awarded. The new jury awarded $1.5 million ($62,500 per recording infringed). However, in July 2011, the judge again reduced the jury's damage award to $54,000. As of the date of this book's writing, it seems likely that the RIAA will appeal this ruling, so while Thomas' liability for infringement seems clear, the amount of damages she should be liable for remains in dispute.

### (2) Sony BMG Music Entertainment v. Tenenbaum[13]

In the second filesharing case to reach a trial decision, Joel Tenenbaum was sued by the RIAA. Unlike, Jammie Thomas (who, despite substantial evidence indicating otherwise, continues to deny having illegally shared copyrighted music), Tenenbaum ultimately admitted he had used file-sharing software to download and share recordings. Tenenbaum testified that he started using the Napster filesharing software in 1999 to download copyrighted recordings from other Napster users and also made copies of recordings stored on his computer available to other users. After Napster shut down, Tenenbaum used several other filesharing software networks (including Morpheus, Kazaa, and LimeWire) through 2007 and, in total, downloaded and made available to others thousands of copyrighted recordings. The RIAA contacted Tenenbaum in 2005, demanding that he stop his infringing activity and offering to settle the matter. Tenenbaum refused the settlement offer and continued to use filesharing software to download copyrighted recordings.

In August 2007, the RIAA sued Tenenbaum, limiting their claims to 30 of the recordings they apparently had strong evidence Tenenbaum infringed. Tenenbaum initially denied having downloaded the recordings, claiming that someone else must have used his computer to do so. As in the *Thomas* case, the court did not find Tenenbaum's claim that someone used his computer to download music to be credible. Instead, the court concluded that, knowing that his actions were illegal, Tenenbaum attempted to blame family members and other people who had access to his computer and repeatedly lied under oath in an effort to escape liability for his actions. Tenenbaum later admitted that he downloaded the files and made them available to others through filesharing networks. He also admittedly lied in responses to discovery requests and made misleading and untruthful statements in deposition testimony, such as claiming that a computer he used to download and distribute songs through Kazaa had been destroyed when it had not. Tenenbaum's lawyer then asserted some novel but meritless defenses, arguing that Tenenbaum was a kid (he was actually a college student at the time of his filesharing activity) and that the record industry was to blame for being too slow to adapt to Internet technology.

In July 2009, a jury found that Tenenbaum willfully infringed the 30 copyrighted recordings and awarded $675,000 ($22,500 per recording infringed) in statutory damages. The court found that Tenenbaum's infringement was willful because before using Kazaa and other filesharing software, he understood that Napster had closed because it was facilitating copyright infringement. He was also warned about illegally sharing copyrighted works by a student handbook published by his undergraduate university. Despite this, he continued to use filesharing software to infringe copyrights even after receiving a letter from the RIAA demanding that he stop. Tenenbaum's attorney indicated that he would appeal the jury verdict on the grounds that the amount awarded was excessive and unconstitutional. The district court judge apparently agreed and in July 2010 reduced the award to $67,500. Both parties appealed, and as discussed in Chapter 12, the appeals court reinstated the original $675,000 damage award but also left open the possibility of another trial on damages unless a reduced amount can be agreed on by the RIAA.

The *Thomas* and *Tenenbaum* cases make it clear that using filesharing software to download copyrighted works without the copyright owner's authorization is illegal. In fact, the judge in the *Tenenbaum* case repeatedly stated that the law was overwhelmingly on the record companies' side and warned Tenenbaum against continuing to litigate without legal basis. However, the judges in both decisions also believed that the juries' awards of statutory damages were excessive and reduced the awards to amounts they felt more appropriate. All of the jury awards were within the amount permitted by the statutory damages provision of the Copyright Act, so it will be up to appellate courts to reach some decision on whether the jury decisions should be upheld, whether judges can reduce such awards, and hopefully give some clear guidance on how statutory damages should be determined in cases involving filesharing.

## E. *Grokster* and *Streamcast*, Part Three: Filesharing D-Day

As discussed earlier in this chapter, the RIAA's decision to sue individuals for illegal filesharing was a response to the 2003 *Grokster* court decision that insulated filesharing companies from indirect liability for copyright infringement. However, that decision was appealed to the U.S. Supreme Court, which in mid-2005 issued its decision.[14] The district and appellate courts had ruled that the Grokster and Streamcast companies, which provided filesharing software, were not liable for copyright infringements committed by users of their software. However, the Supreme Court held that the lower courts misapplied the law and reversed their decision. Instead of deciding the case based on the *Sony* precedent, which the lower courts had relied on, the Supreme Court held that Grokster and Streamcast are likely guilty of contributory copyright infringement by inducing and encouraging users of their software to infringe. The Court's unanimous opinion holds that:

> [O]ne who distributes a device with the object of promoting its use to infringe copyright, as shown by clear expression or other affirmative steps taken to foster infringement, is liable for the resulting acts of infringement by third parties.

---

**Note:** Interestingly, the Court seemed split on whether the case should have been resolved according to the *Sony* standard. A concurring opinion by Justice Ginsburg (joined in by Justices Rehnquist and Kennedy) indicates that Grokster and Streamcast might be liable for contributory infringement even absent inducement because they failed to present evidence that their filesharing software is capable of substantial noninfringing use. This view is contradicted by Justice Breyer's concurring opinion (joined by Justices Stevens and O'Connor) favoring a more lenient interpretation of substantial noninfringing use.

---

The Supreme Court's decision appears to strike a balance between allowing copyright owners to enforce their rights against infringers while also allowing for the existence of new technologies that may be used by people to infringe. Under the Court's inducement theory of infringement, merely supplying a technology that can be used to commit copyright infringement is not enough to be liable as a contributory infringer. Instead, the distributor must take affirmative action to encourage users of its technology to infringe. The Court found that Grokster and Streamcast encouraged users of their filesharing software to commit copyright infringement, stating that Grokster and Streamcast's unlawful intent was "unmistakable."

According to the Court, inducement often occurs through advertisement or solicitation that is intended to encourage people to commit infringement. The Court stressed three items of evidence supporting this intent. First, Grokster and Streamcast were intended to take the place of Napster, which was known to be used predominantly for copyright infringement. Additionally, Grokster and Streamcast made no attempt to use filtering tools to reduce infringing use of their software.

Finally, Grokster and Streamcast's business was based on selling advertising, and the price they charged for ads was directly proportional to the number of users of their software. In essence, their business depended on infringement because the vast majority of filesharing use is to commit copyright infringement. Although non-infringing uses exist, if Grokster or Streamcast had to rely on these uses to support their business, they would surely go out of business.

Although the Supreme Court sent the case back to the District Court, Grokster decided to surrender rather than risk a trial where it would be almost certain to lose based on application of the Supreme Court's inducement standard. Under a settlement agreement, Grokster agreed to stop distributing its filesharing software and to pay $50 million to the music and film industry associations.[15]

The *Grokster* decision was promptly criticized as a severe blow to technological innovation. However, the Court's decision does not establish a rule that will lead to liability for any company that creates or distributes a new technology that is capable of being used for illegal purposes. Such a rule would certainly chill innovation. Instead, *Grokster* establishes that a company can be held liable for copyright infringements committed by users of its technology only if the company takes active steps to induce the infringement. The Court specifically states that liability will not be imposed merely due to knowledge of potential or even actual infringing use.

A few months after the *Grokster* ruling, the RIAA sent letters to several other popular filesharing companies, including eDonkey, LimeWire, WinMX, and BearShare, warning them to stop encouraging infringement. Under the Supreme Court's inducement standard for contributory copyright infringement, whether these companies are liable would depend on whether they took active steps to encourage infringement by users of their software. Although the Supreme Court clearly believed that such evidence existed with respect to Grokster and Streamcast, their decision leaves room for other filesharing companies, even though their products may be used for overwhelmingly infringing purposes. If a company distributes filesharing software that has non-infringing uses and does not actively market it for infringing use, it is unlikely that it would be liable for infringements committed by users of its software. A technology company's liability will depend not on the technology itself or even how the technology is used but on the company's actions in marketing its technology to users. As long as a company does not take steps intended to encourage infringement, it should be protected from most claims of contributory infringement regardless of how the technology is actually used.

LimeWire was another filesharing program that became extremely popular beginning in the early 2000s and was one of the recipients of the RIAA's warning letters to filesharing companies to discontinue inducing direct infringement by users of filesharing software. After the Supreme Court's *Grokster* decision, LimeWire chose to continue operating. Consequently, a group of record companies sued LimeWire in 2006.[16] In 2010, a judge ruled that LimeWire was liable for inducing copyright infringement.

The court followed the *Grokster* Supreme Court precedent and found that "there was overwhelming evidence that LimeWire engaged in purposeful conduct that fostered infringement." The evidence showed that LimeWire was aware that its software was used overwhelmingly for infringing purposes (nearly all files shared contained copyrighted music and other content) and failed to adopt any meaningful measures to limit infringing use of its software. Further, LimeWire set out to build a business based on copyright infringement. LimeWire marketed its software to people known to use filesharing programs for illegal downloading and sharing. Most importantly, LimeWire purposefully designed its search functions to identify copyrighted music and sometimes assisted users by responding to user requests to help find copyrighted recordings.

The court ordered an injunction prohibiting the further distribution or support of the LimeWire software. Before a trial on damages, LimeWire reached an agreement to pay $105 million, which is likely much less than the amount the court would have found LimeWire liable for due to the enormous number of copyrighted works infringed over a 10-year period. Interestingly, a study found that illegal filesharing of music dropped dramatically after LimeWire was shut down.[17]

## F. The Emergence of an International Standard

On September 5, 2005 (10 weeks after the U.S. Supreme Court's *Grokster* decision), an Australian court ruled that filesharing company Sharman Networks (which owns and distributes the Kazaa filesharing software) violated the Australian Copyright Act. The Kazaa filesharing software became extremely popular after the demise of Napster; over 900 million files were available on the Kazaa filesharing network at its peak popularity in 2003.

The Australian record industry sued Sharman Networks, a company based in Australia but incorporated in the country of Vanuatu. Apparently, Sharman picked Vanuatu as its corporate location in order to keep the identity of its owners secret and to make it difficult to pursue legally. The Australian court ruled that Sharman was liable for infringements committed by users of the Kazaa filesharing software. The court stated that it was in Sharman's financial interest "to maximize, not minimize music filesharing" and that Sharman actively encouraged users to share files, the vast majority of which contained copyrighted music.

Under Australian copyright law, infringement occurs when someone other than the copyright owner "copies a sound recording, causes it to be heard in public, or communicates the recording to the public, or authorizes anyone else to engage in any of these acts without the copyright owner's permission." Sharman was held liable for authorizing others (i.e., users of its software) to infringe. Sharman authorized Kazaa users to infringe by encouraging them to share files and promoting Sharman's "Join the Revolution" campaign, which sent a message that users should disobey the law by downloading copyrighted works without permission. The "Join the Revolution" campaign included the distribution of photographs of a person wearing a T-shirt with the following battle cry:

> THE KAZAA REVOLUTION
> 30 years of buying the music they think you should listen to.
> 30 years of watching the movies they want you to see.
> 30 years of paying the prices they demand.
> 30 years of swallowing what they're shoveling.
> 30 years of buying crap you don't want.
> 30 years of being sheep.
> Over. With one single click.

*Peer 2 peer, we're sharing files.*
*1 by 1, we're changing the world.*
*Kazaa is the technology.*
*You are the warrior.*
*60 million strong. And rising.*
*Join the revolution.*
*KAZAA*
*Share the revolution[18]*

Like the U.S. Supreme Court in *Grokster*, the Australian court indicated that its ruling merely holds a business liable for encouraging users of its product to engage in illegal activity and does not impose any restrictions on filesharing for legal purposes. Despite the finding that Sharman is liable for infringements committed by Kazaa users, the court ruled that Sharman could continue to operate the Kazaa filesharing system if it modified its software to filter out unauthorized recordings from its search results. Evidence introduced at trial indicates that such filtering software existed, and although it would not eliminate all illegal filesharing, it would significantly reduce the amount of illegal filesharing. Although it was clearly technologically possible for Sharman to use filtering technology, it was just as clear that it would not be in Sharman's interest to do so because its business was based on infringement. As the court noted:

> *Kazaa is apparently sustained by advertising revenue. It is a fundamental of advertising marketing that price is sensitive to the exposure likely to be achieved by the advertisement. The more shared files available through Kazaa, the greater the attraction of the Kazaa website. The more visitors to the Kazaa website, the greater its advertising value and the higher the advertising rate able to be demanded by Sharman. And what is more likely to attract large numbers of visitors to the website than music, especially currently popular 'hits'?*

The result of the Australian decision is similar to the *Grokster* decision in that it holds the distributor of filesharing software liable for infringements directly committed by users of the software. Although the legal reasoning used to hold Sharman liable by the Australian court is not exactly the same as the Supreme Court's reasoning due to differences between Australian and U.S. copyright law, liability in both cases is based on the conduct of a particular company rather than being based on the technology itself. The *Sharman* ruling is extremely important because it is the first case against a filesharing company to proceed through a full trial and, although arrived at based on somewhat different law, it achieves essentially the same result as the *Grokster* decision in the United States.

After the Australian decision against Sharman, other filesharing companies were found liable for copyright infringement in different countries. For example, a Korean court ordered filesharing company Soribada to either take steps to stop unauthorized filesharing over its network or shut down. Additionally, a Taiwanese court convicted filesharing company Kuro of criminal copyright infringement. Kuro was a bit unique in that it not only allowed files containing copyrighted works to be traded but also profited directly from the infringements because it charged users a subscription fee without obtaining permission or paying anything to the copyright owners or creators of the works being traded. The owners of the company were sentenced to up to three years of imprisonment as well as a $90,000 fine.

Another important non-U.S. case involved The Pirate Bay, a filesharing website founded by a group of Swedish anti-copyright proponents called Piritbriyan (Piracy Bureau) that began in late 2003. By 2008, it had become one of the world's most popular filesharing websites and was ranked in the top 100 most-trafficked websites worldwide. As its name indicates, The Pirate Bay has always made it very clear that its main purpose is illegal filesharing of copyrighted works.

Although publicizing itself as a Robin Hood–type organization, which exists to free creative works from their greedy owners, it seems clear that The Pirate Bay's owners were motivated largely by monetary considerations. Like most filesharing companies, The Pirate Bay made money by posting advertisements on its website, and in 2007, a reporter posing as a potential advertiser estimated that The Pirate Bay was earning up to $85,000 a month.[19]

In March 2006, Swedish police raided The Pirate Bay's offices to investigate claims of copyright infringement, seizing truckloads of computer file servers. As a result of the investigation, Swedish authorities charged three of The Pirate Bay's creators and one of its financiers with facilitating copyright infringement. In a 2009 trial, all four men were found guilty of criminal copyright infringement, sentenced to one year in jail, and fined $3.5 million. An appeal in 2010 resulted in a lowering of the jail sentences, but an increase in the fine to about $7.1 million.

These as well as other foreign court decisions in addition to the *Grokster* decision in the United States indicate that a global legal standard is emerging. Although the specific provisions of copyright law and standards for liability in these countries vary, the courts have reached similar results by holding that companies that actively authorize, facilitate, or encourage people to infringe copyrights can be held legally responsible for the infringing conduct.

## G. Have the Filesharing Lawsuits Helped?

So far, copyright owners have been winning the war against illegal filesharing, at least from a legal perspective. The strong initial victory in the Battle of *Napster* was followed by several smaller easier victories, some with filesharing companies surrendering without a shot being fired.[20] The filesharing allies (Grokster and Streamcast) mounted a successful counterattack that for a while looked like it might turn the tide. However, the copyright owners modified their battle plan, launching a blitzkrieg of lawsuits against individual filesharers. While these individual attacks continued and spread throughout the world, the Supreme Court dropped a bomb in their reversal of the *Grokster* decision, followed shortly after by a similar blast in Australia's *Sharman* decision.

Although the war rages on, the copyright owners have been the clear legal victors so far. Just as clearly though, illegal filesharing has not been eradicated and, according to some estimates, has experienced an overall increase since the RIAA began suing individuals. So what practical effect has all the litigation achieved?

### (1) Decrease in Illegal Filesharing?

The immediate result of the initial round of filesharing lawsuits by the RIAA in 2003 was a fairly substantial decrease in filesharing. However, there has since been a resurgence with people moving to newer filesharing networks. Looked at from a more narrow perspective, the RIAA lawsuits against individual filesharers have clearly caused a decrease in filesharing over the filesharing networks targeted. Filesharing activity on the Kazaa and Morpheus networks decreased by about 15 percent one week after the first round of lawsuits were announced, and Kazaa use decreased by over 40 percent within a few months.[21] This indicates that if the RIAA continued to file lawsuits targeting users of the most popular filesharing systems, there may ultimately be a decrease (or lesser increase) in illegal filesharing. Combined with lawsuits against the major filesharing companies, which after the Supreme Court's *Grokster* decision seem extremely likely, illegal filesharing may eventually be limited to a smaller scale.

It also seems that the RIAA's litigation campaign has been effective in convincing casual filesharers that illegally downloading a few songs here and there is not worth the risk of being sued. While there may be a mindset among many prolific filesharers—especially young, technology-oriented individuals—that they're too clever to get caught, less-active filesharers are more likely to be deterred.

Another likely reason for the eventual increase in filesharing after the RIAA campaign began is that the lawsuits were initially limited to the United States. At the same time, filesharing was increasing outside the United States due to growing broadband Internet access in foreign countries and the knowledge that the RIAA lawsuits were limited to filesharers in the United States. In addition to the fact that many people outside the United States download files illegally, many filesharers in the United States download files made available on computers located in other countries.

Because the Internet is a worldwide communications network and filesharers can trade files contained on computers all over the world, the only potentially effective legal deterrent may be a worldwide litigation campaign. In 2004, after a yearlong public awareness campaign and warnings of impending lawsuits, a worldwide litigation campaign began, with various foreign record industry associations initiating lawsuits against filesharers in countries such as France, the United Kingdom, Germany, Italy, Denmark, Sweden, and Austria. Because the foreign lawsuits, like those filed in the United States, have been targeted at people who make large numbers of illegal songs available through filesharing networks, this litigation strategy may eventually have a significant impact on the amount of filesharing because it could result in a large decrease in the amount of copyrighted music available worldwide.

**Note:** In June 2004, the Societe Civile des Producteurs Phonographiques, the French record industry trade organization, filed 21 lawsuits against filesharers.

Additionally, the Motion Picture Association of America (MPAA) also began suing filesharers of copyrighted movies in the United States.

## (2) Public Awareness

One indisputable result of the RIAA lawsuits against filesharers is a tremendous increase in public awareness that unauthorized filesharing of copyrighted works is illegal. Although the music industry had initiated public awareness campaigns before the RIAA started suing filesharers, litigation has proved to be a much more effective way to make people aware not only of the illegality of unauthorized filesharing, but also that there are practical consequences. The amount of media coverage, although generally portraying the record industry as evil for suing its customers, has worked to the industry's advantage in terms of creating public awareness.

Although there are people who will not be deterred and continue to share copyrighted works illegally, many other people try to obey the law, assuming they are aware of it. Since many filesharing lawsuits have been filed against college students—who take advantage of university high-speed Internet access—many universities have adopted policies and enforcement methods to prevent illegal filesharing. Further, universities have entered into deals with legitimate online music companies to provide music to students at reduced prices.

Many parents who didn't even know what filesharing was before the RIAA lawsuits should now realize that their children could be using their computers to illegally download music. Knowing that this could potentially subject them to a lawsuit, parents are likely talking to their children about their online behavior, paying closer attention to their computer use, or removing filesharing software from their computers.

As a result of the increased awareness, consumer attitudes may be changing to some extent. Due to knowledge of illegal filesharing and the risk of being sued, some consumers are also migrating to legal online music services.

### (3) Legitimate Alternatives

While the record industry has been fighting its war against illegal filesharing, it has also been trying to establish a legitimate online music market to provide people with ways to obtain music legally online. By 2010, over 400 companies worldwide were legally selling music online.[22] Legal online music services offer a huge variety of music in a variety of ways. Some such as Apple's iTunes allow customers to download individual songs, while others (Pandora, Spotify, etc.) allow customers to listen to many songs, either for free (supported by advertising) or for a monthly subscription fee.

The main obstacle many legal online music services face, especially paid download and subscription services, is illegal filesharing, because many people will not be willing to pay for something they can easily get for free. However, the possibility of being sued for illegal filesharing and paying thousands in settlement fees makes paying 99 cents to download a song a much more attractive option to many people.

> **Example 15.2**
>
> Shortly after the first round of RIAA lawsuits, traffic to BuyMusic.com increased by 30 percent; other legitimate online music sites experienced similar growth.

Companies that encourage illegal filesharing have significant advantages over legitimate online music companies. Legitimate companies must obtain licenses from the copyright owners of each song and sound recording they sell. Although much of this licensing is done on a collective basis, it is still a complicated and time-consuming process. Additionally, many contracts between record labels and recording artists entered into before online music became a reality do not contain provisions dealing with online sales; these must be renegotiated.

According to a worldwide survey, 2004 was the first year of any significant revenue from online music sales.[23] Although online music sales generated about $330 million worldwide, this represented only 1 percent of total sales for the music industry By 2010, online music sales generated revenues of about $4.6 billion worldwide, accounting for 29 percent of total music revenues.[24] The challenges in making music legally available online will gradually diminish as the legal market for online music continues to increase and licensing standards continue to develop.

## II. Three Strikes and You're Out?: The Role of Internet Service Providers

Despite all of the efforts by the music industry to limit the illegal availability of their content online, various forms of online infringement remain rampant. The record industry has successfully sued many of the most popular filesharing companies. However, new filesharing networks have continued to arise as well as other ways for people to illegally obtain music online. The RIAA's lawsuit campaign against individual filesharers brought unprecedented attention to the issue and has resulted in some legal victories that may provide some deterrent effect to people considering illegally downloading.

In a 2008 keynote speech at an international music industry conference (Midem), U2 manager Paul McGuinness called for Internet Service Providers (ISPs) to play a more active role in assisting copyright owners in addressing online infringement:

> *Network operators, in particular, have for too long had a free ride on music—on our clients' content. It's time for a new approach—time for ISPs to start taking responsibility for the content they've profited from for years. And it's time for some visionary new thinking about how the music and technology sectors can work as partners instead of adversaries, leading to a revival of recorded music instead of its destruction.... Why does all this matter so much? Because the truth is that whatever business model you are building, you cannot compete with billions of illegal files free on P2P networks. And the research does show that effective enforcement—such as a series of warnings from the ISP to illegal file-sharers that would culminate in disconnection of your service—can address the problem.... I think the failure of ISPs to engage in the fight against piracy, to date, has been the single biggest failure in the digital music market. They are the gatekeepers with the technical means to make a far greater impact on mass copyright violation than the tens of thousands of lawsuits taken out against individual filesharers by bodies like BPI, RIAA, and IFPI.... ISPs, Telcos, and tech companies have enjoyed a bonanza in the last few years off the back of recorded music content. It is time for them to share that with artists and content owners.[25]*

McGuinness' speech helped push momentum for an effort previously begun by the record industry to convince ISPs to play a more cooperative role in limiting illegal filesharing. It is important to note that ISPs are generally protected from indirect liability for copyright infringements committed by their subscribers by a provision of the Digital Millennium Copyright Act (discussed in Chapter 14) and similar provisions in the copyright laws of some other countries. ISPs therefore have no responsibility for copyright infringements committed by their subscribers and no legal obligation to send warning notices on behalf of copyright owners. However, ISPs have indirectly benefited from illegal filesharing, because such activity requires high-speed Internet connections and has helped drive customers to pay higher prices for broadband Internet access.

For several years, the music and other copyright industries have been trying to persuade ISPs to take a more active and cooperative approach by sending warning notices to their subscribers suspected of engaging in illegal filesharing. Since these efforts have been mostly unsuccessful, copyright industries around the world have also lobbied governments to enact laws requiring ISPs to send warning notices and ultimately to penalize people who receive multiple notices but fail to stop infringing. Although specific proposals vary, the basic idea is to implement what is often referred to as either a "graduated response" or a "three strikes" system to address online infringement, which would require ISPs to send a number of warnings to their subscribers who are identified by copyright owners as engaging in illegal filesharing. Such proposals work essentially as follows:

- Copyright owners (or their agents) would provide evidence of ISP's subscriber accounts allegedly responsible for online infringement.

- ISPs would then be required to send warning notices to such subscribers, notifying them that they have been identified as a potential source of online infringement, providing informational material on copyright infringement, and possibly warning of the potential consequences. The initial notice would be a warning, explaining what the alleged illegal conduct is and requesting that the subscriber stop any illegal filesharing. Subsequent identification of a subscriber as a "repeat infringer" would result in harsher warnings.

- If a subscriber were to receive a third notice (or final notice as specified by the applicable proposal), the subscriber would face some type of penalty, such as a suspension or limitation of Internet access and/or a fine.

There are several potential advantages to a graduated response system compared to instituting legal action against filesharers. First, it would be a more educational approach, with early notices simply notifying subscribers of alleged infringement and requesting that they stop. Second, copyright owners could target a much larger number of online infringements this way (although this might be a disadvantage to ISPs). Third, even the harshest penalty imposed (loss of Internet access for some time period or fines) would likely be much less than the amount of financial liability a subscriber would normally incur if sued successfully for copyright infringement.

Since ISPs have generally not been receptive to graduated response proposals, copyright owners have also tried to convince governments to enact new laws requiring them. France began implementing such a law in late 2010; it provides that after two warning notices, alleged infringers can be referred to court. If the court finds that the subscriber has infringed, the court can impose a fine and order suspension of Internet access for up to 12 months.[26] The United Kingdom, South Korea, and Taiwan have also enacted gradual response laws, and several other countries have proposed, but not yet enacted, such laws. In other countries, voluntary agreements are being discussed between copyright owners and major ISPs.

The RIAA has been trying for several years to persuade ISPs in the United States to adopt a graduated response system to address illegal filesharing. These efforts were persistently resisted until mid-2011, when an agreement between a group of major ISPs (AT&T, Comcast, Verizon, etc.) and the music and film industries was announced. (See Chapter 14 for an outline of the notice provision under the agreement and a discussion of regulatory environment precipitating the agreement.) Overall, this agreement appears to be a very conservative approach to dealing with illegal filesharing, which has required a great degree of compromise, especially on the part of copyright owners. Although it has taken a long time to reach such an agreement, this provides an example of self-regulation that may prevent legal enforcement from being needed except in exceptional circumstances (i.e., where subscribers repeatedly ignore notices and continue engaging in large-scale online infringement).

In addition to graduated response systems, copyright owners have also been working with ISPs (as well as mobile phone service providers) to provide legal subscription music services. For instance, as part of a settlement to a lawsuit by the Irish record industry association, Internet service provider Eircom offers its subscribers a free music streaming service. Eircom also agreed to adopt a graduated response system as part of its settlement. By combining more easily accessible legal music services with graduated response systems, the music industry hopes to convert users of illegal online music services to legal ones.

## III. Copyright Education

In addition to legal enforcement, it is crucial that the music industry educate the public about the importance of copyright. If people have at least a basic understanding of how copyright benefits society, they will be more likely to respect it. For instance, many people still do not perceive downloading an unauthorized copy of a recording for free in the same way as they view shoplifting a CD from a record store. They may believe that because they have not deprived anyone of any physical piece of property, they are not hurting anyone. However, if they realized that copyright law makes it possible for creators, such as songwriters and recording artists as well as the companies that spend enormous amounts of money making and promoting recordings possible, they may be a bit less likely to download illegal files.

Any educational effort should be primarily based on ethical considerations behind copyright law rather than on legal intricacies of the law. Unfortunately, the greatest challenge to educating people about copyright law is that it is not simple. In order for people to comply with the law, they must be able to understand it, at least to the extent that it applies to their individual behavior. Copyright education should stress the reasons for copyright (i.e., allowing creators and companies that invest in the creation of copyrighted works to make a living, which ultimately results in greater availability of works to the public), the basic rights copyright owners have, the ways in which those rights are commonly violated, and the types of uses people may legally make.

In recent years, various music industry organizations have implemented educational programs. Some of these programs and initiatives include:

- **Music Matters (http://www.whymusicmatters.org/):** An organization formed by the United Kingdom music industry that offers videos from artists about the value of music. Music

Matters also has a trust mark program that is intended to help UK music fans determine whether online music is legally offered or not.

- **Pro-Music (http://www.pro-music.org/):** A music industry–supported organization that provides information about online music and legal online music services.

Although efforts at educating the public about copyright are commendable, the main challenge to these efforts is the complexity of copyright law. Instead of providing clear rules that people can easily follow, many provisions of copyright law are difficult to understand and subject to numerous exceptions and limitations. For instance, although most people seem to believe that making copies of copyrighted works for personal use is legal, copyright law does not specifically address this. Some personal copying is permitted by the Audio Home Recording Act, and the fair use defense may apply, but expecting people to understand laws that copyright experts and judges often disagree on is not a practical goal. Ideally, if Congress could amend the Copyright Act to specify that some common uses of copyrighted works that are reasonable for people to make (e.g., making backup copies of legally acquired works, making copies for personal use on different media such as portable digital music players, etc.) qualify as fair use, there would be some simple rules that people could easily understand and follow. Unfortunately, any attempts to do so would inevitably be mired down by lobbying by copyright industries and organizations opposing them.

Many people seem to believe that copyright law benefits only rich, famous musicians and giant record companies. In reality, for each famous recording artist, there are thousands of relatively unknown musicians—not to mention songwriters, record producers, and others who contribute to the creation of music—who, although they make much less money, are dependent on the protection that copyright affords for their livelihood. Similarly, for each major record company, there are thousands of small record companies and other businesses based on the ownership of copyrighted works. Although the public isn't generally sympathetic to major corporations, these companies employ thousands of people who earn their living largely due to the existence of copyright. Although copyright certainly benefits large companies that own popular copyrighted works, it is important to understand that many small businesses and individuals benefit from copyright as well. In reality, musicians (whether famous or not) and businesses (whether large or small) are hurt by large-scale infringement of copyrighted works, and in many cases, the small-scale players are hurt the most because they are often struggling to stay in business in the first place.

## IV. Conclusion

Copyright law is becoming increasingly important to individuals and to society at large. Technological innovations have brought about new ways in which copyrighted works can be used and distributed. The beginning of the twenty-first century has been a great challenge for copyright, but despite copyright owners' fears of piracy and the copyright-critics establishment's cries of a free music revolution, copyright will likely continue to survive, and businesses will continue to adapt to new ways in which their products can be used and distributed.

Copyright has survived numerous technological advances over the past several centuries. Often, these new technologies have posed challenges to copyright law's applicability. Although copyright has not always adapted immediately and smoothly, it has not prevented any of these technologies from thriving. Similarly, copyright will survive the challenges posed by the Internet and the digital distribution of music. However, its application will certainly change as new legislation is passed, court precedents are established, and new business models continue to arise and develop.

As always, copyright law must balance the competing interests of copyright owners and the public. Just as the public needs to become educated about copyright law, the music industry needs to educate itself about new ways that music can be made available. Although the music industry should not be blamed for protecting its property, it should also be open to new possibilities to make music legally available in ways that consumers desire. Although initially resistant to making music available online, the illegal availability of online music has forced the music industry to be more flexible and open to new technologies and business models. If copyright owners are open to new technologies and technology companies are willing to respect copyright owner's rights, innovative new forms of technology can be used to enhance the creativity of artists and increase the dissemination of music to the public. This is exactly what copyright is intended to accomplish.

## Endnotes

1. "Music Piracy: Singing a Different Tune," *The Economist,* Nov. 12, 2009, available at http://www.economist.com/node/14845087.
2. Music's lost decade: Sales cut in half, David Goldman, February 3, 2010, available at http://money.cnn.com/2010/02/02/news/companies/napster_music_industry/.
3. See, e.g., Stan Liebowitz, Will MP3 Downloads Annihilate the Record Industry? The Evidence So Far, 29–30 (June 2003) (a study examining possible causes of the decline in record sales from 1999 to 2002 and concluding that illegal downloading is the only likely cause).
4. *A & M Records, Inc., et al. v. Napster, Inc.,* 114 F. Supp. 2d 896 (2000).
5. 464 U.S. 417 (1984).
6. *Zomba Recording Corp. v. John Deep*, Complaint No. 01CV4452 (S.D.N.Y. 2001).
7. *MGM Studios v. Grokster, Ltd.,* 259 F. Supp. 2d 1029 (C.D. Ca. 2003) and 380 F. 3d 1154 (2004).
8. *MGM Studios, Inc. v. Grokster, Ltd.,* 380 F.3d 1154 (9th Cir. 2004).
9. 464 U.S. 417 (1984).
10. When it began suing filesharers, the RIAA relied on § 512(h) of the Digital Millennium Copyright Act (DMCA), which required Internet service providers to identify subscribers alleged to be committing infringements. The DMCA subpoena provided a quick and inexpensive way to identify alleged infringers. This provision of the DMCA was challenged by Verizon (an Internet service provider), and a court ruled that the RIAA could not use the expedited subpoena provision. See *Recording Indus. Ass'n of Am., Inc. v. Verizon Internet Servs.,* 351 F.3d 1229, 1236 (D.C. Cir. 2003). After the *Verizon* ruling, the RIAA was

forced to file *John Doe* lawsuits relying on alleged infringers' Internet addresses in order to obtain a subpoena. This procedure is more time consuming and costly. Although Verizon claimed it resisted the DMCA subpoenas to protect the privacy of its subscribers, the practical result has been that the increased costs incurred by the RIAA seem to have somewhat increased the settlement amounts the RIAA is willing to accept from filesharers.

11. *BMG Music et. al. v. Gonzalez,* 2005 U.S. Dist. LEXIS 910.
12. 579 F. Supp. 2d 1210 (2007).
13. 721 F. Supp. 2D 85 (D. Mass 2010).
14. *MGM Studios, Inc. v. Grokster, Ltd.,* 125 S. Ct. 2764 (2005). Because the Supreme Court's decision was limited to whether the lower courts had properly granted summary judgment, unless Streamcast settles, as Grokster did after the Supreme Court's decision, the case will go back to the district court for a trial to determine whether Streamcast is in fact liable according to the standard specified by the Supreme Court and, if so, to determine the amount of damages for which Streamcast is liable.
15. Grokster's co-defendant, Streamcast Networks, which refused to settle with the RIAA and MPAA, was ultimately found liable for copyright infringement.
16. *Arista Records, LLC v. Lime Group, LLC,* 715 F. Supp. 2D 481 (2010).
17. Sandoval, Greg, "Study: Limewire Demise Slows Music Piracy," CNET News, March 23, 2011, at http://news.cnet.com/8301-31001_3-20046136-261.html#ixzz1UZsZEcEt.
18. *Universal Music Australia Pty. Ltd. v. Sharman License Holdings Ltd.,* (2005) FCA 1242 (5 September 2005).
19. Olsson, Staffan, "Pirate Bay drar in miljonbelopp" (in Swedish). Svenska Dagbladet. http://www.svd.se/nyheter/inrikes/pirate-bay-drar-in-miljonbelopp_334410.svd (July 8, 2006).
20. See, e.g., *Arista Records v. MP3Board.com,* 2002 U.S. Dist LEXIS 16165 (S.D.N.Y. 2002); *Twentieth Century Fox v. Scour, Inc.,* (S.D.N.Y. filed July 20, 2000).
21. Press Release Netratings, Inc., "File-Sharing Application Usage Dips After Warning from the Recording Industry" (July 14, 2003), available at http://www.nielsen-netratings.com/pr/pr_030714.pdf; Lee Rainie & Mary Madden, Pew Internet Project and comScore Media Metrix Data Memo 6 (Apr. 2004), available at http://www.pewinternet.org/pdfs/PIP_Filesharing_April_04.pdf.
22. See Promusic at http://www.pro-music.org/Content/GetMusicOnline/.
23. IFPI Digital Music Report 2005, available at http://www.ifpi.org/site-content/library/digital-music-report-2005.pdf.
24. IFPI Digital Music Report 2011, available at http://www.ifpi.org/content/library/DMR2011.pdf.
25. The full text of McGuinness' speech can be accessed at http://www.billboard.biz/bbbiz/content_display/industry/news/e3i062b16e707aa9991bc2d3ece70427dc6.
26. The French law is known as the Creation and Internet Law in English. The French text of the law is available at http://www.senat.fr/dossier-legislatif/pjl07-405.html.

# Index